Tom Cowling

LETTERS FROM
A DYING TOWN

Bridal Veil, Oregon
(1955-1960)

The Bridal Veil Heritage Collection

The Bridal Veil Heritage Collection

Bridal Veil, a once-flourishing company mill town born in 1886 in the heart of the Columbia River Gorge, was one of the most difficult achievements in Oregon's lumbering history.

Although the town died 75 years later in 1960, the rich history of Bridal Veil has been brought back to life in **The Bridal Veil Heritage Collection.** Combining a treasure chest of rare photographs, historic maps, newsletters and magazine and newspaper articles, **The Collection** recalls an exciting era when Oregon lumbermen overcame enormous obstacles to bring Larch Mountain timber to market.

The building of three mills and company towns (one burned down in 1902), log chutes, flumes, skid roads and several miles of narrow gauge railroad for the four locomotives in the logging operation is vividly brought back to life in **The Bridal Veil Heritage Collection.** Welcome to my hometown, Bridal Veil!

Tom Cowling

The Bridal Veil Heritage Collection

STORIES OF BRIDAL VEIL: A Company Mill Town (1886-1960). Tom Cowling, 2001.

LETTERS FROM A DYING TOWN: Bridal Veil, Oregon (1955-1960). Compiled by Tom Cowling, 2006.

LETTERS FROM
A DYING TOWN

by **Tom Cowling**

Acorn Publishing Company
Portland, Oregon

The Bridal Veil Heritage Collection

LETTERS FROM A DYING TOWN

To receive our **FREE Bridal Veil Newsletter,** with stories of Bridal Veil's rich history, book announcements and other news of interest, email info@bridalveiloregon.com or register at our website, www.bridalveiloregon.com.

ISBN No. 0-9708701-1-6

Published and Distributed by:
Acorn Publishing Company
3140 SW 97th Ave. Portland, OR 97225
(503) 297-5337
info@bridalveiloregon.com
www.bridalveiloregon.com

Printed in the United States of America

Bridal Veil was a company mill town.
It was a good place to live, work and play.
May its memory live on.

Acknowledgments

The people of Bridal Veil were no strangers to newsletters. The article below shows clearly that company management had a desire to share matters of general interest, both business and social, with its employees.

NEW HOUSE ORGAN APPEARS

Square Edge & Sound is the title of a new house organ being issued by the Wind River Lumber Co., Bridal Veil Lumbering Co. and the Douglas Fir Lumber Co., of Portland, all affiliated companies.

The purpose of the little publications is to record company affairs, both business and social, and to treat matters of general interest to the employes. (The Timberman, October 1920).

This book is a collection of newsletters representing the final years in the life of the company mill town, Bridal Veil. The town's rich history covered seventy-five years (1886 to 1960). These newsletters recorded faithfully the five-year struggle of Bridal Veil Lumber & Box Co. to survive in an increasingly difficult business environment.

The newsletters were an important communication link between the company and its employees. The entire Bridal Veil community received current information as the fate of the town became evident. Because of the newsletters, the company was able to enlist the support of its employees and, at the same time, provide information enabling individuals to make their own plans for the future. Many families, including mine, lived in Bridal Veil during its last years as a company mill town.

Today, more than forty years after Bridal Veil's demise, I am thankful for Mr. Kraft's decision to use the newsletter as a tool for helping us look beyond a hopeless situation, and the end of an era, to a more promising future. It exemplified the paternalistic approach that he used with the employees of the mill, and their families, when times were good and when they were not.

The task of assembling a complete set of newsletters was made more difficult with the passage of time. I would like to thank Jim Bowen and Chuck Kraft for adding their collections to mine so that each volume could be represented in this book. Chuck wrote the Introduction, providing additional insight on Leonard Kraft's decision to publish the BRIDAL VEIL LUMBER & BOX CO. NEWS LETTER.

Tom Cowling

Front cover: The post office at Bridal Veil, February 2006. It is one of the smallest in the United States.

Inside front cover: This aerial photograph was taken of the mill at Bridal Veil in the early 1950's. It was later used on the cover of the December 1956 issue of the BRIDAL VEIL LUMBER & BOX CO. NEWS LETTER.

Introduction
By
Chuck Kraft

Because of the <u>BRIDAL VEIL LUMBER & BOX CO. NEWS LETTER</u>, the company's last five years (1955-1960) are rather better known than are its earlier years. Publication began in July 1955, and the last issue appeared in February 1960. The company went into liquidation in March 1960.

In the first issue, company president Leonard Kraft penned a brief sketch of the firm's history. The firm began in Portland in March 1936 as Wood Specialties Company and made the box shook for Kraft cheese. In 1937 the company changed its name and moved its operation to Bridal Veil. One tale in the family, perhaps apocryphal, alleges that the reason for the move was because J. L. Kraft, the president of Kraft Cheese Company, in a romantic moment thought it would be great to have cheese boxes made in a town called Bridal Veil. To this day, wedding invitations are mailed from the local post office (one of the town's survivors) so as to carry the Bridal Veil postmark.

Copies of the <u>News Letter</u> were sent to customers, but in its March 1956 issue, Mr. Kraft explained that the main reason for its publication was internal. "We have long felt that there are many things about his employer that an employee should know," he wrote, "and yet he can't find out if the employer has no means of letting him know. In fact, we are inclined to say...that the more the employee knows about his employer, the better.

"...What are the chances of running out of lumber? What is the condition of the Order file? What are the business prospects for the coming year?" Answering questions like these frankly, even when the news is bad, at least removes doubt, and the employee can tell where he stands and thus plan his personal affairs to better advantage."

Depending on content, the <u>News Letter</u> would vary between four and eight pages (a couple of issues actually ran to twelve). Generally it would lead off with an opinion or commentary piece by Mr. Kraft.

Regular items included stories of visitors to the company; biographical sketches of employees celebrating 10, 15, or 20 years at Bridal Veil (with photographs); frequent articles highlighting the operations and crew of this or that department in the mill: and a gossip column, called "Rips and Trims," where the reader would find mention of new parents, or who had been hunting or fishing (and with what results), or who had recently totaled his car (this happened a surprising number of times). The employee seniority list appeared several times each year, and birthdays each month were noted. Articles emphasizing industrial safety appeared frequently, and also included were reprints of letters from satisfied customers. Don West edited the News Letter until August 1958, when he left for High Sierra Pine Mills in Oroville, California. He was followed as editor by Sarah Mahn.

After almost a quarter century of operation, Bridal Veil, as noted above, went into liquidation in March 1960, for reasons of simple economics. Although the company consistently delivered a superior product, the mill was on the one hand too far from its supplies of lumber, Ponerosa pine from forests in Eastern Oregon, and on the other hand it was too far from its customers, who were mainly in the Middle West or on the east coast. The result was that the company, particularly in its final years, rarely operated at a profit.

Liquidation did not come altogether as a surprise. In the October 1959 News Letter, Mr. Kraft announced that the company was leaving the millwork business in favor of producing the cut stock from which other companies would fashion the finished millwork. Bridal Veil was competing with millwork operations that were either more centrally located to suppliers and customers, or that paid lower wages, or both. The same announcement also noted that this new arrangement would also require fewer employees. Unfortunately, a dip in home construction in 1959 and 1960 further undermined the company's prospects, and the directors accordingly agreed to cease operations entirely.

****

Chuck Kraft was born in Longview, Washington, December 6, 1935, son of Leonard Kraft and Annette Thompson. He came to Bridal Veil with his parents when cheese box production was moved there in June 1937. He completed sixth grade at Corbett Grade School, but in November 1947 the family moved to a home built on four acres near Lake Oswego (the house is, like the one they lived in at Bridal Veil, no longer there). He graduated from Riverdale Grade School in 1949, Lincoln High School in 1953, and Lewis and Clark College in 1957. During summers he worked at the mill in Bridal Veil, and in the summer of 1957, while awaiting orders to active duty with the Navy, he worked briefly on the News Letter.

Following military service he received a master's degree in history from the University of Oregon and then taught for two years at a college in Michigan's Upper Peninsula. For 28 years he was at Portland Community College, until retiring in 1994. He lives in Portland with his wife, Jackie. Their daughter, Shannon, also lives in Portland. Their son, Kevin, and his family live in Menlo Park, California. Chuck and Jackie have two grandchildren, Andrew and Grace Kraft.

BRIDAL VEIL LUMBER & BOX CO.

News Letter

Volume 1, Number 1   BRIDAL VEIL, OREGON   JULY, 1955

Introducing . . .

Bridal Veil Lumber and Box Company was incorporated under the laws of the State of Delaware on October 24, 1935 under the firm name of "Wood Specialties Company". Its purpose was to manufacture wooden boxes for the Kraft Foods Company.

The organizers and original stockholders were Mr. J. L. Kraft, Mr. C. H. Kraft and Mr. H. E. Leash.

Operations were started in March of 1936 at 2805 SE 14th street in Portland, Oregon. The building was leased from the Star Drilling Machine Company. The original equipment was four California push type cut off saws.

Early in 1937, the company bought the facilities of Bridal Veil Timber Company at Bridal Veil, Oregon. After spending the summer installing equipment, production was started at the new location in August of 1937.

On April 1, 1937, amended articles of incorporation were filed with the State of Delaware changing the firm name to "Bridal Veil Lumber and Box Company."

During the war years Bridal Veil production was largely channelled into ammunition boxes for the Army and Navy, and reached a peak of 1,-250,000 feet in February of 1943.

During the first four months of 1943, Bridal Veil operated an assembly plant at The Dalles, Oregon for the semi-assembling of ammunition boxes from shook produced at Bridal Veil.

In the immediate post-war period, our plant was swamped with orders for our old standby, cheese boxes. However, as our customers gradually converted to fibre cheese containers, our market began to shrink. We were faced with the necessity of finding new products.

After sampling several lines of products in the next few years, our production was converted to window and door frames during the fall of 1950. The first car of window frames was shipped to R. O. W. Distributors at Rocky Mountain, Virginia, January 26, 1951.

Since our first hand-made frames of the 1951 period, we have steadily improved our equipment and product, and increased our volume to the point that we are now able to produce and ship 18 car loads of frames per month.

Now that the change over has been successfully completed we can reflect on the part that all of us played in making the success. We were warned by many experts that it was not possible to convert a box factory to a millwork plant. Had we known at the time what we were getting into, we would have been inclined to agree.

However, the change over was made successfully and everyone of you who worked with us through those trying years deserves the credit for helping to accomplish the impossible.

Len Kraft

Luggage Shook Order Doubles

You may have noticed increased activity around the clamp carrier the past couple of weeks. The A. K. Gibbon Lumber Co., who purchases all of our luggage shook, has asked that we try to double our production of this stock. It seems that they are opening a new plant somewhere in the East and will require as much shook as they are using in their present plant. We have been producing three cars of luggage shook a month and they estimate they will need six to eight cars a month in 1956. So we should be in pretty good shape for orders of this kind for a good while.

Don West

20 Months -- Perfect Safety Record

Congratulations are in order for the Yard Crew, who hung up the enviable record of over 43,000 hours without an accident. Two men were on vacation at the time of this picture: Jim Kendrick and Glenn Willoughby.

Reading from left to right: Charles Lofstedt, Vrytle Kuntz, Leslie Polzel, Roland Morgan, Joe Cote, Walter Stolin, James Eversull, Ray Cote, Orval Johnson, Larry Smazal, Walter Pachal, Fred Crouser and Dean Burkholder.

Bridal Veil Visitors

Mr. David Jacobson, president of the Concord Lumber Co., Albany N.Y., and the Concord Millwork Corp., of Rochester N. Y., stopped by to inspect plant facilities and discuss delivery schedules. Mr. Jacobson, our largest single customer, incidentally, was returning to Albany, N.Y., from a vacation in Acapulco, Mexico. The Concord Lumber Co., purchased 19 carloads of window and door frames from us in 1954, and we expect purchases to total about 40 cars this year. Needless to say, we rolled out the red carpet.

After an 18 month absence, Mr. Leo J. Donnelly of the Contact Lumber Co., Portland, paid us a visit.

William I. (Bill) Carr, of the Harbor Sales Co., Baltimore, Maryland visited the plant and commented favorably upon our modernization program.

Mr. E. W. Ruddick, Pacific Mutual Door Co., Tacoma, Washington, who both buys from us and sells lumber to us stopped by for a while.

Frank Paxton Lumber Co., Des Moines, Iowa sent Mr. Keepers, one of their buyers, to see us. He was very high in his praise of our products.

Mr. Wilson, retired president of Becker Builders Supply Co., Willington, N. C. who is taking it easy on a year's vacation (imagine that) stopped by to pay his respects to old friends. He asked to have an extra car shipped in the next 60 days, which as far as we are concerned at the moment is just like asking for your right arm. We'll try.

These are all Very Important People because they are our Customers. The impression they receive in touring the mill reflect later on the plus side of the ledger in sales. For the first time many of them understand the diversity of individual skills that is required to produce a car load of frames. We can all take pride in our success in building customer confidence in our organization.

Let's Look at Safety

With all of our efforts and attention having been channelled in other directions over the past several years — new products—new machines — new methods — large scale repairs and modernization — our safety record has steadily deteriorated.

We can no longer point to Bridal Veil Lumber & Box Co., with a feeling of pride as a safe place to work.

Our relationship to the national millwork industry, as reported by the Bureau of Labor Statistics of the U. S. Department of Labor, is reflected in these figures:

Period	Accidents Per Million Man Hours
1st Quarter, 1953	14.7
2nd Quarter, 1953	60.2
3rd Quarter, 1953	40.8
4th Quarter, 1953	74.2
Bridal Veil Average	**45.9**
1st Quarter, 1954	53.4
2nd Quarter, 1954	68.7
3rd Quarter, 1954	46.4
4th Quarter, 1954	44.8
Bridal Veil Average	**52.6**
Industry Average, 1951	28.0
Industry Average, 1952	23.8

As can be seen from the above figures, our Lost Time Accident Frequency Rate is approximately twice the average for the millwork industry.

A good Safety Record automatically will result from the combined efforts of everyone concerned. By being alert and attentive, we can still beat the industry average in 1955.

Mel Mallinson

July Birthdays

Many Happy Returns of the Day!

Harold Vogel	Lester Anderson
Bob Bird	Paul Detrick
Art Schroder	T. Van Hee, Sr.
Lillie Yerion	Rodney Clayton
Willie Bowen	Bob Layton
George Leash	Jim Cowling
Alan Brown	A. R. Kimbley, Sr.
Tom Cowling	

New Employees

A hearty welcome is extended to the following new employees added during June:

Albert E. Barlett	Fredrick Bailey
David Clark	John Smith

Order File Plugged

It is the general consensus of opinion that the current building boom will extend into 1956. It may be a little early to predict just how the market will be this winter, but, barring unusually cold weather, it should be as good as last year. We have a three or four month backlog of orders at this time and as yet at least, it has shown no signs of slackening. One of our biggest customers, Concord Lumber Company, at one time this year, had twelve carloads of frames on order. Pease Woodwork Company had eight or nine at the same time. We have another fairly big customer in Dekker-Brish Millwork Company, who has been buying frames at the rate of two cars per month, and they would like to increase that to four cars a month. To top it off, we have many smaller customers, and they alone could keep us fairly busy. So it can be readily seen that we are going to be pretty busy the rest of this year.

Don West

Lots of Lumber in Sight

One of the two major causes for curtailing production in the past has been a shortage of lumber. This was a matter of real concern this year as our old standby at Heppner went out of production during the last week in April and will not be in production again until late August.

However, it is a pleasure to learn that our June receipts will be well over 1,500,000 FBM. To get this volume has required shipments from nineteen different mills scattered all the way from Yakima, Washington on the North, to Boise, Idaho on the East and to Chico, California on the South.

Summer Replacements

Leo Hageman, Jr. has finished his college career, and thus also has left the student ranks. However, as Uncle Sam has first call on his services, he will be filling in here for the moment.

Chuck Kraft is back for his third summer at Bridal Veil and Allan Weston and Lynfred Crouser are now second summer men.

Newcomers to the student ranks include Harry Visse, Jr., Bob Bird, Tom Cowling, Jim Yerion, and Ronald Evans.

Rips and Trims

Anyone interested in fishing lessons should see **Jim Cowling**. Jim has a new method which we're sure he will be glad to demonstrate.

Can't report any new automobiles this month, but thought we'd pass along that **Riley West** is the proud owner of a new bike. Reported to have Power Brakes (foot).

Hope the **Ralph McCredie** family enjoy their new home. They purchased the Spike Emerson property in Corbett.

Do-It-Your-Self **Jarvis Kilness** has the foundation poured at his new house at Coopey Falls.

Len Kraft, you all know him, went on a fishing trip to Bowron Lake, B. C. Len reports lots of trip and very little fishing.

Hear that the **Potter's** and the **Gross's** are heading to Canada also. Expect to hear a better fishing report when they return.

Jim Bowen and **Rodger Seegar** attended the National Guard camp at Ft. Lewis, while **Chuck Kraft** went south to San Diego for two weeks with the Naval Reserve.

Einar Mickelson and family are currently enjoying a 3 week trip to Iowa.

Eleanor Taylor spent a week with her Mom and Dad at Cathlamet. We didn't check, but she reports a dandy sunburn on her back.

Leo Hageman likes Bridal Veil so well he stayed right here for his vacation. Spent most of his time trying to avoid Ade who wanted him back on the job.

Patty Cowling spent a week in Pendleton. Ask Patty for details.

Congratulation to **Herb Courter** who was appointed Grand Pursuivant of the Grand Lodge of Masons of the State of Oregon.

Walt Keller coming along fine with his new beach cottage. The noise you heard over the 4th was hammering, not fire crackers.

Glen Willoughby and family vacationed in Arizona.

Welcomed back after long illnesses were **Martha Jones** and **Inez Houchin.**

Willy and **Annie Bowen** are traveling down the coast for a visit with their son **Kenny** and family. Kenny worked here at Bridal Veil as a cutter and is now employed at Consolidated Aircraft in San Diego.

Eldon Neilson and family have returned from a trip to Tuscon Arizona, welcome back Eldon.

Fred Crouser reports that his son **Bruce** is up and around after a serious attack of rheumatic fever.

The **Jim Kendricks's** are due to return shortly from a 3 week vacation in Texas.

Hear that **Mrs. Elmer Ayles** is working at Gresham Berry Growers during the berry season.

The **Van Buskirks** spent a week roughing it on the Deschutes trying for some fish to substantiate their stories.

We understand that **Homer Walker** spent Memorial Day in Reno. Did Harold's Club pay for the trip, Homer?

Walt and **Lillian Norgard** unlimbered their clam guns at Long Beach a couple weeks back. Knowing Walt they probably got their limit.

Good Work!

We received the following congratulatory letter from the Eaton-Young Lumber Co. in Eugene.

"You have recently shipped an extremely large car of frames to Lumber Dealers in Kansas City and I want to report that they received this difficult car in excellent condition. Add to that the quality product produced by your concern and you and the fellows in the mill can take justifiable pride in a job well done.

Just want you to know we and Lumber Dealers are appreciative of this nearly extinct personal attention you and the men in the mill must give to our business."

Signed
Eaton-Young Lumber Co.
E. Lee Bennett
Manager, Pine Department

We all know that it takes the concentrated efforts of everyone in the plant to produce the above results and here's hoping we may get many more letters such as this one.

Is there a cartoonist in the house? Steady highly regarded positions on the staff of the News Letter are open, see Don West for details.

Do you like to write? If so, see Don West, the News Letter needs reporters.

BRIDAL VEIL LUMBER & BOX CO.

News Letter

Volume 1, Number 2   BRIDAL VEIL, OREGON   AUGUST, 1955

Creating More Jobs

Our program to bring our plant and equipment up to date may be divided into two kinds. Let's call one kind voluntary and the other involuntary. Late in September of 1953 we had a good example of the involuntary sort, when we returned from lunch to find that some 80,000 FBM of ripped lumber and a finger-lift had come to rest approximately twenty feet below the floor level in the sorting building.

Of course, we ended up with a dirt fill in the sorting building, and from that time on we were no longer concerned about getting lumber piled too high. But up to that time we hadn't planned very seriously to do that particular job.

Another type of involuntary modernization was forced on us by rulings of the Oregon Insurance Rating Bureau. The circulating underground mains, the 750,000 gallon reservoir, and the two 1500 GPM pumps are the result of the necessity for either modernizing our fire protection system or else going without fire insurance protection. This is the hardest kind of modernizing to do since pumps, pipes, and valves are tremendously expensive, and since the investment does not show up in new productive equipment, increased production, on lowered costs.

So much for the headaches and heartaches of the involuntary improvement. More fun to talk about and more fun to participate in is the kind of modernization which can be planned ahead of time and which winds up with more productive results. Since we entered into the manufacture of window and door frames, many new machines have been added. The first was the Greenlee double-end tenoner, with framing and sill horning attachments. The Mattison eight-inch moulder soon followed.

Meantime we were increasing our cut-off equipment from four Irvingtons to eight, and following these with the Morgan 72" Nailer, Porter Router, another Greenlee Tenoner, and box-factory hog and conveyor.

The work done on our buildings starting at the Cutter line is a spectacular improvement accomplished within the last year. The new floor, new lights, lack of posts and improved ceiling height all combine to provide a safer and more pleasant work area. This particular improvement is most showy and productive of favorable visitor reaction.

Now the interesting thing about these purchases of modern equipment is that they have not caused anyone to lose his job. Ordinarily we think of new machines as being "labor saving", whereas they are actually "labor creating" machines. It is reassuring to note that our seniority lists over the past five years carried:

102 names at July 10, 1950

103 names at April 18, 1951

95 names at May 22, 1952

124 names at June 1, 1953

120 names at Aug. 11, 1954

149 names at May 17, 1955

Here is a definite showing of the job-creating results of modernization.

A couple of years ago one of our wholesale frame outlets asked me what I thought of the prospects for what was then the coming year. My reply went something like this: "I don't know whether the home construction industry is going to have a better or poorer year than last year. But this I do know: Bridal Veil is going to do 25 percent more business next year than last."

We can make a statement like that
(Continued on page 3)

Bridal Veil Visitors

Reedy Berg of Dant & Russell was a recent plant visitor. Some of you may remember Reedy as a former University of Oregon basketball star.

Mr. Rudy Ruddick of Pacific Mutual Door Co. also visited us. As a matter of interest Pacific Mutual Door Co. is handling the Animal Trap Co. account.

C. W. Kraft, Len's brother, and family were Bridal Veil visitors on Saturday, July 9. They were returning to their home in California after a vacation in Alaska. They drove to Fairbanks, Alaska and then flew to Barrow, the northernmost town on the American continent.

Mr. Kraft is president of the Kraftile Co. of Niles, California and a director of Bridal Veil Lumber & Box Co.

Doug Walwyn of Smith & Crakes of Eugene, Oregon, o u r insurance agents, stopped in at Bridal Veil Friday July 15, to "bring our insurance records up to date." Doug found himself practically unemployed as Walt Norgard's records were in perfect shape. Says Doug, "Walt is the first office manager I have ever known to keep his insurance records up." Take a bow, Walt.

August Birthdays
Many Happy Returns of the Day!

Fred H. Long	Vera Nell Ball
Roger Seegar	Ralph Lamke
George Bennett	Roy Anderson
Ann Keller	Theophile Van Hee
Lester Howell	Theodore Van Hee
Jarvis Kilness	Harry Densmore
Dean Burkholder	Paul Levan
Archie Davies	Ralph Ellis

The hillbilly one day walked into the sheriff's office with a jug in one hand and a shotgun in the other. He turned the gun on the sheriff and demanded: "Here, friend, take a drink outa my bottle!"

The sheriff refused, but a healthy prod of the shotgun brought results.

The sheriff took a big swallow, shuddered, turned green a n d sputtered: "Oof, what awful stuff!"

"Ain't it tho?" agreed the hillbilly. "Now hold the gun on me until I take a gulp!"

Lloyd DeMain

10th Anniversary

Lloyd DeMain, night foreman of the Moulding Department will observe his 10th anniversary at Bridal Veil Lumber & Box Company on August 27th.

Lloyd was born in Benson, Minnesota in May 1914. He was one of five children. When he was still a small boy the family moved to Souix City, Iowa. He attended school in Souix City and Klamath Falls, Oregon, having moved to the Orgeon country when he was fifteen years old.

His hobbies are fishing and playing the guitar. It is well known that he is either one of the best or luckiest fisherman in this area: He consistently catches lots of salmon so maybe it isn't all luck. He is also quite accomplished with the guitar, and has played at many dances in and around the Gorge.

Lloyd has a fine family consisting of his wife, Emma, and two children, Linda and David.

We might also mention that the DeMains have a parakeet.

He who whispers down a well
About the goods he has to sell
Wont reap as many golden dollars
As he who climbs a tree and hollers

Let's Look at Safety

Three lost time accidents marred our chances of improving our safety record during June, and raised our accident frequency rating from 82.4 per million man hours to 86.0 per million man hours. While our accident rate has mounted sharply during 1955, we note a steady decline in the rate for our industry as reported by the Bureau of Labor Statistics of the U.S. Department of Commerce to 21.2. Our accident rate is now 4.1 times the industry average.

Mel Mallinson

Creating More Jobs

(Continued from page 1)

and back it up with performance because we are a young and expanding factor in the frame market. All we have to do is make a better frame at a competitive price, and the business is ours for the taking.

And so it is that your management makes this promise: No one will lose his employment because of modern machines or methods. Past history provides us with the proof that greater efficiency spells greater opportunity and steady and expanding employment. On the other hand, failure to keep pace with our competition spells disaster.

Len Kraft

With the plant using 1,250,000 FBM of lumber per month at an average cost of $112.50 per thousand feet, each per cent of cut-away costs $1,562.60.

A Fire Today—No Job Tomorrow.

Build a Better Mouse Trap

ROUGH ON RATS

We have added the Animal Trap Company of Lititz, Pennsylvania to our list of customers. Their initial order calls for 400,000 Mouse Trap Bases and 200,000 Rat Trap Bases.

The Animal Trap Co. estimates their yearly requirement of mouse traps to be around 15,000,000 or roughly five cars. We do not know how many rat traps they will want but would guess that it will run somewhere in the neighborhood of 1,000,000.

This is a definite shot in the arm for us as the mouse and rat trap bases come from essentially the same stock that would ordinarily go into core blocks, yet they are worth almost three times as much!

We have been, and will continue, to explore the markets for items of this nature whereby we can realize the full utilization of our raw material at the highest market price.

Don West

Push Out the Walls

Last month, in reporting on the availability of lumber, we hazarded a guess that our June purchases would be in excess of 1,500,000 FBM. The figure turned out to be 1,919,415 FBM. As a matter of general interest that lumber cost $208,715.01 FOB mill, and by the time we added inbound freight of $17,696.96 to it, our FOB Bridal Veil lumber bill was $226,411.97.

Houses started in 1955 are expected to exceed a total of 1,300,000.

DEPARTMENTAL SAFETY RECORD

January 1 - June 30, 1955

	Factory	Millwork	Yard	Shipping	Maint.	Total Plant
Date of Last Accident	6-9-55	6-14-55	11-4-53	5-8-55	1-24-55	6-14-55
Man Hours Since Last Accident	9718⅜	4107½	45,773¼	2,359¾	15,944½	16,601
Total Manhours This Year	72187½	37770½	16,924¾	5,784¼	18,518	151,185
No. Accidents This Year	3	6	0	1	3	13
Accident Frequency	41.6	158.8	0	17.3	162	86

H & W Fund Trustees

The operation of the Health and Welfare Fund is under the supervision of a Board of Trustees, which performs its duties through an administrator which the Board of Trustees appoints.

While there are six Trustees, three being representatives of Millmen's Locals and three being employer representatives, Bridal Veil Lumber and Box Co. comes within an eye-lash of having a majority of the board with three men. Ade Jones, Leo Hageman and Len Kraft make up the Bridal Veil contingent. Just about coralled the offices too, with Len as Chairman and Leo as Secretary.

Toys Galore

We just received a reorder for 3 cars of toy stock for the Hampshire Mfg. Co., through our Chicago representatives the R. T. Feltus Lbr. Co. This will take care of their 1956 requirements for roof slats for Lincoln Log sets. This is a good order for us because it calls for 9,000,-000 pieces of one size and the piece is quite small. The first car is due to ship in January.

This is the fifth reorder we have had from this company, which points out how attention to details in producing a quality product directly results in more sales.

New Employees Hired in July

A hearty welcome is extended to the following new employes added during July.

    Nina Chamberlain

    Paul Levan

    Leon Dunlap

Woman motorist, stalled in traffic, to impatient male behind her: "If you are smart enough to start my car, I will try to be stupid enough to lean on your horn while you do it."

As many as 400,000 housing units disappear each year from such causes as fire, flood, razing, etc.

New Female Performer: "This is my first circus job. Better tell me what to do to keep from making mistakes."

Circus Owner: "Well, don't undress in front of the bearded lady."

BASEBALL: Marv Jackson, manager of the Blue Lake Baseball Team, will lead his aggregation into action in the ABC tournament on August 10, 7:00 p.m. at Westmoreland Park. Marv's team won the 1955 championship of the Greater Portland Baseball League, and are one of the top seeded entries in the ABC tourney. This is a regional tournament, and the winner will go to Watertown, South Dakota to compete for the national championship.

NICE VACATION: Marv, Dorothy and Cristal Jackson are leaving Monday night, August 1st., via United Air Lines, for Lima, Ohio to pick up a new school bus for Corbett school District No. 39. It is a 66 passenger bus so there should be plenty of room for the Jacksons on their way home. Marv estimates that they will be on the road six days.

LUGGAGE SLOWDOWN: The luggage business we were bragging about last month has nearly come to a standstill. We have been informed that the customer shut their plant down for a two week vacation, so is only temporary. They are also still working on their new plant and do not have it in opera tion, yet.

Machine Operators Must Not Wear Gloves.

Rips and Trims

CANDY CRANE, daughter of Marge and Steve Crane, former employee, underwent a serious operation for a spinal injury on August 3rd. A definite cause of the injury has not been determined but it left her spine curved and misshapen. It is expected that she will be in a cast for at least three months and in the hospital a total of six months. All of our best wishes to Candy for a speedy recovery.

KERMIT KLINGER, a former operator of the Bridal Veil store, now has a grocery store on SW Capitol Highway near Multnomah. He and his wife did have a television store in Northeast Portland but gave that up in favor of the grocery. They have rented their Portland home and are living above the store.

ADE JONES and family spent the 4th of July fishing on the Metolius River.

MR. AND MRS. VYRTLE KUNTZ celebrated their 20th wedding anniversary with a picnic at Blue Lake. Congratulations.

CRISTAL JACKSON spent a couple of weeks visiting the Frank Bacon family at Celilo.

JEAN MURRAY underwent surgery in Providence Hospital and at last report, is doing fine.

THELMA ROWE has been on the sick list, but, we are glad to report that she is recovered and back on the job.

Boy Scouts attending Camp Merriweather were Jim Hambrick, Don Hageman and Fred Mickelson. Fred cut his foot and had to have some stitches taken.

Girls attending camps this month were Claudia Hambrick, Lenann Kraft, Diana Taylor, Patty Cowling and Marcella Steele.

NORMAN and SUSIE KELLER and family were visitors at the Walter Kellers over the 4th. Mrs. Keller's brother and wife from St. Paul, Minn. were also visitors.

The TED HANSON family spent their vacation at a Camp Meeting at Gladstone.

VYRTLE KUNTZ, CLARENCE LOFSTEDT, JERRY ROBERTS, JACOB VAN ORSOW and CHESTER WOODARD were also on vacation in July but we have been unsuccessful in finding out what they did so you might try asking them. If you find out let us know.

MARY LEE TAYLOR recently returned from a two week's stay with her grandparents in Cathlamet, Washington. Ralph and Eleanor went after her and traded Diana, who will now stay for two weeks. Wonder how long they can keep that up and we also wonder why we didn't think of an angle like that.

DURWARD AND RUTH LITTON spent a recent weekend salmon fishing off the Southern Oregon coast. They picked up four nice salmon and one of them caught a slight case of seasickness before they returned to shore.

RALPH SANDERS had a good story about a bout with a rattlesnake. We were going to put it in this issue but unfortunately didn't have room. It may be a good thing we didn't because since then he encountered two more of the critters. To make a long story short we'll let Ralph fill in the details.

HARRY ADOLPH and family spent their vacation here in Oregon, reportedly trying to find some sunshine. Wonder how they made out.

The ELMER AYLES family motored to Montana. No report on the weather, so we assume it was a good trip.

VERA NELL BALL flew to Tulsa, Oklahoma on her vacation.

Heard that PEARL CLOE and family spent a week trying for fish at East Lake. Any luck, Pearl?

LESTER HOWELL and family are also reported to be fishing enthusiasts and spent some time at the coast trying their luck (or skill).

RALPH McCREDIE spent his holidays the hard way, working on his new home in Corbett.

MIRA NIELSON spent some time at the coast during her vacation. Fishing or just taking life easy, Mira?

MARVIN STOLIN and family drove to Tolley, North Dakota. We tried to locate Tolley on the map but didn't have much luck.

MARY WOODARD and her mother visited relatives in Montana during Mary's vacation. Now they have relatives visiting them from Montana. Must be some sort of reciprocal trade agreement.

GARY LONG left July 8th for U. S. Army Reserve Camp and Leo Hageman, Jr. left July 22nd for Fairchild Air Base in Spokane. Leo will ge gone a month.

WALT and LILLIAN NORGARD are proudly announcing the birth of a grand-

(Continued on page 6)

Cutting Department Increases Production

The cutting department racked up a 10 percent increase in hourly production in the second quarter of 1955 over the first quarter.

Even though there was a wage raise in March this increased production actually lowered costs nearly 7 percent. Left to right is Clyde Hambrick, foreman; Marvin Van Orsow, Fred Harp, Eldon Nielson, Howard Hunt, Fred Crouser, Roy Eveland, Richard Jacobson, Harold Jacobson and Lester Anderson. Jerry Roberts, also a cutter, was on vacation at the time this was taken. We'll catch him next time.

Rips and Trims

(Continued from page 5)

son, David Bruce on July 19th. After a trip to Richland the following week-end they pronounce him "the biggest and best".

Just cast those envious eyes on the following list of new hot rods and wish. That's all we can do:

Ted Van Hee—Mercury
Clarence Noble—Plymouth
Tom Britton—Studebaker
Joe Van Orsow—Pontiac
Jerry Roberts—Mercury

Grease Monkey: "My boss said I was a young man who would go far."
Date: "You'll go just so far—no matter what your boss says."

Our payroll for Memorial Day (a paid holiday) was $2,179.36.

A Careless Move May Mean a Shattered Life.

Publicity

The Dow Chemical Co., manufacturers of Penta, which is used in Toxic Treat, ran a nice story of Bridal Veil in the July issue of The Wood Saver. A copy has been posted on the bulletin board by the store if anyone would like to read it. We feel quite honored for having been chosen for this story from among the many frame manufacturers throughout the country.

H & W Fund Trustees Meet

At a meeting of the Trustees of Mill-workers' Health & Welfare Fund held June 28, 1955 at the Labor Temple in Portland, the following actions were taken:

(1) Final arrangements were made to provide for complete processing of claims in the office of the Administrator of the Fund.

(2) Renewal of the contract with Bankers Life was authorized.

BRIDAL VEIL LUMBER & BOX CO.

▸News Letter

Volume 1, Number 3   BRIDAL VEIL, OREGON   SEPTEMBER, 1955

'If You Care--Share'

When October rolls around it will be time for the annual United Fund Campaign. In the past the Company has evidenced its interest in and support of the United Fund by arranging for representatives of the United Fund to make a short half-hour presentation on behalf of the United Fund on company time, and by later providing for in-plant subscriptions on the Payroll Allotment Plan. The program during the coming campaign will be similar to that of the previous years.

During the past it has been difficult for us, living at some distance from Portland, to associate ourselves with the Portland United Fund. Many of the agencies receiving support were purely local in nature, and did not seem to concern us. This year, however, the United Fund Campaign is being designated as the "Tri-County United Fund" and is being expanded to include sixty-eight service agencies in Washington, Multnomah and Clackamas Counties. This action should clear the way for the whole-hearted support of all of us. Now we know that we have a stake in the outcome.

The 1956 Tri-County United Fund Campaign goal has been set at $3,003,644.00. The OREGON JOURNAL for August 31, 1955 carries a comment in B MIKE's column that an eastern financial publication rates West Slope as the fastest-growing area in the United States. Yet the United Fund has increased its budget by less than nine per cent over last year, and has added the county agencies of Washington, Multnomah and Clackamas Counties. The goal is realistic—we can't afford to fail.

Here is an interesting item. It has been estimated that it costs $10.00 a year to keep a scout in scouting, but it costs $1,600.00 a year to keep a

boy in jail. J. Edgar Hoover, head of the Federal Bureau of Investigation and Warden E. Laws have always stated that they have never known of a criminal either to be incarcerated as a felon or to come to the attention of the F. B. I. for any particular major crime who has been an active boy scout or a member of the YMCA. A dollar spent for prevention of juvenile delinquency eventually saves you at least $100.00 in taxes used for punishment and treatment. We can't afford to fail.

Who is behind the United Fund Campaign? It is a campaign of volunteers. This is a volunteer organization of over 8,000 men and women who serve their community and fellow citizens without pay. The United Fund, the Agency Board of Directors, the Budget Committee, the Campaign Organization, all are volunteers.

The reasons why people support the United Fund are probably as varied as the people themselves. Some give because they know that the budgets of all United Fund agencies are examined carefully by a budget committee of representative citizens which makes sure that every dollar is needed to provide essential services. Others give because they know that the United Fund way is the economical way to provide operating funds for essential community services. Last fall the local campaign costs were 3.3 per cent of the goal—among the lowest in the nation. Many people give to the United Fund because they know personally about the work of one or more of the agencies it supports. Still others give because they know that adequate health, welfare, recreation and rehabilitation services make their community a better place in which to live, to do

(Continued on page 2)

Bridal Veil Visitors

Dean Sherman, managing editor of the Timberman visited the plant on August 8. The Timberman has a story of Bridal Veil in its September 1955 issue. See Bulletin Board?

H. E. Webster, president of the H. E. Webster Lumber Co. of Kansas City, Mo., was also an Aug. 8 visitor. The same day he gave us an order for a carload of luggage shook and since then has sent in orders for two more cars. We are now making luggage shook for two concerns.

Mr. Cecil Barger of Stateville, No. Carolina paid us a visit August 17th. Mr. Barger is one of our window frame customers and usually makes a tour of his various suppliers once a year.

Mr. T. C. (Ted) Gevaart of Portland was out a few weeks ago to discuss the possibility of making cheese box shook for a company we used to supply with shook.

Mr. L. E. Dunn, of Mid-West Mill and Supply Co. of Tulsa, Okla., stopped by to see if perhaps we could supply them with their window frame and inside door jamb requirements. They too, are former customers.

'If You Care--Share'

(Continued from page 1)

business, to work, and to rear their children.

Living in the United States is a priviledge granted to relatively few of the persons inhabiting the face of this earth. And the priviledge also carries stern responsibilities, one of which is to express our concern for the less fortunate among us in a tangible way. We feel this so strongly that in addition to the estimated $150.00 it will cost to meet the payroll during the presentation by the United Fund representatives, and in addition to the cost of operating the Payroll Allotment Plan, which many companies refuse to do because of the cost, the company has undertaken to match every dollar contributed by its employees.

We can't afford to fail.

Len Kraft

Our payroll in July was the highest in the history of the company: $80,-882.29.

15th Anniversary

Kenneth L. (Connie) Meyer

On September 16, this year Kenneth L. (Connie) Meyer will observe his 15th anniversary at Bridal Veil.

Connie was born and raised in Nelson, Nebraska. He has one brother and one sister. In August of 1938 Connie and Maxine Carroll were married in Nelson. They have one daughter who is now 16 years old.

In 1940 the Meyers moved to Corbett, where they still live. Bridal Veil is the only place Connie has worked since coming to Oregon. At the present time he is an operator of one of the cleat saws.

Connie has only lost one day of work due to an accident since he has been here and has never missed a paycheck.

Connie manages to keep himself occupied in his spare time by working around the house and on top of that he is an active member of the Multnomah County Sheriff's Reserve, having joined that organization in 1952.

Second Call

In our first issue, we appealed for reporters and cartoonists for the Newsletter. Since the response hasn't been overwhelming we are still in need of more volunteers. If any of you would like to join the staff of the paper, stop and see Don West.

10th Anniversary

Lawrence A. (Pete) Peterson

September 24th will be Lawrence A. (Pete) Peterson's tenth anniversary at Bridal Veil. Pete is one of the operators of the glue clamp carrier. Pete was born in Stanley, Wisconsin on May 4, 1903, one of eleven children. He received his education in Stanley. In fact Pete lived there just 40 years, leaving in 1943 and coming to Oregon.

Pete and his wife, Ethel, were mar-

Let's Look at Safety

There were no lost time accidents in the month of July. We have accumulated 46,103 man-hours since our last lost time accident, thus lowering our accident frequency from 58.9 per million man-hours worked to 49.6 per million man-hours.

While our accident rate is still 2.3 times the industry rate, with continued efforts toward safety, by the end of the year we can still come close to our industry average.

Mel Mallinson

DID YOU KNOW? That you do not pay any part of the Unemployment Compensation Tax. It is not part of your deductions and should not be confused with Social Security, one-half of which you do pay.

. . . . That the company pays all the tax for Unemployment Compensation.

. . . . That the company is in favor of Unemployment Compensation for those entitled to it—those who are out of work through no fault of their own.

ried in Stanley in March of 1927 and have two children, Don, 22 years old, and Alice, 19 years old.

Pete tells us his hobby is working around their Troutdale home, doing such things as home repair and gardening.

1955 SAFETY RECORD

	Lost Time Accidents	Man Hours Worked	Accidents Per Million Man Hours
January	4	28,772	139.9
February	0	24,023	0
March	0	24,253	0
First Quarter 1955	4	77,048	51.9
April	1	28,179	35.5
May	2	30,721	65.1
June	3	33,905	88.5
Second Quarter 1955	6	92,805	64.7
July	0	31,950	0
Total for Year 1955	10	201,803	49.6

Rips and Trims

Walt and Lillian Norgard are on a three week vacation in Canada. They went to the wedding of one of Walt's grandnieces in Edmonton, Alberta. After a round of entertainment, they will relax a few days at Lake Louise and Banff. They plan to return by way of the Frazier River to Vancouver. Walt is expected back on the job Sept. 6.

Einar Mickelson and **Jim Cowling** took their families to Long Beach, Washington for a weekend of clam digging. Wonder if they got any.

Ann Keller, Evelyn and sons **Tommy** and **Danny** spent a few days in Vancouver, B. C. visiting relatives. Ann will be leaving in a few days for a visit with Norman Keller and his family in Great Falls, Montana.

We finally found out what will bring people home in a hurry from their vacation. **Mrs. Don Senter,** daughter of **Mr. and Mrs. Clarence Noble,** gave birth to a baby girl, **Dona Jean,** on Mrs. Noble's birthday. It didn't take the Nobles long to get home.

Mr. and Mrs. Merrill Hartshorn are the proud parents of a baby girl, **Rebecca,** born at noon on August 30. Papa is really beaming.

Kenny Elliott was home for the Labor Day weekend. Kenny is attending the St. Mary's school for boys at Beaverton.

The **Kraft** family, with the exception of **Len** and **Chuck,** are enjoying a vacation at Gleneden Beach. Len's mother was with the family for a week and is now in California visiting the Chuck Kraft family.

Ade Jones and his wife are tentatively planning to take in a game or two of the world series this year. Because of the close race in the American league they can't tell where the series will be played, so their plans, at this time, are somewhat flexible.

Len is now a proud member of the "Gallon Club" of the Red Cross. On August 31st he gave his ninth pint of blood.

Don West has a saddle horse. He says it is a Tennessee Walking horse. We have an idea that if he actually rides this horse he'll be glad to do his own walking. Don't ask why he has a horse or what he is going to do with

Sept. Birthdays

Many Happy Returns of the Day!

Tom Choate	Chester Woodward
Howard Hunt	Larry Smazal
Robert Godat	John Hancock
William Rogers	Albert Kimbley, Jr.
Lloyd Frazier	Ade Jones
Joseph Cote	Steve Kuzmesky
Leonard Kraft	Milford Collins
Jim Yerion	James Scrivner
Merrill Hartshorn	Roley Zumwalt
Orval Johnson	Edsel Kinonen
Lou Cowling	

Help!   Help!
News Depends Upon Its Readers

If anyone has an item, article, story or what have you, be it long or short, of interest to the readers, please get in touch with Lou Cowling. This is **your** paper, and to make it more enjoyable, we need your suggestions and contributions. Believe us when we say, they will be greatly appreciated.

Our shipments for the first 8 months of the 1955 fiscal year totaled 6,980,-080 FBM. In the same period last year our shipments were 5,504,463 FBM— a gain of 27 per cent.

During fiscal 1954 27.9 cents out of every sales dollar went for payroll. For the first eight months of fiscal 1955, the figure is 30.3 cents.

---

it because personally we don't think he knows.

Tom Britton and family are enjoying a three week trip to Wyoming and Nebraska visiting relatives.

The **Lloyd DeMains** are on vacation at Depoe Bay. Lloyd is trying his hand at deep sea fishing. Lloyd's brother has a commercial fishing boat.

The following people took vacations in August but we have had no report of what they did or where they went: **Fred Harp, Lawrence Peterson, Ray Schneringer, Noah Atchley, Louis Bissel, Frank Bowen, Pete Ellis, Mabel Hills, Stanley Hills, Hiram Layton, Durward Litton, Bob Polzel, James Scrivner, Theophile Van Hee, Jr., Theophile Van Hee, Sr., Joe Van Orsow, Walt Stolin.**

In case you are wondering who painted the front of the store and office, it was the Standard Oil Co. Bridal Veil store is now selling Standard gasoline.

Nomenclature and Definitions

Many industries have a special vocabulary, designed specifically to convey ideas between the initiated, and which is "Greek" to the outsider. Here is the "lingo" of the frame industry, as reported by the United States Department of Commerce and the National Bureau of Standards:

Sash.—A sash is a single assembly of stiles and rails made into a frame for holding glass, with or without dividing bars to fill a given opening. It may be either open or glazed.

Window.—A window consists of two or more single sash made to fill a given opening. It may be either open or glazed.

Window unit.—Window unit means a combination of the window frame, window, weather strip, balancing device, andv, at the option of the manufacturer, screen and/or storm sash, assembled as a complete and properly operating unit.

Measurement:

Between glass. — The measurement across the face of any wood part that separates two sheets of glass.

Face measurement — Measurement across the face of any wood part exclusive of any solid mold or rabbet.

Finished size. — Measurement of any wood part over-all, including the solid mold or rabbet.

Outside opening.—The measurement of any given article from outside to outside.

Wood allowance.—The difference between the outside opening and the total glass measurement of a given window or sash.

Stiles.—The upright, or vertical, outside pieces of a sash or screen.

Rails.—The cross, or horizontal, pieces of the framework of a sash or screen.

Check rails.—Meeting rails sufficiently thicker than the window to fill the opening between the top and bottom sash made by the check strip or parting strip in the frame. They are usually beveled and rabbeted.

Bar.—A bar may be either vertical or horizontal and extend the full width or length of the glass opening.

Muntin.—A muntin applies to any short or light bar, either vertical or horizontal.

Solid sticking.—A mold that is worked on the article itself.

Frame (wood).—A frame is a group of wood parts so machined and assembled as to form an enclosure and a support for a window or sash.

Jamb.—That part of any frame which surrounds and contacts the window or sash that the frame is intended to support.

Side jamb.—The upright member forming the side of the opening.

Head jamb.—The horizontal member forming the top of the opening.

Rabbeted jamb.—A jamb with a rabbet run on one or both edges to receive a window or sash.

Sill.—The horizontal member forming the bottom of the frame.

Pulley stile.—A side jamb into which a pulley is fixed and along which the sash slides.

Casing.—Molding of various widths and thicknesses used to trim window openings.

Parting stop.—A thin strip of wood let into the jamb of a window frame to separate the sash.

Drip cap.—A molding placed on the top of the head casing of a window frame.

Blind stop.—A thin strip of wood machined so as to fit the exterior vertical edge of the pulley stile or jamb and keep the sash in place.

Extension blind stop.—A molded piece, usually of the same thickness as the blind stop, and tongued on one edge to engage a plow in the back edge of the blind stop, thus increasing its width and improving the weather-tightness of the frame.

Dado.—A rectangular groove cut across grain of a frame member.

Jamb liner.—A small strip of wood, either surfaced 4 sides or tongued on 1 edge, which, when applied to the inside edge of a jamb, increases its width for use in thicker walls.

Fabricator.—The person or firm that assembles all of the component parts of the window unit.

Manufacturer — The person or firm that manufacturers any of the component parts of the window unit.

Our contributions for Federal Old Age and Survivor's Insurance during the fiscal year ended November 30, 1954 were $10,024.10.

Meet the Band Saw Crew

These people play an important role in the production of such items as luggage shook, mouse traps, cleats, cheese box shook, and vegetable crating. Together they represent a combined total of 79 years of service at Bridal Veil. Reading from left to right they are: Clyde Hambrick, foreman; Bertha Davis, Mira Nielson, Martha Jones and Verl Bird.

Bridal Veil Standard Frame

On August 9, 1955, we received our first order for a Bridal Veil standard window frame from Firpine Products Co., representing the Frank Paxton Lumber Co. of Des Moines, Iowa. The frame they have chosen has been designated the MS-607. The Paxton Company previously used the BV-500 frame.

In designing standard window frames, we incorporated the most desirable features from the standpoint of patterns and specifications. From four basic standard frames, the parts of which are interchangeable, twenty-one different styles may be obtained. This interchangeability will provide the customer with a wide variety of patterns from which he may select the frame of his choice.

This is definitely a milestone in the advancement of manufacturing window frames at Bridal Veil. If we continue to promote and sell these frames, it will greatly reduce the possibility of error; allow us to build up an inventory of complete frame parts and consequently give better service to our customers.

Don West

Our payroll for July 4 (a paid holiday was $2104.20.

Winter Precaution

As we go to press, the Portland area has enjoyed some thirty-five rainless days, and it might seem like a poor time to talk about winter. However, in a few more days we will be halfway to the shortest day of the year, and we are reminded of frozen pipes. It will be a lot easier to prepare them now rather than after the damage has been done, and with the temperature below freezing.

Ade Jones

New Employees Hired in August

A hearty welcome is extended to the following new employes added during August.

Paul Watts
Francis Cook
Clem Hancock
George Knieriem
Jerry Minch
Max Nelson
Elmer Spencer

Our contributions to the Millmen's Health & Welfare Fund during the fiscal year ended November 30, 1954 amounted to $13,359.91.

BRIDAL VEIL LUMBER & BOX CO.

News Letter

Volume 1, Number 4   BRIDAL VEIL, OREGON   OCTOBER, 1955

Community of Interest

Whatever else may be said about the American way of doing business, there is one fact that stands out beyond the realm of contradiction—this American way has produced the highest standard of living of any country in the world. This American way has many descriptive names, and among these are "the free enterprise system" "free competition" or "the profit system".

All these descriptive names arise from placing the emphasis on some one particular characteristic of the American way. It is interesting to note that the result of these characteristics is the very high level of productivity of American workers, and since they are more productive than those of other countries, the high standard of living is possible. One thing we cannot get around is the impossibility of distributing wealth that has not been created.

The American system is peculiarly well adapted to the stimulation of ways and means to increase individual productivity. In a competitive situation, with customers constantly shopping for the most advantageous buys, manufacturers must be constantly alert to new methods. The automobile industry provides a most striking example of how increasing productivity has resulted in lower prices and better value, which in turn has stimulated greater sales and thus made possible not only far greater employment but also a steadily improving standard of living for those engaged in the auto industry.

This situation is not a unilateral benefit to employers only or to employees only. Both are equally concerned with the results of increasing productivity—the employer gains by way of better profits and the employee by way of larger paychecks. If, however, a manufacturing concern fails to increase its productivity—at least to the extent of keeping pace with its competition—the resulting stagnation in time places that concern in an impossible situation, and employer and employes alike suffer.

While at first blush it might appear that an employee doesn't have an important stake in the prosperity of his employer, it is always a fact that the employee does have an investment of five, ten or fifteen years of his life, years of seniority, and a place in his community, all of which he stands to lose.

Although much has been written on the conflict of interests between employer and employee, it seems that there is a definite and critical community of interest. The interdependence of each upon the other cannot be over-emphasized. They will stand or fall together.

Len Kraft

What's With 1956

There are as many forecasts covering the 1956 residential building outlook as there are guessers in the field. They all seem to be agreed that 1956 will be a good year, although there is some disagreement on how good. The two Washington News Letters to which we subscribe estimate residential starts at 1,100,000 to 1,200,000, while a Portland news service quotes the September issue of House and Home magazine as estimating that 1956 home building may surpass 1955.

When it comes to forecasts, you pay your money and take your choice. It is encouraging that the prospects look good for the coming year.

10th Anniversary

Lawrence (Larry) Smazal, operator of the band rip saw on the swing shift, observed his 10th anniversary with Bridal Veil Lumber and Box Co. on the 2nd of October.

Larry was born in Milladore, Wisconsin, on September 9, 1920, and was one of seven children. He was to remain in Milladore for the next 24 years, until 1944, when he came to Oregon. During the war, he worked at the Swan Island shipyard as a pipe-welder.

Larry knew his bride-to-be, Irene, in Wisconsin. She was already working at Swan Island when Larry came to Oregon. They were married in December 1944.

They didn't believe they wanted to stay in Oregon after the war so in May 1945 they went home to Wisconsin. But, as so often happens in these cases, they soon found out they liked Oregon much better, so in September 1945, they returned to make Oregon their home.

They lived in Bridal Veil a while and then bought a home in Boring. Later on, they sold that and purchased their present home in Latourell. They started out with 8 acres but have now

increased that to 34, so it seems safe to say that Larrys' hobby is farming.

The Smazals have one child, a very lovely daughter, Bobbi, who will be three years old in November.

Mrs. Smazal was also employed at Bridal Veil, working nearly 6-½ years before she retired to become a housewife.

Larry has a sister living in Bridal Veil, Mrs. Harold Vogel.

October Birthdays

Many Happy Returns of the Day.

Emmett Bottoms	Chester Rogers
Ward Dull	Herb Courter
Daryl Cox	James Clark
Don West	Michael Kriska
Charles Gaymon	Bob Polzel
Richard Davis	Carl Walker
Marvin Van Orsow	Dean Davis
Einar Mickelson	H. G. Willoughby
Wesley Adams	

New Employees Hired in October

A hearty welcome is extended to the following new employees added during September.

John A. Kerslake	Virgil Dobson
Ed L. Wendler	Richard Flanagan
James M. Layton	Emmett Bottoms

New Arrivals

Mr. and Mrs. Allan James Grant have announced the birth of a son, Brian James Grant, born October 1, 1955. The young fellow weighed in at a strapping 7 lbs. 6 ozs. Congratulations. Mr. Grant is the designer of the Bridal Veil standard window frame patterns.

"X" Marks the Spot

Gus and Ole, at a Northern fishing resort, rented a hotel boat and found great fishing at a certain spot in a nearby lake, so great that they decided to mark the place and come back for more sport the next day. At the dock Gus said, "Ole did you mark the spot?"

"Yah," replied Ole. "Ay put a chalk mark on this side of the boat."

"Boy, are you dumb!" exclaimed Gus. "Maybe ve von't get the same boat."

Fifteen Years Ago

We have a copy of the **Sunday Oregonian** for October 28, 1940, which lists registrants under the Selective Service Act, by way of preparing for the gold-fish bowl lottery of Tuesday, October 30, 1940. How many old timers can you recall from this list of Bridal Veil employees who registered with local board No. 12 at Gresham?

14 Henry Crampton
59 Clifford Nelson
110 Bruce Klock
142 Walter Stolin
143 Ernest Buchanan
186 Eldon Hepburn
189 Alfred Mourton
226 Stanford Nielson
241 Marion Butler
294 William Nielson, Jr.
316 James B. Hartshorn
372 John Van Orsow
406 Raymond Crampton
407 Ralph Taylor
408 Russell Moulter
409 John Powers
410 Howard Schimmel
468 Carl Cossman
501 Walter Murphy
514 Everett Evans
552 Edmond Wheatley
573 Gilbert Nelson
574 Alton Taylor
583 Ray Hotchkiss
584 Ward Dull
593 Carl Johnson
616 Dean Burkholder
648 Harvey Crouser
649 Archie Lewis
718 James Davis
738 Robert Weston
740 Carl White
743 Leonard Kraft
745 Donald James
748 Albert Davis
749 Fred Crouser
750 Jack Frainey
823 Murray Evans
824 Orval Klock
825 Burton Dunken
835 Delbert Dunken
897 Albert Soderstrom
932 Edgar Cox
934 Theodore Hanson
937 John Fauver
956 Floyd Powers
982 Charles Weaver
983 Adrian Jones
1002 Harold Burkholder
1004 Paul Tomlin
1012 John Thorpe

1051 Lewis Faught
1060 Howard Gilson
1089 Norwood Johnson
1107 Chester Nelson
1126 C. Earle Knipfel
1149 Hugh Douglas
1150 Josiah M. Barnes
1152 Fred Larson
1154 Donald Harp
1185 Veryl Stone
1207 Franklin Bowen

Bridal Veil Visitors

Pictured above is Mr. R. U. (Bob) Tuohy, president of the R. T. Feltus Lumber Co. of Chicago. Mr. Tuohy visited us on September 21. Some of you will recall that his son, Robert, worked here the past two summers.

Fred McBride of Firpine Products was also a September visitor.

Leo Donnelly of the Contact Lumber Co. was out on the afternoon of Sept. 26.

George Mackin and John Couch of Oregon Moulding and Lumber Co. were out to see us a week or so ago. George and John have a new outlet for one of our standard window frames.

Rips and Trims

Tom and **Beulah Choate,** together with their son and daughter-in-law, vacationed in Las Vegas, Nevada. Beulah reports they had a wonderful time in that most fabulous of places.

Ralph, Eleanor, Mary Lee and **Diana Taylor** were lucky enough to be able to attend the Pendleton Roundup. They enjoyed the show very much. It is quite a spectacle.

The **Don Wests** visited relatives at Walla Walla over Labor Day weekend. It was so hot that, to escape the heat, on the return trip they left Walla Walla at midnight, arriving here at 6:00 a.m. a little sleepy.

E. R. (Ernie) Farrari, saw filer, is filling in for J i m C o w l i n g while J i m has gone deer hunting somewhere north of Burns. Ernie was a long time employee a n d resident of Bridal Veil, w o r k i n g here for many years. Upon leaving Bridal Veil, Ernie moved to Vancouver, where he now makes his home. Ernie holds the patent on the saws we use on the band saw line.

The **Jim Cowling** family visited friends and relatives around Eugene, then went camping above Westfir on the Willamette over Labor Day. They report that Westfir was the hottest spot in the state at that particular time.

Alice Elliott has moved to Beaverton and is living with her brother and sister-in-law. Alice is interested in opening a yardage good shop in Gresham. Bridal Veil will miss you Alice.

Harry Densmore took a week off and got in some fishing on the coast. Harry must not have had too good of luck. Weren't they biting, Harry?

Donald Hageman was one of the Journal carriers that got to go to the Pendleton Roundup this year.

Mr. and Mrs. Ralph (Pete) Ellis motored to Minnesota on their vacation. Mrs. Ellis went on to New York to visit her daughter.

The Corbett high school students elected class officers for the year. Children of Bridal Veil employees elected were the following: Senior Class President: **Jim Yerion,** son of **Lillie Yerion.** Vice President of Senior Class: **Bob Bird,** son of **Mr. and Mrs. Verl Bird.** Vice Pres. of Junior Class: **Don Bowen,** son of **Mr. and Mrs. Frank** Bowen. Secretary-Treas. of sophomore class: **Philip Schneringer,** son of **Mr. and Mrs. Raymond Schneringer. Barbara Mickelson,** daughter of **Mr. and Mrs. Einar Mickelson,** is secretary of the Freshman class.

It's beginning to look like spring around Bridal Veil what with all the new cars showing up. **Eldon Gross, Eldon Neilson** and **Elmer Ayles** are sporting new Fords. **Dean Davis** has a new Chevrolet and **Harold Jacobson** a new Studebaker.

Ralph Sanders won a blue ribbon for his display at a rock show at Yakima. Ralph says that this was only his third entry, so to come up with top honors is pretty good. Nice going Ralph.

Lula Cowling

Let's Look at Safety

Two lost time accidents in the month of August again marred our chances of improving our safety record and raised our accident frequency rating from 49.6 per million man-hours to 50.6 per million manhours.

In going back over accident reports we find that there has been some accidents where hands or fingers have been injured. We also note that in some cases gloves were being worn at the time of the accident. In one or two of these incidents, gloves were the indirect cause of the accident, therefore we must be doubly careful when wearing them. In the winter months gloves are somewhat of a necessity but, lets not forget, they also create an extra hazard for saw and other machine operators. If you find it necessary to wear gloves, perhaps it would be a good idea to keep in mind the fact that if the gloves you are wearing are snug fitting, you will be less apt to get your fingers caught in a saw, gear, or other type of machinery.

Mel Mallinson

Payments to railroads for freight charges during the fiscal year ended November 30, 1954 were $204,648.33.

Ten Years Ago in Gresham Outlook

Orders Swamp Firm;
Labor Badly Needed

Lifting Of Cheese Rationing Brings Order Rush.

BRIDAL VEIL, September 20, 1945 —With more than 3,000,000 orders on hand for cheese boxes of all sizes, the Bridal Veil Lumber and Box Company is preparing to speed up its post war program.

Biggest handicap now is the shortage of workers, said Leonard Kraft, president of the organization.

Orders for cheese boxes have been swamping the Bridal Veil concern ever since the rationing on cheese was lifted last week. Within 24 hours after cheese was taken off the ration list, telegrams ordering more than a half million boxes had been received by company officials. By early this week orders were over the three million mark. To gear the plant to full peace time production, Mr. Kraft this week made a plea for workers.

J. M. Barnes, representative of the firm, will be at the city hall in Gresham Saturday morning from 10 a.m. to 12 noon to interview residents of the Gresham area for full-time, permanent employment at the Bridal Veil plant.

To help solve transportation problems, Portland Stages, Inc., will begin operating a bus between Gresham and the plant on Monday. The bus will leave here about 6:30 a.m., arriving at the plant before 7:15 a.m., when the day shift starts. It will make a stop in Fairview Homes. The bus will return with workers in the evening.

"We are offering permanent employment to residents of the area," Mr. Barnes declared. "This is not war work; it is peacetime work with an established company."

The work week at the box plant is 49 hours with the unskilled wage rate 85 cents an hour with time-and-a-half over 40 hours. All work is inside, Mr. Barnes explained.

The finished suit case shook produced from a blank 6/4x7¾x25¾ has a value of 46 cents.

A finished window sill for a 2-4 opening Dekker-Brish frame has a value of $1.15.

Total salaries and wages paid during the fiscal year ended November 30, 1954 were $637,257.14.

Total payments to suppliers for lumber during the fiscal year ended November 30, 1954 were $1,181,656.54.

Our payroll for the first 8 months of the 1955 fiscal year was $531,598.69. In the same period last year it was $379,679.80—a gain of 40 per cent.

1955 SAFETY RECORD

	Lost Time Accidents	Man Hours Worked	Accidents Per Million Man Hours
January	4	28,772	139.9
February	0	24,023	0
March	0	24,253	0
First Quarter 1955	4	77,048	51.9
April	1	28,179	35.5
May	2	30,721	65.1
June	3	33,905	88.5
Second Quarter 1955	6	92,805	64.7
July	0	31,350	0
August	2	35,625	56.0
Total for Year 1955	10	237,803	49.6

Corbett Football Highlights

Bridal Veil Lumber & Box can well be proud of the boys who play on the high school football team at Corbett. Not only are these boys doing a fine job representing the school, they are also supplying the team with nearly ¼ of the players. Three of the boys in the starting backfield are from Bridal Veil with Bob Cowling at quarterback, Tom Cowling at right halfback, and Dewayne Kilness at left halfback.

Other Corbett players whose fathers or mothers are employed at the mill include Don Hageman, Don Bowen, Jim Yerion, Bob Long, Marvin Howell, and Garfield Pearson, who is living with the Louis Wilsons'.

This is a good football team. They have made mistakes, and will undoubtedly make more, but we must remember that this is only the second year of football at Corbett. The boys have good team spirit and are giving their best when they are in the game. As they gain experience, these boys are going to give a lot of football teams plenty of anxious moments. In the first four games, which Corbett won, their opponents were blanked in the first three.

There are several outstanding players on the squad. Some of them will be lost through graduation next year. One boy who will be around for two more seasons and should develop into an outstanding player is Bob Cowling, who shows lots of promise.

$5.56 Per Minute

On a random day in August, 1955 (Wednesday, 17th) our straight time payroll was $2,671.67. If someone were to flip you a five dollar gold piece every minute for eight hours a day (a nice way to make a living), you would catch $2,400.00 in the 480 minutes of the working day. On the other hand, if you stopped catching for ten minutes morning and afternoon you would be short $100.00 at the end of the day. In a twenty-day month you would end up $2,000.00 short, and in twelve months, it would be $24,000.00.

Ade Jones

Our paid vacations during the fiscal year ended November 30, 1954 totaled $15,284.01.

We should all make it a practice to attend all the games we can. The boys appreciate a good crowd, and besides, they put on quite a show.

Tom Cowling

10th Anniversary

This is the 10th anniversary of Howard Hunt, cutter in the box factory. Howard is somewhat of a rarity in Bridal Veil inasmuch as he is a native Oregonian. He was born in Portland on September 4, 1897. He was educated in Portland and Estacada.

In 1917, Howard moved to Baker where he worked for what was then the Baker White Pine Lumber Co.

Howard and Mrs. Hunt were married in Baker and both of their children, boy and girl, were born there. They now have six grandchildren.

The Hunts have their home in Corbett. Howard is a 1st lieutenant in the Multnomah County Sheriffs' Reserve and has been in that organization for fourteen years. So between that and the eleven acres on their place, Howard manages to keep fairly well occupied. We also understand that Howard is quite a fisherman.

BRIDAL VEIL LUMBER & BOX CO.
News Letter

Volume 1, Number 5   BRIDAL VEIL, OREGON   NOVEMBER, 1955

Board of Directors Meet

Left to right—Leonard Kraft, H. B. Hardy, A. D. Jones, H. W. Winfree and C. W. Kraft.

The semi-annual meeting of the Board of Directors of Bridal Veil Lumber & Box Company was held at Bridal Veil Wednesday, October 26. The board consists of five men who are elected by the stockholders or owners of the company to represent them in directing the management of the company. The board of directors, in turn, appoints the officers who are charged with the responsibility for the day to day operation of the company.

However, the Board of Directors does not just hire the operating officials of the company, and then forget the whole thing, leaving it up to the local manager to "carry the mail". Since the directors are the representatives of the stockholders, it is their duty to the stockholders to see that the company is operated efficiently and profitably. In order to discharge their duties the directors are required to give thoughtful consideration to the problems confronting their management and to counsel and guide them in the interests of the company.

Since the above might sound like a lot of fancy talk with very little actual meat in it, I would like to outline a few of the directors' objectives. It is the announced intention of our board to create at Bridal Veil a woodworking plant that will be a pace-setter in our industry. Of course, such a goal has as its first step the matter of providing the necessary capital to finance a series of improvements which will still extend over a period of several years into the future. The problem of how to best equip and house the operation is one requiring the attention of the board. In some cases the equipment to do our job does not even exist and steps must be taken to cause it to be constructed.

While creating a long term program for the development of Bridal Veil,

(Continued on page 2)

Temporary Slowdown

As reported in one of the earlier editions of the Newsletter, at one time this year we had 44 carloads of window frames on order. That would amount to almost three months of production.

Now we have only 11 cars of window frames on order. That means roughly one month's production. Ordinarily, by this time we would be getting orders for shipment in December. If these orders aren't forthcoming shortly it could mean a rather lean month as far as making window frames is concerned.

What is the reason for this? There are several factors involved, especially at this time of the year.

As we all know, this has been a particularly bad year in the east weatherwise. There were two or three hurricanes that badly damaged the east coast. Following that there were a series of floods and torrential rains that virtually paralyzed the north-eastern section of the country. We ship a large percentage of our mill-work to those areas, and it will take time for them to recover from those reversals.

As usual, at this time of year, some dealers attempt to pare their inventories to avoid having to pay an inventory tax (levied in some states) at the end of the year.

These factors add up to a slowdown in everything, including the construction of new homes.

These things are not as bad as they sound. Customers have repeatedly assured us of more orders in 1956 than we have had this year. Business experts predict housing starts next year will come close to equaling those of this year.

If we do experience a slowdown in December we are certain it will be a very temporary thing, maybe less than a month in duration.

On the Eastern Front

On my recent trip east I visited the Wichita Building Materials Co. in Wichita, Kansas, Pease Woodworking Co. in Cincinnati, Ohio, Luce Manufacturing Co. and Martin Materials Co. in Kansas City, Mo., Dekker-Brish-Lumber Co. in Chicago, Concord Millwork Corp. in Rochester, New York, Concord Lumber Co. in Albany, N. Y. and The Becker Builders Supply Co. in Wilmington, N. C.

In each instance my visit was welcomed by representatives of the various companies, and each one of them seemed glad to take the time to discuss with me the various problems that we have and to make any changes in their details or their method of operation, to make our production problems simpler.

In almost every instance I find, while watching a customers operation, that there are items that they need, that we would like to produce to round out our own operation.

The high light of my entire trip this year, as well as last year is the fact that all of our customers like our window frames. Our Millwork is tops. The texture of our material cannot be beat and the careful way our pro-duct is loaded in the boxcars brings forth a lot of favorable comment.

The big cry at each place is More frames, faster, in their busy season.

So, it seems that if we continue our high quality of workmanship, keep on a competitive price basis and ship on schedule we will have these cus-tomers for a long time.

Incidentally, I also attended two world series games at Ebbets field in Brooklyn.

Ade Jones

Board of Director Meets

(Continued from page 1)

the board also concerns itself with the current operating program and coun-sels and guides the management in its efforts to take the long term pro-gram in stride and produce current profits at the same time.

The board recognizes that great strides are being made in the proper direction and is proud of the fine cooperation the entire organization is giving toward attainment of the ulti-mate goals. With continuation of this splendid spirit our calendar for pro-gress and growth may be speeded up considerably.

Seniority List

1. Atchley, Noah 3-23-36	58. Murray, George 4-21-47	114. Kuntz, Vyrtle 5- 4-54
2. Dull, Ward E. 5-18-36	59. Lofstedt, Charles 4-23-47	115. Long, Fredrick H.... 6- 2-54
3. Noble, Clarence 7-27-36	60. Jones, Martha A. 5-14-47	116. Kilness, Jarvis 6- 2-54
4. McCredie, Ralph H. 8-27-36	61. Choate, Thomas 5-15-47	117. Fawcett, Fred 8-16-54
5. Harnam, Ed 3-22-37	62. Van Hee, Theo. V. 9- 9-47	118. Zumwalt, Roley 9- 7-54
6. Davis, D. Fay 3-22-37	63. Rowe, Thelma Y. ...11-12-47	119. Cox, Daryl 9-13-54
7. Jackson, Marvin T. 4- 8-37	64. Dunken, William L. 9-15-47	120. Crane, Franklin T..... 9-13-54
8. Stolin, Walter F. 5-11-37	65. Hills, Mabel M. 1-14-48	121. Davis, Richard 9-13-54
9. Rhodes, James D. 6- 8-37	66. Davis, Dean F. 9-31-48	122. Walker, Carl 9-20-54
10. Bowen. Franklin M. 8-19-37	67. Jacobson, Richard 11-29-48	123. Wilson, Louis 9-20-54
11. Crouser, Fred 8-30-37	68. Hills, Stanley B. 1-15-51	124. Rees, David 9-23-54
12. Bird, Verl W. 9-20-37	69. Ball, Vera Nell 1-15-51	125. Spitzengel, Richard 9-23-54
13. Taylor, Ralph L. 11-22-37	70. Granberg, Larry A. 1-15-51	126. Godat, Robert D. ...10- 6-54
14. Hanson, Theodore N. 4-18-38	71. Van Orsow, John H. 1-15-51	127. Morgan, Roland B. 12-14-54
15. Van Orsow, Jos. M. 4-22-38	72. Kimbley, A. R. Jr. 2-19-51	128. Kriska, Michael 1- 3-55
16. Dunken, James D. 7-18-38	73. Van Treek, Paul 2-27-51	129. Long, Gary R. 1- 5-55
17. Courter, Herbert D. 2-13-39	74. Van Hee, Theo. Sr. 2-27-51	130. Polzel, Leslie D. 1- 5-55
18. Burkholder, Ken. D. 2-22-39	75. Schneringer, Ray 10- 8-51	131. Gaymon, Charles N. 3-29-55
19. Meyer, Kenneth L. 9-16-40	76. Walker, Homer F. 10- 9-51	132. Kreman, Jack L. ... 3-30-55
20. Hartshorn, Merrill 1- 8-41	77. Frazier, Lloyd 10- 9-51	133. Collins, Milford G..... 4- 6-55
21. Harp, Fred 5-21-41	78. Eveland, Roy D. ...10-15-51	134. Kruckman, Harry D. 4- 7-55
22. Mickelson, Einar ... 7- 1-41	79. Catlin, Kenneth V. 10-18-51	135. Clayton, Rodney L. 4-11-55
23. Roberts, Jerald G. 9- 8-41	80. Anderson, Lester 5-19-52	136. Reischel, Robert W. 4-11-55
24. Van Orsow, Jacob M. 9-29-41	81. Emmons, Dale 5-20-52	137. Seeger, Roger 4-11-55
25. Ellis, Ralph 10- 9-41	82. Kimbley, A. R. Sr. 6- 2-52	138. Pitts, Orien 4-13-55
26. Latourell, Clifford.... 3-23-42	83. Howell, Lester B. .. 6-23-52	139. Rogers, William 4-18-55
27. Vogel, Harold A. 3-25-42	84. Hutchison, Earl 6-23-52	140. Dull, Thelma 4-25-55
28. Nielson, Eldon F. 4-21-42	85. Van Buskirk, Norman 7-28-52	141. Adams, Wesley 5- 9-55
29. Davis, Bertha M. 5- 6-42	86. Preston, Grant 8- 4-52	142. Dooley, Paul D......... 5- 9-55
30. Rhodes, Louise I. 5-28-42	87. Hancock, Loren 9- 2-52	143. Schroder, Arthur H. 5-11-55
31. Hartshorn, Dorothy 7-14-42	88. Long, Fred M. 9- 9-52	144. Hageman, Leo C. 6- 1-55
32. Bowen, Anna 9-30-42	89. Cote, Joseph 9-10-52	145. Smith, John W. 6- 9-55
33. Woddard, Chester E. 11- 2-42	90. Adolph, Harry ....- 9-22-52	146. Bailey, Fredrick C. 6-20-55
34. Anderson, Roy J. 2-11-43	91. Godat, Harold M. 9-25-52	147. Clark, David 6-27-55
35. Hageman, Leo F. 7-14-43	92. Willms, John G. 9-29-52	148. Levan, Paul F. 6-28-55
36. Yerion, Lillie P. 7-19-43	93. Potter, Eugene H. 10-28-52	149. Dunlap, Leon C. 7- 5-55
37. Houchin, Wilbur O. 7-26-43	94. Johnson, Orval K. 3-23-53	150. Heatherington, M..... 7-26-55
38. Cloe, Pearl P. 11-12-43	95. Wells, Glen 3-23-53	151. Clark, James P. 7-29-55
39. Eversull, James A. 12-17-43	96. Crane, Jack L. 3-30-53	152. Rogers, Chester 8- 9-55
40. Britton, Thomas C. 12-20-43	97. Davies, Archie L..... 4- 1-53	153. Cook, Francis P. ... 8-10-55
41. Nielson, Mira J. 1-23-44	98. Bissell, Louis W. 5- 1-53	154. Hancock, Clem A..... 8-15-55
42. Litton, Durward L. 5- 9-44	99. Layton, Bob 5-28-53	155. Minch, Jerry L. 8-22-55
43. DeMain, Lloyd E..... 8-27-45	100. Bissell, Max 6- 1-53	156. Watts, Paul A. 8-22-55
44. Peterson, Lawrence 9-24-45	101. McCawley, William 7-27-53	157. Knieriem, George S. 8-24-55
45. Hunt, Howard G. ...10- 1-45	102. Sanders, Ralph L..... 8- 3-53	158. Nelson, Max D. 8-24-55
46. Smazal, Lawrence A. 10-2-45	103. Ayles, Elmer L. 8- 4-53	159. Spencer, Elmer D..... 8-25-55
47. Stolin, Marvin J. 3-28-46	104. Willoughby, H. G.... 8-24-53	160. Cox, Ernest M. 8-29-55
48. Van Hee, Theophile 4-17-46	105. Gross, Elden 8-27-53	161. Kerslake, John A..... 9- 6-55
49. Polzel, Robert E. 5- 1-46	106. Mannthey, Walter... 9-14-53	162. Wendler, Ed L. 9- 6-55
50. Kendrick, James B. 5-13-46	107. Kuzmesky, Steven.... 9-15-53	163. Layton, James M.... 9- 7-55
51. Woodard, Mary R. 6- 3-46	108. Lamke, Ralph 1-25-54	164. Dobson, Virgil 9- 7-55
52. Houchin, Inez M. 9- 5-46	109. Hancock, John 3- 2-54	165. Flanagin, Richard J. 9- 7-55
53. Jacobson, Harold R. 9-16-46	110. Bennett, George O. ..5- 4-54	166. Bottoms, Emmett.... 9-13-55
54. Choate, Beulah 10- 7-46	111. Bowen, James E. 5- 4-54	167. Clabaugh, David ...10-26-55
55. Layton, Hiram 11-13-46	112. Burkholder, Harold 5- 4-54	168. Westlake, Donald 10-17-55
56. Steele, Edward J..... 1-14-47	113. Kinonen, Edsel 5- 4-54	169. Reinsch, David 10-21-55
57. Lofstedt, Clarence.... 1-16-47		170. Swanson, Robert ...10-24-55

The Filing Room

There is only one way to file a saw, and that is the right way. At Bridal Veil that job is entrusted to the two men pictured above. **Ralph Taylor** on the left and **Jim Cowling** on the right.

We (the writer) found out we didn't know very much about saw filing. It is quite a complicated and delicate thing, when it is done right.

First we started with the band saws. Jim explained that when a saw is first brought in to be sharpened, the first thing he does is put it on the Band Saw Stretcher. This machine puts the proper amount of tension in the saw.

He also checks the saw for bumps, and if any are found, they must be hammered out. Bumps are caused by small chips and slivers getting between the saw and the wheel.

To get back to the tension angle, if a saw does not have the proper amount of tension it is apt to get hot and wobble or flutter, or, as sometimes happens, the saw will break.

Next the saw is taken to the Automatic Band Saw Grinder, where, if needed, the saw is swaged (pronounced swedge). This expands or broadens the teeth. Then comes the shaper which puts the proper shape on the teeth, particularly on the sides. After that the teeth are gauged to assure proper alignment and last the saw is ground to the proper degree. The band rip saws are set for a 3-32" kerf and the band resaws are set for a 1-16" kerf.

From there Ralph took over as "teacher" and began describing how a round or circular saw is handled. When they are brought in he checks the tension and smoothness. After that the set is checked and this as well as the tension is done with a hammer.

Then the saw is placed on an arbor and side dressed. This hones down the side of the teeth for kerf and smoothness.

The saw goes to the hand gummer next, (hope that is spelled right) which grinds between the teeth, joints the top of the teeth and faces the teeth. Ralph finishes the job by hand filing the tips of the teeth.

Circular saws are often kerfed for a particular job, depending on the thickness of the lumber. The kerf might be 3-32, 7-64 or 1-8". At the time of this writing, Ralph had a set of saws kerfed at 13-128' for a special job. We couldn't even measure something like that, let alone do it.

We have circle saws ranging from 2-½" to 26" in diameter in varying thicknesses.

Jim and Ralph, as you know, have both been at Bridal Veil for many years. Jim, the head filer, has been in the filing room since 1938 and Ralph since 1951.

We have been making cheese box shook for seventeen or eighteen years. We have been making noveltoy stock for nine or ten years. The noveltoy is circle resawn and the cheese box shook is band resawn. The customers know when they order they will always get the same fine job of resawing whether it is circle or band. That is probably one of the most important reasons why we have had reorders for these many years.

Back to School

With a view toward doing something to correct our poor safety record, the State Industrial Accident Commission is going to put on a series of classes on accident prevention.

The school will consist of three two-hour sessions conducted at one week intervals starting Thursday, November 10, and will be attended by all foremen.

A Man and a Machine

The man in the picture is **George Leash,** machinist for Bridal Veil, and the machine is the new splitter George recently completed. The splitter is now situated just east of the band resaw line in the box factory.

The new splitter was specifically designed with the idea in mind of running roof slats for Lincoln Log Sets. The Hampshire Mfg. Co., to whom we ship these roof slats, is a highly valued customer, therefore we are constantly looking for ways and means of improving the quality of this item.

We began shipping roof slats in February, 1948 through the R. T. Feltus Lbr. Co. of Chicago and they have been and are still handling the account.

George put many long hours, lots of experience and perhaps even a little patience into his splitter. At any rate, we think he did a fine job, and

George Leash

deserves a great big "well done" for his efforts.

Bridal Veil Visitors

Reedy Berg of Dant & Russell was out on the 6th of October. He brought with him a sample window frame for us to look over and, if possible, quote on.

Maury Isted, Sales Manager of Pine Products at Prineville, who supply us with a great deal of lumber was a visitor on October 5.

George Wicker, of George Wicker, Inc., Portland, was a visitor on October 3.

George Close, Sales Manager of the Kinzua Corporation, was here on October 18, to discuss lumber shipments to Bridal Veil.

W. M. Clem, of the Clem Lumber and Distributing Co. of Cincinnati and Alliance, Ohio, was here on Oct. 18, to discuss purchase of millwork items for their distribution yards.

John Shearon, of Shearon Lumber Sales, Des Moines, Iowa visited us on Oct. 18. Mr. Shearon was interested in buying window frames. We made the necessary drawings, price lists and specifications and forwarded them to his office.

When work goes out of style we may expect to see civilization totter and fall.

—John D. Rockefeller.

Nov. Birthdays

Many Happy Returns of the Day.

Clem A. Hancock	Fay Davis
Ralph Sanders	Fred Harp
Harry Adolph	David Clabaugh
Harold Burkholder	Kenneth Meyer
Verl Bird	Louis Bissell
Harold Godat	Walt Norgard
Richard Jacobson	Bill Dunken
Louise Rhodes	

Keep the Seniority List

On page three of this issue of the newsletter, we have printed the seniority list for the benefit of the employees. This will be a regular feature of the newsletter and will appear three or four times a year. For your own information it might be a good idea to pull out this page and tack it up some place for ready reference.

The most important part of every business is to know what ought to be done.

—Columbella.

School Bus Stops

Motorists Reminded of 1949 Law

Some 1800 Oregon school buses are carrying pupils to their various schools. Under Oregon law, since 1949, all motorists are required to come to a full stop when meeting or overtaking a school bus which has stopped to load or unload.

The summer-long absence of school buses from the highway, except as used carrying farm workers and for summer outings, may have caused some motorists to forget the law. There is one situation in which traffic is not required to stop and that is that approaching traffic on opposite side of a four lane roadway may proceed with caution but in case of doubt, stop! At all other times, both inside and outside of cities, traffic must stop and remain stopped as long as children are leaving the bus or are on the highway.

Paid Holiday Recap

The cost of the three paid holidays can now be totalled up, and the figures look like this:

Memorial Day	$2,179.36
Fourth of July	2,104.20
Labor Day	2,155.80
Total	$6,439.36

Modernization Program

Among the projects considered for early scheduling by the Board of Directors at the October 26 meeting were the following:

Hog for Moulding Department	$ 3,754.75
Bow string Truss Roof west of factory	30,000.00
Revamp Moulding Department blower	8,631.00
Paving of Yard and Driveways	5,092.50
Scissor Lifts for Ripping Operation	3,526.00
Sprinkler Ripping Building	8,500.00
Sprinkler Truss Roof	8,000.00
Revamp Ripping Department Blower	1,725.00
Total	$69,229.25

Let's Look at Safety

Two lost time accidents in the month of September raised our accident frequency rating from 50.6 per million manhours to 51.9 per million manhours.

September ends the third quarter of 1955 and with the industry average of 21.2 per million manhours, we are 2.4 times the industry average.

1955 SAFETY RECORD

	Lost Time Accidents	Man Hours Worked	Accidents Per Million Man Hours
January	4	28,772	139.9
February	0	24,023	0
March	0	24,253	0
First Quarter 1955	4	77,048	51.9
April	1	28,179	35.5
May	2	30,721	65.1
June	3	33,905	88.5
Second Quarter 1955	6	92,805	64.7
July	0	31,350	0
August	2	35,625	56.0
September	2	31,716	63.1
3rd Quarter, 1955	4	98,691	40.5
Total for Year 1955	14	269,519	51.9
Industry Average, 1954			21.2

CHARLES W. KRAFT

"Chuck" Kraft is President of Kraf-tile Company, Niles, California. He was elected to the Board of Directors March 19, 1953 to represent 39 percent of the capital stock held by G. Howard Kraft.

HERBERT W. WINFREE

"Herb" Winfree is a partner in the law firm of Winfree, McCulloch, Shuler & Sayre of Portland. He was elected to the Board of Directors March 19, 1953 as legal counsel of the company.

HOWELL B. HARDY

"Ben" Hardy is a partner in the law firm of Snyder, Chadwell & Fagerburg of Chicago, Illinois. He was elected to the Board of Directors March 19, 1953 to represent 39 percent of the capital stock held by Erwin P. Snyder.

Meeting of Health and Welfare

A meeting on health and welfare, to which all employees were invited, was held in the community hall on October 14. Mr. Herman Schmunk, business representative of Millmen's Local 1120 and Administrator for the Board of Trustees of the Millmen's Health and Welfare Fund was on hand to explain the necessity for the proper completion of the doctor and hospital report forms, which, in turn, assures payment of legitimate claims.

It was also discovered, and brought out, that the union is to provide a safety committee in the plant, as well as the one provided by the company. **Theophile Van Hee, Jr.** was elected unanimously.

New Employees Hired in November

A hearty welcome is extended to the following new employees added during October:

Donald Westlake   David Reinsch
     Robert Swanson

Rips and Trims

Paul Van Treeck suffered a light heart attack October 16, and is having to take it easy awhile. We hope and trust it is not too serious and that Paul will be back with us shortly.

Mrs. Noah Atchley recently spent a few days in the hospital. We are glad to report that she is now able to be home.

Leonard and **Gerry Kraft, Jack Flaucher, Jack Flaucher Jr.** and **Lefty Hansen** of Multnomah Falls, went deer hunting at Izee. Report has it that they were all successful.

Dorothy Jackson spent a few days in the hospital but is now home and reported doing fine.

Verl Bird was on jury duty off and on during the month of October.

Art Molter, a former employee of Bridal Veil, was a recent visitor. Art worked here many years but is now retired and living in Portland.

Quite a few of the boys enjoyed a successful deer season. Some were not so lucky. Here are a few of the reports we have been able to come up with: **Marvin Van Orsow** got a forked horn in the Eastern part of the Ochoco National Forest. **Ralph Sanders** and **Dewey Spencer** each got a doe east of Madras. **Herb Courter** tells us he got a small three point 60 miles south of Pendleton. **Jim Cowling** got a 4 point in the Myrtle Park area in Eastern Oregon. **Marv Stolin** missed the only shot he had somewhere on Larch Mt. **Archie Davies** got a fawn in the Lapine area. **Harold Godat** got a doe in Clackamas county. **Howard Hunt** got a doe in Lake County. **Elmer Ayles** got a 4 point buck somewhere near Kinzua. **Louis Wilson** and **Harold Burkholder** are reported to have each gotten a deer but unfortunately we were unable to contact them to find out when and where. **Bob Bird** got a doe while hunting the area around Kinzua.

Except for the coastal country these boys pretty well covered the state.

Pictured above is what we would call a fairly decent catch of steelhead. The fish were taken on the Rogue River. The fishermen (in the background) are Len and Gerry Kraft and Doug Walwyn of Smith & Crakes of Eugene.

Back in the Fold

Welcomed back on our list of customers after a nine year absence (last car shipped April 6, 1948) is the Borden Company at Van Wert, Ohio, who recently placed an order for 120,000 3. Cream Cheese boxes and 30,000 Liederkranz boxes. The order was placed through Quality Box Service Company for assembly by Lynch Box Company, Ltd. of Wrenn, Ohio.

It is the studying that you do after your school days that really counts. Otherwise you know only that which everyone else knows.

—Henry L. Doherty.

UNITED FUND REPORT

Here is how our United Fund campaign ended this year as compared to last year:

Year	No. of Employees	Employees Pledge	Company Pledge	Total Pledge
1955	192	$632.16	$632.16	$1264.32
1954	158	$638.60	0	$ 638.60

BRIDAL VEIL LUMBER & BOX CO.

News Letter

Volume 1, Number 6   BRIDAL VEIL, OREGON   DECEMBER, 1955

There Is a Difference

As we look about us and compare the standard of living in America with what we know about conditions in other countries around the world, we come to be more and more impressed with the conclusion that the high level which we enjoy can best be wrapped up in one word — "productivity".

Some years ago I had the pleasure of a trip to Mexico City, and thus had an opportunity to observe a building project not far from the hotel at which we were staying. Somebody apparently had dumped a load of sand in the wrong place and there was a move on foot to transfer the sand pile about 50 feet. The method employed involved a man with a shovel, who attacked the pile and shovelful by shovelful built a new pile a few feet away. At this point another man armed with a shovel took over and repeated the process and then another, and another, with men scattered along the entire distance. Thus, bucket brigade fashion, the pile was ultimately moved. I didn't stay long enough to see the project completed.

In this country it would have been a matter of a few minutes for one man with a scoopmobile to do the job. And the one man wouldn't have been exhausted when the job was done, either.

This sort of an example serves to pinpoint the story of productivity. American workmen are paid more because they produce more and thus there is more wealth to share. They produce more because they have the tools to work with, and lots of horse power to help them. An American contractor attempting to use bucket brigade techniques would go broke at 25 cents an hour wages regardless of how hard his men worked. They just wouldn't have the productivity necessary.

In the past many schemes have been introduced to boost production per man per hour, and many plans have withered on the vine because they were headed in the wrong direction. Some of these plans simply tried to increase productivity by increasing the speed of the workman so that if you wanted to cut cost 20 per cent you simply required 25 per cent more work per man. That worked fine up to the point where workmen looked more like whirling dervishes, and it was impossible to go any further since both the plan and the workmen had broken down.

Consequently we find that there is a vast difference between the modern day attempts to increase productivity and the "speed-up" techniques employed thirty years ago. Today the emphasis is placed on improving the tools available, cleaning up the work area, positioning tools and materials and generally making it possible to produce more with less actual physical effort. Today a stationary engineer in a large plant can report to work in a white shirt, sit at a desk, and by pushing a few buttons, stoke half a dozen coal-fired boilers.

Surely this type of job improvement is one that can be welcomed by all segments of society, as it is the key to increasing productivity, higher wages, less physical effort, better working conditions, and a higher standard of living for all.

The methods employed by industry today to improve production are the result of a long period of evolution that started when the first factory was established. During the evolutionary period many means were tried and almost as many means have been dis-

(Continued on page 2)

Back to School

The State Industrial Accident Commission has started a series of three, two hour safety classes at Bridal Veil, which are being presented by C. B. Huskey and E. C. Thomas of the commission.

Attending the classes are:

Leonard Kraft, Clarence Noble, Ade Jones, Walt Norgard, Clyde Hambrick, Don West, Paul Detrick, Mel Mallinson, Dean Burkholder, Einar Mickelson, Jim Cowling, Leo Hageman, Jacob Van Orsow, Willie Bowen, Verl Bird, Theophile Van Hee, Roley Zumwalt, Lloyd DeMain.

The material being presented consists of a series of lectures and films designed to acquaint our supervisory personnel with the need for a complete safety protection program. Included in our plans for the immediate future is the establishment of a safety committee which will be responsible for making safety inspections and safety suggestions and also for making investigations of lost time accidents.

Mel Mallinson

In addition to lost production when we have a power failure, each ½ hour of shut down costs $78.93 in wages paid out.

There Is a Difference

(Continued from page 1)

carded as being unsatisfactory. Some were discarded as being out-and-out mistakes. The evolution has not been completed yet by any means, and further improvements are yet to come. The industrial environment of the year 2005 will be as different from 1955 as 1955 is from 1905.

The object today remains as it was fifty years ago — to increase the product of every man. The big difference is in the "how". One man (weight 125 lbs. wringing wet and with his pockets full of stones) can dig a ditch faster and easier than ten men (weight 200 lbs. stripped to the waist) could at the turn of the century.

Yes, there is a difference.

Len Kraft

Let's Look at Safety

Three lost time accidents in the month of October raised our accident frequency rating from 51.9 per million man hours to 63.4 per million man hours.

With the industry average being 21.2 per million man hours, we are three times the industry average.

1955 SAFETY RECORD

	Lost Time Accidents	Man Hours Worked	Accidents Per Million Man Hours
January	4	28,772	139.9
February	0	24,023	0
March	0	24,253	0
First Quarter 1955	4	77,048	51.9
April	1	28,179	35.5
May	2	30,721	65.1
June	3	33,905	88.5
Second Quarter 1955	6	92,805	64.7
July	0	31,350	0
August	2	35,625	56 0
September	2	31,716	63.1
3rd Quarter, 1955	4	98,691	40 5
October	3	30,223	99.3
Total for Year 1955	17	299,752	63.4

Health and Welfare Coverage

The following employees worked at least 80 hours in October so are covered by Millworkers Health & Welfare Insurance for the month of December 1955:

Wesley Adams
Harry Adolph
Lester W. Anderson
Roy J. Anderson
Noah Atchley
Elmer Ayles
Vera Nell Ball
George O. Bennett
Verl W. Bird
Louis Bissell
Max Bissell
Emmett Bottoms
Anna Bowen
Franklin M. Bowen
James E. Bowen
Thomas Britton
Harold Burkholder
Kenneth Burkholder
Kenneth Catlin
Beulah Choate
Thomas Choate
David Clabaugh
David Clark
James P. Clark
Rodney Clayton
Pearl P. Cloe
Milford Collins
Francis P. Cook
Joseph Cote
Herbert Courter
Daryl W. Cox
Ernest M. Cox, Jr.
Franklin T. Crane
Jack Crane
Fred Crouser
Archie Davies
Bertha M. Davis
D. Fay Davis
Dean Davis
Richard Davis
Lloyd DeMain
Virgil Dobson
Paul Dooley
Thelma Dull
Ward Dull
James D. Dunken
William Dunken
Leon C. Dunlap
Ralph Ellis
Dale Emmons
Roy Eveland
James Eversull
Fred Fawcett
Richard Flanagin
Lloyd Frazier
Charles N. Gaymon
Harold M. Godat
Robert D. Godat
Larry Granberg
Elden Gross
Leo C. Hageman

Leo F. Hageman
Clem A. Hancock
John W. Hancock
Loren Hancock
Theodore N. Hanson
Ed Harnam
Fred Harp
Dorothy Hartshorn
Merrill Hartshorn
Manford Heatherington
Mabel M. Hills
Stanley B. Hills
Inez M. Houchin
Wilbur O. Houchin
Lester B. Howell
Howard G. Hunt
Earl Hutchison
Marvin T. Jackson
Harold Jacobson
Richard Jacobson
Orval K. Johnson
Martha A. Jones
James Kendrick
John Kerslake
Jarvis Kilness
A. R. Kimbley
Albert Kimbley, Jr.
Edsel Kinonen
George Knieriem
Jack Kreman
Michael Kriska
Harry D. Kruckman
Vyrtle C. Kuntz
Steven Kuzmesky
Clifford Latourell
Bob Layton
Hiram Layton
James M. Layton
George M. Leash
Paul Levan
Durward L. Litton
Charles Lofstedt
Clarence Lofstedt
Fredrick H. Long
Fred M. Long
Gary Long
Walter Mannthey
William McCawley
Ralph McCredie
Kenneth Meyer
Einar Mickelson
Jerry Minch
Roland B. Morgan
George Murray
Max Nelson
Eldon Nielson
Mira Nielson
Clarence Noble
Lawrence Peterson
Orien Pitts

Leslie D. Polzel
Robert E. Polzel
E. H. Potter
Grant Preston
David G. Rees
Robert Reischel
James D. Rhodes
Louise Rhodes
Jerald Roberts
Chester Rogers
William Rogers
Thelma Rowe
Ralph Sanders
Raymond Schneringer
Arthur Schroder
Roger Seegar
Lawrence Smazal
John W. Smith
Elmer D. Spencer
Richard Spitzengel
Edward J. Steele
Marvin J. Stolin
Walter F. Stolin
Ralph L. Taylor
Norman Van Buskirk
Theodore Van Hee
Theophile V. Van Hee
Theophile Van Hee, Sr.
Jacob Van Orsow
John Van Orsow
Joseph M. Van Orsow
Paul Van Treeck
Harold A. Vogel
Carl Walker
Homer F. Walker
Paul Watts
Glen Wells
Edward Wendler
Don Westlake
John Willms
H. G. Willoughby
Louis A. Wilson
Chester E. Woodard
Mary Woodard
Lillie Yerion
Roley Zumwalt
Fredrick Bailey
Willis Bowen
James Cowling
Lula Cowling
Harry Densmore
Paul Detrick
Clyde Hambrick
A. D. Jones
Ann Keller
Walter Keller
Leonard Kraft
Ralph Lamke
Melvin Mallinson
E. W. Norgard
Eleanor Taylor
Don West

Rips and Trims

Fred Crouser had a narrow escape on Thanksgiving day. Fred was working on his car when some gasoline exploded, burning his face quite badly.

On a recent hunting trip, **Fred Bailey** and his son each got an elk. Fred's had a nice rack of horns.

We understand that **Ralph Lamke** has been having good luck duck hunting.

Mr. and Mrs. Don West went to Walla Walla Nov. 25 and 26 to see Don's sister and family of Riverside, Calif., who are going to Naples, Italy to live for three years.

The Leonard Kraft family flew to San Francisco for the Thanksgiving holidays. They had dinner with the Charles Kraft family and report fifteen were present for the dinner.

Mr. and Mrs. Walt Norgard had their family home for Thanksgiving. Their son David and family from Richland, Wash., and son George and his wife of Portland.

Ward and Thelma Dull are spending their vacation in Nevada. They visited Hugh and Georgia Douglas, former Bridal Veil employees, one weekend. They also took a trip through Death Valley.

Mr. and Mrs. Fay Davis are sporting a new Ford automobile.

Archie Davies has purchased the car the Davis' family formerly owned.

The Corbett High School Seniors gave their class play on November 22nd. The following boys and girls who had parts in the play were: **Dorothy Cote,** daughter of Mr. and Mrs. Joe Cote; **Jim Yerion,** son of Mrs. Lillie Yerion; **Tom Cowling,** son of Mr. and Mrs. Jim Cowling; and **Garfield Pearson,** who lives with Mr. and Mrs. Louis Wilson

The **Ralph Taylor** family motored to Cathlamet, Wash., to spend Thanksgiving with Mrs. Taylor's parents.

Dean Burkholder recently was ill for about two weeks but is now back on the job and reports he is feeling much better.

Richard Davis is driving around in a pretty, new Studebaker.

Mrs. Bird Asked to Serve: Mrs. Verl Bird has been asked to be the headquarters for the Cancer Society in this part of Multnomah County.

The work of the society is to inform

While on a recent tour of western mills, the salesmen of the R. T. Feltus Lumber Co., our wholesale outlet in Chicago, stopped by to look over our plant. They are, from left to right, Ed Gross, Jay Burch, George Kohlbacher and John Dean, Sales Manager.

the public of the help available to them. For instance, how many of us know that bandages are available for patients needing them, and that there is a lending closet located in Portland which has articles needed in the home of a patient.

Mrs. Bird is attending a three day conference in Portland this week so she will likely have lots more information when she returns.

Dec. Birthdays
Many Happy Returns of the Day.

Clyde Hambrick	Francis Cook
Eugene Potter	Hiram Layton
Glen Wells	Walter Keller
Jack Crane	Paul Watts

Employees are reminded that the Company makes the $8.50 per month contribution to the Millmen's Health and Welfare Fund for all employees who have worked a minimum of 80 hours per month. In case you have not worked 80 hours in any month, you may keep the benefits in effect by making the payment yourself at the office of the Fund in the Labor Temple or, if more convenient, at the company office.

Remember to buy and use Christmas Seals.

BRIDAL VEIL LUMBER & BOX CO.

News Letter

Volume 1, Number 7   BRIDAL VEIL, OREGON   FEBRUARY, 1956

Corporate Finance

Bridal Veil Lumber and Box Co., is currently involved in cleaning up the details attendant to negotiating a three year term loan from the United States National Bank of Portland. By way of general information, the amount of money involved is $100,000.-00, the interest rate is 5 percent, and the repayment schedule calls for 20 percent of the principal amount the first year, and 40 percent the second and third years. The note is being secured by a first mortgage on the plant and equipment of the company.

To those for whom the words "Corporation" and "Wealth" have the same meaning, it may come as a surprise to find that our company would find it necessary to resort to a mortgage loan to help finance its operations. However, the reasons for such a course of action becomes obvious upon examination.

Under ordinary circumstances, a small company such as ours has several sources of funds. In the original instance, the stockholders put up the necessary money to get the company started. However, it frequently happens that a business may require additional capital beyond that provided at the time of organization. This need may arise out of a desire to improve the production facilities or may be required by the expansion of the physical volume of merchandise manufactured and sold. Another cause for needing additional funds may be the appearance of the inflation factor. It obviously costs more to carry 1,000,000 FBM of lumber at $115.00 per M ($115,000.00) than it did when the same lumber could be handled at $20.00 per M ($20,000.00). The difference is $95,000.00. Presuming the company is successful, money becomes available through profits, through bank credit, or perhaps the stockholders might be willing to put up additional capital.

During the year just past we continued our program of modernization at Bridal Veil. The year 1955 saw the installation of the second double-end tenoner, the purchase of a new finger lift, the completion of the lighting and rewiring program in the box factory, and continuing the renewal of concrete footings under the moulding factory, which increased our investment by $88,467.12. While we were doing all this we also increased our volume of business to the highest level in the history of the company, and that involved increasing the amount of money involved in inventories by $203,571.-41.

While our plant operation has been very modestly successful over the past several years, our results have not been adequate to support what we have been trying to do. Since our profit is not enough to finance our improvements and expansion on a "pay-as-you-go" basis, we must turn elsewhere for funds.

The bulk of the capital stock of our company is presently concentrated in the estates of two of the company's founders. As our conversion program has taken all our funds and, accordingly, the company has been unable to pay a dividend for many years, it would not make sense to the administrators of these estates to put up more money.

That leaves the bank as a source of funds. However, the bank also is interested in our profit experience as a measure of our efficiency and of future ability to prosper. When they go over our statements for prior years and discover a rather liberal use of red ink from time to time, they conclude that our earnings record does

(Continued on page 4)

Safety Program for 1956

In the December issue of the News-letter we told of our plans for the establishment of a safety committee which will be responsible for making safety inspections and safety sugges-tions and also making investigations of all lost time accidents.

Thursday, January 26, 1956 a safe-ty committee was formed and will meet bi-weekly. The committee is composed of nine members selected at random throughout the plant, and is representative of all departments and all levels of authority and respon-sibility. The term of office shall be three months and all employees will be called to serve on the committee at one time or another.

For the first three months, Jim Cowling will be the chairman and Don West will be the secretary. The rest of the committee will be divided into two sub-committees: A plant in-spection sub-committee which will make plant inspections at frequent intervals to correct and enforce safe-ty rules. The members of this com-mittee are: Willie Bowen, Ed Kinon-en, Eldon Nielson and Fred Long, Jr. The accident investigation sub-com-mittee will investigate all lost time accidents and will report on them at the regular safety committee meet-ings. The members of this committee are Durward Litton, Leo Hageman, and Lloyd DeMain.

As can be seen by 1955 Safety Rec-ord chart our accident frequency rate was almost three times the industry average. With this in mind, let's all work with our safety committees and not only make Bridal Veil a safe place to work but the safest in the industry.

Mel Mallinson

English Hospital Care Not Quite Cricket

If you were a patient in St. Thomas Hospital in London, you would be ask-ed to bring with you:

Admission form card, two night-dresses or two pairs of pajamas, dressing gown and slippers, two wash-cloths and soap, hairbrush and comb (men, shaving equipment), toothbrush and toothpaste, small mirror, Nation-al Health Service Medical Record; and to arrange for your own launder-ing of personal clothing and towels.

Be allowed visitors (two only) on Wednesdays and Sundays.

—Oregon Blue Cross News Letter

1955 SAFETY RECORD

	Lost Time Accidents	Man Hours Worked	Accidents Per Million Man Hours
January	4	28,772	139.9
February	0	24,023	0
March	0	24,253	0
First Quarter 1955	4	77,048	51.9
April	1	28,179	35.5
May	2	30,721	65.1
June	3	33,905	88.5
Second Quarter 1955	6	92,805	64.7
July	0	31,350	0
August	2	35,625	56 0
September	2	31,716	63.1
3rd Quarter, 1955	4	98,691	40 5
October	3	30,223	99.3
November	2	25,350	79.9
December	1	19,963	50.0
Fourth Quarter 1955	6	75,536	79.4
Total for Year 1955	20	344,080	58.1
Average for the industry 1954			21.4

Bridal Veil Visitors

The four men pictured above favored us with a visit on February 6th. They are, from left to right: Reedy Berg of Dant & Russell; Burton Pease of Pease Woodwork, Inc., Cincinnati, Ohio; Carl Crane, Pease employee, and Dick Stoner of Dant & Russell's Columbus, Ohio office. Pease Woodwork is one of our oldest customers and the visit was a thoroughly enjoyable one.

Other very welcome visitors to Bridal Veil have been: Harvey Knapp and Buck Pryor of Dant & Russell; Fred McBride of Firpine Products Co. (whom we hope to have a picture of next month) and Ted Gevaart of Quality Box Service Co.

Order Line Lagging

As we go to press we have only twelve carloads of millwork on order, and of those twelve there are only six that could be considered window frame orders. The others are a mixture of door frames, door jambs and some fingerjointed stock.

This is a source of major concern for we believed that, by this time, business would be considerably improved. It seems to be, simply, that inventories just aren't moving. We have had many promises of orders, but perhaps those promises were based on forecasts rather than on actual needs.

Prominent nationwide business forecasters have predicted only a slight drop in volume from the staggering total of 1955, which would still be a very good year. From these predictions we assume that business will be good. However, a downturn at this time of year is normal.

All we can do is maintain constant contact with our customers and hope that things improve in the very near future. We'll keep you posted.

Correction

In the December issue of the Newsletter we printed a paragraph on page four on the Millmen's Health and Welfare Fund. The statement that 80 hours of work were required to qualify was in error. The Company makes the $8.50 contribution for all employees who have worked a minimum of 60 hours in any month.

Complete Safety Training Course

The above group of men recently completed a safety training course conducted by the State Industrial Accident Commission.

Back row, standing left to right: Roley Zumwalt, foreman frame department; Lloyd De Main, night foreman; Theodore Van Hee, set-up man—moulding; Einar Mickelson, foreman crosswork department; Jacob Van Orson, floor man; Willis Bowen, shipping clerk, Dean Burkholder, yard foreman; Clarence Noble, circular saw set-up; Ade Jones, production superintendent; Clyde Hambrick, box factory foreman; Melvin Mallinson, layout draftsman; Paul Detrick, maintenance foreman; Verl Bird, band sawyer; Mr. Huskey, A. P. D. representative. Seated: L. Kraft, president; Don West, sales manager; James Cowling, saw filer and first aid; E. W. Norgard, office manager.

Corporate Finance

(Continued from page 1)

not justify unsecured credit. Hence, the loan secured by a mortgage.

There is an old saw to the effect "Nothing succeeds like success". Certainly it is true of a business venture. A successful company automatically has funds for normal growth; and in times of extraordinary needs, the stockholders and the bankers are anxious to help. In a successful company the employees gain the security of knowing that they are a part of an efficient and prosperous company that is not in danger of going out of business. Our own future is wrapped up in our ability to operate efficiently and to produce an adequate profit consistently. The best job security in the world, and quite possibly the only job security, lies in being a part of a successful company; the more successful the better.

Profits foretell the future!

Len Kraft

Here Is a Good Thought

Competition whose motive is merely to compete, to drive some other fellow out, never carries very far. The competitor to be feared is one who never bothers about you at all, but goes on making his own business better all the time. Businesses that grow by development and improvement do not die. But when a business ceases to be creative, when it believes it has reached perfection and needs to do nothing but produce — no improvement, no development — it is done.

Henry Ford

Vacations for 1956---by Months

JANUARY:		Days
1	Fred Crouser	10
3	Michael Kriska	5
5	Gary Long	5
5	Leslie Polzel	5
5	Inez Houchin	10
8	Merrill Hartshorn	10
14	Martha Jones	10
18	Kenneth Catlin	10
23	Mira Nielson	10
27	Dean Davis	6

FEBRUARY:		Days
3	Grant Preston	7
13	Herbert Courter	10

MARCH:		Days
1	Roy Anderson	10
1	George Leash	10
1	Ralph Taylor	10
2	John Hancock	6
15	Stanley Hills	10
15	John Van Orsow	10
22	Fay Davis	10
22	Ed Harnam	10
23	Orval K. Johnson	7
23	Clifford Latourell	10
25	Harold Vogel	10
28	Marvin Stolin	10
29	Charles Gaymon	5
30	Jack Kreman	5

APRIL:		Days
1	Archie Davies	7
6	Milford Collins	5
7	Harry D. Kruckman	5
11	Rodney Clayton	5
11	Robert Reischel	5
11	Roger Seeger	5
13	Orien Pitts	5
15	Vera Nell Ball	10
17	Theophile V. Van Hee	10
18	Theodore Hanson	10
18	William Roegrs	5
21	Eldon Nielson	10
22	Joseph Van Orsow	10
23	Glenn Wells	7
30	Jack Crane	7

MAY:		Days
1	Louis Bissell	7
1	Robert Polzel	10
4	George Bennett	6
4	James E. Bowen	6
4	Harold Burkholder	6
4	Edsel Kinonen	6
4	Vyrtle Kuntz	6
6	Bertha Davis	10
9	Durward Litton	10
9	Wesley Adams	5
9	Paul Dooley	5
11	Walter Stolin	10

MAY: (Continued)		Days
11	Arthur Schroder	5
13	James Kendrick	10
13	Hiram Layton	10
17	William Dunken	6
18	Ward Dull	10
19	Lester Anderson	8
20	Dale Emmons	8
21	Fred Harp	10
27	Theophile Van Hee, Sr.	10
28	Louise Rhodes	10

JUNE:		Days
2	Jarvis Kilness	6
2	A. R. Kimbley	8
2	Fred H. Long	6
3	Mary Woodard	10
8	James Rhodes	10
9	John W. Smith	5
20	Paul Van Treeck	10
23	Lester Howell	8
27	David Clark	5
28	Bob Layton	7
28	Paul Levan	5
30	Anna Bowen	10

JULY:		Days
1	Max Bissell	7
1	Einar Mickelson	10
5	Leon Dunlap	5
14	Leo F. Hageman	10
18	J. Delbert Dunken	10
19	Lillie Yerion	10
27	Clarence Noble	10
28	Norman Van Buskirk	8
29	James P. Clark	5

AUGUST:		Days
2	Larry Granberg	8
9	Theodore Van Hee	10
9	Chester Rogers	5
10	Francis Cook	5
14	Edward Steele	10
15	Clem Hancock	5
16	Fred Fawcett	6
19	Franklin Bowen	10
21	George Murray	10
22	Jerry Minch	5
22	Paul Watts	5
24	George Knieriem	5
24	Max Nelson	5
26	Wilbur Houchin	10
27	Lloyd DeMain	10
27	William McCawley	7
27	Ralph McCredie	10
29	Ernest M. Cox	5

SEPTEMBER:		Days
2	Loren Hancock	8
4	Elmer Ayles	7
6	John Kerslake	5
6	Ed Wendler	5

SEPTEMBER: (Continued)		Days
7	James Layton	5
7	Virgil Dobson	5
7	Richard Flanagin	5
7	Roley Zumwalt	6
8	Jerald Roberts	10
9	Fred M. Long	8
10	Joseph Cote	8
13	Emmett Bottoms	5
13	Daryl Cox	6
13	Franklin Crane	6
13	Richard Davis	6
16	Kenneth Meyers	10
20	Verl Bird	10
22	Harry Adolph	8
20	Louis Wilson	6
20	Carl Walker	6
23	Richard Spitzengel	6
23	David Rees	6
23	Charles Lofstedt	10
24	H. G. Willoughby	7
24	Lawrence Peterson	10
25	Harold Godat	8
27	Elden Gross	7
29	Jacob Van Orsow	10
29	John Willms	8

OCTOBER:		Days
1	Howard Hunt	10
2	Lawrence Smazal	10
3	Ralph Sanders	7
4	Marvin Jackson	10
6	Robert Godat	6
9	Ralph Ellis	10
9	Lloyd Frazier	10
9	Homer Walker	10
14	Mabel Hills	10
14	Walter Mannthey	7
15	Steven Kuzmesky	7
17	Donald Westlake	5
21	David Reinsch	5
26	David Clabaugh	5
28	E. H. Potter	8

NOVEMBER:		Days
2	Chester Woodard	10
8	Raymond Schneringer	10
12	Pearl P. Cloe	10
15	Roy Eveland	10
16	Harold Jacobson	10
23	Richard Jacobson	7
23	Earl Hutchison	8
24	Clarence Lofstedt	10

DECEMBER:		Days
7	Beaulah Choate	10
12	Thelma Rowe	10
14	Dorothy Hartshorn	10
14	Roland B. Morgan	6
17	James Eversull	10
20	Thomas Britton	10
31	Thomas Choate	10

Rips and Trims

Since the last edition of the News-letter there have been quite a few new cars purchased by employees. If we have overlooked any, let us know and we'll put them in the next issue. Martha Jones, Plymouth; Tom and Beulah Choate, Cadillac; Noah Atchley, Dodge; Ade Jones, Chevrolet; Verl Bird, Mercury; Leo Hageman, Sr., Chevrolet; Leo Hageman, Jr., Chevrolet; Merrill Hartshorn, Dodge; Harold Burkholder, Jeep.

Walt and **Ann Keller** left Friday evening, Feb. 3 by train for a visit with their son, Norman, and family of Great Falls, Montana. They expect to be gone about one week.

Mr. and Mrs. **Ralph Taylor** and family spent Christmas with Eleanor's parents in Cathlamet, Wn. Eleanor and the girls, Mary Lee and Diana, stayed on through the week to be with Eleanors' mother, who underwent surgery.

Gerry Kraft and **Bob Cowling** exchanged visits over the holidays.

The **Don Center** family of Hood River were guests of **Mr. & Mrs. Noble** during the holiday season. Mrs. Center is a daughter of the Nobles.

Mrs. Paul Dooley, daughter of **Mr. & Mrs. Eugene Potter,** was ill for some time, and during her recuperation, the Dooleys were guests of the Potters. We hope she is completely recovered by now.

Mr. and Mrs. Jack Kennedy of Medford and **Bert Cowling** of Powers, were guests of the **Jim Cowlings** over the holidays.

The **Ralph Taylor** family were dinner guests of the **Cowlings** on New Years Day.

Mr. and Mrs. Walter Norgard were guests of **Mr. and Mrs. George Norgard** during the Christmas season.

Alice and **Kenny Elliott** were guests of the **Don Wests** during the holidays.

Mrs. Ade Jones entered t h e University of Oregon State Tuberculosis hospital on Monday, February 6, for what may prove to be a rather extended stay. Our best wishes go out to Mrs. Jones for a complete and speedy recovery.

15th Anniversary

January 8 marked the fifteenth anniversary for Merrill Hartshorn, cleat saw operator.

Merrill was born and raised in Lucas, Iowa.

He has lost time only once since he began working at Bridal Veil, and that was only for a day or two when he cut his fingers.

Merrill is married to the former Dorothy Burkholder and they have two lovely daughters: Sharon, a sixth grade student at Corbett, is eleven years old and baby Rebecca, aged five months.

Merrill is an ardent and persistent fisherman. He has spent many trying hours on the Columbia fishing for salmon but, like several others we know, he hasn't been too successful. He does have good luck trout fishing on the Deschutes however, and brings back some fine catches. He also does quite a little bird hunting.

January Birthdays
Many Happy Returns of the Day!

Tom Britton	Loren Hancock
Ralph McCredie	Thelma Rowe
Bertha Davis	Larry Granberg
Pearl Cloe	George Murray
Clarence Lofstedt	Mira Nielson
Roy Eveland	Marvin Jackson
Eldon Nielson	Mel Mallinson
Eleanor Taylor	

BRIDAL VEIL LUMBER & BOX CO.

News Letter

Volume 1, Number 8   BRIDAL VEIL, OREGON   MARCH, 1956

The Newsletter

I have heard that there is a question in the minds of some as to the reason for publishing the Newsletter. Some of our people are of the opinion that the Newsletter is primarily a sales instrument, and was designed to help get our story over to our customers. Others have felt that it is a house organ of interest principally to our own group.

It is true that we have a mailing list of customers, suppliers and other interested parties to whom we regularly send copies of the Newsletter. There is no doubt in my mind but that there are some incidental benefits to be derived from this mailing. Surely as our customers come to know us better and to understand our plans and goals for the future, their confidence in us and in our ability to produce quality merchandise on schedule and at the right prices is strengthened.

However, that is not what prompted us to undertake the publication of the monthly Newsletter. We have long felt that there are many things about his employer that an employee should know, and yet he can't find out if the employer has no means of letting him know. In fact, we are inclined to go further than that, and say that the more the employee knows about his employer, the better.

With this thought in mind we have endeavored to put into the Newsletter items which we know to be matters of concern to our employees. What are the chances of running out of lumber? What is the condition of the Order file? What are business prospects for the coming year? Answering questions like these frankly, even when the news is bad, at least removes doubt, and the employee can tell where he stands and thus plan his personal affairs to better advantage.

Here is an item that has been brought to my attention in the past few days. The Portland papers have carried an article announcing that the Dant & Russell interests are contemplating the sale of their properties and have given an option to interested parties which may be exercised sometime in the next three or four months. I did not realize it, but it appears that many of our employees are under the impression that Dant & Russell owns a "substantial" stock interest in our company, and that the above announcement has c a u s e d concern among our employees as to the effect of a Dant & Russell sale on the ownership and policies of Bridal Veil Lumber & Box Co.

It is a fact that our company has enjoyed a very close working relationship with Dant & Russell, extending back over many years. Up to the time of the retirement of Mr. Robert Dant, our company profited through his advice and counsel and our business was transacted on a very personal basis. The Dant & Russell Organization also gave us much needed financial help on several occasions.

However, it is not true that Dant & Russell owns any part of us. We expect to continue to buy lumber at market prices, to manufacture our regular line of products, and to sell our products at market prices regardless of who owns or controls Dant & Russell.

I am happy to have an opportunity to set forth the facts in the above case. I would also be deeply appreciative of an opportunity to answer any other questions our employees may have. I will do my best to give a frank and straightforward answer.

Len Kraft

Bridal Veil Visitors

An always welcome and familiar face at Bridal Veil is Fred McBride of Firpine Products Co., Oswego, Ore-

gon. Fred has visited us many times but this is the first opportunity we have had to get a picture of him. He has been in the lumber business for thirty years, and in nearly all the various phases of production. This wide background, vast knowledge, and understanding of window frames, is an invaluable asset to Fred in his sales efforts. He is perhaps the leading proponent of the Bridal Veil standard window frame.

————79————

March Birthdays

Many Happy Returns of the Day!

Martha Jones   Jack Kreman
Dale Emmons   John W. Smith
Fred Fawcett   Elden Gross
Walter Stolin   Ed Harnam
Paul Dooley   Richard Spitzengel
Noah Atchley   Gary Long

Safety Program

In the establishment of the safety committee, a committee composed of nine members was selected at random throughout the plant. The committee was divided into two sub-committees—a plant inspection committee and an accident investigation committee.

To get our safety program started three members were to serve one month, three members two months, and three members three months. By rotating in this manner, we would have experienced safety members at all times. After three safety meetings they find that a six member committee can do the job.

We would like to mention that Mr. C. B. Husky of the S.I.A.C. attended our first safety meeting Jan. 26, 1956. His comment was that he attended to help kick off the safety program but this committee performed like they had been doing safety work for years.

February completed 79 consecutive days without a lost time accident— This isn't a record yet—but let's make one.

————79————

LOOK

The Red Cross Bloodmobile will be at the Corbett grade school gym to accept blood donations on Friday, March 16, between 3 and 6 p.m.

Any employee who will volunteer to give a pint of blood will be excused from work at 4:00 o'clock, but will be paid for the hour between 4:00 and 5:00. Night shift employees who sign up may come to work at 6:00, but their pay will start at 5:00.

Blood donations are urgently needed, so let's all get together and have a good turnout this time. Remember, you or some member of your family might need blood one of these days, and it's comforting to know it would be available.

Pay attention to the job at hand!

1956 SAFETY RECORD

	Lost Time Accidents	Man Hours Worked	Accidents Per Million Man Hours
January	0	16,297	0
February	0	20,821	0

20th Anniversary

March 6 will mark the 20th anniversary for Leonard (Len) Kraft, president and Chairman of the Board of Bridal Veil Lumber and Box Co.

Len was born and raised in Chicago,

Illinois and is one of five children. He was graduated from the University of Illinois.

He came west in January 1934 to work for International Wood Products Co. in Cathlamet, Washington. His first position was that of cost clerk. In February 1936 he reported to work at Wood Specialties Co. in Portland as assistant manager.

Early in 1937 the company purchased the facilities at Bridal Veil and changed its name to Bridal Veil Lumber and Box Company. Len came to Bridal Veil as assistant manager in June of 1937. On October 8, 1941 he was elected to his present position of president of the company.

Len married the former Annette Thompson of Chicago, on August 31, 1934, in Vancouver, Washington. They lived in Portland and later moved to Bridal Veil where they lived until moving to their present home near Oswego. There are three children in the family: Charles, 20, a junior at Lewis and Clark college; Gerry, a sophomore at Lincoln high school; and Lenann, a fifth grade student at Riverdale school.

Len has served in several capacities in addition to his business interests. He served on the Corbett school board from 1940 until 1946. He is also active in church work, having been an elder of the Palatine Hill Presbyterian church since 1948. He is chairman of the board of trustees of the Millmen's Health and Welfare Trust and vice-president and member of the executive committee of the Woodwork Employers Association.

As for hobbies, Len is an ardent and unusually lucky fisherman, which the picture in our November issue will verify.

————79————

Plant Inspection

The Plant Inspection Sub-committee of the Safety Committee, consisting of Jim Cowling, Fred Long, Jr., Eldon Nielson and Willie Bowen, made its regular inspection February 8, 1956.

Four unsafe conditions were noted and recommendations covering these were presented to the Safety Committee at its regular meeting of February 9, 1956. The four suggestions were approved by the Safety Committee and referred to the Management. Actions required to remove three of the unsafe conditions have already been completed, and the fourth condition, having to do with fencing the pond, which will require a capital expenditure, will be considered along with the plant improvement program for 1956.

Management has been very cooperative in complying with the Safety Committee in this effort of making Bridal Veil a safer place to work.

Let's all strive to help with this program and make Bridal Veil a 100% safer place to work.

Willis Bowen

————79————

February Birthdays

Many Happy Returns of the Day!

James Dunken	Richard Flanagin
Vyrtle Kuntz	Ed Wendler
Kenneth Catlin	Norm Van Buskirk
Louis Wilson	Mary Woodard
Paul Van Treeck	Elmer Ayles
Mabel Hills	Beulah Choate
Fred Crouser	

————79————

Don't let an accident strike you out! Think, listen, ask about Safety!

ORGANIZ

BRIDAL VEIL

B

BRIDA

S T

BOARD

Leona

C. W. Kraft

H. B. Hardy

GEN

Leonard K

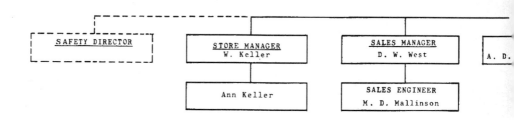

SAFETY DIRECTOR	STORE MANAGER W. Keller	SALES MANAGER D. W. West	A. D.
	Ann Keller	SALES ENGINEER M. D. Mallinson	

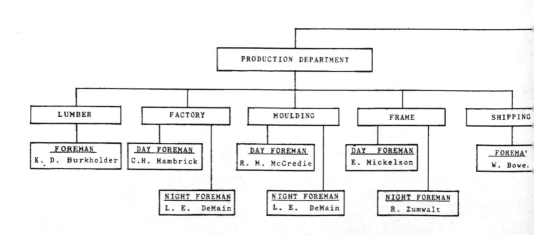

PRODUCTION DEPARTMENT

LUMBER	FACTORY	MOULDING	FRAME	SHIPPING
FOREMAN K. D. Burkholder	DAY FOREMAN C.H. Hambrick	DAY FOREMAN R. M. McCredie	DAY FOREMAN E. Mickelson	FOREMA' W. Bowe
	NIGHT FOREMAN L. E. DeMain	NIGHT FOREMAN L. E. DeMain	NIGHT FOREMAN R. Zumwalt	

ƆN CHART

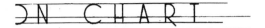

Box Company

REGON

R S

ƆTORS

rman

A. D. Jones

H. W. Winfree

A G E R

--President

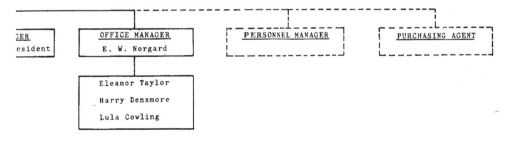

GER | OFFICE MANAGER | PERSONNEL MANAGER | PURCHASING AGENT

esident   E. W. Norgard

Eleanor Taylor

Harry Densmore

Lula Cowling

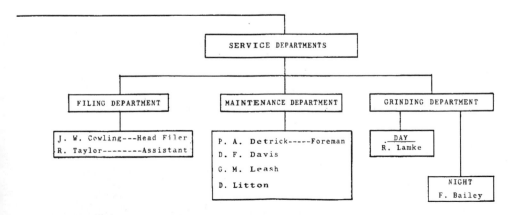

SERVICE DEPARTMENTS

FILING DEPARTMENT

J. W. Cowling---Head Filer
R. Taylor--------Assistant

MAINTENANCE DEPARTMENT

P. A. Detrick-----Foreman
D. F. Davis
G. M. Leash
D. Litton

GRINDING DEPARTMENT

DAY
R. Lamke

NIGHT
F. Bailey

10th Anniversary

On March 28, Marvin Stolin, sticker feeder, will have been with Bridal Veil Lumber and Box Co. ten years.

Marv was born in Corbett. When he was 6 months old the family moved to Latourell where he lived until he married. Marv attended grammer school in Latourell and high school in Corbett.

Marv and the former Mae Rowland of Tolley, North Dakota were married on October 3, 1942. They have one son, Loren, two years old.

Marv was in the Army during world war 2, and served with the Aviation Engineers in the China-India-Burma theater of operations for 21 months. Shortly after his discharge the family moved to Bridal Veil, where they make their home.

Marv is perhaps one of the most devoted outdoor sports enthusiasts in this area. He spends a good deal of his spare time either hunting or fishing, in fact, he has a total of five bears to his credit which he bagged in the Larch mountain area.

"Did you get that pane of glass for the kitchen window today?"

"No, I wanted a twelve by fourteen size, and all they had was a fourteen by twelve."

"Why didn't you buy it? You could have put it in sideways."

20th Anniversary

On March 23, 1956, Noah Atchley, cut-off sawyer, will have been with Bridal Veil Lumber and Box Co. for twenty years.

Noah was born in Knoxville, Tennessee and spent the early part of his life there. On September 23, 1910, he married the former Lola Larrence of Knoxville, and shortly afterward they came to Portland.

Noah has one brother who lives in Tennessee and works for a utility company.

Mr. and Mrs. Atchley own their own home just east of Coopey Falls. Noah's hobby, the past year or so at least, seems to be carpentry, as he has been building an addition to their home. He is doing a fine job and seems to be pretty well along on it.

Mr. and Mrs. Atchley are active in church affairs and are members of the Bethel Baptist Church in Gresham.

————79————

The new guest at a hotel was given a room directly above that of a temperamental poet, and was warned that noises disturbed the latter. On retiring, the guest forgetfully dropped a shoe on the floor, but then recalled the occupant below. He set the other shoe down gently. Several hours later, he answered the door, and was asked, "Will you please drop the other one so I can get to sleep?"

Minimum Wage Increased

A couple of weeks ago **The Oregonian** printed an item reminding us that the Congress has voted an increase in the minimum wage law from 75 cents to $1 an hour under the 1938 federal wage law, and that the increase is slated to go into effect March 1, 1956.

The result of this action will be that on March 1, 1956 over 2,100,000 Americans living all over the country will get an automatic pay boost. It will run as high as 25 cents an hour in some cases, and it is expected to average out to 13 cents an hour. It will add an estimated half billion dollars to the annual wage bill of the employers involved.

To most of us in the Northwest lumber industry, who have long ago passed the $1 an hour mark, it comes as shock to realize that in this high cost of living era so large a number still make substantially less than that. Yet, in the sourthern lumber industry alone, 84 per cent of the workers are earning less than $1 an hour and will be in line for a raise.

And therein lies our interest in the $1 an hour minimum. There are many parts of the country in which we can sell our product only at a distinct disadvantage because the freight rates are against us or because of the wage rate differential that amounts to over 100 per cent of the southern lumber industry rate. Sometimes the disadvantage incudes both freight and wage rates.

As the gap closes, our competitive position improves.

———79———

Statement of Company Policy

The management of Bridal Veil Lumber and Box Company, after careful consideration of the problem, has decided that beginning immediately we will initiate and maintain a complete accident prevention program in this plant. We wish it to be known that this program will become a basic part of our management policy and will govern our judgment on matters of operation equally with considerations of quality, quantity, personnel relations, and other recognized phases of our management problem.

Further, we wish you to know that the success of our accident prevention program depends upon the cooperation of every person in the organization just as surely as does the success of any production program. We are asking for this cooperation and at the same time assuring you that your efforts and suggestions toward the end that this plant be kept free of accidents will be sincerely appreciated and considered a worth-while contribution from each of you.

———79———

HOUSING GOAL: Albert Cole, the housing and home finance administrator, let his prediction arrow go flying. Mr. Cole says the government sets 1,250,000 home starts as a goal in 1956 and that, if necessary, moves to loosen housing credit would be taken to achieve this figure. This one and a quarter million home starts is about 100,000 down from this year's. Mr. Cole did not elaborate on when easier credit steps might be taken, but he did say that if home building should rise above this total, the government would tighten the reins again and make every effort to hold the line at 1,250,000 starts.

The Order File

It is beginning to look as if March will be about the same as February as far as shipments are concerned. Orders are still coming in, but they are rather spasmodic, making it difficult to determine just what kind of shape we'll be in the following month. We are still getting favorable reports about how soon business will pick up, but from all we can gather it is mostly guesswork.

———79———

Consult Your Foreman

Anyone wishing to take time off from work for such things as dental or doctor appointments or other necessary situations, may do so by making arrangements with their foreman. These arrangements should be made as far in advance as possible.

———79———

REMEMBER—The best safety device ever invented is located about nine inches above your shoulders — USE IT!

Health and Welfare Coverage

The following employees worked the required number of hours in November to become eligible for Health and Welfare coverage and will be covered on the first day of January, 1956. Employees who did not work the required hours will become ineligible the same day. Additions: David W. Reinsch, Robert W. Swanson. Deletions: Thelma Dull.

The following employees worked the

Rips and Trims

Clyde Hambrick reports that they expect to get started building their new home in Gresham, sometime in March and hope to have it finished during the summer.

—79—

Joe Van Orsow has purchased a home on SE 175th Place. Tom Britton and family are expected to move into Joe's present home in Wood Village, soon.

—79—

Mr. and Mrs. Ralph Ellis expect to be moving into their new home in Wood Village sometime in April.

—79—

In order that we might get some badly needed news items for this column, we would sincerely appreciate it if the employees would jot down items of interest, (about their family, friends, etc.) and turn them in to their foremen; they in turn can report them to the office. These items need not be of earth-shaking importance; anything of interest to the employees is of interest to the paper. Let's all try to report at least one item a week to our foreman.

————79————

New Cutter Foreman

Effective March 5, 1956 Marvin Van Orsow has been made foreman of the Cutter line. The balance of the Box Factory consisting of the push rips, cleat saws, band resaws, circular resaws, splitter, printer, clamp carrier, etc., are under Clyde Hambrick.

Congratulations, Marv, on your new responsibility.

————79————

On the tombstone of an atheist: "All dressed up and no place to go."

required number of hours in December to become eligible for Health and Welfare coverage and will be covered on the first day of February, 1956. Employees who did not work the required hours will become ineligible the same day. No additions. Deletions: Harold M. Godat, Robert D. Godat, Manford Heatherington, A. R. Kimbley, Sr., Max D. Nelson, Arthur Schroder, Elmer D. Spencer, Robert W. Swanson.

The following employees worked the required number of hours in January to become eligible for Health and Welfare coverage and will be covered on the first day of March, 1956. Employees who did not work the required hours will become ineligible the same day. Additions: Harold Godat, Robert Godat, Albert Kimbley, Sr., Arthur Schroder. Deletions: Leo C. Hageman, Jarvis Kilness, David W. Reinsch.

————79————

Health and Welfare

In the February issue of the Newsletter we printed a correction to a paragraph which appeared in the December issue, on Health and Welfare. With a red face we must now admit that both were wrong, and we will attempt to correct the correction by quoting directly from the Union Agreement as follows: The employer agrees to contribute $8.50 for the current month for each employee who has worked eighty (80) hours or more in the previous month, (and after three (3)) months' employment, the Employer agrees to contribute $8.50 for the current month for each employee who has worked sixty (60) hours or more providing such employee is not permanently terminated) to the Millworkers Health & Welfare Fund, for the purpose of hospitalization, medical and surgical group insurance benefits, together with $25.00 per week indemnity for non-occupational injuries and non-occupational illnesses. Hospitalization, medical and surgical group insurance benefits shall also apply to the eligible employees' wife and children, including all Foremen who are members of Millmen's Unions.

————79————

Think of safety **every day** in 1956.

BRIDAL VEIL LUMBER & BOX CO.

News Letter

Volume 1, Number 9   BRIDAL VEIL, OREGON   April

Meet the Boss

In the February issue of THE NEWSLETTER I made the comment that a successful company automatically has funds for normal growth. The phrase "normal growth" doesn't mean much by itself and must be applied to a specific situation. Then it gives rise to questions such as, "how big should a company get?" and "why grow at all?"

About as nice a handling of the cause of growth as I have seen was written by my brother "Chuck" in the March 1955 issue of the Kraftile Company Newsletter THE KRAFTSMAN. "Chuck" in addition to being president of Kraftile Company is also a director of Bridal Veil Lumber & Box Co. Here are his comments:

"Fundamentally, a business grows because it has more customers than it can take care of with its present facilities. Sometimes you will run into a management that by conscious choice decides for reasons of its own that it doesn't want to get any bigger and so it turns the extra customers away and remains a nice 'comfortable' size. This is a dangerous proceeding because it leads to complacency and rather than stand still as the management hoped, it begins to lose business. Most businesses elect to keep pace with their possibilities and most especially is this true of the companies that grow to large size.

"The popular notion is that 'big businesses' are big because people poured a lot of money into them and this made them big. Like many popular notions, we see, though, that this is false. The big business is supported by a lot of customers—not by a lot of stockholders. As we saw last month, a person invests his money in a business so as to earn dividends. Certainly, very few would do so out of a de-sire to make it the biggest in the world! Because it is favored by a lot of customers, it attracts the necessary stockholders to finance the additional facilities.

"This presupposes that the management knows how to operate at a profit—otherwise, the more customers, the faster it will go 'broke' which is another way of saying that it cost more to produce the article or service than the customer thought it was worth. In my desk is a cartoon showing an ordinary looking kind of guy wearing a smug smile and a crown and underneath is the inscription, 'The Customer is King.'

"Mr. Customer King doesn't know much about business—after all he's the same guy that has a lot of screwy notions about economics—but he does know whether he likes your product and your service, and he also knows how much money he has to spend for that sort of thing and how anxious he is to spend it for that purpose instead of something else. So you see it's immaterial to him what it cost you to make it. A business to grow must produce at a price at which a growing number of people are able—and willing—to buy.

"So a business will grow just as big as its customers will let it.

"There are, of course, some other factors involved. The dividing line between 'big' and 'little' business is often spoken of in terms of employees—more or less than 500. This varies by industry, however; and so a steel mill with only 500 employes would be small; whereas, a structural clay products plant with 500 employes would be large. Indeed there is probably none that big in the entire country.

"Relative size in this connection is

(Continued on page 3)

NEWS LETTER

Published on the 10th of each month by
Bridal Veil Lumber & Box Co.
Bridal Veil, Oregon

Editor . . . . . Don West

Bloodmobile Visit

The company is very grateful to the people who either donated or attempted to donate blood during the visit of the bloodmobile at the Corbett school on March 16th. The Red Cross is also grateful as you can see by their letter which is posted in the lunchroom.

Following is a list of those who gave or attempted to give.

Lester Anderson	Lillie Gross
Elmer Ayles	Lester B. Howell
Fred Bailey	Leonard Kraft
Max Bissell	Steve Kuzmesky
Richard Caffrey	Bob Layton
Lou Cowling	Mel Mallinson
Fred Crouser	Eugene Potter
Dean Davis	Eleanor Taylor
Fay Davis	N. Van Buskirk
Lloyd DeMain	Harold Vogel
Ward Dull	Don West
Elden Gross	

The reward of knowing you have helped someone less fortunate than yourself is great compared to the small amount of discomfort involved in giving blood.

————22————

Safety Shoes

Safety shoes are strongly recommended by the Oregon State Industrial Accident Commission, also by our own safety committee.

It is quite reasonable that a shoe with a steel capped toe could save a lot of injured toes.

From our own record of injuries, we find that in the past two weeks several employees have injured their feet by dropping trays on them. In these cases a lot of discomfort could have been avoided, had they been wearing safety shoes.

Safety shoes are good looking, comfortable, reasonably priced and available in several different styles.

A representative of a reliable company that sells safety shoes will call on us, at the mill, and anyone who wishes may purchase shoes for cash or by payroll deduction.

Ade Jones

Health and Welfare Coverage

The following employees worked the required number of hours in February to become eligible for Health and Welfare coverage and will be covered on the first day of April, 1956. Employees who did not work the required hours will become ineligible the same day. Additions: Jarvis Kilness. Deletions: Emmett Bottoms, David Clabaugh, Milford Collins, Ernest M. Cox, Virgil Dobson, Richard Flanagin, John Kerslake, A. R. Kimbley, Albert Kimbley, Jr., James Layton, William Rogers, Edward Wendler and Donald Westlake.

————22————

April Birthdays
Many Happy Returns of the Day

Jim Eversull	Dorothy Hartshorn
Wilbur Houchin	John Willms
Ted Hanson	Harry Kruckman
Grant Preston	Robert Reischel
Fred M. Long	Clarence Noble
Joe Van Orsow	David Reinsch

————22————

Student Visitors

Recently we had the pleasure of conducting a tour of the plant for the freshman class of Corbett High School. The boys and girls showed a great deal of interest and asked many questions. A few days later we received a letter thanking us for the visit. The pleasure was all ours.

whatever you do —
WATCH WHERE YOU'RE GOING!

Safety Rules

1. Report all hazardous conditions or unsafe work practices to your foreman at once.

2. Replace all guards before starting up machines.

3. Goggles are provided by the company and shall be worn wherever flying particles are a hazard.

4. Do not use guards for clothes racks or storage shelves.

5. Never oil or adjust a machine until it has been shut down.

6. Lock out and tag machine control switches with "Do not start" signs before making adjustments or repairs on machines.

7. Keep tools in good shape. Replace cracked or broken handles. Dress down mushroomed heads.

8. Gloves are provided by the company for handlers at the dip tank.

9. Use push sticks provided for feeding saws.

10. Unless authorized, do not attempt to operate any machine on these premises.

11. Use of air hose to clean clothing or play practical jokes is prohibited.

12. Do not remove or make inoperative any guard or safety device furnished for your protection.

13. Report every injury immediately to your foreman. Get first aid treatment at once, no matter how slight the injury.

14. Employees working underneath any hazard shall wear hard hats.

15. Do not stand in line with stock being fed into saws.

16. Only authorized employees shall cross over sorting chains.

17. Handrails on stairways are for your protection, **use them**.

18. Learn the location of the fire extinguisher closest to your station. Do not pile material in front of it, nor hang anything over it.

19. Operators of lift trucks and jitneys must slow down at blind corners and sound horn.

20. Only authorized employees are permitted to ride on, or hang onto, company vehicles.

21. Never raise pressure rolls on edger while cants are going through.

22. Poor housekeeping causes accidents. Keep your work area neat.

23. Open-toes and tennis shoes are prohibited.

24. Horse-play, scuffling or practical jokes prohibited.

25. Block throwing is prohibited.

26. Anyone under the influence of intoxicants or in possession thereof will be removed from the job.

Showered

At a bridal shower given by Donzella Nielson for Vera Nell Ball, the evening of March 9th, the following co-workers and friends were present: Mrs. A. J. Perkins and Mrs. Earl Stone from Hood River; Mrs. Nadine Dunn of The Dalles; Mabel Hills, Mary Woodard, Juanita McCauley, Ruth Litton, Faye Harp, Mrs. Ed Wiebold, Thelma Rowe, Anna Bowen, Mrs. Einar Mickelson, Mrs. Keith Roberts, Mrs. Clarence Noble and Mrs. Iris Potter.

Those sending gifts but unable to attend were Lillie Yerion, Bertha Davis, Thelma Pitts, Martha Jones, Louise Rhodes, Mrs. Ralph Ellis, Mrs. Daryl Cox, Margaret Stevens and Mira Nielson.

————22————

The greatest service any company can render society is steadily to improve its efficiency.

Meet the Boss

(Continued from page 1)

dependent upon the best size for efficient operation. The maximum size of a business will still be determined by the point at which it can do the best job for its customers.

What about Kraftile? As calculated by Stanford Research Institute, after a study of 20 years of operation, we are rowing at the rate of 8.6% per year. This means that we double our size every 8½ years. This is by no means automatic; but if we continue our efforts to please our customers in every way—price, quality and service — we may expect this rate of growth to continue—indeed, accelerate."

Chuck Kraft.

————22————

Accidents don't just happen — they are caused!

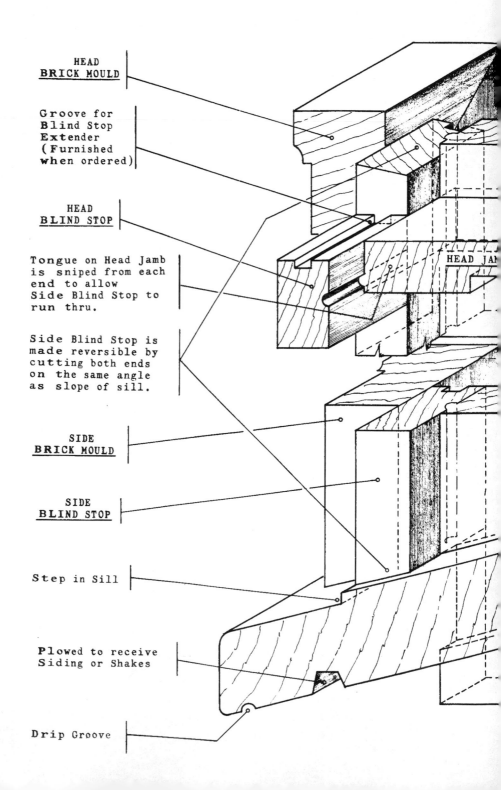

HEAD
BRICK MOULD

Groove for
**Blind Stop
Extender**
(**Furnished
when** ordered)

HEAD
BLIND STOP

Tongue on Head Jamb
is sniped from each
end to allow
Side Blind Stop to
run thru.

Side Blind Stop is
made reversible by
cutting both ends
on the same angle
as slope of sill.

SIDE
BRICK MOULD

SIDE
BLIND STOP

Step in Sill

Plowed to receive
Siding or Shakes

Drip Groove

HEAD JA

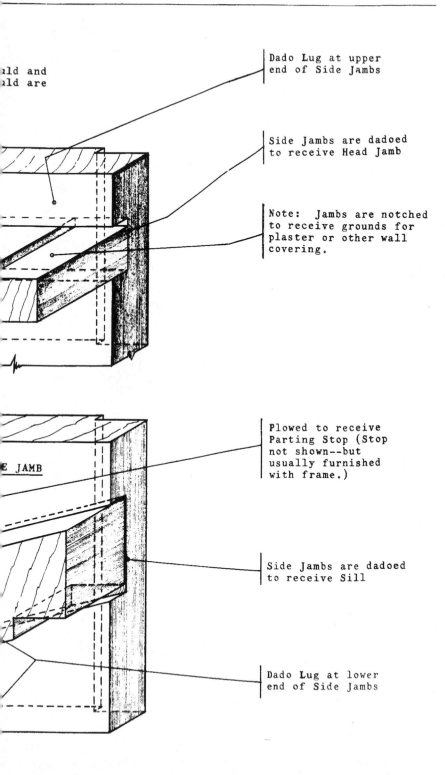

ld and
ld are

Dado Lug at upper
end of Side Jambs

Side Jambs are dadoed
to receive Head Jamb

Note: Jambs are notched
to receive grounds for
plaster or other wall
covering.

Plowed to receive
Parting Stop (Stop
not shown--but
usually furnished
with frame.)

E JAMB

Side Jambs are dadoed
to receive Sill

Dado Lug at lower
end of Side Jambs

10th Anniversary

Theophile Van Hee was born in Gresham, August 28, 1926. At the time the family lived in Corbett and, ex-

cept for three years, Theophile's home has always been Corbett. The other three years were spent in Ocosta, Washington.

Theophile is married to the former Patricia Patterson of Burke, Idaho. They have two children, Tommy, 8, and Betty, who is 7. They are expecting a third child, which we will report on upon arrival.

Theophile enlisted in the Navy on his seventeenth birthday, August 28, 1943. He received his boot training at Farragut, Idaho. While there he attended gunnery school. He then transferred to Treasure Island, California for completion of training and schooling, after which he was assigned to the destroyer Jaccard, in the Atlantic fleet. While on patrol duty in the Atlantic he was injured and sent to the Navy hospital in Chelsea, Mass. Upon release from the hospital he was assigned to the famous battleship Missouri and, while there, witnessed the historic signing of the surrender of the Japanese to the U. S. forces. He stayed on the Missouri until his discharge from the Navy on March 28, 1946.

Theophile came to work at Bridal Veil on April 17, 1946. His older broth-

Health and Welfare

At the March 21 Health and Welfare meeting, the following items of interest to employees and their dependents were acted upon.

It was moved, seconded, and carried that the Trustees adopt the increase offer for Dependents under date of March 8, 1956, by the Bankers Life Company to become effective May 1, 1956. The new benefits to be purchased are as follows:

DEPENDENTS BENEFITS

Present		Increased to:
$ 10.50	Hosp. daily room	$ 13.50
(35 days)	and board	(35 days)
200.00	Hosp. extras	300.00
70.00	Hosp. Maternity	90.00
	(including insured)	
240.00	Surgical Schedule	300.00
200.00	Blanket accident	300.00

It was moved, seconded, and carried that the Administrator spell out individual payment on employees out of work effective with the April premium.

Individual payment would be as follows: Any individual who is out of work through no fault of his own but remains in the industry and is available for work, unless prevented by illness or accident or on leave of absence, and thereby not eligible for payment by any Employer, may pay his own premium to the Millworkers Health and Welfare Trust Fund, subject to the approval of the Administrator. Such individual payments are to remain at the $8.50 rate but are subject to change if and when the Board of Trustees find it necessary to amend or revoke this action.

It was moved, seconded and carried, that the present officers continue for another year. Leonard Kraft is chairman of the board and Leo Hageman is secretary.

It was moved, seconded and carried that the Chairman investigate bonding of the Administrator.

————22————

A South American was describing his country to an American woman:

"Our most popular sport is bullfighting," he told her.

"Isn't it revolting?" she asked.

"No," smiled the man, "That's the second most popular Sport."

er (by twenty minutes) and his father are also employed here.

Safety Program for 1956

The figures for March are not complete, but February completed 79 days and 37,118 manhours worked without a lost time accident and an accident frequency of "0". For the same period in 1955 we had 4 lost time accidents with a frequency of 75.7.

At the March 22 safety meeting 3 new members, who are Dean Burkholder, Fay Davis, and Ward Dull, were chosen to replace the 3 outgoing members, Leo Hageman, Durward Litton and Lloyd DeMain.

Since the organization of our safety program, 68 safety suggestions have been made and 48 have been approved and corrected. Several more of the suggestions have been approved and will be taken care of in our 1956 modernization program. This question was raised at the last meeting—are we making too many suggestions that are not important? We think not. Any suggestion in regard for safety is important. The more safety suggestions we receive and correct the safer place we have to work.

While the figures for March are not complete, we did have one lost time accident. After an accident investigation it was found that faulty equipment was partly to blame. Since the accident that piece of equipment has been repaired and brought to our attention several pieces of equipment that should be checked more closely.

Even though we have weekly plant inspection by a safety team, we can all help to prevent accidents by reporting any faulty piece of equipment or any hazardous condition to our foreman immediately.

Our lost time accident ended 87 consecutive days without any lost time accidents—we now have 22 days! —Let's keep it going.

————22————

Notice

At the next PTA meeting at the Corbett Grade School on April 11th at 8:00 P.M., there will be two motion pictures on Cancer, shown. The two films are "Warning Shadow" and "Man Alive." Dr. Jack Battalia will be present to answer any questions you might have.

Evelyn Bird

————22————

Father (to suitor): "Young man, the one who marries my daughter will get a prize."

Suitor: "May I see it, sir?"

The picture above is one taken of our new safety sign that will soon be put up just north of the boiler room at the entrance to the mill. This will really give us something to shoot at, now that we have a visible sign showing how we are doing in our safety campaign. We hope we run the figure up into four or more numbers even though, if we do, we'll have to get a new sign.

Rips and Trims

Vera Nell Ball and **Jerald Roberts**, Bridal Veil Lumber & Box Co. employees for several years, were married St. Patrick's day (March 17th) at the Lutheran church in Shelton, Washington.

The bride was given in marriage by her brother, **Leroy Newman. Donzella Nielson** was her sister's matron of honor and **Keith Roberts** was best man for his brother.

Following a reception in the church, dinner was served in the Newman home by **Mrs. Jonetta Moore.**

Mr. and Mrs. Roberts are living with Jerry's father in Gresham.

Richard Caffrey, who works on the cut off line, and the former **Inga Elvsaas** of Bainbridge Island, Washington, were married Thursday night, March 29, in Vancouver, Washington. The couple is now living at Coopey Falls. Our best wishes to them for happiness and prosperity.

There have been a lot of flu bugs going around and **Louis Bissell** must have had the granddaddy of them all, as he has been off work for a week. There have been others that have had flu in the last couple of weeks: **William McCawley, Dale Emmons** and **Howard Hunt.** However, they managed to get rid of theirs in a day's time.

Harold Burkholder returned to work looking thinner—no lack of food, just lack of teeth: Harold had had his "lowers" pulled the day before.

Jim Rhodes had a bout with the flu for a few days, then came back to work apparently too soon—he's now laid up again. Get it all out of your system this time, Jim.

Martha Jones has had "flu symptoms" and is home trying to combat the bug.

Paul Detrick was a patient at Portland Sanitarium for a week and is home, now. After two blood transfusions and a series of tests the doctors have not yet reached a verdict as to the cause of his illness.

Bud Kimbley has taken a trip to Arizona to try to get rid of a bad case of arthritis. Hope the sun does you a lot of good, Bud.

New cars in Bridal Veil are a black Ford for **Steve Kuzmesky** and an orchid and ivory Dodge for **Robert Godat.**

The **Les Polzels'** dog "Poochie" disappeared for a few days, to produce a family. By diligent watching and trailing, **Ruth Hambrick** found her hiding place under the front porch of a local resident. Les is trying to get the family home.

————22————

Safety Committee

We received the following commendatory letter from the State Industrial Accident Commission, relative to the safety program now in progress at Bridal Veil. "We note with great interest the progress being made in your accident prevention program. The copies of the minutes of your safety committee meetings seem to us to indicate a very active and efficient safety organization in your plant.

Our representatives Mr. C. B. Huskey and Mr. E. C. Thomas have advised us of the keen interest which your employees exhibit and the business-like manner in which your committee meetings are conducted.

It is through this type of organized effort of all employees and their continued interest in accident prevention that we feel Bridal Veil Lumber and Box Company will be one of the outstanding companies in the area in their accident prevention program.

We very sincerely wish to commend all the members of your safety committee for their efforts and cooperation and to congratulate you for your fine organization in accident prevention.

Should we be of further assistance to you and your organization, we trust that you will not hesitate to communicate with us."

Some of the men responsible for the fine start on this campaign are Jim Cowling, Eldon Nielson, Willis Bowen, Edsel Kinonen, Fred Long, Jr., Lloyd DeMain, Durward Litton, Leo Hageman and Don West. These men are the "pioneers", so to speak, of the program. It is hoped that eventually, all or nearly all of the employees will participate as active members of the safety committee.

————22————

It's not the RIGHT way if it isn't the SAFE way.

RIDAL VEIL LUMBER & BOX CO.

News Letter

lume 1, Number 10   BRIDAL VEIL, OREGON   May

Automation Makes Progress

The term "automation was coined few years ago to describe automatic otion, or control by machinery. hen a machine stamps out a part r an automobile or a television chass, frequently the part has to be rewed or otherwise fixed into place an assembly—by hand. When other achinery is developed to transport e part to the assembly and autoatically fix it into place, this is tomation.

It is merely an extension of the odern machine tool concept of manfacturing which was pioneered in merica—a healthy, logical step in roduction progress. And yet some eople are viewing automation with larm, declaring that it will create ast unemployment and cause a disster in America. Such viewing with larm has accompanied many phases f America's industrial development.

When the blacksmiths' shops began o go out of business as the automoile replaced the horse and buggy arly in this century, there were oans of alarm from many quarters. ven President Wilson, then a profesor at Princeton University, spoke out ith misgiving about the automobile's evelopment. The prevailing thought mong alarmists was that there would e no jobs for the people temporarily isplaced in the wagon and buggy inustry and this meant disaster.

Some of today's economics textooks state that it is questionable vhether inventions are good for the ation, particularly new industrial production machines which cut down on uman labor. All this seems to be ather short-sighted or even blind easoning. The facts about the development of the automobile are available. The automobile made 10,000 jobs or every one which it eliminated in he wagon and buggy industry. The same is true as regards the other steps in America's technological progress.

Machine tools as developed through the ingenuity of American industrialists have been mankind's greatest material boon. The increased production of wealth in America can be traced directly to them. The fact that Americans enjoy a living standard five times better today than a century ago can be traced to the growth of "automation" — which has increased man-made production. The fact that nearly 65,000,000 Americans are employed today is a commendation for advances in "automation" during the last 20 years.

Harnessing the machine has opened almost limitless opportunities for the production of new products. Nylon would have been virtually worthless in the spinning-wheel era. Today it accounts for perhaps 100,000 good paying jobs. Air condtioning plants could be sold only to Sultans and Kings—if automation didn't produce units at a price within the reach of millions of home owners. Hundreds of such examples could be cited. The new products to make living more pleasurable also make jobs more plentiful. Automation, then, could be said to be merely a new word for progress!

Len Kraft

————6————

The Order File

Situations can and do change rapidly. A couple of months ago our order file was rather thin but now we have twenty-one carloads of window frames on order. In other words we are sold for nearly sixty days, right now. This siuation should remain healthy, at least until Fall.

————6————

Overconfidence results in accidents!

NEWS LETTER

Published on the 10th of each month by
Bridal Veil Lumber & Box Co.
Bridal Veil, Oregon

Editor . . . . . Don West

Rambling Around

Mrs. West (Barbara) and I are leaving the 18th of May on a business trip to the East. Some of the places and customers we plan on visiting are Chicago; Dekker-Brish in South Holland; Hill-Behan and Mann Sash & Door Company in Aurora; McGill Metal Products in Marengo, Illinois; Concord Millwork Corporation in Rochester, New York; New York City; Clearfield Cheese Company in Curwensville, Pennsylvania; Pease Woodwork Company in Cincinnati and the Borden Company in Van Wert, Ohio; Luce Manufacturing Co. and the Millwork Company in Kansas City, Missouri.

We will return by way of San Francisco.

It should be an interesting and informative trip and I hope to be able to give a more detailed report after we get back, sometime after the first of June.

Don West

————6————

Some **DUMB BUNNIES** depend on LUCK to prevent accidents.

20th Anniversary

Adrian D. (Ade) Jones, Production Superintendent, was born at Oregon City, and now owns the farm on which

his parents lived at that time. His mother lives on the farm at the present time. Ade received his education in Oregon City. He has one sister who is living in Portland.

Ade worked in quite a few different places in the Northwest as a member of a survey party. He also tried his hand at logging, truck driving and millwork. In 1928 he worked for the Bridal Veil Timber Co. at the Palmer mill. While there he worked as a choker setter, fireman, and ran a drag saw. The mill was located some two miles up on the hill in back of Bridal Veil. Ade began working at Wood Specialties Co. in Portland on May 6, 1936 and in September 1937 transfered to Bridal Veil where he has remained.

Ade and his wife, Jane, now live at 1831 N. E. 142nd St. in Portland. They have three daughters, Judy, a student at Washington high school; Linda 8 and Dianne 6.

Mrs. Jones is, at the present time, recuperating from an illness in the University of Oregon hospital and must, of necessity, remain there for some time.

————79————

A job isn't done right if it isn't done SAFELY.

The 'Fringe'

Payroll costs during 1955 were as follows:

Health and Welfare	$17,201.91
Industrial Accident Insurance	9,375.98
Unemployment Compensation	9,551.60
Federal Old Age Benefit	13,644.43
Aetna Group	1,793.99
Vacation Pay	18,818.70
Paid Holidays	6,454.16
Total	$76,840.77

Since our total payroll in 1955 was $835,423.12, these costs were 9.2% of the total payroll.

———6———

Games of Chance

All games of chance aren't played with the pasteboards, galloping dominoes or roulette wheel. One popular pastime consists of seeing how close you can come to danger without getting hurt. It can be played at home, on the street, or in the plant in more ways than you can use a deck of 52 cards plus the joker.

According to the law of averages, you will break even in most games if you play long enough and the game is on the square. In playing with Accident, the law of averages works the other way around—it will get you in the end.

———6———

Worker's Paradise

A remark attributed to Walter Reuther during his recent trip to India went something like this: "The difference between Communism and Capitalism is that in Russia the workers own the factories and the bosses own the cars, while in the United States the bosses own the factories and the workers own the cars."

———6———

May Birthdays

Many Happy Returns of the Day!

Leo Hageman	Jim Rhodes
Lawrence Peterson	Leslie Polzel
Leon Dunlap	David Clark
Lloyd DeMain	Frank Bowen
Homer Walker	Inez Houchin
Cliff Latourell	Charles Lofstedt
Marvin Stolin	David Rees
John H. Van Orsow	Stanley Hills
Ralph Taylor	Ed Steele
Anna Bowen	Fred Bailey

20th Anniversary

May 18th will be the 20th anniversary for Ward Dull at Bridal Veil, and in all that time he has not been

off work from a lost time accident. So far, that is the best safety record we have found. He was recently appointed to the safety committee at Bridal Veil.

Ward was born at Penawawa, Washington and has lived all his life in the Northwest.

Ward worked for the International Wood Products Company in Cathlamet, Washington from 1933 to 1936. He then moved to Portland in May 1936 to work for Wood Specialties Co. He came to work at Bridal Veil the first of September 1937.

Ward joined the Navy Seabees in November 1942 and received his training as a carpenter in Providence, Rhode Island. He served overseas in Dutch Harbor, Alaska; Ulithi Atoll, Saipon and Marcus Island. He was discharged the 26th of November, 1945.

Ward is married to the former Thelma Harrison. They have two boys and one girl. Jerry works in Portlang, Tom is in the Air Force and daughter Val Rae is a student at Gresham High school.

They own their home and ten acres two miles southwest of Gresham. Ward is a member of the Corbett V. F. W. post.

10th Anniversary

May 13th will mark the 10th year at Bridal Veil for Jim Kendrick, band rip sawyer. Jim was born and raised

in Houston, Texas. He left there in December of 1942 and joined the Army. He was assigned to the 104th Infantry Division, which trained at Camp Adair, near Corvallis. He served overseas in the European theatre of war, and, while there, was awarded the Silver Star and Purple Heart for gallantry in action. Though wounded, Jim stayed at his post for eighteen hours before being relieved.

On July 8, 1944, Jim married the former Augusta Lofstedt. They have two daughters, Patty, 10, and Roxie, 4. The Kendricks home is a mile or so east of Corbett on the old Columbia River highway. Jim is a member of the volunteer fire department at Corbett and is also a member of the V. F. W.

———————6———————

Daylight Time

For the benefit of our friends who are on the mailing list for the NEWS-LETTER we would like to point out that Bridal Veil Employees have voted to move our working hours ahead one hour for the twentieth consecutive year.

Effective April 30, regular hours are 7:00 to 11:00 AM and 12 noon to 4:00 PM.

Health and Welfare

The following employees worked the required number of hours in March to become eligible for Health and Welfare coverage and will be covered on the first day of May, 1956. Employees who did not work the required hours will become ineligible the same day: Additions: Richard Caffrey. Deletions: Wesley Adams, David Clark, Rodney Clayton, Francis Cook, Daryl Cox, Franklin Crane, Richard Davis, Paul Dooley, Leon Dunlap, Fred Fawcett, Robert Godat, Jarvis Kilness, George Knieriem, Jack Kreman, Michael Kriska, Harry D. Kruckman, Vyrtle C. Kuntz, Paul F. Levan, Fred H. Long, Gary Long, Jerry Minch, Roland Morgan, Orien Pitts, Leslie D. Polzel, David G. Rees, Robert Reischel, Chester Rogers, Arthur Schroder, Roger Seeger, John W. Smith, Richard Spitzengel, Carl L. Walker, Paul Watts, Roley Zumwalt.

———————6———————

Flower Fund

Thanks to collections recently made, the Bridal Veil Employees Flower Fund is again in the black. Here is a brief report on activity in the Fund since the previous collection in May of 1954:

Balance Forward (Short) ....$(15.90)		
Collections, May 1954		$63.37
Flowers—N. Elliott (Dad)	8.75	
" Norgard (Brother) ..	7.50	
" Elliott	7.95	
" Taylor (Mother)......	8.30	
" Eveland (Mother)	7.30	
" Kinonen (Dad)	7.30	
Collections, October 1955		2.00
Flowers, H. Leash	8.55	
Heart Fund, Jones (Dad)	10.00	
Flowers, McCredie (Gene)	7.80	
" Washburn	7.80	
Collection—April 17, 1956		43.16
" 18		14.36
" 19		2.88
" 23		1.00
" May 1		7.38
Total Collections		134.15
Paid out		97.15
Balance		$37.00

Jim Cowling

———————6———————

Three cell mates in a Red prison were talking things over. The first said that he was accused of absenteeism for being late to work; the second told how he had come to work five minutes early, and was accused of spying; and the third said, "I came to work on time and they accused me of buying an American watch."

Absence Report

During March, the first month for which we have compiled such a figure, our rate of absence was 1.8%.

Individual absence rates ran all the way from zero to 25.9%. Over 80% of our employees had a perfect attendance record, while 20% lost a total of 42 days.

Judging from our experience with absence rates, we could well be on the road to hanging up an enviable record in that department.

————6————

Housing starts in January 1956 were lower than a year ago, but contract awards were more than in January 1955. This means more activity in from four to six months.

————6————

See Ade Jones for details on Safety-Toe Shoes.

New Director

Mr. Erwin P. Snyder of the law firm of Snyder, Chadwell and Fagerburg of Chicago, was elected to the Board of Directors of Bridal Veil Lumber and Box Co. at the stockholders meeting, which was held in Bridal Veil on April 10, 1956. Mr. Snyder succeeds Mr. Howell B. Hardy in this position.

————6————

A lot of farmers think they have a right to a decent income. They're wrong. They only have the right to earn a decent income.

—Charles Shuman

BRIDAL VEIL LUMBER & BOX COMPANY
BRIDAL VEIL, OREGON

Operating Statement - Company Store
For the Year ended November 30, 1955

	Amount	% of Total Sales	Amount	% of Total Sales
TOTAL SALES			$85,392.16	100.00
DEDUCT: Cost of Goods Sold			72,673.02	85.11
GROSS PROFIT:			12,719.14	14.89
Deduct Expenses: (See Footnote)				
Salaries and Wages	$9,158.36	10.73		
Payroll Taxes	268.60	.31		
Insurance	422.00	.49		
Industrial Accident Insurance	68.53	.08		
Paper, string, etc.	172.23	.20		
Repairs and Maintenance	452.67	.53		
Laundry	118.03	.14		
Advertising	48.57	.06		
Excise Taxes	49.89	.06		
Licenses	75.50	.09		
Miscellaneous	250.50	.29		
Total Expenses			11,084.88	12.98
NET PROFIT			$ 1,634.26	1.91

Footnote:

No charge made for heat, light, real property taxes, personal property taxes, depreciation, insurance on buildings and equipment, health and welfare, or cost of trucking merchandise from Portland to Bridal Veil in company truck.

Bridal Veil Visitors

Pictured above is John M. Chase, Sales Manager of the Millwork Department of Dant & Russell. John has been a welcome visitor at Bridal Veil many times but this is the first opportunity we have had to get a picture of him. Reedy Berg accompanied John on his visit.

Another visitor was Rex Caffall of Milwaukie Box and Veneer Co. for whom we have been making cleats for several years.

Walter Mann of Mann Sash & Door Co. of Aurora, Illinois and Don Michaelson of Pacific Mutual Door Co. were also visitors during the month.

———6———

Blood Donor Data

Have you ever wondered just how rare a creature you really are in this bloody old world?

Well, here's the Awful truth . . .

Blood Donors needed to get 1 pint of:

O POS	2.6	B POS	11.1
O NEG	13.0	B NEG	55.5
A POS	3.0	AB POS	32.4
A NEG	15.0	AB NEG	161.2

You AB NEG folks are really rascals. Just think how hard it is to find you! An an ethical basis, you owe it to the world to stay away from accidents.

———6———

See Jim Cowling for Ear Plugs.

15th Anniversary

Fred Harp, cutter, was born in Leon, Iowa, one of six children. When he was five the family moved to Creston, Iowa. It was there that Fred received his education. Fred has two sisters living in Puyallup, Washington, one brother in Yakima, and two sisters in Iowa. His mother also lives in Puyallup and recently observed her 90th birthday.

Fred served in the 71st Army Artillery Regiment in World War I. He was stationed near Boston and also spent some time in France. Later he worked as a boilermaker for seventeen years on the Burlington railroad.

Fred and the former Fay Jeffers were married on December 8, 1916. They have two children, Don and Shirley. Don and Shirley's husband, Jerry Lambert, are partners in the Northwest Tire Co. in Portland.

In 1936 the family moved to a dairy farm outside of Cathlamet, Washington, which they operated for four

years. Later they moved into town and it was from there they moved to Bridal Veil, where Fred began working as a car loader.

Fred and Fay own their home which is located about a quarter of a mile north of the 12-Mile Corner, near Gresham.

———6———

Accidents don't just happen to THE OTHER GUY!

10th Anniversary

Bob Polzel, night watchman at Bridal Veil Lumber and Box Co. whose tenth anniversary was May 1st, was

born in Otis, Colorado. Bob was one of twelve children. When he was thirteen years old his family moved to Salem, where Bob remained until 1940. Bob's parents still live in Salem.

In September of 1940 Bob joined the Army and spent three years serving in Alaska and the Aleutian Islands.

On December 25, 1953, Bob and the former Velma Hargis of Portland were married in Vancouver, Washington. They have an adopted son, Tommy, who is nine years old. Their home

Safety Program

The month of March ends the first quarter for the year 1956. A total of 55,253 man hours worked with one lost time accident gives us an 18.1 accident frequency rating for the quarter which is below the national average of 21.4 for our industry.

At the April 19th safety meeting, three members who are Ralph Taylor, Clarence Noble and Mel Mallinson were chosen to replace Jim Cowling, Don West and Eldon Nielson. Fay Davis will serve as Chairman for three months; Mel Mallinson as secretary.

In the first quarter a total of 88 safety suggestions were made and 65 have been approved and corrected.

As can be seen by the 1955 and 1956 safety record charts interest for safety has paid off and will continue to do so.

Mel Mallinson

is at 320 NE 92nd Place in Portland.

Bob lists gardening and fishing as his hobbies and tells us he has better luck with the first one.

One of his brothers, Leslie, is also employed here at Bridal Veil.

————6————

The Diamond Match Company at Cusick, Washington reduced its Accident Frequency Rate from 23.91 accidents per million man hours in 1954 to 0.0 in 1955.

————6————

The Crown Zellerbach Corp. at Camas, Washington boasts a five year accident frequency rate of 4.50.

1955 SAFETY CHART

	Lost time Accidents	Man Hours Worked	Accident Frenquency
January	4	28,772	139.9
February	0	24,023	0
March	0	24,253	0
Ist Quarter 1955	4	77,048	51.9

1956 SAFETY CHART

	Lost time Accidents	Man Hours Worked	Accident Frenquency
January	0	16,297	0
February	0	20,821	0
March	1	18,135	55.1
Ist Quarter 1956	1	55,253	18.1

Rips and Trims

Dale Hanson, son of Ted Hanson, was lucky and won two tickets to the opening ball game of the Portland Beavers.

Mr. and Mrs. Chester Woodard and Mary have moved to their home southeast of Corbett. A fire, last week, burned a hole in the roof of the house they moved from.

George Leash had to return to the hospital after a week at home. George had a rather bad case of shingles. Our best wishes to George for a speedy recovery.

The Ralph Taylor family recently spent a weekend in Cathlamet with Eleanor's parents.

On the same weekend Walt and Lillian Norgard visited their son and family in Richland, Washington.

Some of the seniors of Corbett high school who recently visited colleges they plan to attend were Jim Yerion, Garfield Pearson and Tom Cowling. All reported a very nice time.

Mrs. Don Aldrich, Lou's sister, visited at the Cowling home for a week. While here, she also visited her father and mother. Her father is in a hospital in Salem, but nearly well enough to go home.

Sons and daughters of Bridal Veil employees who were in the Junior Class play were Don Bowen, Dewayne Kilness, Mary Lee Taylor and Carol Meyer.

The Kraft family spent a fairly successful opening day trout fishing on the McKenzie river.

The Gross' opened the season by fishing the lower Deschutes.

The Clarence Nobles have had Mrs. Ethel Tupper of Vancouver, B. C., as a visitor for the last two weeks.

Tom and Beulah Choate are building a barn to house their new cow. Beulah says she is going to drink lots of milk.

The Godats small son Curtis has missed one week of school, due to a bad case of "flu."

The six Hancock brothers got together at Calvin Hancock's home in Portland to celebrate a visit of Claud who has been in the U. S. Army fifteen years. Present were Calvin, Claud, Clem, Loren, John and Roy.

Matrtha Jones' daughter, Marilyn, is now recovered from an attack of pneumonia which kept her confined five weeks.

Mr. and Mrs. Ray Kreuger and son, of Portland, were weekend guests of the Verl Birds. Ray reports that his firm, Western Wood Products, is very busy at this time.

Bertha and Fay Davis are celebrating their 31st wedding anniversary May 7th. Congratulations to both of them. The next thirty-one should be easy.

Mrs. Ed Harnam returned from Emanuel hospital on Monday (7th), having been there since April 27th. Son, Ralph Sanders, says she feels much better now.

Ralph Sanders and wife, Betty, will leave May 21st for a two week vacation. They will go to Fortuna, California for a few days to visit their son and grandchildren; then back to Oregon and on to Weiser, Idaho, to visit friends and attend a "Rock show" at Caldwell.

Ed Harnam began his vacation on Monday, May 7th. Ed is going to spend his vacation at home, taking care of his wife, who is convalescing from a recent illness.

————6————

Inviting an Accident

Many a workman is reporting for work in clothes with hazards built-in-garments that were unsafe for work in the first place or have become so through neglect.

Consider the loose or dangling sleeves, the floppy pocket flaps or loose apron strings. It's tempting fate to wear them around moving machinery. And when garments are not kept in repair, the hazard is increased. Rips, tears and lost buttons leave loose ends to catch in moving parts and on obstructions. Long, loose sleeves, neckties and gloves rank high on the list of hazards. Cuffs on trousers may cause tripping or catch on something. Ripped or torn clothing can catch on projections.

The most important safety factor of all is the human factor. If a man is properly trained and indoctrinated, he's much more apt to die of old age than if he gives little thought to the subject.

BRIDAL VEIL LUMBER & BOX CO.

News Letter

Volume 1, Number 11   BRIDAL VEIL, OREGON   JUNE

Wood vs. Aluminum

All authorities agree that a dark surface absorbs heat and becomes warm when exposed to the sun, so we can eliminate dark surfaces without further discussion.

The National Bureau of Standards of the Department of Commerce exposed various surfaces to the sun, and determined the temperatures of each. The results of this survey have been published by the Bureau in "Building Materials and Structures Report BMS-64", entitled "Solar Heating of Various Surfaces".

BMS-64 states that a surface covered with glossy white paint was cooler than any other tried, and that one covered with flat white was nearly as cool. This report also states that a surface covered with aluminum foil was cooler in the sun than another covered with aluminum paint, but both were considerably warmer than the white painted surface. It is reasonable to believe, as is assumed in BMS-64, that the tendency of an exterior covering to impart heat to a house is increased as its temperature increases.

The report concludes that oxidation of the aluminum and soiling of the painted surfaces would reduce their insulation effectiveness some, and states that the best protection against the heat of the sun would be a white painted surface.

Most aluminum siding is pre-coated or painted on the outside surface. This immediately changes the reflective property of the siding from the value of aluminum to that of whatever color of coating is used, and seldom is that color white—that best of all reflectors.

The above information has to do with radiant heat from the sun, which is the category in which it was previously supposed that aluminum was better as a protection against summer sun.

When it comes to heat conduction, wood painted or unpainted is so far superior to aluminum as an insulator that it is positively amazing. Figures in the Refrigerating Data Book of the American Society of Refrigerating Engineers show that, in a given length of time, aluminum of a given thickness and area will transmit almost two thousand times as much heat as will a piece of wood of the same dimension; and this means hot sun heat into the house in the summer and expensive furnace heat out of the house in the winter.

Is it any wonder that those with windows of aluminum (or, for that matter, any metal) cannot sit within several feet of them on a cold winter day without feeling the full force of Jack Frost's attack? These cold surfaces create drafts and also we lose at least a small amount of our body heat to them by radiation, thus adding to our discomfort.

Unfortunately, this condition is made worse by infiltration around the edges of metal windows and storm sash due to contraction of the metal because of the low temperature. Aluminum is worse than steel in this respect as it shrinks twice as much as steel. And to aggravate the condition still more, the aluminum and steel shrink in the winter when we would like them to swell to make a tight joint, and then expand in the summer, causing sticking, when we would prefer a little looseness.

Investigation by the Pittsburgh Testing Laboratory disclosed that, when placed over the same window, a make of wood storm sash marketed throughout the nation was more than five times as effective in preventing cold air infiltration as the best of the alu-

(Continued on Page 4)

NEWS LETTER

Published on the 10th of each month by
Bridal Veil Lumber & Box Co.
Bridal Veil, Oregon

Editor . . . . . Don West

20th Anniversary

June 12th will be the twentieth anniversary at Bridal Veil for Clyde Hambrick, box factory foreman.

Clyde was born in Steubenville, Ohio and when he was eight years old the family moved to a small town near Bellingham, Washington. Clyde received most of his education in Anacortes, Washington.

When he was sixteen years old Clyde went to Alaska, where he worked in a gold mine, foundry and box factory. He also workd in box factories in Everett, Seattle, Portland, San Francisco and Los Angeles. He has worked in many more places that we haven't mentioned so you can readily see that Clyde is well travelled.

After working from Mexico to Alaska, Clyde settled in Seattle in 1933. On June 9, 1934 he and the former Ruth Branstrom were married in Seattle. There is quite a story behind that wedding. It seems that they were to be married n th City Hall but they needed to have witnesses. Clyde went out in the hall to find someone and asked a man if he would help them. The man

Storage Tank Installed

The month of May saw the installation of an 8000 gallon storage tank for the mineral spirits used to dissolve the toxic and water repellant treat for our millwork. The total cost of the job has been estimated at $1,700.00 and has been financed by Standard Oil Company on an interest free basis requiring the repayment of $170.00 every six months for five years.

These "small" jobs have a way of getting involved. That big dike around the tank is a requirement of the Oregon Insurance Rating Bureau, which requires a dry lake large enough to hold the contents of the tank plus 10 per cent.

Most important, however, is that we will save 3 cents a gallon on the mineral spirits plus the hauling expense.

————37————

Going fishing this week-end? You probably already have your license and know the fishing laws. But, do you know the fire laws? It's against the law to throw away a lighted cigarette or leave a campfire burning! Continued good fishing is dependent on green forests. When in or near the woods, always be mindful of the danger packed in a lighted cigarette, match or campfire. HELP KEEP OUR FORESTS GREEN AND GROWING!

he asked happened to be the publicity agent for Olson and Johnson of stage fame. Olson and Johnson were at the City Hall to receive the keys to the city, where their show was playing for a week. Olson and Johnson wanted Clyde and Ruth to be married on the stage during one of their performances. Ruth declined but Olson and Johnson were still witnesses to their wedding.

The Hambricks came to Portland in 1935. Clyde worked for Portland Box Co. and then on June 12, 1936 went to work for Wood Specialties Co. In July 1937 they came to Bridal Veil.

The Hambricks have two children, Jim 14 and Claudia, 12. Both are students at Corbett school.

The Hambricks are building a home on S. W. Walters Road in Gresham, which is scheduled for completion late this summer.

————37————

Whatever you do — watch where you're going!

10th Anniversary

Walt Norgard will observe his tenth anniversary at Bridal Veil on the tenth of June.

Walt was born and raised in Eau Claire Wisconsin. In 1911 he came west to Everett Washington. After his arrival in Everett he attended business college. Walt worked in a bank in Everett until he entered the Army in August of 1918. He was in the Army six months, which time was spent at the Presidio in San Francisco. Walt was discharged from the service due to the illness of his father. He went back into banking and worked in Everett, Seattle and Los Angeles.

In 1927 he went to Ketchikan, Alaska where he was Assistant Cashier in the First National Bank. Because of an illness in the family he had to return to Everett in 1928, where he remained until 1938. From there he went to Kinzua, Oregon, where he was private secretary to the president and general manager of the Kinzua Pine Mills. In 1942 he was engaged in war work in Portland and from 1944 until he came to Bridal Veil he was office manager of Upper Columbia Logging Co.

On December 30, 1922, Walt and the former Lillian Schuberg of Everett were married in Mt. Vernon, Washington. They have two boys, Dave and George.

Dave is a scientist at the Hanford

June Birthdays

Many Happy Returns of the Day!

Max Bissell	R. Schneringer
George Knieriem	Durward L. Litton
Harold Jacobson	William McCawley
Jerald Roberts	Walter Mannthey
Roland Morgan	James Kendrick
James Bowen	Earl Hutchison
Frank Crane	

————37————

Safety Program

The month of May completes 37 consecutive days without a lost time accident. This is the longest period since March 9, when we had racked up 95 days without any lost-time accidents— Let's keep the string going!

Since the organization of the safety program, a total of 93 safety sugestions have been made and 72 of them have been completed. Of the remaining 21 suggestions, most of them will be taken care of by the modernization program.

Along with the accident frequency rate, we have added the accident severity rate. Both of these rates are figured on the basis of per million man hours worked. The accident frequency rate is figured by the number of accidents per million manhours worked while the severity rate is figured by the number of days lost per million manhours.

————37————

Absence Report

The fine attendance record of March has been extended in April. The April figure was 1.9% compared to 1.8% in March—only one tenth of one percent more. Here is how the two months compare:

Month	Hours Present	Hours Absent	Total Hours	% of Absence
March	17,969	336	18,305	1.8%
April	19,393	382	19,775	1.9%

Atomic Works and he and his family live in Richland, Washington. They have three children, two girls and one boy.

Their other son, George, is a student at Portland State college. This fall he will enter Oregon State to complete his work in electrical engineering.

Walt is a long time member of the American Legion and is past commander of Bonneville Post No. 88. He is also a member of the Central Lutheran Church of Portland.

10th Anniversary

June 3rd will be the tenth anniversary at **Bridal Veil Lumber & Box Co** for **Mary Woodard**, tail-off in the millwork department.

Mary was born in Ekalaka, Montana. The family lived on a farm at the time. When she was six years old the family moved to Toppenish, Washington. In 1941 they went back to Montana for one year. In 1942 they moved to their present home a few miles south of Corbett. They also lived in Bridal Veil for several years but also maintained their home at Corbett.

Mary received her education in Toppenish and Corbett. Mary has not had a lost time accident since she has been working at Bridal Veil, nor has she ever missed a paycheck.

Mary enjoyed a brief period of local fame in the fall of 1954 when she won a one-thousand pound white face steer in a raffle at Corbett.

Health and Welfare

The following employees worked the required number of hours in April to become eligible for Health and Welfare coverage and will be covered on the first day of June, 1956. Employees who did not work the required hours will become ineligible the same day. Additions: Rodney Clayton, Daryl Cox, Franklin Crane, Fred Fawcett, Robert Godat, Jarvis Kilness, Jack Kreman, Harry Kruckman, Vyrtle Kuntz, Fredrick Long, Roland Morgan, Orien Pitts, Leslie Polzel, David Rees, Robert Reischel, Richard Spitzengel, Carl Walker, Roley Zumwalt. Deletions: Larry Granberg.

————37————

Wood vs. Aluminum

(Continued from Page 1)

minum storm sash and those of other metals.

When it comes to keeping heat from the sun out in summer and heat from the furnace in during the cold months, the above data merely confirm actual experience that wood is by far the best answer.

And it looks better, too.

Len Kraft

————37————

Band Rip Saw Moved

During May we moved the No. 1 Band Rip Saw seven feet to the East. The additional space between the two saws will give us room for two additional rips.

At the price we pay for our lumber, each ⅛" of width on a 6-4 board costs three cents. The additional two loads will permit us to rip our lumber closer to the finished widths required, and we hope to save quite a few ⅛ inches per day.

————37————

Horseplay never pays!

1956 SAFETY CHART

Month	Tot. Pd. Man Hrs.	Hourly Accidents	Lost Time Accident Freq.	Days Lost	Accident Severity
January	16,297	0	0	0	0
February	20,821	0	0	0	0
March	18,135	1	55.1	5	276
April	19,749	2	101.3	7	354
TOTAL	75,002	3	40.0	12	100

Seniority List

1. Atchley, Noah 3-23-36	49. Choate, Beulah 10-7-46	97. Gross, Elden 8-27-53
2. Dull, Ward E. 5-18-36	50. Layton, Hiram 11-13-46	98. Mannthey, Walter 9-14-53
3. Noble, Clarence 7-27-36	51. Steele, Edward J..... 1-14-47	99. Kuzmesky, Steven 9-15-53
4. McCredie, Ralph H. 8-27-36	52. Lofstedt, Clarence.... 1-16-47	100. Hancock, John 3-2-54
5. Harnam, Ed 3-22-37	53. Murray, George 4-21-47	101. Bennett, George O. 5-4-54
6. Davis, D. Fay 3-22-37	54. Lofstedt, Charles 4-23-47	102. Bowen, James E...... 5-4-54
7. Jackson, Marvin T. 4- 8-37	55. Jones, Martha A. 5-14-47	103. Burkholder, Harold.... 5-4-54
8. Stolin, Walter F. 5-11-37	56. Choate, Thomas 5-15-47	104. Kinonen, Edsel 5-4-54
9. Rhodes, James D. 6- 8-37	57. Van Hee, Theodore V. 9-9-47	105. Kuntz, Vyrtle 5-4-54
10. Bowen, Franklin M. 8-19-37	58. Rowe, Thelma Y. 11-12-47	106. Long, Fredrick H..... 6-2-54
11. Crouser, Fred 8-30-37	59. Hills, Mabel M. 1-14-48	107. Kilness, Jarvis 6-2-54
12. Bird, Verl W. 9-20-37	60. Dunken, William L. 9-15-48	108. Fawcett, Fred 8-16-54
13. Taylor, Ralph L. 11-22-37	61. Davis, Dean F. 9-31-48	109. Zumwalt, Roley 9-7-54
14. Hanson, Theodore N. 4-18-38	62. Jacobson, Richard 11-29-48	110. Cox, Daryl 9-13-54
15. Van Orsow, Jos. M. 4-22-38	63. Hills, Stanley B. 1-15-51	111. Crane, Franklin T.... 9-13-54
16. Dunken, J. Delbert 7-18-38	64. Roberts, Vera Nell.... 1-15-51	112. Wilson, Louis 9-20-54
17. Meyer, Kenneth L. 9-16-40	65. Van Orsow, John H. 1-15-51	113. Rees, David 9-23-54
18. Hartshorn, Merrill 1-8-41	66. Van Treeck, Paul 2-20-51	114. Godat, Robert D.... 10-6-54
19. Harp, Fred 5-21-41	67. Van Hee, Theo. Sr. 2-27-51	115. Morgan, Roland B. 12-14-54
20. Mickelson, Elnar 7-1-41	68. Schneringer, Ray...... 10-8-51	116. Polzel, Leslie D. 1-5-55
21. Roberts, Jerald G..... 9-8-41	69. Walker, Homer F. 10-9-51	117. Gaymon, Charles N. 3-29-55
22. Ellis, Ralph 10-9-41	70. Frazier, Lloyd 10-9-51	118. Kreman, Jack L. 3-30-55
23. Latourell, Glifford.... 3-23-42	71. Eveland, Roy D. 10-15-51	119. Kruckman, Harry D..... 4-7-55
24. Vogel, Harold A. 3-25-42	72. Catlin, Kenneth V. 10-18-51	120. Clayton, Rodney L. 4-11-55
25. Nielson, Eldon F. 4-21-42	73. Anderson, Lester W. 5-19-52	121. Reischel, Robert W. 4-11-55
26. Davis, Bertha M. 5-6-42	74. Emmons, Dale 5-20-52	122. Seeger, Roger 4-11-55
27. Rhodes, Louise L. 5-28-42	75. Caffrey, Richard 5-21-52	123. Pitts, Orien 4-13-55
28. Hartshorn, Dorothy 7-14-42	76. Kimbley, A. R., Sr. 6-2-52	124. Adams, Wesley A..... 5-9-55
29. Bowen, Anna 9-30-42	77. Howell, Lester B...... 6-23-52	125. Dooley, Paul D........ 5-9-55
30. Anderson, Roy J. 2-11-43	78. Hutchison, Earl 6-23-52	126. Schroder, Arthur H. 5-11-55
31. Hageman, Leo F. 7-14-43	79. Van Buskirk, Norman 7-28-52	127. Hageman, Leo C........ 6-1-55
32. Yerion, Lillie P. 7-19-43	80. Hancock, Loren 9-2-52	128. Smith, John W.......... 6-9-55
33. Houchin, Wilbur O. 7-26-43	81. Long, Fred M. 9-9-52	129. Clark, David D........ 6-27-55
34. Cloe, Pearl P. 11-12-43	82. Cote, Joseph 9-10-52	130. Levan, Paul F. 6-28-55
35. Eversull, James A. 12-17-43	83. Adolph, Harry 9-22-52	131. Dunlap, Leon C. 7-5-55
36. Britton, Thomas C. 12-20-43	84. Godat, Harold M. 9-25-52	132. Clark, James P. 7-29-55
37. Nielson, Mira J. 1-23-44	85. Willms, John G........ 9-29-52	133. Rogers, Chester 8-9-55
38. Litton, Durward L.... 5-9-44	86. Potter, Eugene H. 10-28-52	134. Cook, Francis P...... 8-10-55
39. Peterson, Lawrence 9-24-45	87. Wells, Glen 3-23-53	135. Hancock, Clem A.... 8-15-55
40. Hunt, Howard G. 10-1-45	88. Crane, Jack L. 3-30-53	136. Watts, Paul A. 8-22-55
41. Smazal, Lawrence A. 10-2-45	89. Davies, Archie L. 4-1-53	137. Knieriem, George S. 8-24-55
42. Stolin, Marvin J. 3-28-46	90. Bissell, Louis W....... 5-1-53	138. Cox, Ernest M........ 8-29-55
43. Van Hee, Theo. V. 4-17-46	91. Layton, Bob 5-28-53	139. Wendler, Ed L........ 9-6-55
44. Polzel, Robert E. 5-1-46	92. Bissell, Max 6-1-53	140. Dobson, Virgil 9-7-55
45. Kendrick, James B. 5-13-46	93. McCawley, William 7-27-53	141. Bottoms, Emmett 9-13-55
46. Woodard, Mary R..... 6-3-46	94. Sanders, Ralph L..... 8-3-53	142. Westlake, Donald 10-17-55
47. Houchin, Inez M....... 9-5-46	95. Ayles, Elmer L........ 8-4-53	143. Reinsch, David W. 10-21-55
48. Jacobson, Harold R. 9-16-46	96. Willoughby, H. G. 8-24-53	144. Clabaugh, David 10-26-55

Engineering

In case you have wondered just what the term "Insurance Engineering" covers, we print the above picture of "Doug" Walwyn of Smith & Crakes making an inspection of our fire protection reservoir.

According to Doug the results of this survey indicate:

   (a) There is water in the reservoir,

   (b) There are fish in the water.

ACCIDENTS DON'T JUST HAPPEN
— they are caused!

Bridal Veil Visitors

Fred McBride of Firpine Products Company conducted a tour of our mill for Stanley Anderson, Jr., Del Stutz and Ivan Jones of Fall Creek Lumber Company, May 29th. The Fall Creek Lumber Company is a manufacturer of fir window frames.

————37————

Play Ball

With only five returning "regulars", Corbett High School's baseball team started the 1956 season on rather "shaky" legs. The team, being a young one, was considered by many as a "darkhorse", or "the team that didn't have a chance". Two pre-season scrimmages with Parkrose and Cascade Locks seemed to prove these theorys correct as the Corbett squad lost both of them by lop-sided scores.

However, undaunted, the boys worked even harder in practice and when the first league game rolled around, a new team made its appearance and Corbett won by an easy margin.

With "desire to win" filling in where "experience" left off, Corbett literally "breezed" through the league schedule and in the process they knocked over all of last year's "league powers". Corbett was the first team, in the history of the Hill River Valley League, to go through an entire season, undefeated.

But the trail did not end here, and as the Cardinals downed Mill City 4-0, they found themselves playing Siletz for the district title.

On May 15, the team traveled to Toledo (a neutral field) and proceeded to "squeek" by Siletz 1-0 in an eight inning contest. "All good things must end" and Corbett went down in defeat in the State Quarterfinals, losing to Gaston 3-0.

All concerned seem to agree that big things are in store for next year's baseball team at Corbett High School.

Corbett baseball players whose fathers are employed at Bridal Veil Lumber and Box Company are: Don Bowen, Bob Bird, Tom Cowling, Bob Cowling, Bob Long, Don Hageman and Marvin Howell.

Tom Cowling

————37————

Let Safety show through whatever you do.

CONTACT LUMBER COMPANY . *Western Forest Products*
719-720 CORBETT BUILDING · PORTLAND 4, OREGON · CAPITOL 8-7361

June 1, 1956.

Bridal Veil Lumber & Box Company,
Bridal Veil, Oregon.

Gentlemen:

       Referring to our order M-1761, your M-982, we have the following
letter dated May 28th from customer, and which we quote:

> "You may accept this letter as our complete
> approval, without any changes of the frame
> specifications submitted by Bridal Veil
> Lumber & Box Company, and applying to your
> order M-1761. We hope you do everything
> you can to expedite delivery.
>
> We surely admire the thoroughness that
> Bridal Veil Lumber exercised in submitting
> these specifications."

       The writer had an opportunity yesterday to briefly page through the
extensive report prepared by a statistical organization for the National
Lumber Manufacturers Assn., entitled "IMPROVING MARKET OPPORTUNITIES FOR
THE LUMBER INDUSTRY". Perhaps you have a copy, or could obtain one direct
from the Western Pine Assn. Understand the report cost $130,000.00.

       What you have done in preparing detailed specifications on a millwork
order, besides eliminating the possibility of error or misunderstanding, goes
a long way towards solving some of the problems set forth in the above report.
Certainly it does bridge the gap—too often left open—between the buyer and
user and the manufacturer. It is a distinct job of selling confidence and
good will.

               Yours very truly,

               CONTACT LUMBER COMPANY

LJD-j   BY: Leo J. Donnelly

Rips and Trims

Two Bridal Veil boys won the honors in the Senior Class at Corbett. They are **Tom Cowling**, valedictorian and **Jim Yerion**, salutatorian. These two boys started in the first grade together and have gone on through high school. Jim plans to go to Monmouth next year and Tom to the U of O.

Norman Van Buskirk will start his vacation May 29th. He plans to spend two days in the mountains fishing, and the rest of the time working on the place they bought on 143rd, one block north of Burnside.

Paul Van Treeck vacationed four days at Siltcoos Lake in May. He reported that the fishing was not too good, but that he enjoyed boat riding. He spent the remainder of his vacation at home working.

Mr. and Mrs. Walter Mannthey, son and wife (**Dave** and **Jeannie**) and their baby daughter **Alta**, spent their vacation on a trip east. Stopping in Butte, Montana they visited relatives. They spent six days in Alta, Montana and Clear Lake, South Dakota visiting friends and relatives. They returned by way of the Black Hills, the Badlands, and Yellowstone National Park.

Rodney Clayton is back to work after being on vacation. He spent most of his time working on his car. He did a little fishing in the local streams but didn't have very good luck.

Fred Harp was off four days to have a growth removed from his nose. He only planned on being off two days but it didn't heal up like it should and he was off four days, instead.

Daryl Cox, Ed Wendler and his son spent the 26th and 27th fishing on Crane Prarie. They got 40 trout, which averaged 12 to 14 inches. They said it was very cold and windy, there.

Theodore Van Hee left the 25th of May for Virginia. His mother and sister made the trip with him. They will visit with Ted's brother and family. Ted planned to make it back there in six days and may return by plane, leaving his car for his sister to drive back.

We have news for those who think it is necessary to travel to catch fish. Young **Terry Ayles**, son of **Elmer Ayles**, caught a six pound steelhead in Bridal Veil Creek, Saturday, May 19th.

George Knieriem is scheduled to leave for the Annual National Guard Summer Field Training at Camp Clatsop June 16th to 30th.

Marvin Jackson, Chairman of the school board at Corbett, presented diplomas to the grade school graduating class Thursday evening, May 31.

Connie Meyers is taking the balance of his vacation (6 days). Connie says he is going to show his mother the high-lights of the State of Oregon, including Mt. Hood, Crater Lake and the Oregon beaches. Hope it compares well with Nebraska, Connie.

Bridal Veil is plagued with high water from the flooding Columbia River, again, bringing back memories of the 1948 flood. **Paul Detrick's** crew worked Sunday, June 3rd, raising the motor of the box-factory fan. They were able to re-install it Monday morning, however, as the water level remained practically the same. We are keeping our fingers crossed for the remainder of the month.

Martha Jones has been off work for the last week with a bursitis condition in one arm.

Jim and **Louise Rhodes** are off work to take Louise's mother to a doctor. Jim says her condition seems to indicate a light stroke.

It is graduation time again in our schools and Bridal Veil is pretty well represented with graduates in the Corbett schools. **Tom Cowling, Jim Yerion** and **Bob Bird** were graduated from Corbett high school and **Fred Mickelson, Jim Hambrick, Sharon Catlin** and **Cristal Jackson** were graduated from the eighth grade.

Bob Layton starts his vacation the 21st of June. On the 23rd of June he will be maried to **Dona-Rae Schneringer**, of Corbett, at Stevenson, Washington. They will honeymoon at the coast.

John and **Marvin Van Orsow** spent the week end fishing in Central Oregon. East Lake proved so unsuccessful that they changed to Crane Paririe on Sunday and brought home the limit.

Mr. and Mrs. Eldon Nielson and children are leaving Friday, the 8th, for Oklahoma for a visit with Mrs. Nielson's relatives. They plan to be back in Bridal Veil the 25th.

BRIDAL VEIL LUMBER & BOX CO.
News Letter

Volume II, Number 1   BRIDAL VEIL, OREGON   JULY, 1956

Wood vs. Aluminum—Part 2

The material printed last month was largely taken from an article written by Mr. John Reno, Utilization Director, The Pacific Lumber Company, and printed in The Hoosier Board and Brick in the July 1953 issue. After publication of the above article, the manufacturers of metal windows and siding disputed some of the conclusions in the article. Mr. Reno answered their comments by point as follows, with figures from accepted authorities.

1. Comment: Metal windows have made great inroads into the wood window market—Miami, Florida, is given as an example.

Mr. Reno's answer: The use of aluminum windows above the basement in the USA dropped from 9 per cent in 1940 to 5 per cent in 1950 and and only 1 per cent of the basement windows are of aluminum. This in spite of the almost irresistible force of millions of dollars of advertising, promotion, and publicity in behalf of aluminum building materials in the last 15 years. Advertising can sell initially but customer satisfaction governs in the end.

These data are in the U. S. Government Housing & Home Finance Agency report, "The Material Use Survey," dated November, 1952.

2. Comment; It is the window glass, not the metal frame that transmits the the heat and cold; and condensation caused by the frame is of secondary importance.

Answer: The fact is that window glass is 260 times better as an insulator than is aluminum. Heat or cold goes through aluminum of a given thickness 260 times as fast—and 260 times as much—as through window glass of the same thickness. That is why frost gathers on the aluminum so often instead of on the glass

in spite of their different thicknesses. You will notice they admit there is condensation on the metal frame but call it "of secondary importance." There is no condensation on wood frames.

No. Aluminum cannot compare to wood for window use.

3. Comment: The Pittsburgh Testing Laboratory annually tests aluminum window products of the members of the Aluminum Window Manufacturers Association to check air-infiltration against a standard.

Answer: How strict is the standard? It is this same Pittsburgh Testing Laboratory that proved by tests that the modern wood storm sash tested was more than five times as good in preventing infiltration of cold air as the best of the aluminum units.

4. Comment: It is hinted that infiltration of cold air around windows is desirable because it permits water vapor to escape from the house.

Answer: This is an amazing statement. Here we modernize wood windows by weather-stripping them and the metal manufacturers try to equal the efficiency of the wood window by various types of designs and when unsuccessful they say, "Oh, well, the cold air should be allowed to come in anyway because it reduces the humidity in the house."

Yes, we should reduce this humidity but it should be done scientifically. An article on this subject is appearing in the trade press under the title of "Getting Humidity Out of the House."

5. Comment: Figures in the authoritative Guide of the American Society of Heating and Ventilating Engineers show that non-weatherstripped wood windows with their 1/32 inch crack have greater infiltration than metal windows.

(Continued on Page 3)

NEWS LETTER

Published on the 10th of each month by
Bridal Veil Lumber & Box Co.
Bridal Veil, Oregon

Editor . . . . . Don West

The Half Way Mark

If you've come through the first six months of 1956 without having had a serious injury—either on or off the job—your being careful has already paid off!

But whether or not you made a resolution on January 1st to be careful during the year, the half-way mark of 1956 is a wonderful time to resolve to stay safe on and off the job for the second half of the year.

Almost everyone knows how to be careful on the job.

The trouble is that often we come to think of accidents as a matter of luck. The fact that we've always gotten by without a serious injury sometimes lulls us to sleep — sometimes makes us feel that we can take a chance with safety.

Anyone who ever thinks that accidents won't happen to him or who thinks that he doesn't need to be careful cannot be sure from one minute to another when an accident will happen.

Yet you can all but guarantee your own safety on the job to the rest of 1956 by remembering that you can't count on luck in preventing accidents.

There is no substitute for being careful every day on every job! July has still another importance to the safety of everyone. It is the start of the summer months—the season of long weekends, vacations, and outdoor living — the time when off-the-job accidents are most apt to happen.

No one wants to be a kill-joy and say "Have a good time!" and then list all of the things that can happen. But long experience shows that accidents never take a vacation—or indeed any time off at all!

And that's just as true in off-the-job activities as it is on-the-job.

In short, it's worth remembering that keping safety in mind is the best insurance for having a good time during the summer months.

REMEMBER — being careful pays off "off-the-job" as well as "on-the-job!"

Re-Inspection

Here we have visual proof of the terrific concentration required in verifying the results of Doug Walwyn's re-

cent engineering survey of our fire protection reservoir. Len Kraft, pictured above, is giving the subject matter his undivided attention.

Len, never one to shirk a duty, reports that the results of his re-survey indicate:

(a) There is water in the reservoir.

———43———

One American in ten works in a forest-dependent industry. More than one and a half million people earn their livings working in woods and mills alone. Probably five times that many work in businesses, trades or industries that are partially dependent on forest products. They live in homes like yours, in neighborhoods like yours. They have children and attend churches of their own choice. In short, these people—like the industries they represent—are part of the democracy that is America. These are reasons why every citizen has a stake in helping woodland owners grow continuing crops of trees for tomorrow's harvest.

———43———

Professor: "What are the bones in your hand called?"

Medical Student: "Dice."

———43———

A Crutch May Support You, But It Will Not Support Your Family.

Wood vs. Aluminum---Part 2

(Continued from Page 1)

Answer: This is comparing a 1930 wood window with a 1953 metal one.

In my comparison I have used the modern aluminum window and the modern wood window for my examples.

The modern wood window is weather-stripped and does not stick in winter or summer.

It does not decay because it is made of a naturally durable wood or of other woods that have been toxic treated to prevent decay.

Actually the Guide shows that modern weather-stripped metal windows have air leakage 1 1/3 times as much as weather-stripped wood windows in the double-hung type, while metal casement air leakage is 1½ to 2 times that of wood casements. In the nonweather-stripped variety the superiority of the wood window is even more pronounced.

These figures are for metals that are more stable dimensionally and that will stay tighter than aluminum. The aluminum manufacturers apparently have made no effort to have special tests made on aluminum windows, and the inference is they are content to "let sleeping dogs lie" and to use the more favorable figures of other metals, even though these show up poorly compared to wood. This policy also seems to apply to aluminum siding.

6. Comment: In commenting on total heat losses of aluminum and wood windows an advantage of only 4% was given to wood.

Answer: This figure is evidently just a statement of the aluminum people themselves as no authority was given for it. Also they said "neglecting infiltration of air." Of course this infiltration of cold air is one of the disadvantages of aluminum storm sash and windows and must be considered when comparing aluminum with wood.

7. Comment: F.H.A. Bulletin UM-6 accords insulation value to aluminum siding with its two bright faces.

Answer: F.H.A. Bulletin UM-6 and F.H.A. Tech. Circular No. 7 show that walls identical, except for the siding, have greater insulation value when wood siding is used than they do with aluminum siding.

8. Comment: Aluminum siding is applied over other siding because of paint blistering on the latter due to moisture being driven through the wall from the inside.

Answer: Water blisters on paint should be remedied by correcting the conditions which cause the water to be present—the corrective measures are given in an article entitled, "Paint Troubles on Redwood Siding—Causes & Cures."

If aluminum siding is applied over other siding troubled with water blisters, the water will continue to be driven into the wall and when stopped by the aluminum siding will merely build up in quantity with bad effect on the entire wall. The least harmful result is an unpleasant, musty smell. The best remedy is to remove the cause of the unwanted moisture and then no trouble from paint blistering will occur on any type of siding.

9. Comment: Wood had better be painted for reasons other than appearance if it is to be serviceable for any length of time.

Answer: Any well informed lumberman knows wood is painted for appearance only. Painting gives a different color to wood and it prevents the wood weathering. Weathering is the roughening and darkening of the surface of the wood. Unpainted wood houses are still sound and sturdy although more than 100 years old; or for that matter more than 200 and 300 years old. There are many of these fine old wood houses in this country. Salt air has no bad effect on wood. Actually wood tanks are used for the storage of salt water, acids and alkaline mixtures.

In closing I would like to comment that the truth is aluminum production has increased so greatly in the last few years for war purposes that the aluminum manufacturers are panicky in their efforts to find new peace-time uses to absorb this production, and have in some instances promoted it for purposes where other materials do a better job.

For many purposes aluminum is good. For instance, we recommend aluminum nails for nailing house siding.

———43———

Two camels plodded along side by side in a caravan crossing the burning desert. Finally one looked around furtively and said: "I don't care what anybody says, I'm thirsty."

Our Eastern Trip

Mrs. West (Barbara) and I left Portland May 18th to begin our eastern sales trip. We traveled to Chicago on the Union Pacific's "City of Portland", which is by far the finest train we saw on our entire trip.

We arrived in Chicago just before noon on Sunday, and as soon as we could get checked into the hotel, we headed for the baseball game between the Chicago White Sox and the Boston Red Sox, which we really enjoyed. Boston won.

The following morning the "work" began, for me at least. While Barbara and Mrs. John Dean explored Chicago, John and I called on Dekker-Brish Millwork Co. It was a thoroughly enjoyable visit, as all the calls on the customers were.

The next two days were spent calling on the McGill Metal Products Co. of Marengo, Illinois and the Mann Sash & Door Co. of Aurora, Illinois.

Wednesday evening we left Chicago for Fort Wayne, Indiana, where we rented a car and drove to Van Wert, Ohio, to see a cheese box customer at the Borden Co. From Van Wert, our travels took us to Rochester, New York to call on Mr. Stanley Rainka and Mr. David Jacobson of the Concord Millwork Corporation. In Rochester we were pleasantly surprised to learn that business is ahead of last year's record volume.

After a very nice dinner and evening with Mr. and Mrs. Rainka, we boarded the train for New York City where we spent the weekend. Saturday found us staring at the wonders of that city. On arriving at the hotel in New York we were presented with tickets to a stage play and a ball game through the courtesy of Dant & Russell, Inc. I'm afraid I was little tired by this time and was probably the only one in the theatre to sleep through "Damn Yankees". Anyway, Barbara enjoyed the play, if not my company.

The next day it rained so we couldn't see the ball game, so we rested until train time that night, when we left for Pennsylvania, where we called on the Clearfield Cheese Co.

On leaving Pennsylvania, we headed for Cincinnati, Ohio where we arrived on the morning of May 30th, Memorial Day. It was hot that day but luckily we had an air conditioned room in our hotel. The next day was spent at the Pease Woodwork Co. in company of Mr. Burton Pease. Burt took us on a tour of the plant where they make prefabricated houses and we also inspected the model homes in a tract adjacent to the factory. It was an informative and interesting visit.

Next we flew to Kansas City, Missouri, where we visited Luce Mfg. Co. and the Millwork Co. Although our visit to these places was enjoyable, by this time we were getting tired and a little homesick.

On Friday evening, June 1, we boarded the train for San Francisco, where we relaxed for a day before coming home.

We made many new acquaintences on our trip and learned things which we feel will lead to a better understanding of the problems which confront our customers as well as ourselves.

Don West

Pictured above is the storage tank for the mineral spirits used to dissolve the toxic and water repellant treat for our millwork. The installation was recently completed and the 8000 gallon tank is now ready to use.

"Safety" is a fight against heartache and economic loss. Let's not be bored by it.

Former Employee Solos

A former employee who worked here during school vacations, has made his first solo flight as a Navy pilot. He is Ensign Robert U. Tuohy, Jr., son of Mr. and Mrs. Robert U. Tuohy. He attended Northwestern University before entering the service. Before leaving Whiting Field Naval Auxiliary Air Station, Milton, Florida, for more advanced training, he will have received instruction in precision air work along with his regular solo flights.

———43———

Scenic Columbia River Highway

In the past forty years I have traveled over this road thousands of times, and today its beauty means as much to me as the first time I ever saw it.

I have been told by people who have traveled all over the world that it is the most beautiful in the world.

There are a good many retaining walls built along this road, no two alike. They were built by masons imported from Italy who were masters of their craft, and the walls will stand for all time.

I have noticed, since the express highway was built, that there have been numerous phases of neglect in the maintenance of this road, especially in winter. Shame on the State Highway Department.

I would venture to say that if our highway and scenery were within thirty miles of New York City, all the money in the would couldn't buy it.

Roy J. Anderson

What's Good for GM

Possibly you will recall Tae Yong Min, the Korean student from Lewis and Clark College who spent a summer working at Bridal Veil a few years back. That particular summer the frame business had fallen on evil days for one reason or another, and the problem of lagging frame sales troubled Min (that's his first name) to the extent that he turned his mind to the search for a solution.

One morning Min came up with the answer. Here it is as he wrote it:

"The house building and automobile industry have met depression according to the paper.

"It is my imagination that you could adopt the same yearly fashion system as the automobile industry did, i.e., the system of 1952 Buick, 1953 Plymouth, and so on.

"If the house building industry could adopt the same yearly fashion system as 1953 Bridal Veil (window frame), 1954 Bridal Veil ("), and so forth, then there would be no depression in this industry for you.

"Nobody pays attention, when they look at the house, to the roof, or wall, they do pay attention to the windows of the house. Really window is the face of the house. And everybody wants to keep their faces clean and nice. Especially the showwindows, windows of the public buildings and inns and motels are in that need."

———43———

The sergeant of a new company of recruits stuck his head in the barracks. "Any of you guys good at shorthand?" he asked.

Four men stepped forward.

"O.K.," snapped the sergeant. "Report to the mess hall right away—they're shorthanded."

1956 SAFETY CHART

Month	Tot. Pd. Man Hrs.	Hourly Accidents	Lost Time Freq.	Accident Days Lost	Accident Severity
January	16,297	0	0	0	0
February	20,821	0	0	0	0
March	18,135	1	55.1	5	276
1st Quarter	55,253	1	18.1	5	91
April	19,749	2	101.3	7	354
May	24,255	1	41.2	7	289
TOTAL	99,257	4	40.2	19	191

10 Points for Traffic Safety

If you find traffic conditions a headache, don't be too optimistic about things looking up. After a look into the future, the National Safety Council has come up with these disconcerting figures for 1966:

15th Anniversary

July 1 will be the fifteenth anniversary at Bridal Veil for Einar Mickelson, foreman of the cross working department.

Einar was born in Scranton, Iowa, one of twelve children. There were five boys and seven girls in the family. When Einar was four years old the family moved to Perry, Iowa.

On May 9, 1938, Einar and the former Bernice Ebrecht, of Perry, were married in Scranton.

The Mickelsons came west to Cathlamet, Washington, May 24, 1938. In Cathlamet, Einar worked for International Wood Products Co., where he stayed until he came to Bridal Veil. Since he has been at Bridal Veil he has worked in every department in the mill with the exception of the maintenance department.

The Mickelsons have three children: Nancy 17, Barbara 15, and Freddie 14. All are students at Corbett school.

Einar is a member of the Masonic Lodge.

(a) 82,000,000 vehicles will jam the roads, 20,000,000 more than now.

(b) 90,000,000 drivers will pilot them.

(c) They will travel approximately 825 billion miles a year.

(d) The traffic toll will be about 53,000 unless some genius sells safety to those drivers.

Since the traffic toll is interwoven inseparably with the flow of traffic, the Council has announced a safety program based on engineering, education, and enforcement.

(1) Convince every individual to drive and walk safely and encourage others, through organized efforts.

(2) Give communities facts on how their traffic program compares with recognized standards.

(3) Quickly, build many miles of safe, modern, accident-resistent roads.

(4) By using traffic engineering and law enforcement, make existing highways more foolproof and safe.

(5) Obtain uniform vehicle laws so one set of traffic rules can be followed and enforced, coast to coast.

(6) Require driver education in the schools.

(7) Tighten regulations so only completely qualified persons can obtain drivers' licenses.

(8) Revoke the license of anyone not driving decently and sensibly.

(9) Back traffic courts to the limit.

(10) Encourage auto design improvements for easier safe driving.

The Council states the traffic situation can improve only as the public accepts these ten objectives. However, safety, like everything worthwhile — costs time, money, and effort.

————43————

Teamwork

A man stepped on a nail in a board and hurt his foot. Two persons were responsible for the accident—the man who left the nail in the board, and the other who did not look where he was stepping. It really took teamwork to get results: but how much better it would have been to use the teamwork idea in starting a good, sound, healthy, effective, enthusiastic safety organization in the plant. The value of such organizations has been proved in many plants.

July Birthdays

Many Happy Returns of the Day!

Harold Vogel	Virgil Dobson
A. R. Kimbley, Sr.	T. Van Hee, Sr.
Art Schroder	Rodney Clayton
Lillie Yerion	Bob Bird
Willie Bowen	Bob Layton
Lester Anderson	Tom Cowling
Paul Detrick	Orien Pitts
Jim Cowling	

————43————

Health and Welfare

The following employees worked the required number of hours in May to become eligible for Health and Welfare coverage and will be covered on the first day July, 1956. Employees who did not work the required hours will become ineligible the same day. Additions: Wesley Adams, David Clabaugh, David Clark, Francis Cook, Ernest Cox, Virgil Dobson, Paul Dooley, Leon Dunlap, George Knieriem, Paul Levan, Chester Rogers, Arthur Schroder, Roger Seeger, John W. Smith, Paul Watts, Edward Wendler and Donald Westlake. Deletions: Orval K. Johnson, Grant Preston, Richard Spitzengel, Carl Walker and Chester Woodard.

————43————

Rips and Trims

Mrs. Ade Jones was released from the hospital Thursday, June 21, where she has been convalescing following an operation. It will be another six months or so before she is completely recovered, however. Ade reports she is feeling pretty good now.

Dale and **Dick Hanson** won third and seventh prizes, respectively, in "Why I'd like to be a bat boy for the Beavers" contest.

Recent guests at the **Jim Cowling** home were Mr. and Mrs. Henry Cowling of Oakridge, and Jim's sister, Alice Ragsdale, of Spokane.

The **Jack Cranes** have a baby boy in their family now, making them three girls and a boy and Jack says he wants an even dozen.

Walt and **Lillian Norgard** just returned from a week of vacation spent at Sun Lakes State Park in Washington.

————43————

ALERT TODAY--ALIVE TOMORROW

20th Anniversary

July 27 will be the 20th anniversary at Bridal Veil for Clarence Noble, set-up man on the circular resaws.

Clarence was born in Grinell, Iowa. In 1910 he and his mother came west to Vancouver, British Columbia, where Clarence remained until 1936.

From 1921 to 1924, Clarence owned and operated a passenger bus line between New Westminster, B. C., and Fort Langlie.

In 1925 he began working for the International Wood Products Co., in a box factory, at New Westminster. He remained there until July, 1936. The family then moved to Portland where Clarence worked at Wood Specialties Co. for a year before coming to Bridal Veil.

Clarence and the former Gertrude Forman of Coghlan, B. C., were married on September 10, 1921. They have two daughters, Thelma and Verna. They also have two grandchildren, Bobby and Donajean.

As near as he can recall, Clarence has not had a lost time accident since he has been at Bridal Veil.

————43————

"What's the matter with you," the wife demanded. "Monday you liked beans, Tuesday you liked beans, Wednesday you liked beans; now Thursday, all of a sudden, you don't like beans."

Rips and Trims

Fay and **Bertha Davis** had as week-end guests, Captain and Mrs. Vassey. Mrs. Vassey, Nora, is Fay's sister and was employed here during the last war. They are enroute from Okinawa and left Monday, June 25th, for Oklahoma.

Verl Bird and wife, **Evelyn**, visited son **Bob**, at Camp Clatsop, Sunday, June 24th, where he is undergoing two weeks National Gunard training. Bob was doing KP and enjoying it.

Robert Godat was in a wreck involving five cars and came out of it in very good shape. Bob says it cost him only $100 and he has a brand new Dodge.

Fay and **Bertha Davis** entertained with a pot-luck dinner Sunday evening, June 24th, for nearly all their brothers and sisters and families.

Anna and **Willis Bowen** attended a wedding reception for **Bob Layton** and his bride at the **Ray Schneringer** home in Corbett, Saturday afternoon, June 23.

Mira Nielson is vacationing on the beach at Newport, starting July 2nd. Mira says she is going to do nothing but "loaf."

Connie Meyers is still not up to par, from the effects of his operation. His doctor says he will have to be careful for about a year.

Charles Gaymon is leaving for his vacation July 5th. Charlie and family will do some traveling. Don't know where but will let us know when he gets back.

Mrs. Van Hee, Sr., just came back from a trip to Virginia with son **Ted**, where they visited another son, Bob. Bob was in a car wreck and is recovering from a broken hip and leg.

T. Van Hee, Sr., will vacation at their house at Seaside starting July 9th. Phil says he will make improvements on the house.

Lawrence Peterson will start his vacation July 16th. Pete says he is going to have his teeth pulled, and rest the balance of the time.

Ralph Sanders is the proud owner of a new Swedish "Husquvarna" rifle. It is chambered for the famous .270 Winchester ammunition. Lok out deer!

Louise Rhodes spent one week of her vacation taking care of her mother. Louise is back at work now and will take the rest of her vacation later this summer.

Clarence Noble says he has a nest of chipmunks in their laundry room. He hopes they move soon, as they keep him awake nights.

Dorothy and **Merrill Hartshorn** enjoyed a very pleasant trip to Yakima over the week-end. They visited with Merrill's brother, Ray.

Vera Nell Roberts had a bout with a sun lamp and ended up losing. She received painful burns around her eyes which resulted in their swelling quite a bit. She missed a week of work as a result.

Dale Emmons vacationed the week of June 4th.

Leo Hageman started June 15th on his vacation. The family is on a trip to the Black Hills of South Dakota. On the way they spent one night in Spokane and visited Mrs. Hageman's sister and niece in Great Falls, Montana.

Arthur Schroder and family spent the last four days of his vacation at Siltcoos Lake, along the Coast. They brought back forty trout, some of them 14½" long.

Orien Pitts starts his vacation the 27th of June. His oldest and youngest sisters are visiting here from Wisconsin and he plans to take them to the coast for a few days. The visitors are a little frightened of the hills as they have never seen any like them.

Lester Anderson and family are driving to Wisconsin to visit relatives.

Eldon Nielson and family returned from a two week trip to Oklahoma. The weather was good, with only one day of rain. While there, they visited relatives and on the way home they stopped at several national parks.

Roy Eveland cut his finger on the cutoff saw, but not bad enough to cause him to lose time from work.

Roger Seeger is spending his vacation at National Guard summer training camp.

Donald Westlake suffered serious injuries when his car hit the end of the railing on the approach to the Bridal Veil overpass. The accident occurred Monday evening, June 25, as he was returning to work after his lunch hour.

-----43-----

Think ahead for Safety!

BRIDAL VEIL LUMBER & BOX CO.

News Letter

Volume II, Number 2   BRIDAL VEIL, OREGON   AUGUST, 1956

Salute

It is our pleasure this month to use a good portion of The Newsletter to introduce the Pease Woodwork Company, Inc. to our employees. We start-shipping window and door frames to Pease in December of 1952, and since that time we have shipped them in excess of seventy cars of millwork valued at over three quarters of a million dollars.

When all is said and done, the success of any business venture depends upon the ability of the organization to sell its product at a profit. Starting as we do, with rough lumber, and ending up with finished millwork, the processes in between largely involve the addition of value to the rough lumber by the application of the efforts and skills of our employees. When these efforts and skills are properly employed, we end up with a saleable product.

What makes a product saleable? In the final analysis it takes three factors to interest a customer: Price, Quality and Availability. When any one of these elements is missing the customer rapidly loses interest. His reaction to too high a price, or poor quality or late delivery is the same as any individual. Being customers ourselves, we know how mad we get when we feel we have been "taken," and the bad taste remains long after. Somebody has lost a customer.

The inescapable conclusion is that all segments of the business community are best served with the efficient production and marketing of good products. Upon efficient production and marketing hinges the marketability of the services of all those who have helped put the product together.

We at Bridal Veil can take particular pride that our product has been found acceptable by a firm of the calibre of Pease Woodwork Company, Inc. Stable, progressive and successful customers are our best insurance for our continued existence. Pease is such a customer. May the coming years see Pease, Bridal Veil, and the employees of both prospering through the production and marketing of top quality merchandise at a price that will sell. Herein lies the heart of industry.

Len Kraft

The Pease Story

Early in the year 1893, Charles Harlow Pease, then a young man of 27, established himself as a dealer in Sash and Doors at Second and Water Streets, Cincinnati, Ohio. So far as we know, this was the first business of its kind to be established in Cincinnati. All Sash and Doors, like other millwork, having been made by local carpenters in their shops. The need for such a service was great as evidenced by the immediate growth of the firm. Even before the turn of the century, the Pease Company was forced to move twice into larger quarters. By 1910 the office force had grown to 30 and the warehouse crew to 50 or more—enough men to unload and ship several carloads of Building Millwork every day. During the next decade, horse drawn wagons gave way to trucks, more and more business was transacted over the telephone and a gradually widening circle of customers and friends spread the word which encouraged still others to write for prices and to purchase trial orders. Throughout the growth of the company, a reputation for dealing in only the highest quality of materials was obtained and maintained.

The desire to provide an even more sound method of assuring their customers of the highest quality materials at the lowest possible prices led the Pease Woodwork Company, during World War I, to adopt a merchandising plan that is as sound today as it was then. The "PEASE PLAN", as it became known is based on the accepted basic principle in business that only by operating on a strictly cash basis and under minimum expense can lowest prices be reached and maintained. As a result, the company evolved into a mail-order business operating under these points of the "Pease Plan": Highest quality building materials in every case; Maximum economy through selling by mail; Prompt, personal handling of inquiries and orders; Lowest prices through selling strictly for cash. Now known as the Building Materials Division of the Pease Woodwork Company, the mail-order business continues to operate under the plan and provides a major part of the over-all operation. Their four warehouses and office building are located in the Northside community of Cincinnati. One hundred and ten persons are employed by the division.

The Pease Homes Division was a natural step from selling all component parts of a house to selling the complete house. Customers were ordering, on a single order, all materials needed to be shipped at one time to avoid delays at their building sites. As a service for eliminating as much work as possible at the building site. Pease originally offered a pre-cut home package for builders. This package was produced from the builder's own plans or those drawn by Pease draftsmen from illustrations or merely written specifications. Convinced of the merits of the objectives—package shipments and reduction of labor at the job site—the officers of the company made the decision to produce and offer prefabricated homes.

A former foundry building in Hamilton, Ohio, was acquired in 1940 to provide space for manufacturing. The aim of the company has always been toward the improvement of the millwork and materials they market in order to build better homes cheaper. In keeping with this policy, after considerable study of the most modern automobile factories, the plant was set up on a production line basis. In doing so, the first builder of prefabricated homes in Ohio became the first in the prefabricated home industry to use this method. The production line is still used although the architectural design of the Pease Home has undergone a change.

The first homes produced were called "Peaseway Homes" and fabricated in entire wall, ceiling and floor sections. Both exterior and interior walls were shipped with plywood sheathing installed. The Peaseway Homes were sold through franchised builder-dealers only. The "Pease Homes" of today are built of smaller panel units that permit greater flexibility in floor plan and design. Floor and ceiling

materials are shipped un-assembled and only the exteriors of outside wall panels are plywood sheathed at the factory. Dry wall or rock lath for plastering has replaced plywood on the interior surfaces. These changes enable the Pease Home to be finished in a conventional manner that makes it very hard to distinguish it from a completely conventionally built home. Pease no longer sells through franchised dealers. Anyone, individual, builder or contractor, can purchase one or many homes direct from the factory.

Improvement of Pease Homes is constantly sought and the materials used uphold the Pease Woodwork Company's reputation for quality. This quality is protected by proper handling and storage. The materials are unloaded at a sheltered dock, moved by mechanical equipment, stored entirely under roof and out of the weather, and by constant turnover is kept new, clean and prime grade. Not until they arrive at the job site and the transport tarpaulin removed are they exposed to the weather. Interior matrials are shipped by enclosed trailers which arrive after the home is under roof.

The recognition that Pease Homes enjoys as a leader in the prefabricated home industry is largely due to the way the company entered the field. Since they approached prefabrication through the conventional building field, and with fairly conservative objectives in mind, Pease has managed to avoid the pitfalls that have handicapped some of their competitors. They have always maintained a determined effort to keep their homes conventional in appearance and avoid a "prefab" look. Their refusal to become involved in radical departures from conventional home design, and their adherence to the strictest conventional construction standards, has paid off in a successful prefabricated home business.

Recognizing the need for such strict adherence if prefabricated homes were to ever become popular, James L. Pease, Sr., then President, now Chairman of the Board, helped found the Prefabricated Home Manufacturers' Institute in 1943. He served as President of the Institute in 1945 and 1946, as did John W. Pease in 1948

(Continued on Page 4)

The Pease Story
(Continued from Page 3)

and 1949. The Institute was organized for the specific purpose of setting up commercial standards for the industry and eliminate substandard products. The success of the PHMI is best described by one of its requirements for membership which states that each and every home produced by a member must conform to the Commercial Standard for Prefabricated Homes as published by the National Bureau of Standards—the world's greatest testing laboratory—a branch of the United States Department of Commerce.

Today, the Pease Homes Division, still in their original but expanded home in Hamilton, Ohio, is a busily operating and thriving business. Three hundred and fifty persons are employed. Recently the general offices of the company were transferred to Hamilton. The offices and factory now cover almost three full city blocks, and include the distinctive "Street of Pease Display Homes", with guest parking area. The factory itself covers 250,000 square feet of floor space under roof, and is located on the Baltimore & Ohio Railroad. Four private switches handle 24 box cars a day, while eight fully enclosed loading docks accommodate sixteen trailer trucks at one time. The "Street of Pease Display Homes" is an entire block on which are constructed nine Pease Homes. They are open seven days a week. Thousands of families visit them each year, making themselvs at home while they plan, select, study and compare homes in "America's most unique and permanent model home showroom". One of the homes is even partially cut away inside to demonstrate every quality feature from top to bottom. There is also a sales room with representatives on hand to furnish any information desired or to assist in placing an order.

The line of Pease Homes had grown to thirteen basic homes which encompass thirty-four separate plans. Ranch, contemporary or colonial styles; 2, 3 or 4 bedrooms; L-shaped, T-shaped or rectangular plans are included. They are available for construction on basement, crawl space or slab foundation. Their design permits such a variety of exterior treatment, in wood or masonry, that the customer has a practically endless selection. Each year, new models are added and changes made to insure that current demand is met. Economy as well as styling and design is a prime consideration of Pease Homes. High speed equipment and large scale production machinery, mechanical handling under controlled working conditions make factory assembly possible in less than one-third of the time usually consumed in on-site construction. This saving in dollars and cents is reflected in the final cost of a Pease Home when due allowance is made for the number of carpentry hours spent on the job. Pease Homes are made faster and better by careful planning and more efficient use of skilled labor. Thus, through better production comes better value at lower cost to the customer. The status of Pease Homes in the prefabricated home industry is best reflected by the increased number of sales of homes in the deluxe or luxury class home. It is a true indication of customers receiving "more house for their money".

The Pease Woodwork Company is a family company. The four sons of Charles H. Pease are in active direction. After the death of the senior Pease, in 1936, James L. Pease assumed the Presidency until 1954, when he relinquished the office to John W. Pease to become Chairman of the Board. Harvey P. Pease serves as Vice-President and David H. Pease as Secretary. A member of the third generation, James L. Pease, Jr., holds the position of Treasurer. The organization aso includes Burton R. Pease, David H. Pease, Jr., and son-in-laws George R. Smith, William B. Heffner, James V. Rice and Henry C. Seasholes. Good employee relations are both a policy and a practice at Pease; the "open door to the boss's office" is a working reality, and everyone is known by his or her first name. In 1945, the employees were encouraged to form a labor union under the AF of L, and Pease Homes carry the AF of L label. Pease management has established a broad group of employee benefits wholly paid for by the company—a pension trust, hospital care family plan, group insurance up to $10,000 per employee and paid vacations.

The Story Behind Our Jobs

The story behind our jobs is the story of making our customers want to buy our products. It's easy to forget sometimes that our jobs actually depend on our products being sold. Naturally, if they are not sold, we cannot go on producing. And in order to be sold, our products must meet the competition of others who are trying to sell similar items.

Our company is not alone in this. Every other company faces the same problem. And, of course, there is nothing new about it either, it has always been that way.

What makes it so important today is that competition is keener. That's why our sales organization is putting forth greater effort than ever before. And it is easy to see that anything we can do to help make that selling easier helps us too. Let's take a look at how we can help.

When we go into a store to buy something, we want to get our money's worth. We know how we feel when something we buy isn't as good as we thought it would be when the quality we expect isn't there.

Our customers feel that way too, and that's where we come in. For quality is built into our product, directly or indirectly, by every one of us. Whatever our part in the finished product may be, doing a good job every day helps make ours the product the customer wants to buy. The price tag certainly means a lot to us when we buy something and it is also a big factor in selling our customers. We all know, of course, that the price we have to charge for our products depends on how much it costs to make them. That's where every one of us comes into the picture again. We can help keep our selling prices competitive by eliminating as much waste and spoilage as possible, as well as suggesting better ways of doing our job.

Many of us have had the experience, as customers, of having had to wait for something beyond the time when delivery was promised. Naturally we didn't like it, and neither would our customers like it if it should happen to them.

When we cut down the number of times we are absent or tardy, when we avoid accidents and do all we can to maintain our equipment properly, we are helping to eliminate production delays which might prevent the promised delivery of our products to the customer. The real story behind our jobs is the ability of our Company to satisfy our customers with quality products, at a price they will pay and with delivery when they want them.

It may be true that in our particular job, we may never have occasion to meet the customer in person. But it is also true that each of us, every hour of every day, can help do our part in making our customers want to buy our products.

When our customers continue to buy, then and only then, can we continue to produce!

———74———

August Birthdays

Many Happy Returns of the Day!

Fred Long	Jarvis Kilness
Roger Seeger	Dean Burkholder
George Bennett	Archie Davies
Ann Keller	Donald Westlake
Ralph Ellis	Vera Nell Roberts
Lester Howell	Ernest Cox, Jr.
Roy Anderson	Ralph Lamke
Theodore Van Hee	Theophile Van Hee
George Perry	Harry Densmore

———74———

Health and Welfare

The following employees worked the required humber of hours in May to become eligible for Health and Welfare coverage and will be covered on the first day of August, 1956. Employees who did not work the required hours will become ineligible the same day. Additions: Anthony Angelo, Donald M. Bowen, Leroy Brenneke, Thomas Cowling, Lynfred Crouser, Ronald K. Evans, Dean Jacobson, Charles Long, Garfield Pearson, George Perry and James Yerion. Deletions: Herbert Courter, Martha Jones, Edsel Kinonen, Paul Levan, Louise Rhodes, Theodore Van Hee.

———74———

Capitalism is the unequal distribution of benefits. Socialism is the equal distribution of misery.

—Winston Churchill

NEWS LETTER

Published on the 10th of each month by
Bridal Veil Lumber & Box Co.
Bridal Veil, Oregon

Editor . . . . . Don West

Rips and Trims

Mr. and **Mrs. Floyd Jones** and daughter, **Marilyn,** recently returned from a three week vacation visiting relatives and friends in Idaho, Montana, Iowa, and Nebraska. Reported a thoroughly enjoyable trip.

The **Eldon Nielson** family and the **Floyd Jones** family attended the Iowa picnic at Jantzen Beach Park.

Clarence and Gert Noble and **Fred and Fay Harp** are vacationing from Aug. 18th over Labor Day. They will go to Grand Coulee Dam for a few days, then to Lake Chelan and on into Canada. They hope to visit Lake Louise then travel down the Fraser River and on to Vancouver, B. C. From there they plan to go to Nanaimo on Vancouver Island, down to Victoria, then by ferry to Port Angeles in good old U.S.A. Sounds like lots of miles, but a wonderful vacation trip. Have fun.

Merrill and Dorothy Hartshorn had one week of their vacation the first part of August. Merrill did a lot of fishing at Bonneville, but isn't talking much about his luck.

Anna and **Willis Bowen** vacationed the last two weeks of July. Anna's sister, Mrs. Woolf, went with them. Anna said Willie played the slot machines but didn't make his fortune. Then they went on to Yellowstone Natl.

Safety Program

At the July 26 meeting of the safety committee, two new members, Roley Zumwalt and Marvin Jackson, were chosen to replace Ward Dull and Dean Burkholder. Fay Davis, chairman, Ralph Taylor and Clarence Noble are also on the safety committee.

While it is the duty of the safety committee to make plant inspections and safety recommendations, you can help them by reporting to them any unsafe conditions or unsafe acts.

Bill Bohlender of the S.I.A.C. made a plant inspection and also attended the safety meeting of July 26.

If you are wondering if safety pays off, our accident frequency rate for the first 6 months of 1955 was .86 and .33 for the first 6 months of 1956, a reduction of 62 percent.

July 31 completed 74 consecutive days without any lost time accidents.

————74————

The Cover Picture

The picture on the cover shows the Pease Homes Division of the Pease Woodwork Company. The plant is located in Hamilton, Ohio, just a few miles from Cincinnati. The line of homes above and left of the plant itself is the Pease "Street of Homes" display, which is open for public inspection seven days a week. The Pease story appears in this issue.

Park and saw "Old Faithful" spout. On to Salt Lake City, visited the Mormon Temple. Anna says the organ music was wonderful. They then returned home and to work. Had a wonderful time.

1956 SAFETY CHART

Month	Tot. Hourly Pd. Man Hrs.	Lost Time Accidents	Accident Freq.	Days Lost	Accident Severity
January	16,297	0	0	0	0
February	20,821	0	0	0	0
March	18,135	1	55.1	5	276
1st Quarter	55,253	1	18.1	5	91
April	19,749	2	101.3	7	354
May	24,255	1	41.2	7	289
June	23,360	0	0	0	0
2nd Quarter	67,364	3	44.5	14	208
TOTAL	122,617	4	32.6	19	155

20th Anniversary

August 27th will be the twentieth anniversary for Ralph (Mac) McCredie, foreman of the moulding department, at Bridal Veil Lumber and Box Co.

Mac was born in St. Paul Minnesota. When he was four years old the family moved to Oregon, where his father was employed by what is now the Portland General Electric Co. He has two sisters and one brother.

Mac went to school in Portland, Bull Run and Gresham. After his schooling he worked at various jobs before coming to Bridal Veil.

On December 18, 1937, Mac and the former Erma Bacon of Santa Rosa, California were married in Vancouver, Washington. They had one child, Ermagene, who passed away early this year. She would have been sixteen on August 28th.

The McCredies purchased the Spike Emerson place at Corbett where they now make their home.

Mac is a licensed ham radio operator. He regularly communicates with his brother, who is also a radio operator and who lives in Kennewick, Washington.

Mac is a member of the Masonic Lodge and the Eastern Star. During the war he was a member of the Multnomah County Sheriff's Reserve.

Mac has worked in nearly every department since coming to Bridal

Rips and Trims

Einar Mickelson will start his vacation August 13th. He is expecting visitors from Iowa so will spend his time showing them the sights of Oregon and Washington.

Lenann Kraft was at Camp Namanu at Sandy, Oregon from July 28th to August 10th.

Walt and Lillian Norgard spent the weekend of August 4th clamming at Long Beach, Washington.

Jack Kreman was married to Marie Ellis of Ranier, Oregon, in that city on July 21, 1956. They honeymooned on the Olympic Peninsula in Washington.

Elmer Ayles and family took a trip to Sheridan, Wyoming. Elmer got in three days of fishing and caught some big ones (he says).

Clarence Lofstedt took one week of his vacation starting July 23rd. Clarence said he was going to do some fishing but we have had no report on the results.

Ted Hanson also started his vacation on July 23rd. He planned to spend one week camping on the Clackamas river and the remainder of the time visiting various parts of the state.

Bill Dunken is on vacation now and is visiting relatives in California.

George Murray is going to spend part of his vacation working on his house and the rest of the time at the beach.

Eldon Gross says he hasn't done any fishing yet this year so will spend his entire vacation fishing on the north fork of the Clackamas river.

John Willms has retired from the ice cream business, at least temporarily. He and his wife operated the John Willms Ice Cream Store from August 1, 1951 until July 30, 1956. The store was located at 12328 SE Division St., Portland. They have stored their equipment for the time being. John says it just like being on vacation now that he only has one job.

The **Kenneth Catlin** family have had relatives from Nebraska visiting with them the past two weeks.

Veil. When he was hired he was told it was only temporary. Twenty years is a long time to be on a temporary job.

BRIDAL VEIL LUMBER & BOX CO.

News Letter

Volume II, Number 3   BRIDAL VEIL, OREGON   SEPTEMBER, 1956

You and Your Neighbors

This year, contributors to the United Fund-Red Cross campaign are being asked to consider the people being helped by their pledges as neighbors who might need a lift. This idea may be difficult to understand in a three-county area in which there are about three quarter million people. What relation could there be between a burned-out family of strangers in Gresham and a UF contribution in Northwest Portland or in Forest Grove?

Consider this section of Oregon a hundred years ago. Just what constituted a neighbor in 1856? In general, neighbors were people who lived anywhere within a day's travel by wagon. The **nearest** neighbor might live one or two miles further up a muddy wagon road. The pioneer housewife would be more likely to borrow a bag of flour than a cupful, because it might be a month before the family made its next trip to the mill or store.

More important was the attitude toward these neighbors, whether they lived a mile, five or twenty miles away. In addition to the fact that the pioneers just plain wanted to be of help when needed, there was a very practical reason why they "turned to" when a fire wiped out a neighbor's possessions. These were times when men **had to** help each other in order to survive . . . very few independent souls could survive for long as "lone wolves" against the wilderness forces of nature.

Actually, it's not much different today. The problems are changed, but the principle is the same. We also must "turn-to" when a neighbor needs help, for the survival of our way of life is at stake. If you disagree, consider the alternatives. Communism is one possibility—let "the government" take care of everybody. That system has been tried for centuries, and it

hasn't worked yet. Another possibility would be to let everyone take his own chances that he can continue to care for himself and his family. That system might look good to the healthy, secure (and selfish) person with a good income until he begins to wonder where the money comes from for research on such ills as heart disease and cancer.

Nobody will insist that the United Fund method of taking care of ourselves and our neighbors is perfect. But as long as humanity exists there will be a need for a man to consider his neighbor. When he stops thinking about his neighbor, civilization will collapse, and men will go through more "dark ages". In the meantime, it is the belief of hundreds of thousands of home-loving people in the Multnomah - Clackamas - Washington County corner of the State of Oregon that this method does the best and least expensive job of preserving the better parts of humanity. We have studied a lot of ways to do the job, and this one still looks best to us.

To give ourselves something to shoot at, here is the record for the past two years:

Year	No. of employees	Employees Pledge	Co. Pledge	Total Pledge
1954	158	$638.60	———	$638.60
1955	192	632.16	$632.16	1264.32
1956	154	?	?	?

Continuing the practice instituted last year, the Company will undertake to match the contributions of all the employees.

The United Fund Campaign will be held at Bridal Veil during the latter part of September. Let's give earnest consideration to our degree of participation in this worthy cause between now and campaign time. It would be a marvelous achievement to have our total pledges this year add up to twice last year's total.   Len Kraft

NEWS LETTER

Published on the 10th of each month by
Bridal Veil Lumber & Box Co.
Bridal Veil, Oregon

Editor   . . . . Don West

What Is an Accident?

The State Industrial Accident Commission has defined an accident as "Any unplanned event which iterferes with production". From this definition we can infer that there are several degrees of accidents.

For example, there can be an accident in which there is no personal injury. This might involve a couple of finger - lift trucks colliding, which would result in stock being spilled, with no personal injury being involved.

The next step in the degree of seriousness might involve an accident as above, with an injury to one of the operators requiring first aid or professional medical treatment of a minor nature which would permit the injured operator to return to work the same day, or at the latest, the following morning.

If the injury is so severe that the injured person cannot return to work the following day, we have what is known as "a lost time accident". This is the type of accident upon which industrial safety records are based.

The range of accident severity goes on through those causing temporary or permanent partial disability, temporary or permanent total disability, and death.

While our safety records are based upon "lost time accidents" as described above, we are concerned with all accidents. The accident that causes no injury is still a potential killer, and is valid subject for our time and effort in our accident prevention campaign.

————105————

KEEP UP YOUR GUARD!

That means not taking safety for granted no matter how familiar we are with our jobs—the moment we get careless, even about the little everyday things, danger pops up.

What Is a Year?

There are probably as many ways of figuring the number of straight time hours in a year as there are people who figure it. We would do it this way:

Days in a year . . . 365 days
Deduct: Sat. & Sun. 104 days
    Average vacation   8
    Paid holidays   6
    Av. absence (2.8%) 7

    Total   . . . . 125 days

Working days   . . . 240 days
Working days x 8 . . 1920 hours
————105————

Counting the Cost

For the past several months, our average straight time hourly wage rate (not counting the so-called "fringes") has been running around $2.11 per hour. This $2.11 figure can be used as a starting point in computing cost to the individual of a day's absence. Each day lost amounts to $16.88 in direct wages. Those who lose an average of one day a month (an absentee rate of roughly 5 per cent) end up $202.56 short at the end of the year.

————105————

Trees are a crop in America. Each year more than 500 million forest tree seedlings are planted on farms, industrial forests and public-owned properties. For each tree planted by man, millions more spring up naturally from seeds. If these young trees are protected from fire, our forestlands will continue to grow all the wood we need. You can do your part by always being careful with fire in the woods. HELP KEEP OREGON GREEN!

————105————

Pease Story

Credit for "The Pease Story" goes to Mr. Raymond H. Porter, assistant advertising manager of Pease Woodwork Co. Mr. Porter's name was inadvertantly omitted in the August issue of the News Letter.

————105————

The Diamond Match Company at Metaline Falls, Washington operated the entire year 1955 without a lost time accident.

10th Anniversary

September 5th will be the 10th anniversary at Bridal Veil for Mrs. Inez Houchin, box factory.

Mrs. Houchin was born in Morland, Kansas. Her father was a wheat and cattle rancher.

In 1908 she married R. A. Collin. They had five children, including two sets of twins. One of her daughters, Mrs. Lillie Yerion, works in the moulding department.

Mrs. Houchin came west to Idaho in 1935 and in 1942 she came to Oregon. She worked at the Kinzua Pine Mills for two years before coming to Bridal Veil to be with her daughter, Lillie, whos husband was in the hospital.

The Houchins were married June 10, 1950 in Stevenson, Washington. They have their home and 5½ acres two miles northwest of Corbett. Mrs. Houchin lists gardening as a hobby. At Bridal Veil she works with her husband on a push-rip saw.

————105————

DON'T TAKE A CHANCE!

Too often we say to ourselves "This won't take a second" and we don't bother with the necessary safety device. Or even worse, we tell ourselves that "It won't happen this time" and then take an unsafe short-cut, or ignore a safety rule because we can't "be bothered."

15th Anniversary

September 8 will be the fifteenth anniversary at Bridal Veil for Jerry Roberts, cleat saw operator.

Jerry was born in Lucas, Iowa, one of three children. His brother, Keith, lives in Portland and works for the Western Fire Equipment Co. His other brother, Chuck, is in the Air Force and is stationed at Cheyenne, Wyoming. Jerry's father lives at Depoe Bay.

In 1937 the famiy moved to Corbett, where Jerry attended high school. On November 7, 1942 Jerry joined the Army Signal Corps. He received his training at Miami Beach, Florida and then spent a year at Freso, California. He was then sent to Ascot, England, attached to the Ninth Air Force, where he remained until the Normandy invasion. He was also in the Luxemboug and Germany campaigns. He was stationed at Creil, France for one year. Jerry was discharged from the Army January 4, 1946.

On March 17, 1956, Jerry and Vera Nell Ball were married at Shelton, Washington. Vera Nell is also employed at Bridal Veil. They make their home in Gresham.

Fishing and hunting are Jerry's hobbies. He says he does a lot of both but without much success.

————105————

No one's too tough to practice Safety.

10th Anniversary

September 16th will be the tenth anniversary at Bridal Veil for Harold Jacobson, cutter.

Harold was born and raised in Osceola, Nebraska. At the age of 27 he went to Deer Trail, Colorado where he farmed for ten years. After that the family moved to Gresham. After arriving in Oregon, Harold worked at the Swan Island shipyards for one and one-half years. Later on, before coming to Bridal Veil he worked on a bulb farm.

Harold and Leola Archer were married in Imperial, Nebraska on January 24, 1930. They have seven children; Richard, who also works here, Marjorie, Rodney, a former employee, Charles, Dean, Daniel and Cheryl.

Harold has lost time only once as the result of an accident. He had a sliver in his knee and it became infected. He has worked in nearly every department at Bridal Veil.

————105————

An old man drove up to a filling station in a dilapidated old car.

"Give me a dollar's worth of gas, Henry," he said.

"Why don't you fill her up, Dave?" the attendant asked.

"Wa-a-l, Henry," he replied, "I'm afraid she might not run that fur."

20th Anniversary

September 29 will be the fifteenth anniversary at Bridal Veil for Marvin Van Orsow, foreman of the cutter line.

Marv was born in Dundas, Minnesota, where he was raised and educated.

Joe Van Orsow, tenoner operator, advised Marv that he might be able to get a job so Marv came here directly from Dundas and went to work. Three months later his parents also came to Oregon from Minnesota.

Marv joined the U. S. Army Air Corps in July 1942. He received his training at Camp Kearns, Utah. After going overseas he was transferred to the infantry. This occurred during the Battle of the Bulge. Marv was in three campaigns during the war. He was in the Normandy invasion, the Central Europe and the Northern France campaigns. Marv was one of the unfortunate soldiers, in that he had no leaves or furloughs while he was in the Army.

On March 23, 1946 Marv and the former Gayle Hartshorn were married in Vancouver, Washington. They have two children, Donald 8 and Linda 6. Their home is at 16335 SE Lincoln street in Portland.

Marv is an ardent fisherman and hunter.

————105————

Accidents never take a vacation!

Bridal Veil Visitors

Pictured are Robert E. Dant, chairman of the board, and D. M. Warnock, president, of the newly formed Dant & Warnock Co. Their offices are located in Menlo Park, California.

Another visitor to Bridal Veil was Mr. Harry L. Grove of Weyerhaeuser Sales Co. of Chicago.

————105————

Do you know that nine out of every ten forest fires are caused by careless people who think of themselves as law-abiding citizens? Remember, when you go into a forest to fish, hike or picnic always be careful with fire. When a forest burns, everybody loses. Crush out that cigarette or pipe ash! Break your match! Put out your campfire! HELP KEEP OREGON GREEN.

Sept. Birthdays
Many Happy Returns of the Day!

Merrill Hartshorn	John Hancock
Tom Choate	Steve Kuzmesky
Howard Hunt	Joseph Cote
Robert Godat	Roley Zumwalt
Ade Jones	Edsel Kinonen
Lawrence Smazal	Leonard Kraft
Lloyd Frazier	Lula Cowling

————105————

Three Figures!

For the first time in our present safety campaign the number of accident-free days has crossed the 100 mark. We think this milestone in our war on accidents is worthy of extra special comment in our recorded history.

The 105 days noted on the sign is the result of the care and cooperation of **everyone**. It is a record all of us have had a part of, and is the sum of every individual's safety record over the past 105 days.

Having reached 100 days, the goal is now moved ahead to 250 days. Let's see to it that we have to move it ahead again to 500 days.

————105————

Can you crow about YOUR Safety record?

Health and Welfare Coverage

The following employees worked the required number of hours in June so are covered by Millworkers Health & Welfare Insurance for the month of September, 1956:

Wesley Adams
Harry Adolph
Lester W. Anderson
Roy J. Anderson
Anthony Angelo
Noah Atchley
Elmer Ayles
George Bennett
Verl W. Bird
Louis W. Bissell
Max Bissell
Anna Bowen
Donald Bowen
Franklin Bowen
James E. Bowen
Leroy Brenneke
Thomas Britton
Harold Burkholder
Richard Caffrey
Kenneth Catlin
Beulah Choate
Thomas Choate
David Clabaugh
David Clark
James Clark
Rodney Clayton
Pearl Cloe
Francis Cook
Joseph Cote
Thomas Cowling
Daryl W. Cox
Ernest Cox, Jr.
Franklin Crane
Jack Crane
Fred Crouser
Lynfred Crouser
Archie Davies
Bertha Davis
Fay Davis
Dean Davis
Virgil Dobson
Paul Dooley
Ward Dull
James Dunken
William Dunken
Leon Dunlap
Ralph Ellis
Dale Emmons
Roy Eveland
James Eversull
Fred Fawcett
Lloyd Frazier
Charles Gaymon
Harold Godat
Robert Godat
Elden Gross

Leo F. Hageman
Clem Hancock
John Hancock
Loren Hancock
Theodore Hanson
Ed Harnam
Fred Harp
Dorothy Hartshorn
Merrill Hartshorn
Mabel Hills
Stanley Hills
Inez Houchin
Wilbur Houchin
Lester Howell
Howard Hunt
Earl Hutchison
Marvin Jackson
Dean Jacobson
Harold Jacobson
Richard Jacobson
Martha Jones
James Kendrick
Jarvis Kilness
Edsel Kinonen
George Knieriem
Jack Kreman
Harry Kruckman
Vyrtle Kuntz
Steven Kuzmesky
Clifford Latourell
Bob Layton
Hiram Layton
George Leash
Durward Litton
Charles Lofstedt
Clarence Lofstedt
Charles L. Long
Fred H. Long
Fred M. Long
Walter Mannthey
William McCawley
Ralph McCredie
Kenneth Meyer
Einar Mickelson
Roland Morgan
George Murray
Eldon Nielson
Mira J. Nielson
Clarence Noble
Garfield Pearson
George Perry
Lawrence Peterson
Orien Pitts
Leslie D. Polzel
Robert Polzel
E. H. Potter

David G. Rees
Robert Reischel
James Rhodes
Louise Rhodes
Jerald Roberts
Vera Nell Roberts
Chester Rogers
Thelma Rowe
Ralph Sanders
Raymond Schneringer
Arthur Schroder
Roger Seeger
Lawrence Smazal
John W. Smith
Edward Steele
Marvin Stolin
Walter Stolin
Ralph Taylor
Norman Van Buskirk
Theodore Van Hee
Theophile V. Van Hee
Theophile Van Hee, Sr.
John Van Orsow
Joseph Van Orsow
Paul Van Treeck
Harold Vogel
Homer Walker
Paul Watts
Glen Wells
Ed Wendler
Donald Westlake
John Willms
H. G. Willoughby
Louis Wilson
Mary Woodard
James Yerion
Lillie Yerion
Roley Zumwalt
Fred Bailey
Willis Bowen
Kenneth Burkholder
James Cowling
Lula Cowling
Lloyd DeMain
Harry Densmore
Paul Detrick
Clyde Hambrick
A. D. Jones
Ann Keller
Walter Keller
Leonard Kraft
Ralph Lamke
Melvin Mallinson
E. W. Norgard
Eleanor Taylor
Jacob Van Orsow
D. W. West

Rips and Trims

Martha Jones was off work August 30th, having a tooth pulled

Jim Rhodes helped his son work on his home over Labor Day.

Fay and **Bertha Davis** entertained relatives over Labor Day.

Verl Bird's father, Andrew F. Bird, is convalescing in Portland from a light heart attack. He is 86 years young and everyone wishes him a speedy recovery.

The **Kraft** family have just returned from a two week vacation at Gleneden. **Len** joined them over the holiday.

————105————

How Accidents Can Be Avoided

It would be a wonderful thing if, by waving a magic wand, it were possible to eliminate all accidents.

Unfortunately, of course, it's not as easy as that. Accidents just can't be wiped out by a wish.

Many accidents can be avoided by the use of safety devices and personal protective equipment.

But the prevention of most accidents has only one answer—YOU! Every study of accidents ever made has proved that most of them are caused by personal carelessness.

Yet that's the best break you could possibly have.

It means that you can do something about preventing accidents from happening to you. Your own personal safety is, for the most part, in your hands. hands.

The timber beam which has supported the 2000-pound Liberty Bell in Philadelphia's Independence Hall for generations was examined recently and found to be in excellent condition.

1956 SAFETY CHART

Month	Tot. Pd. Man Hrs.	Hourly Accidents	Lost Time Accident Freq.	Days Lost	Accident Severity
January	16,297	0	0	0	0
February	20,821	0	0	0	0
March	18,135	1	55.1	5	276
1st Quarter	55,253	1	18.1	5	91
April	19,749	2	101.3	7	354
May	24,255	1	41.2	7	289
June	23,360	0	0	0	0
2nd Quarter	67,364	3	44.5	14	208
July	24,576	0	0	0	0
TOTAL	147,193	4	27.2	19	134

Rips and Trims

Homer Walker and family have moved to Coopey Falls where they and their son, Carl, are now operating the service station. Good luck in your new venture, Homer.

Mel Mallinson just returned from two weeks vacation during which he painted his home. If anyone needs any tips on painting, see Mel.

Harry Densmore enjoyed a week's vacation fishing in the coastal streams and reportedly had very good luck.

Ralph Sanders attended the convention of the Northwest Mineral Show at Boise, Idaho, over the Labor Day weekend and took a red ribbon for his exhibit. Columbia Gorge Rockhounds of Corbett took third prize among club displays. An estimated 8000 visitors attended the show.

Eldon Nielson and family spent Labor Day weekend camping out with the Blue Lake baseball club at John Day.

Paul Dooley spent his week's vacation fishing at Newport and reports the fishing very poor. There's an honest fisherman!

Mrs. Leon Dunlap injured herself from a fall in a bathtub. Best wishes for a speedy recovery.

Ed Wendler spent the weekend Steelhead fishing. He caught one that weighed fourteen pounds.

Mrs. Virgil Dobson and sons have been visiting relatives in Spencer, Iowa, the past month.

Mr. and Mrs. Ray Eveland spent the weekend of August 16th visiting relatives in Seatttle.

Noah Atchley spent one week of his vacation fishing at several lakes in the Bend area. The fishing was not too good as the weather was cold.

Arthur Schroeder decided to try his luck at fishing down on the coast at Newport over Labor Day. However, it was too cold so he came back and went trout fishing. '

Mr. and Mrs. Howard Hunt had a very nice Labor Day weekend fishing on the White river. Reported their luck was very good.

Harold Jacobson and family spent the Labor Day weekend visiting relatives in Klamath Falls.

The Charles Gaymon family visited relatives in Eugene over Labor Day.

Lester Anderson recently added a fireplace to his home.

Marvin and Gayle Van Orsow, daughter Linda, and Mrs. H. Hartshorn motored to Lucas, Iowa to attend the funeral of Mrs. Hartshorn's sister, Florence Talbot, on August 10th. While there, Marvin drove to Minnesota for a week to visit relatives and friends. Marvin reports a pleasant trip except for two lightning storms which they encountered.

Mr. and Mrs. Kenneth Bowen and family of San Diego, California, were guests of **Willis and Anna Bowen** the last week of September.

Stanley and Mabel Hills spent one week of their vacation in Reno, Nevada. The other week was spent visiting relatives in Portland and Stanwood, Washington.

Mr. and Mrs. Glenn Willoughby and son Robert spent their vacation in Clovis, New Mexico and points of interest between here and there. They reported a very enjoyable trip which totaled 4800 miles.

Louis Bissell plans to do some fishing during his vacation and also to work on a new addition to his house.

Ward Dull's plans are somewhat incomplete at this time but says he plans to attend a few car races during his vacation.

Walter Stolin and family spent several days at Ocean Park, Washington, digging clams. They then visited relatives in Kennewick, Washington, and Idaho.

Jim Kendrick spent one week of his vacation working on his home, located two miles east of Corbett.

Jerry Roberts spent Labor Day fishing on the Dechutes river.

Marv and John Van Orsow fished at Wickiup Reservoir over Labor Day with very poor luck.

Harold Godat and **John Hancock,** it is rumored, picked a winning quinella on the dogs and came home $100 to the good.

Roy Anderson is vacationing for the next two weeks. Ray says he may spend part of the time in Seattle.

Merrill Hartshorn did his fishing from a boat over Labor Day. Wonder if Merrill found where the Salmon are hiding.

BRIDAL VEIL LUMBER & BOX CO.

News Letter

Volume II, Number 4   BRIDAL VEIL, OREGON   OCTOBER, 1956

Automation--Part 2

Some time ago we pointed out in these pages that the word "automation" is merely a fancy term for the use of better and better tools. Through the use of better tools we are able to increase production, the only possible route to a higher standard of living.

Indeed, there is every indication that over the next 20 years an expanding population, a rising standard of living and the trend toward increased leisure and a shorter work week will cause a shortage of workers in the future.

If we assume a minimum age of 20 for a worker, then we readily see that every worker for the year 1975 has already been born. The Total is presently fixed—there is nothing we can do about increasing our work force now. It has been estimated that our population will grow another 55,000,000 people in the next two decades. The nation's standard of living has been raising at the rate of 2.5 per cent a year for the last 10 years, while productivity has increased only 2.4 per cent a year in the same period.

In addition, new products are being brought forth at an ever increasing rate and the need for men to produce them is a drain upon our available labor supply. With the progress being made in medical research, our life expectancy is being extended so that a constantly enlarging percentage of our population is in the age group over 65 years of age.

With all these obvious factors staring us in the face, we cannot fail to realize that since at the present time we have very nearly full employment, we do not have a working force large enough to just maintain our present standard of living in the years to come, let alone increase it, unless means are found to increase the output of every man in industry. The answer, of course, is the increase in productivity that comes through the use of constantly improving tools—in short—automation.

Take our own situation, to be specific. Men and management work as a team. We realize that we are in this thing together. Outside of ourselves nobody really cares enough whether Bridal Veil lives or dies to do anything about it. We realize that a man can only do so much with his bare hands and so we constantly strive to provide our workers with better tools and equipment, utilizing greater and greater amounts of electrical and mechanical horsepower instead of human energy.

For the next month or so we will all be treated to a liberal dose of "politicking". In fact is has already started. Many claims and counterclaims will be made and some halftruths and otherwise misleading statements will be made by both sides. Because it is so basic to our standard of living and an understanding of what makes it possible, I want to come down hard on one of them—the idea that either political party can claim credit for increasing wages. Reduced to ABC's, which is the way I can understand it best, the only way that we can have more is to produce more. This results in a higher standard of living which is reflected in higher wages per hour or lower prices for the things we buy or some of both. Obviously a general price increase — inflation — is not the real thing. I would like to hear somebody boast that they had controlled inflation!

True, legislation designed to improve working conditions, hours and wages is passed, but it follows and makes official something that indus-

(Continued on Page 6)

NEWS LETTER
Published on the 10th of each month by
Bridal Veil Lumber & Box Co.
Bridal Veil, Oregon

Editor . . . . . Don West

Special Notice

All employees who worked more then sixty hours in September and who were laid off September 28 will be included in our report to the Health & Welfare Fund on October tenth and will have coverage through November.

Any employee who was laid off September 28 and who is not called back for at least 60 hours during October, may keep his coverage in effect for December by making payment directly to the Health and Welfare Fund prior to November 25.

Leonard Kraft

INDUSTRIAL SAFETY PLEDGE

Believing that great benefits can accrue to myself, my family, and my Community through application of sound Accident Prevention methods in Oregon Industries, I hereby affirm my belief that it is my moral obligation to do all within my power to work safely and help provide the safest possible working conditions.

Pledged by ....

Employed by ....

Address ....
In cooperation with the
STATE INDUSTRIAL ACCIDENT COMMISSION

INDUSTRIAL SAFETY PLEDGE

This Certifies That

....
Employe

....
Employed by
has signed the Industrial Safety pledge, in cooperation with the State Industrial Accident Commission, to work safely for the protection of himself, fellow workers and management.

Employer ....

Title ....

10th Anniversary

October 7 will be the tenth anniversary at Bridal Veil of Mrs. Beulah Choate, box factory.

Mrs. Choate was born and raised in Vienna, Illinois.

On September 5, 1931, she and Thomas Choate were married in Ozark, Illinois. They lived in Vienna for a while and then moved to Elgin, Illinois. In Elgin Mrs. Choate worked as a nurses aide and later in the office of a hospital. Her husband was also employed at the hospital.

The Choates have one son, Thomas Earl, who works in Portland, and who is also going to night school.

Mrs. Choate arrived in Bridal Veil on October 3, 1946 and began working four days later. She has never lost any time as a result of an accident.

The Choate home is located near Latourell Falls. They have seven acres which include an orchard, garden, and pasture for cattle.

Mrs. Choate lists gardening and needlework as her hobbies.

————135————
SAFETY GLASSES

They say there are eleven manufacturers of glass eyes in the United States. If all workers wore their safety goggles, some of these manufacturers would have to take in washing.

October Birthdays

Many Happy Returns of the Day!

Daryl Cox	Jacob M. Van Orsow
Charles Gaymon	Chester Rogers
Einar Mickelson	Ward Dull
Charles Long	Bob Polzel
Glen Willoughby	Dean Davis

————135————

How We Stack

Bridal Veil Accident
    Frequency Rate—1955 ....58.1
Industry Frequency Rate—1955...........24.9
Bridal Veil Frequency Rate—
    First eight months 1956 ....23.4

But just so we don't get the idea that the Accident Prevention job has been completed, the industry average for the first quarter of 1956 has gone down to 22.3.

It is also well to remember that we aren't interested in Safety simply to beat someone else's record—we are solely concerned with making Bridal Veil a safer place to work. When we get our frequency rate to zero, we will have to be ever on the alert to keep it there.

————135————

The Pay Off!

Here is concrete evidence of progress in our war on accidents:

	Hours	Acci-dents	Fre-quency
First 8 months of 1955	237,803	10	496.
First 8 months of 1956	171,128	4	23.4

Percentage-wise these figures show a reduction in our Accident Frequency Rate of 52.8%. These figures mean

Bridal Veil Visitors

Pictured above is John V. Dean of Chicago, Illinois. John is going to sell millwork for Bridal Veil on a commission basis.

Also visiting us in September was John Couch of the Oregon Moulding and Lumber Co. of Portland.

that there has been less than half the chance of being injured this year compared to last year, and most important, less than half the physical suffering.

Martin Material Company

ASBESTOS AND ASPHALT ROOFING ★ **CELOTEX PRODUCTS**

5301 East Ninth Street
KANSAS CITY, MISSOURI
Telephone HU. 9500-1-2-3

Fourth and Messanie
ST. JOSEPH, MISSOURI
Telephone 3-1449

September 19, 1956

Bridal Veil Lumber & Box Co.
Bridal Veil, Oregon

Att: Mr. Don West

Dear Don:

When we received our last car, Order No. 731, Car NYC 180406, and it was unloaded, our foreman at the mill called to our attention the excellent quality of lumber and milling of the material in this car, and the writer went out and inspected same.

We want to compliment your company and especially your employees who produced this merchandise. The milling and quality of lumber are exceptionally good. Although not quite so important as the aforementioned, we also appreciate the care you exercise in loading cars; as a result, material damaged in transit is practically nil.

Millwork produced from quality merchandise, such as received in this car, certainly is a great asset to any company—both in holding old customers and winning new ones.

Yours truly,

LOGAN MASON

MARTIN MATERIAL COMPANY

LM : MS

Quality--The Final Test of Our Products!

Every product that we produce—or at any other company produces—is ended for use by some customer. lat customer may be some other mpany or it may be an individual— e any one of us. If the quality of its orkmanship does not meet the test use, that customer might decide ere and then that he will not pur- ase that particular product in the ture. That goes for every one of us. hen we ourselves are customers, the ings we buy must stand up to our pectations or we just won't buy em again. For the truth is that of l the different kinds of competi- n—the competition of quality is the ost important!

Ony way or another everyone in our organization contributes to the quality of the products we sell. It takes the best workmanship of every individual to build quality into a product. No one individual can do it alone! No matter how small or large a part we may have in actual production—the fin- ished product is going to depend on the thoroughness with which we per- form our particular job. We all help in building the reputation or our pro- ducts and that is why we may all be proud ot it. That reputation is being tested constantly as customers use our products. And that reputation is being maintained every working day of the year as all of us do our very best work on every single job! Our reputa- tion for quality is making possible the continued sale of our products to satis- fied customers—and as a direct result is enabling us to go on producing them.

————135————

Health and Welfare

The following employees worked the quired number of hours in August become eligible for Health & Wel- re coverage and will be covered on e first day of October 1956. Em- oyees who did not work the re- ired hours will become ineligible e same day. Additions: Elvin D. nith. Deletions: George Bennett, obert K. Bird, Donald M. Bowen, odney Clayton, Thomas J. Cowling, ranklin T. Crane, Lynfred Crouser, ean Jacobson, Gerald Kraft, Bill orth, Jr., Garfield Pearson, George erry and James M. Yerion.

————135————

A Careless Move May Mean a Shat- red Life.

Safety Program

At the September 13th safety com- mittee meeting two new members, Mira Nielson and Del Dunken, were appointed to replace Clarence Noble and Ralph Taylor. Marvin Jackson was also appointed to replace Fay Da- vis as committee chairman.

In this issue of the Newsletter you will see a print of the "Industrial Safety Pledge" put out by the State Industrial Accident Commission. The safety committee recommends that all employees of Bridal Veil be asked to sign this pledge.

1956 SAFETY CHART

Month	Tot. Hourly Pd. Man Hrs.	Lost Time Accidents	Accident Freq.	Days Lost	Accident Severity
January	16,297	0	0	0	0
February	20,821	0	0	0	0
March	18,135	1	55.1	5	276
1st Quarter	55,253	1	18.1	5	91
April	19,749	2	101.3	7	354
May	24,255	1	41.2	7	289
June	23,360	0	0	0	0
2nd Quarter	67,364	3	44.5	14	208
July	24,576	0	0	0	0
August	23,935	0	0	0	0
TOTAL	171,128	4	23.4	19	111

Rips and Trims

Bob Bird, Bob Godat and Bill Nelson opened the deer season by bagging a small buck near Kinzua, last weekend.

Louise and Jim Rhodes reported the birth of a fine grandson, Sept. 7th, 1956. Their son and family are living with them till their own home is completed.

Merrill Hartshorn had intended to take a short hunting trip over the weekend but came down with a cold. Merrill says he hunted part of Saturday around Bridal Veil and saw two deer—both does.

Jim Rhodes took a week's vacation last week. Had his eyes examined and got new glasses. The balance of the time was spend working on his son's new hom.

The Roberts (Jerry and Vera Nell) are vacationing at the present time. Vern Nell traveled by plane to Oklahoma to visit relatives and Jerry is spending his time hunting and fishing.

Jim Cowling went to Eastern Oregon for the opening of deer season. Was back on the job Tuesday morning with the report: "No bucks". The season is early yet so Jim still has time to get meat in the pot.

Lou Cowling won the pot on the first game of the world series.

Paul Detrick, Fay Davis and Roy Shultz took a four day hunting trip back of Heppner country and ended up back of Prineville. Didn't see any deer with horns but had a good trip. Had a nice visit with Dwayne and Silvia Whitney.

Durward and Ruth Litton's vacation didn't exactly turn out as planned. Salmon fishing trip to Vancouver Island, B.C. was cancelled because Durward wouldn't leave the wonderful fishing at Bonneville. They caught 196 cans of steelhead. Ruth's sister and brother-in-law spent their vacation here, too.

Len and Gerry Kraft, Jack Flaucher Sr., Jack Flaucher Jr., and Lefty Hansen will leave around the middle of October on their annual deer hunt. If past performances mean anything we may have some outstanding stories for the paper next month.

Mr. and Mrs. Willis Bowen, Jr., were recent visitors at the home of Mr. and Mrs. Marv. Van Orsow.

Fred Crouser spent his vacation putting a roof on his new house.

Jerry Roberts, Daryl Cox, Fred Fawcett and Marv Van Orsow spent the opening weekend of deer season in Eastern Oregon, but without success.

After five years in the office Eleanor Taylor is resigning. She plans to stay home and catch up on her hobbies, which include sewing and gardening. We will certainly miss her around the office.

————135————

Automation---Part 2
(Continued from Page 1)

try has already demonstrated its ability to do. Take the Federal Minimum Wage Law as an example. Not so long ago it was raised from 75c to $1 per hour. Do you know anybody working for $1 per hour in industry? If its a good idea for everybody to receive at least $1 per hour for their labors and a law would do it, why don't they pass such a law in China, or the middle of Africa? The answer if very simple—it won't work. And it won't work because the people involved could not produce even a dollar's worth of value in an hour. No matter what your politics, what school of economic thinking you sucscribe to or what your wishes may be, this fact always gets in the way. So the next time you hear some politician say that he or his party raised your wages you can say, "Nuts, I had more to do with it than you did".

Len Kraft

————135————

DO EVERY JOB THE SAFE WAY!

Getting to know and use the safe method of doing each job—just as we know and use the best method—is one of the secrets of keeping free from accidents.

All the safeguards and safety devices which can possibly be provided cannot themselves eliminate most accidents.

The fact is that the safety of everyone in the organization depends on the realization that personal carelessness is the major cause of accidents.

BRIDAL VEIL LUMBER & BOX CO.

News Letter

Volume II, Number 5   BRIDAL VEIL, OREGON   NOVEMBER, 1956

It Seems to Me

It would seem to me to be a truism that hydro-electric power is cheap power because it is hydro-electric, and not because of the nature of the agency or organization which builds the dam. It is of little consequence to the consumer whether the power project is constructed by the federal government, a local government unit, private enterprise, or any combination of them. On the other hand, since the Bonneville Administration occupies the largest office building in the City of Portland, there is some foundation for the argument that private interests could do the job cheaper. The public utilities do not show a like tendency to end up with such large organizations. Regulatory bodies of the state and federal government still stand between the utility and the consumer, and a large payroll would have to get past the Oregon Public Utilities Commission.

The Hells Canyon—high dam—low dam controversy of the past campaign brought fourth a flood of oratory sufficient to get me pretty well confused, a fact which I offer as my qualification to set everything straight in a couple of paragraphs.

Information checked with the Corps of Engineers and the Bonneville Power Administration indicates that all sources of power generation in the Pacific Northwest can produce approximately 7,500,000 KW. The load in 1936, twenty years ago, was approximately 1,000,000 KW — an increase of 7½ times. Studies indicate that this area will require 11,000,000 KW by 1960 and by 1975 will require 22,000,000 KW.

The September 19 announcement of Bonneville Power Administration advising interruptible users that their power supply would be sharply diminishing during low water flow makes it obvious to all that our need is urgent and that we are running behind now.

Presently under construction are generating facilities that will produce 2,750,000 KW by 1960. Proposed developments could produce an additional 8,000,000 KW by 1975. The controversy does not begin over our present and future needs, as these are generally recognized; the controversy is over federal vs private construction. Said in another way, it is a matter of a high federal Hells Canyon dam vs a series of low private Hells Canyon Dams.

High Hells Canyon has been mentioned as necessary to flood control of the Lower Columbia River. However, the study of the Corps of Army Engineers shows that for the 1956 flow, only two of the five proposed Snake River Dams, Brownlee and Pleasant Valley, would have controlled the Columbia River to the exact same level as high Hells Canyon. In view of this fact we can conclude that the Federal Power Commission is justified in licensing all five of these dams, i.e., Brownlee, Oxbow, low Hells Canyon, Mountain Sheep and Pleasant Valley. It has been estimated that all five of these projects will be constructed for less cost than high Hells Canyon and will produce 2,000,000 KW as against 1,000,000 KW.

Additional storage is needed for flood control. However, storage must be where it will be effective. On June 6, 1956, the middle Snake River peaked at Weiser with a flow of 56,000 cubic feet per second. The lower Columbia had passed its peak at the Dalles on June 2 and was falling. Obviously the middle Snake River did not cause the lower Columbia flood. On the other hand, the Clearwater River peaked at Spalding on May 21,

(Continued on Page 3)

NEWS LETTER

Published on the 10th of each month by
Bridal Veil Lumber & Box Co.
Bridal Veil, Oregon

Editor . . . . . Don West

Pictured above is Eleanor Taylor, Payroll clerk, secretary, filing clerk, stenographer and general all around handy girl. After five years at Bridal Veil Eleanor is retiring to devote full time to being a housewife and from our own experience, that is very nearly a full time job. We can't tell for sure if that is her usual smile or whether it is a little bigger than usual due to the fact that she is retiring. At any rate we'll miss her around the office as some of us have already found out, what with sore fingers brought on by typing, something we are not exactly used to.

IT IS NOW 166 DAYS SINCE
OUR LAST LOST TIME ACCIDENT

WORK SAFELY TODAY

PREVENT ACCIDENTS!

15th Anniversary

October 9 was the fifteenth anniversary at Bridal Veil for Ralph Ellis, power rip saw operator.

"Pete", as he is known, was born in Chatfield, Minnestota. He remained in Chatfield until he was twenty eight years old, then he went to Montana, where he stayed one year. From Montana he went to Deep River, Washington, where he worked for a construction company.

Pete had a friend from Minnesota who worked at Bridal Veil and it was through him that Pete came to work here. Pete stayed in Bridal Veil nearly a year before he got on at the mill. He worked at Bridal Veil for nine months, then left to work in Alaska for a construction company that was building airfields on Sitka. Pete says he only worked a week and living conditions were so intolerable that he was forced to leave. He then returned to Bridal Veil where he has remained since that time.

Pete was in the Army from September 1942 until March 1943.

Pete and Mrs. Ellis own their home in Wood Village, near Troutdale, and Pete spends his spare time working around the house.

Pete has had but one lost time accident since he has been at Bridal Veil.

It Seems to Me

(Continued from Page 1)

1956, at 118,000 c.f.s., over double the flow of the middle Snake. To add to this problem, the Salmon River peaked at Whitebird on May 24 at 105,000 c.f.s. These two did materially contribute to the lower Columbia flood. The combined flows of the Clearwater and Salmon Rivers on May 24, 1956 were 220,000 c.f.s., which was almost seven times the rate of flow of the middle Snake River on that date, it being 32,000 c.f.s.

The conclusion is that effective control of floodwaters in the Columbia Basin will require control of the Clearwater River and, if t h e fish problem is ever solved, the Salmon River, Bruces Eddy and Penny Cliffs dams should be constructed on the Clearwater River as soon as possible by whatever organization or governmental agency that is available to do the job.

Fish interests are concerned with the blocking of any stream tributary to the Columbia where anadromous fish run. However, the Salmon River produces a major portion of the Columbia River salmon run. Therefore, those interested in preserving salmon both for sportsmen and as a major Oregon industry, are especially concerned with any attempt to block the Salmon River. Until better methods have been developed to assure the passage of the salmon both upstream and downstream, we will need to concentrate on the development of other streams.

There seems to be a problem on the Clearwater River regarding the home of a small herd of elk. These elk would be dispossessed of their home by construction of the Bruces Eddy and Penny Cliffs projects. Dislocation of these animals must be balanced against the ravages of the floods caused by the Clearwater River. Idaho sportsmen are also concerned with a steelhead run on the Clearwater River. Again this run must be balanced against the floods.

Irrigation features are not a part of any of the projects mentioned.

It is unfortunate for the over-all economic benefit of the region that political groups have caused great confusion in the minds of many of our citizens. The use of such a phrase as "giveaway" is political demagoguery. No public facility can be given away. Governmental units have the right of eminent domain and can acquire existing facilities through due process of law. Furthermore, the federal government cannot and will not develop all of the feasible power sites. Oregon, Washington and Idaho cannot afford to stake their future on the largess of the other forty-five states; the federal trough just isn't big enough. Local organizations and private industry must be encouraged to undertake as many power projects as possible. A political stalemate could cause the most unfortunate thing that can happen to this area — a lack of power.

Len Kraft

1956 SAFETY CHART

Month	Tot. Hourly Pd. Man Hrs.	Lost Time Accidents	Accident Freq.	Days Lost	Accident Severity
January	16,297	0	0	0	0
February	20,821	0	0	0	0
March	18,135	1	55.1	5	276
1st Quarter	55,253	1	18.1	5	91
April	19,749	2	101.3	7	354
May	24,255	1	41.2	7	289
June	23,360	0	0	0	0
2nd Quarter	67,364	3	44.5	14	208
July	24,576	0	0	0	0
August	23,935	0	0	0	0
September	19,563	0	0	0	0
3rd Quarter	68,074	0	0	0	0
TOTAL	190,691	4	21.0	19	100

Warehouses

PACIFIC MUTUAL DOOR COMPANY

Warehouse and Mill Shipments

PLYWOOD • LUMBER • MOULDINGS • MILLWORK

GENERAL OFFICES:
Washington Bldg.
Tacoma 1, Washington

 QUALITY PAMUDO SERVICE

Telephone: MArket 4108
Teletype: TA 048
MAIL ADDRESS: P. O. Box 1589

Reply To **Tacoma Office**
November 2, 1956

Bridal Veil Lumber & Box Company
Bridal Veil
Oregon

Attention: Mr. Don West

SUBJECT: Car of jambs to Elizabeth

Don, this is just a note to advise you that the car of jambs shipped recently to Elizabeth, New Jersey was considered" the very finest jambs that we have ever received".

We would surely like to thank you and the boys in the plant whose care and consideration and careful workmanship make these things possible.

PAMUDO - TACOMA

E. Lee Bennett

E. Lee Bennett

ELB:meh

Rips and Trims

Mrs. Mildred Phipps was a dinner guest at the **Willis Bowen's** on Monday evening October 29th.

Stan and Mabel Hills became the proud grandparents of a husky baby boy, born October 11th, to their daughter, Mary Jane Shannon. The baby weighed 8 lbs. - 2 ozs. at birth and Mabel thinks there is none other quite like him.

Fay and Bertha Davis are also brand new grandparents. A son was born to their daughter-in-law, Mrs. Robert Davis, at the Emanuel Hospital on October 10th. We weighted 7 lbs. - 4-½ ozs. and Bertha says he is a real blonde, and that they named him Gordon Timothy. Robert Davis is well known in Bridal Veil, having lived here most of his life and was also employed at the plant for a few years.

Earl Hutchison is back on the job after one month off. Earl used up eleven days on a deer hunting trip with his brother. They went to Eastern Oregon where his brother bagged a nice four point buck. Enroute they had serious car trouble. The plug came out of the oil pan, and, not noticing the oil pressure had gone down, all of the bearings burned out.

————166————

Nov. Birthdays

Many Happy Returns of the Day!

Ralph Sanders	Fred Harp
Clem A. Hancock	E. W. Norgard
Harry Adolph	Kenneth L. Meyer
Harold Burkholder	Louis W. Bissell
Verl M. Bird	Louise I. Rhodes
Harold M. Godat	William L. Dunken
D. Fay Davis	

————166————

Health and Welfare

The following employees worked the required number of hours in September to become eligible for Health and Welfare coverage and will be covered on the first day of November 1956. Employees who did not work the required number of hours will become ineligible the same day. Additions: Wayne Zumwalt. Deletions: Leroy Brenneke, Kenneth Catlin, Thomas Choate, David Clabough, James P. Clark, Jack L. Crane, Virgil Dobson, Harry Kruckman, Charles L. Long, Elvin D. Smith, Edward L. Wendler, and Allen W. Weston.

A Perfect Year

The maintenance gang has completed an entire year without a single lost time accident. Reading left to right they are: Pearl Cloe, Elmer Ayles, Paul Detrick, foreman; Fay Davis, Durward Litton, George Leash, Fred Long and Marvin Jackson. Missing from the picture are Bob Polzel and Tom Britton, who were not at work when the picture was taken.

Rips and Trims

Paul Van Treek and Ann Dickert were married at the home of Paul's parents in Gresham on the 29th of September. They honeymooned by driving down the coast highway to Mexico and returned via highway 99. They are now living in Gresham.

Richard Kerslake and Marvin Van Orsow were the only ones to connect with a deer while on a hunting trip in the Buck Springs area of the Ochoco National Forest.

John Van Orsow spent the first four days of the bird season with his son, Clarence, who lives at Culver, Oregon. He came home with seven pheasants, three geese and six ducks.

Mary Woodard and her mother recently took a trip to Arkansas to visit relatives. On the way home they stopped in California to visit relatives also.

Marvin Jackson spent the first week of his vacation hunting pheasants. He hunted near Vale and then near Heppner. Marv came home with a total of some thirty odd birds of varied descriptions. Marvin is going to take the second week of his vacation around the middle of November and is going back east to get a new car. He is going by way of Glacier National Park and will return by a more southerly route through Nevada and California.

Eldon Gross got a four point buck thirty miles out of Paulina in the Ochoco National Forest.

Roley Zumwalt, Wayne Zumwalt and their father got two forked horns and a doe near Mitchell.

Lester Anderson built a new garage during the recent layoff.

Pete Ellis and Hiram Layton spent four weeks in Minnesota visiting with relatives of Pete.

Richard Jacobson is now employed in Denver, Colorado. He is a former employee of Bridal Veil.

Norman Van Buskirk worked on his home during his vacation.

Eugene Potter worked at the Snyder Cannery in Gresham during the lay-off. His niece and her girl friend from Fort Riley visited with the Potter's for a week.

Harry Adolph got a doe near The Dalles. He also had fair luck fishing on the coast, coming up with twenty Jack Salmon.

Howard Hunt and two friends came home with one four point buck.

Willis Bowen Sr., Jimmie Bowen, Max Bissell, Ed and Floyd Kogel spent the weekend of October 27th Elk hunting near Starkey, Oregon. Hunting conditions were very poor. It snowed hard and the wind blew, and there was twelve inches of snow on the ground.

Gean Ann Bowen was the house guest of her grandmother, Mrs. Anna Bowen, the weekend of November 1st.

The Cowling's — Jim, Lou, Bob and Pat, spent three days bird hunting around Ontario and Pendleton, returning with fourteen pheasants, two ducks, and the memory of a pleasant trip.

Bob Cowling and friend Dave Heminger spent a three day weekend around Monument deer hunting, returning with two bucks; a four point and a three point.

Jim Cowling hunted the second weekend of bird season at Heppner and bagged three pheasants.

Merrill Hartshorn, Jerry Roberts, and Keith Roberts opened the pheasant season in eastern Oregon, near Boardman. They had fair luck, coming home with six birds.

The following weekend Merrill went back with Marvin and Walt Stolin but could find no birds. They saw lots of geese which were coming in just out of range. Maybe next time they will come in closer so try again Merrill.

Martha Jones came back to work with a big bandage above her right eye. Martha says she did it on the washing machine pump. Guess we will have to believe you Martha, until we find out differently at least.

Martha's sister, Mrs. Arden Wedwick and family were weekend guests of the Jones'. They are moving from Westport to Pendleton, where Mr. Wedwick is employed in construction work.

Ralph Sanders and Ed Cox (whom many of the older employees will remember) had a nice hunting trip during the deer season. They hunted out of Cove, near Madras. They ran into quite a heavy snowstorm but Ralph says they each brought back a nice doe.

BRIDAL VEIL LUMBER & BOX CO.

News Letter

Volume II, Number 5   BRIDAL VEIL, OREGON   DECEMBER, 1956

More Power

After polishing off the subject of Public Power last month, I ran across an article that indicated support from an unexpected quarter. It seems that the New York State Association of Electrical Workers, a union with 80,000 members and the International Brotherhood of Electrical Workers with 550,000 members throughout America got sufficiently worked up on the same subject to purchase an advertisement which recently appeared in the New York Times. This ad had to do with government development of Niagara River power, and the electrical workers said in effect: "We are afraid of government control of this power resource."

The ten reasons, listed in the ad, why the union employees oppose "public" or government control of Niagara River power are worthy of the careful consideration of every citizen in the Pacific Northwest since our problems are similar:

1. The Niagara project does not involve any legitimate government function—only the generation of power.

2. Private utility companies are ready, willing and able to do the job.

3. If government is authorized to develop water for electric power as a natural resource, other natural resources will eventually be taken over by government.

4. Private power companies pay taxes; government projects do not. The taxes so evaded would have to be made up later by all taxpayers.

5. The rates charged by private companies are regulated by the New York State Public Service Commission: There is no regulation of political operation.

6. Fair and lasting labor agreements are almost impossible with government agencies: Business managed utilities are easier to do business with and the union wants to continue this way.

7. Private development of Niagara is supported overwhelmingly by people of the area; only extremists who want to impose their philosophy on others favor public development.

8. Free enterprise in the power industry deserves to be protected on its record.

9. Government ownership of industry would bring labor under bureaucratic control and tend to make the American worker a servant to his government.

10. The New York State Federation of Labor, with 1,300,000 members has endorsed private development of Niagara.

The electric workers who put up their money thus to have their say, added these powerful words: "We like the free enterprise system that has made America great and the life of the American labor man the envy of the world. Our American system of getting things done makes sense—we want to retain it."

Len Kraft

————196————

New Social Security Amendments

New amendments to the Social Security Law, enacted by Congress during the 1956 legislative session, make it possible for Working Women, Wives of Retired Workers, Widows, and some Dependent Mothers to receive Social Security Benefits as soon as they reach age 62, instead of having to wait until age 65, as formerly. The new law provides as much as 15 years of additional benefits for Disabled Workers, who can now receive payments at age 50, instead of having to wait until age 65, as formerly. Disabled Children can now receive benefits after age 18, instead of up to age 18 only, as was the case under the old law.

NEWS LETTER

Published on the 10th of each month by
Bridal Veil Lumber & Box Co.
Bridal Veil, Oregon

Editor . . . . . . Don West

The Year Ahead

The start of a new year is always a time of looking ahead— of wondering what the new year may hold for each of us. This is so in our personal lives and naturally it is so in connection with our work.

Everyone hopes that 1957 will be a good year. How good it is for all of us who work together in this organization will depend in large measure on the co-operation of every one of us.

Co-operation means realizing that the final judge of the workmanship of every one of us is the customer who buys and uses our products. That's why we are really co-opearating with everyone in our organization when we do our very best on the job.

Co-operation means remembering that customers will buy only if our selling prices are competitive. That's why it is so important to avoid every possible bit of waste or spoilage—and to pass along any ideas which will help to improve production in any way. If the customer is not satisfied and does not continue to buy and use our products, either because of quality or costs, all of us are the losers by the amount of production which is not needed.

Co-operation means helping in every possible way to keep production moving. It means lending a helpful hand to the person next to us when the need arises—passing along any suggestions which might assist our fellow workers on their jobs—working with those whose responsibility it is to supervise production. In short, co-operation means people working together!

Your individual co-operation during the year ahead in doing the best job you can—whatever your part may be —will help everyone in the organization. At the same time, it will help to make 1957 the best possible year for you.

Health and Welfare

The following employees worked the required number of hours in October to become eligible for Health and Welfare coverage and will be covered on the first day of December 1956. Employees who did not work the required number of hours will become ineligible the same day. Additions: None. Deletions: Wesley A. Adams, Harry Adolph, Lester W. Anderson, Elmer Ayles, Louis W. Bissell, Max Bissell, James E. Bowen, Harold Burkholder, Richard A. Caffrey, Francis P. Cook, Joseph Cote, Daryl W. Cox, Ernest M. Cox Jr., Archie Davies, Dean Davis, Paul Dooley, William Dunken, Leon C. Dunlap, Dale Emmons, Roy Eveland, Fred Fawcett, Charles N. Gaymon, Harold M. Godat, Robert D. Godat, Eldon Gross, Clem Hancock, John Hancock, Loren H. Hancock, Mabel M. Hills, Stanley B. Hills, Lester B. Howell, Earl M. Hutchison, Richard Jacobson, Martha A. Jones, Jarvis Kilness, Edsel E. Kinonen, Georger Knieriem, Vyrtle C. Kuntz, Steven Kuzmesky, Bob Layton, Hiram Layton, George M. Leash, Charles Lofstedt, Frederick H. Long, Fred M. Long, Walter Mannthey, William Mc-Cauley, Roland B. Morgan, George Murray, Orien Pitts, Leslie D. Polzel, E. H. Potter, David G. Rees, Robert W. Reischel, Vera Nell Roberts, Chester Rogers, Thelma Rowe, Ralph Sanders, Raymond Scheringer, Arthur Schroder, Roger Seegar, John W. Smith, Theodore V. Van Hee, Theophile V. Van Hee Sr., Paul Van Treeck, Homer F. Walker, Paul Watts, John G. Willms, H. G. Willoughby, Louis A. Wilson, Roley Zumwalt, Wayne Zumwalt.

————196————

Bristlecone Oldest Tree

The oldest living things in the world are three small bristlecone pines high up in the mountains 20 miles northeast of Bishop, Calif., according to a University of Arizona professor.

The pines are 4000 years old, it is estimated by Dr. Edmund Schulman, head of the university's tree-ring laboratory. The giant sequoias of California, current record-holders for old age, are about 3000 years old.

Schulman based his estimate on countings of the pine trees' rings under microscope. He said the trees grow to a maximum height of only 30 feet, with trunks from 25 to 30 inches across. The trunks, he said, grow just an inch across every 150 or 200 years.

Seniority List

1. Atchley, Noah 3-23-36	41. Polzel, Robert E. 5-1-46	81. Davies, Archie L. 4-1-53
2. Dull, Ward E. 5-18-36	42. Kendrick, James B. 5-13-46	82. Bissell, Louis W. 5-1-53
3. Noble, Clarence 7-27-36	43. Woodard, Mary R. 6-3-46	83. Layton, Bob 5-28-53
4. McCredie, Ralph H. 8-27-36	44. Houchin, Inez M. 9-5-46	84. Bissell, Max 6-1-53
5. Harnam, Ed 3-22-37	45. Jacobson, Harold R. 9-16-46	85. Sanders, Ralph L. 8-3-53
6. Davis, D. Fay 3-22-37	46. Choate, Beula 10-7-46	86. Ayles, Elmer L. 8-4-53
7. Jackson, Marvin T. 4-8-37	47. Layton, Hiram 11-13-46	87. Willoughby, H. G. 8-24-53
8. Stolin, Walter F. 5-11-37	48. Steele, Edward J. ... 1-14-47	88. Gross, Elden 8-27-53
9. Bowen, Franklin M. 8-19-37	49. Lofstedt, Clarence ... 1-16-47	89. Kuzmesky, Steven 9-15-53
10. Crouser, Fred 8-30-37	50. Murray, George 4-21-47	90. Hancock, John 3-2-54
11. Bird, Verl W. 9-20-37	51. Lofstedt, Charles 4-23-47	91. Bowen, James E. 5-4-54
12. Taylor, Ralph L. 11-22-37	52. Jones, Martha A. 5-14-47	92. Burkholder, Harold.... 5-4-54
13. Hanson, Theodore N. 4-18-38	53. Van Hee, Theodore V. 9-9-47	93. Kinonen, Edsel 5-4-54
14. Van Orsow, Joseph M. 4-22-38	54. Rowe, Thelma Y. 11-12-47	94. Kuntz, Vyrtle 5-4-54
15. Dunken, J. Delbert....7-18-38	55. Hills, Mabel M. 1-14-48	95. Long, Frederick H. 6-2-54
16. Meyer, Kenneth L. 9-16-40	56. Dunken, William L. 9-15-48	96. Kilness, Jarvis 6-2-54
17. Hartshorn, Merrill 1-8-41	57. Davis, Dean F. 9-31-48	97. Zumwalt, Roley 9-7-54
18. Harp, Fred 5-21-41	58. Hills, Stanley B. 1-15-51	98. Wilson, Louis A. 9-20-54
19. Mickelson, Einar E. 7-1-41	59. Roberts, Vera Nell....1-15-51	99. Rees, David 9-23-54
20. Roberts, Jerald G. 9-8-41	60. Van Orsow, John H. ...1-15-51	100. Godat, Robert D. 10-6-54
21. Ellis, Ralph 10-9-41	61. Van Treeck, Paul.... 2-20-51	101. Morgan, Roland B. 12-14-54
22. Latourell, Clifford 3-23-42	62. Van Hee, Theoph. Sr. 2-27-51	102. Polzel, Leslie D. 1-5-55
23. Vogel, Harold A. 3-25-42	63. Schneringer,Raymond 10-8-51	103. Gaymon, Charles N. 3-29-55
24. Nielson, Eldon F. 4-21-42	64. Walker, Homer F. 10-9-51	104. Pitts, Orien 4-13-55
25. Davis, Bertha M. 5-6-42	65. Frazier, Lloyd 10-9-51	105. Adams, Wesley A. 5-9-55
26. Hartshorn, Dorothy.... 7-14-42	66. Eveland, Roy D. 10-15-51	106. Dooley, Paul D. 5-9-55
27. Bowen, Anna 9-30-42	67. Anderson, Lester W. 5-19-52	107. Schroder, Arthur H. 5-11-55
28. Hagemen, Leo F. 7-14-43	68. Emmons, Dale 5-20-52	108. Hageman, Leo C. 6-1-55
29. Yerion, Lillie P. 7-19-43	69. Zumwalt, Wayne 5-26-52	109. Smith, John W. 6-9-55
30. Houchin, Wilbur O. 7-26-43	70. Kimbley, A. R., Sr. ... 6-2-52	110. Dunlap, Leon C. 7-5-55
31. Cloe, Pearl P. 11-12-43	71. Howell, Lester B. 6-23-52	111. Rogers, Chester 8-9-55
32. Eversull, James A. 12-17-43	72. Hutchison, Earl 6-23-52	112. Cook, Francis P. 8-10-55
33. Britton, Thomas C. 12-20-43	73. Van Buskirk, Norman 7-28-52	113. Hancock, Clem A. 8-15-55
34. Nielson, Mira J. 1-23-44	74. Hancock, Loren 9-2-52	114. Watts, Paul A. 8-22-55
35. Litton, Durward L. 5-9-44	75. Caffrey, Richard 9-2-52	115. Knieriem, George S. 8-24-55
36. Peterson, Lawrence....9-24-45	76. Long, Fred M. 9-9-52	116. Cox, Ernest M., Jr. 8-29-55
37. Hunt, Howard G. 10-1-45	77. Cote, Joseph 9-10-52	117. Wendler, Ed L. 9-6-55
38. Smazal, Lawrence A. 10-2-45	78. Adolph, Harry 9-22-52	118. Dobson, Virgil 9-7-55
39. Stolin, Marvin J. 3-28-46	79. Willms, John G. 9-29-52	119. Westlake, Donald.... 10-17-55
40. Van Hee, Theophile 4-17-46	80. Poter, Eugene H. 10-28-52	

Flower Fund

Following is a report on the employees flower fund since the last collection in May of 1956:

Balance bro't forward
5-1-56 .... $36.90

Flowers—Dunken (mother)
..............................$ 7.50

Flowers—H. Jacobson
(Mother and Dad) 10.00

Flowers—H. Adolph
(Dad) 7.50

Flowers—Roy Anderson 7.50

Phone Calls 2.63

Balance 1.77

Jim Cowling

Dec. Birthdays

Many Happy Returns of the Day

Eugene Potter   Francis P. Cook
Paul Watts   Clyde H. Hambrick
Hiram Layton   Walter Keller

————196————

COLDER DAYS AHEAD

After a taste of the east wind, we are once again reminded of the need to make sure that the water pipes in the houses are adequately protected against the cold weather. If you have not already done so, the mill has material on hand for boxing in pipes and also has sawdust available. It might save many a headache later on to get the job done now.

Rips and Trims

Twin boys were born to **Mr. and Mrs. Dean Burkholder** at 3:00 a.m. December 2, 1956 at Emanuel Hospital. One of the boys weighed 7 lbs-9 oz. and the other weighed 8 lbs.-14 oz. They were not named yet as we went to press. Both the boys and the mother are reported doing fine. **Dean** even looks a little relieved.

Walt Stolin, Bud Polzel and **Edsel Kinonen** got two does and one spike during the special two day deer season in the Ames district.

Orien Pitts and family spent Thanksgiving day at the **Robert Reischel** home in Springdale, Oregon.

Mr. and Mrs. Fred Harp motored to Seattle during Veterans day weekend.

Mr. and Mrs. Fred Harp spent Thanksgiving day at the Wally Evans home in Eugene, Oregon.

Lynfred Crouser spent Thanksgiving day at the home of his parents, **Mr. and Mrs. Fred Crouser** of Latourell.

Laura-Belle Macy and family spent Thanksgiving weekend at the home of her parents, **Mr. and Mrs. Howard Hunt.**

Mrs. Louis Wilson is recuperating at home after eight days in the hospital following an operation.

Mr. and Mrs. John Van Orsow, Marvin and **Donald Van Orsow** and **Mr.**

and **Mrs. Richard Kerslake** spent Veteran's day weekend at the Clarence Van Orsow home in Culver, Oregon. They tried their luck at duck and pheasant hunting but reported very little success.

Clarence Van Orsow and family of Culver, Oregon spent Thanksgiving weekend visiting friends and relatives in the Portland and Corbett area.

James Hartshorn of Port Orford, Oregon was a recent visitor at the home of his mother, Mrs. H. Hartshorn of Portland. James is a former employee of Bridal Veil.

Sounds like **Marvin Jackson** had quite a trip when he went back to Detroit to pick up his new automobile. Marvin visited friends and relatives on the way home and traveled a total of 3531 miles in his new car.

Frank Potter son of **Mr. and Mrs. Eugene Potter,** has entered the Good Samaritan hospital for a series of operations. We wish him every possible success.

Dave Norgard and family of Richland, Washington, plan to leave the first of the year for Madison, Wisconsin where he will do research work for the Veteran's Administration Hospital at the University of Wisconsin. Dave is the son of **Mr. and Mrs. Walter Norgard.**

1956 SAFETY CHART

Month	Tot. Hourly Pd. Man Hrs.	Lost Time Accidents	Accident Freq.	Days Lost	Accident Severity
January	16,297	0	0	0	0
February	20,821	0	0	0	0
March	18,135	1	55.1	5	276
1st Quarter	55,253	1	18.1	5	91
April	19,749	2	101.3	7	354
May	24,255	1	41.2	7	289
June	23,360	0	0	0	0
2nd Quarter	67,364	3	44.5	14	208
July	24,576	0	0	0	0
August	23,935	0	0	0	0
September	19,563	0	0	0	0
3rd Quarter	68,074	0	0	0	0
October	9,449	0	0	0	0
TOTAL	200,140	4	20.0	19	95

BRIDAL VEIL LUMBER & BOX CO.

News Letter

Volume II, Number 6 . BRIDAL VEIL, OREGON   JANUARY, 1957

1957

This is the season of the year when predictions are ten cents a dozen. Drew Pearson, Walter Winchell, Steve Allen, Rodger Babson and a host of others have all had a go at telling what is going to happen during the coming year. While there are many points of disagreement, one conclusion seems to be pretty general— housing won't be any ball of fire.

The big difficulty seems to be that housing is in a poor competitive position for the consumer's dollar and for the lender's dollar. In the battle of the down payments it is much easier to save the down payment on a 1957 model car, a TV set, an outboard motor and boat or a "go now and pay later" vacation than it is to save the kind of money needed for a good substantial down payment on a new home. The home building industry has to figure out a way to make people want a new home more than all the other attractively merchandised items they are constantly being hounded to buy.

From the lenders point of view, it doesn't make sense to loan money at four and a half percent interest and then wait twenty years to get the money back, knowing that there is a good chance that the dollar paid back twenty years from now won't be worth as much as those loaned today. It is far more attractive to loan at six percent or better for items that are paid up in a year or thereabouts.

The credit problem might solve itself if new housing became more popular with the buying public, since lenders might then have surplus funds left over after supplying the credit needs for consumer goods, and in order to lend at all, would be forced to enter home financing. We can be sure that the automobile and home appliance people would fight any such ten-dency tooth and toe-nail, and would do their best to make new models so irresistable that we would just have to have the latest.

Our problem is tied to the "tight money" policy which is but one tool in the kit for preventing a "boom and bust" economy. Nobody quarrels with the objective, but there does seem to be some doubt whether overall quantitative credit control is the fairest kind of control. The theory is that, like rain, it falls on the just and unjust alike, and that would be true if the result were a percentage-wise decrease in credit available for all causes.

Actually, however, over-all credit restriction bears down very hard on some segments of the economy, while it does not affect others. Thus, home building is hard hit, while other types of construction are little affected.

Small business is directly hit. The little fellow finds his credit drastically cut down, but the big corporation is not affected at all. The industrial giants have no difficulty financing their expansion plans. And so it turns out that over-all credit control is in practice highly selective—or at least discriminatory. The truth is that over-all credit control alone is a pretty crude weapon to use in dealing with an economy where not all elements are expanding and not all lives of business need to be discouraged.

There are at least a couple of answers. One way, fraught with danger, is to delegate power to invoke selective controls over too-rapidly expanding segments of the economy. The danger here lies in the possible use of selective controls for coercive or punitive action.

Another answer, on the local level is to go all out to produce the best

(Continued on Page 2)

NEWS LETTER

Published on the 10th of each month by
Bridal Veil Lumber & Box Co.
Bridal Veil, Oregon

Editor . . . . . Don West

10th Anniversary

January 16th will be the 10th anniversary at Bridal Veil for Clarence Lofstedt.

Clarence was born near Corbett, Oregon where his parents still live. His parents have lived there since they were married. His father, Charles, only recently retired from Bridal Veil.

Clarence attended both grammar school and high school in Corbett. He was a member of the 1939-1940 championship basketball team at Corbett.

Clarence entered the Army in August 1942. He was an aviation engineer and served overseas for nearly three years in Scotland, England, France, Belgium, Holland and Germany. He was discharged from the Army in November 1945.

He worked at various jobs until he came to Bridal Veil where he stayed until the Army recalled him in April 1951. He served with the Air Force until November 1952 at the Portland Air Base and at Larson Air Force

Health and Welfare

The following employees worked the required number of hours in November to become eligible for Health and Welfare coverage and will be covered on the first day of January 1957. Employees who did not work the required number of hours will become ineligible the same day. Additions: Wesley A. Adams, Harry Adolph, Lester W. Anderson, Elmer Ayles, Louis W. Bissell, Max Bissell, James E. Bowen, Harold Burkholder, Richard A. Caffrey, Joseph Cote, Archie Davies, Dean Davis, Paul Dooley, William Dunken, Dale Emmons, Roy Eveland, Charles N. Gaymon, Robert D. Godat, Eldon Gross, John Hancock, Loren H. Hancock, Mabel M. Hills, Stanley B. Hills, Lester B. Howell, Earl M. Hutchison, Martha A. Jones, Jarvis Kilness, Edsel E. Kinonen, Vyrtle C. Kunz, Steven Kuzmesky, Bob Layton, Hiram Layton, Charles Lofstedt, Frederick H. Long, Fred M. Long, Roland B. Morgan, George Murray, Orien Pitts, Leslie D. Polzel, E. H. Potter, David G. Rees, Vera Nell Roberts, Thelma Rowe, Ralph Sanders, Raymond Schneringer, Theodore V. Van Hee, Theophile Van Hee, Sr., Paul Van Treeck, Homer F. Walker, John G. Willms, H. G. Willoughby, Louis A. Wilson, Roley Zumwalt, Wayne Zumwalt. Deletions: None.

————227————

1957

(Continued from Page 1)

quality product at the best price, and so to capture a growing percentage of a contracting market. This is the surest method for us.

Len Kraft

Base near Moses Lake, Washington.

On July 28, 1951 Clarence and the former Bertha Snouley of Corbett were married at Corbett. They have two daughters, Connie 4, and Julie, 2. They live at Wood Village where they recently purchased a home. They are members of the Wood Village Baptist church.

Clarence is a member and past commander of the Rooster Rock Post of the VFW.

He is interested in all types of sports. He bowls occasionally and was a member of the Bridal Veil bowling team in 1947. He also played semi-pro baseball for several years.

10th Anniversary

January 14th will mark the 10th anniversary at Bridal Veil for Ed Steele, box factory.

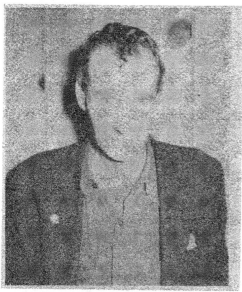

Ed was born in St. Louis, Missouri. When he was four years old the family moved to Tennessee where they remained until Ed came to Oregon in 1935. Ed is the oldest in a family of eleven children.

When Ed came to Oregon he first worked in a sawmill at Hillsboro and

January Birthdays
Many Happy Returns of the Day

Tom Britton	Loren Hancock
Ralph McCredie	Thelma Rowe
Bertha Davis	George Murray
Pearl Cloe	Mira Nielson
Clarence Lofstedt	Marvin Jackson
Roy Eveland	Mel Mallinson
Eldon Nielson	

later on in the woods near Scappoose. Before the war he also worked at Multnomah Falls Lodge. During the war he worked in the shipyards. After the war was over Ed and his brother were in the restaurant business for a time. Then Ed went back to work at Multnomah Falls where he remained until coming to work at Bridal Veil.

On October 22, 1942 Ed and the former Louise Bingham of Latourell Falls were married at Vancouver, Washington. They now have seven children; Edward 14, Donald 13, Marcella 12, Danny 10, Douglas and Debra 3, and Janice. The Steeles have a forty acre farm at Ames, Oregon, which is near Sandy. They have twenty acres under cultivation and the rest is in timber or in the process of being cleared. They have lived there four years and like it very well. The children go to school at Bull Run and to high school at Sandy.

Ed's mother now lives at LaCenter, Washington just north of Vancouver.

1956 SAFETY CHART

Month	Tot. Hourly Pd. Man Hrs.	Lost Time Accidents	Accident Freq.	Days Lost	Accident Severity
January	16,297	0	0	0	0
February	20,821	0	0	0	0
March	18,135	1	55.1	5	276
1st Quarter	55,253	1	18.1	5	91
April	19,749	2	101.3	7	354
May	24,255	1	41.2	7	289
June	23,360	0	0	0	0
2nd Quarter	67,364	3	44.5	14	208
July	24,576	0	0	0	0
August	23,935	0	0	0	0
September	19,563	0	0	0	0
3rd Quarter	68,074	0	0	0	0
October	9,449	0	0	0	0
November	18,401	0	0	0	0
TOTAL	218,541	4	18.3	19	87

STATE OF OREGON
STATE INDUSTRIAL ACCIDENT COMMISSION
SALEM

DATE: November 27, 1956

TO: THE EMPLOYEES AND MANAGEMENT

BRIDAL VEIL
LUMBER and BOX COMPANY

BRIDAL VEIL, OREGON

Your interest in safety as indicated by the 100% endorsement of the Industrial Safety Pledge, is to be commended. We trust you will make this a continuing program by greater participation in the available accident prevention activities.

The combined efforts of all members of your organization directed towards the goal of "NO ACCIDENTS" will result in benefits to all.

STATE INDUSTRIAL ACCIDENT COMMISSION

Chairman   *Wm. A. Callahan*

J. Morris Dunn

L. O. Arens

BRIDAL VEIL LUMBER & BOX CO.

News Letter

Volume II, Number 7   BRIDAL VEIL, OREGON   FEBRUARY, 1957

Motion Time Analysis

During the past week many of you probably have wondered who the stranger was in the mill and what he was writing. Even without an adequate explanation, you have all been very friendly. One man even shared a cup of his good home made coffee on the coldest morning.

I am an Industrial Engineer for the A. B. Segur & Co. Our home office is in Oak Park, Illinois. I came up here from Niles, California where I made a similar study for the Kraftile Co.

We call our study a Motion - Time - Analysis. This should not in any way be confused with a time study, which as you know, is often used to set up standards to get operators to work faster. In making an MTA study the speed at which the operator happens to be working is of no concern. We analyze only the motions that he has to go through to perform his operation. This we usually do in considerable detail because we find that it is the only way to discover t h e difficulties that the operator h a s to contend with on his job. Actually I am studying your equipment and work stations rather than the operators who happen to be on the job. From what I have observed here during these few days, I believe that the operators at Bridal Veil are working as hard as are those of most other industries. In general, very little could be gained by an attempt to just get everyone to work faster.

Your management is also aware of the above, yet they know that something must be done to reduce costs. In a sellers market it is often possible to pass cost increases on to the customer. But in a time like this, men who buy carload lots of millwork are shopping around for the best values, just like we do when we buy a new car at a time when all the lots are

loaded. In fact automobile buyers have probably been the most ruthless in this respect. Out of approximately 7000 concerns that have started out to build automobiles, only about a half dozen now remain. There are rumors now that the buyers may vote that only three are doing a good enough job to survive.

In my contacts with your management, I have detected no feeling of defeatism. In fact they seemed quite determined to make Bridal Veil the most progressive company in your field.

But what is a progressive mill? It would be nice to have a modern building and a chance to revolutionize the layout in one summer with many new pieces of equipment. H i s t o r y has shown however, that this kind of modernization has been the undoing of

(Continued on Page 2)

NEWS LETTER

Published on the 10th of each month by
Bridal Veil Lumber & Box Co.
Bridal Veil, Oregon

Editor . . . . . Don West

Health and Welfare

The following employees worked the required number of hours in December to become eligible for Health and Welfare coverage and will be covered on the first day of February 1957. Employees who did not work the required number of hours will become ineligible the same day. Additions: None. Deletions: Harry Adolph, Lester Anderson, Elmer Ayles, Louis Bissell, Max Bissell, Harold Burkholder, Richard Caffrey, Joseph Cote, Archie Davies, William Dunken, Dale Emmons, Lloyd Frazier, Robert Godat, Eldon Gross, John Hancock, Loren Hancock, Ed Harnam, Mabel Hills, Stanley Hills, Lester Howell, Howard Hunt, Earl Hutchison, Harold Jacobson, Martha Jones, Jim Kendrick, Jarvis, Kilness, Edsel Kinonen, Vyrtle Kuntz, Steven Kuzmesky, Bob Layton, Clarence Lofstedt, Fred Long, George Murray, Mira Nielson, Lawrence Peterson, Leslie Polzel, Robert Polzel, E. H. Potter, David Rees, Vera Nell Roberts, Ralph Sanders, Lawrence Smazal, Ed Steele, Norman Van Buskirk, Theodore V. Van Hee, Theophile Van Hee Sr., John H. Van Orsow, Paul Van Treeck, Homer Walker, John G. Willms, H. G. Willoughby, Louis Wilson, Mary Woodard, Roley Zumwalt, Wayne Zumwalt, Jim Rhodes, Louise Rhodes, Eleanor Taylor, Charles Gaymon, Orien Pitts, Wesley Adams, Paul Dooley, Glen Wells, Jack Kreman.

A football coach accompanied a prospective tackle to the Dean's office where he attempted to get the boy admitted to school without a written examination. The boy, however, could not answer the simplest questions. In desperation the dean asked, "How much is seven and seven?"

"Thirteen," the boy answered.

"Aw, let him in anyway, Dean," pleaded the coach, "he only missed it by two.

Motion Time Analysis

(Continued from Page 1)

many companies. It is far safer to modernize at a rate which is more in line with the earnings of the company. This then calls for doing the best possible job with the present major facilities. When this goal is reached, the profits would justify taking the next step. This is the way all progressive companies grow.

My assignment then is to determine what can be done through simple changes to utilize your present facilities more effectively. How can I hope to do this, when admittedly your people know far more than I about millwork. The only explanation is this, while you were gathering experience in millwork, I have been analyzing operations in over two hundred factories during the last twenty years. We have found that regardless of what industry we happen to be working with, the motions that the operators use can be classified by the seventeen fundamental motions used in MTA. We recognize certain of these motions as effective or useful and others as being ineffective or loss motions. We have certain improvement procedures that we apply to reduce or eliminate these ineffective motions. This usually results in a number of minor changes in the work station to permit the desired motion path.

All of the MTA studies made at Bridal Veil last week showed a high percentage of loss motions. These were no reflection on the operators because in most cases, they couldn't do much differently under the conditions they work. It is too early yet to say what specific changes can be made at this time to improve these conditions. Every effort will be made to initiate some improvements that will illustrate the thinking that we have in mind. Our objective is to have every motion on the part of each operator contribute some value to the product the customer receives. If this goal can be achieved, Bridal Veil will have a progressive mill that need fear no competition.

George Esch

A bewildered man entered a ladies' specialty shop. "I want a corset for my wife," he said.

"What bust?" asked the clerk.

"Nothin'. It just wore out."

Thanks!

The winter so far has brought us more than our normal share of bad weather with its attendant snow and icy roads. The management wishes to express its appreciation for what has been an excellent attendance record in spite of all the difficulties involved in getting to and from Bridal Veil.

Although our order file is not as well filled at the present time as it is in the summer months, we find that our customers do want prompt shipment on the orders they have placed. Good attendance has been a large factor in getting our shipments out in accordance with our customers needs.

Ade Jones

Little Johnnie, being reprimanded by his teacher for being tardy for school, remonstrated with the following excuse: "Ma woke Pa up in the middle of the night saying she heard something in the hen house. Pa, who sleeps in the raw grabbed his loaded shotgun and ran out into the yard. Pa stood there, with his gun pointing at the chicken house, waiting for something to come out when our old hound dog came up behind Pa with his cold nose . . . and we've been cleaning chickens since three o'clock this morning.

February Birthdays
Many Happy Returns of the Day!

Elmer Ayles	Delbert Dunken
Mable Hills	Vyrtle Kuntz
Beulah Choate	Louis Wilson
Fred Crouser	Mary Woodard
Ed Wendler	Paul Van Treeck
Norman Van Buskirk	

One Year of Safety

A year ago the management of Bridal Veil Lumber & Box Co. initiated a safety program and asked cooperation from all employees.

In 1955 our accident frequency was 58.1, which was two and one half times the industry average of 21.4.

In 1956 our accident frequency was 17.6, which was 5.5 points lower than the industry average of 23.1 and is also a 69.7% reduction over 1955.

During 1956 and starting 1957 we racked up 243 consecutive days without a lost time accident. We had one lost time accident in the month of January. However, with the ice and snow, working conditions were more hazardous. So again in 1957, we ask your continued interest and cooperation for safety.

Mel Mallinson

1956 SAFETY CHART

Month	Tot. Hourly Pd. Man Hrs.	Lost Time Accidents	Accident Freq.	Days Lost	Accident Severity
January	16,297	0	0	0	0
February	20,821	0	0	0	0
March	18,135	1	55.1	5	276
1st Quarter	55,253	1	18.1	5	91
April	19,749	2	101.3	7	354
May	24,255	1	41.2	7	289
June	23,360	0	0	0	0
2nd Quarter	67,364	3	44.5	14	208
July	24,576	0	0	0	0
August	23,935	0	0	0	0
September	19,563	0	0	0	0
3rd Quarter	68,074	0	0	0	0
October	9,449	0	0	0	0
November	18,401	0	0	0	0
December	8,115	0	0	0	0
4th Quarter	35,965	0	0	0	0
TOTAL FOR YEAR 1956	226,656	4	17.6	19	84
Average for the Industry 1955			23.1		

Formula

A few days ago the daily papers carried a story reporting that the reserve fund of the State Unemployment Compensaion Commission had been drawn down to a dangerous level. And that leads us to one of the major problems of all seasonal businesses—how can we achieve a steady rate of production on a year around basis:

Since our business is largely dependent upon residential housing we are especially sensitive to the seasonal nature of the construction business. One practical solution is to develop outlets for our products in those areas in which the building season starts earlier in the spring and lasts longer in the fall. The farther south, the longer the building season. In parts of the south, winters are mild enough to have little effect on the building season.

It is unfortnate however, that these areas are also the areas in which the $1.00 an hour minimum wage law had an affect on wage rates in the lumber industry. It was estimated at the time that the $1.00 minimum raised the wages of 80% of the people in the southern lumber industry. Also these same areas are the areas which cost the most to ship to. The freight on millwork to Atlanta, Georgia today on a board measure basis, is twice what we paid for lumber in the late thirties.

While it might sound from the above that we don't have a chance of competing in the deep south, we have been able to ship an occasional car. But it requires a mighty sharp pencil when quoting, and it requires top flight efficiency to ship south with any degree of regularity.

Another answer to the problem of seasonality lies in supplementing our millwork line with other items unrelated to the construction industry. There are a wide variety of items in wood used — the trick is to discover which are wanted at the right time of year and then to produce them at a price the buyer can afford to pay.

The problem of competition is always with us. In quoting new items, as we do from time to time, we are, in effect, pitting our knowledge and skills and efficiency against the same qualities in our competitors all over the country. That some of these competitors have advantages in freight cost or wage rates is merely a stimulant to us to do a better job and to take the business in spite of the competition.

And so the search for better methods goes on. It is a job that will never be finished. Each cost saving idea and every improved method helps our competitive position and helps our chances of reducing the seasonal swing from full production to curtailed operation.

One thing is sure — with the help of all of us we are bound to do a better job of providing full employment and full pay envelopes than the state can. You can't legislate efficient production, and efficient production is the only basis for prosperity.

Len Kraft

Rips and Trims

Mira Nielson has been off work the past two weeks with the flu and an attack of asthma. While at home, she observed her 13th year at Bridal Veil and also celebrated a birthday. Didn't say which one. Anyway, it wasn't a very pleasant way to celebrate, being ill

Phil Van Hee Sr., was off a week with the flu and arthritis. He was lucky in one respect; it occurred during the extreme cold weather.

A window was broken on **Merrill Hartshorn's** car when the wind blew a garage door against it.

Willie Bowen has just completed his term of jury duty, which was for the month of January.

Walt Keller is the (proud) owner of a new Chevrolet.

Mr. and Mrs. Don West are the parents of a new baby boy. Mark Elliot West (pretty fancy name) was born January 28th, at Wilcox Memorial Hospital and weighed in at 9 lbs, 1 oz. at birth.

Lou and **Lucille Snodgrass** (Lou is a former employee), were recent visitors at the Cowling home.

BRIDAL VEIL LUMBER & BOX CO.

News Letter

Volume II, Number 8　　BRIDAL VEIL, OREGON　　MARCH, 1957

You Pays Your Money

It says here that the announcement of the Federal Budget for the coming year has produced widespread consternation in a number of circles. This one, running to some seventy odd billions, is the largest peacetime budget in the nation's history.

Although there is a lot of romance in the basic idea of a reduction in Federal spending—particularly if it would result in a proportional reduction of income taxes—there is really very little reason why we should expect such a thing to come to pass. When most of us think of a reduction of Federal spending, we are really thinking in terms of a reduction of the kind of spending that benefits the other fellow—but don't take anything away from me!

There was an article in the paper the other day that illustrates how this works out. The story said that the Portland Chamber of Commerce had passed a resolution asking the Federal government to appropriate $750,000.-00 for an addition to Timberline Lodge on Mt. Hood. Just why it should be the responsibility of the government to provide skiing facilities on Mt. Hood was not explained in the article.

Apparently the Portland business men belonging to the Chamber of Commerce figure that Abraham Lincoln had become momentarily unhinged when he stated that the government should do only those things for the people which the people cannot do themselves. Surely, if this expansion at Timberline is such a rollicking good investment, the business men involved could pass the hat and round up the money themselves. But such a program would overlook the much more attractive procedure of having the government do the job, and thus "get something for nothing".

The "fat" in the Federal budget that makes it so tough to chew, swallow, digest, and so on, is the sum total of all the goofy projects across the nation sponsored by local interests. These same interests will be back next week making a fuss about high taxes, and suggesting we write our congressman. By golly, we will do that the first time we can think of something to ask him for.

Len Kraft

————42————

Social Security Tax

On January 1, 1957, under the new law, the Social Security Tax which both you and your employer are required to pay on your earnings is increased ¼ of 1 percent, from the present 2 percent rate to 2¼, to pay the added cost of the new disability insurance protection given to employees under the law. The first $4,200 of wages paid you during the year are subject to Social Security Tax—at the new 2¼ percent rate the maximum increase in employer's and employee's tax would be $10.50 on earnings of $4,200 or more.

————42————

GAINS IN LUMBERING SAFETY

The hazardous lumber industry, still at the bottom of the frequency rate list for all industries, continues its steady climb toward safer operations, with member lumber companies reporting a rate of 26.25, against 64.65 ten years ago—an improvement of 60 per cent! By 1950, the rate had been reduced to 46.84, and in 1954 it was 30.88.

————42————

Consumers are getting more for time worked — this will continue to be true.

Example: Dozen eggs cost 20 work minutes in 1951, now cost 19 minutes.

NEWS LETTER

Published on the 10th of each month by
Bridal Veil Lumber & Box Co.
Bridal Veil, Oregon

Editor . . . . . Don West

Health and Welfare

The following employees worked the required number of hours in January to become eligible for Health and Welfare coverage and will be covered on the first day of March, 1957. Employees who did not work the required number of hours will become ineligible the same day. Additions: Harry Adolph, Lester Anderson, Elmer Ayles, Max Bissell, Harold Burkholder, Richard Caffrey, Joseph Cote, Archie Davies, William Dunken, Dale Emmons, Lloyd Frazier, Eldon Gross, John Hancock, Loren H. Hancock, Mabel M. Hills, Stanley B. Hills, Lester B. Howell, Howard Hunt, Earl M. Hutchison, Harold Jacobson, Martha A. Jones, James B. Kendrick, Jarvis Kilness, Edsel Kinonen, Vyrtle Kuntz, Steven Kuzmesky, Bob Layton, Hiram Layton, Clarence Lofstedt, Frederick H. Long, George Murray, Mira J. Nielson, Lawrence Peterson, Robert E. Polzel, E. H. Potter, David Rees, Vera Nell Roberts, Ralph Sanders, Lawrence Smazal, Edward J. Steele, Norman Van Buskirk, Theodore V. Van Hee, Theophile V. Van Hee Sr., John H. Van Orsow, Paul Van Treeck, Homer F. Walker, John G. Willms, H. G. Willoughby, Louis A. Wilson, Mary Woodard, Roley Zumwalt, Wayne Zumwalt. Deletions: James E. Bowen, Charles Lofstedt, Roland B. Morgan.

————42————

WANT TO BE A BARBER?

Or sell real estate or practice law or be a druggist or write insurance? You must first demonstrate that you know something about your calling and obtain a state license. But you can become a politician and direct the industries and lives of your fellow citizens without necessarily knowing anything about anything—except vote catching.

————42————

Oregon's annual output of lumber is around eight billion board feet, enough to build about eight hundred thousand five-room frame houses.

10th Anniversary

The tenth anniversary at Bridal Veil was March 1, for Mel Mallinson, Sales Engineer.

Mel was born in West Salem, Illinois and was one of nine children. He is the only boy in the family.

In 1934 Mel decided to take a look at the country and ended up in San Jose, California where he remained for six years. In 1940 he came north to Portland. He had the restaurant in the old Oregon Bowling Alley in Portland.

Mel joined the Army in October 1942 and received his basic training at Fort Lewis, Washington. In June 1943 he was sent overseas to Hawaii where he was assigned to the Fortieth Infantry Division. He served as Platoon Leader in a heavy mortar platoon. His outfit saw action on Guadalcanal, New Britain, the Phillipines and were later stationed in Korea as occupational troops. In December 1945 he returned to the states and was discharged shortly after.

He first went to work at Wood Specialties Company in Portland, which was later moved to Bridal Veil. In September 1952 Mel was transferred to the office to learn drafting.

On May 24, 1946 Mel and Lillian Nyblod were married in Vancouver, Washington. They have one son. Robert. They live at 3578 S.E. 77th St. in Portland.

15th Anniversary

March 25 will mark the 15th anniversary at Bridal Veil for Harold Vogel, band sawyer.

Harold was born in Redwing, Minnesota, one of two children. When he was still very young the family moved to Visalia, California. After several years in California the family decided to come to Oregon on their vacation and ended up by staying three years. Then they went back to California long enough to sell their holdings and return to Oregon, where they purchased a home in Hubbard. Harold's mother and brother still live in Hubbard.

Harold joined the CCC in 1937 and was in that organization for two years. After that he spent several years working logging camps and sawmills.

March 25, 1942 he came to work at Bridal Veil, where he stayed until he joined the Navy on April 13, 1944. After his training he was assigned to an attack transport. He participated in several Pacific campaigns, among them the Phillipines and Okinawa invasions. He was discharged from the Navy on January 1, 1946.

In June 1946, he and the former Mary Smazal were married in Vancouver, Washington. They now live in Bridal Veil and have three children, Gary 5, Vickie 3, and Harold 1.

Fishing and hunting are hobbies which Harold enjoys whenever he can.

20th Anniversary

March 22, 1957 will be the twentieth anniversary at Bridal Veil for Fay Davis, millwright.

Fay was born in Reno County, Kansas and is one of nine children. Shortly after Fay was born the family moved to Oregon, near Troutdale. The family farmed near Troutdale for a good many years.

Fay was educated at Hurlburt and Corbett. After he was through school, Fay worked for several years in a sawmill south of Corbett and after that for a building contractor in Corbett.

In 1931 Fay came to work at Bridal Veil for the Bridal Veil Lumber Company. He stayed with that company until the present company purchased the plant and then he transferred to this company.

On May 7, 1925, Fay and Bertha Barr were married. They have one son, Robert, who is married and working in Portland.

The Davis' built a home near Corbett in 1954. They have over fourteen acres of ground and each year they raise a big garden. Fay also likes to work in his combination machine and carpenter shop.

Fay is a Mason and a member of the Christian Church of Corbett. He is also a member of the National Rifle Association. During the war he was a member of the Mutlnomah County Sheriff's Reserve.

15th Anniversary

March 23 will be the fifteenth anniversary at Bridal Veil for Clifford Latourell, squeezer operator.

Cliff was born in Latourell Falls, Oregon, just a short distance from where he now lives. Latourell Falls was named after his grandfather, who was the first settler in that community. The name had previously been Rooster Rock. His grandfather came to the area by steamboat, which was the only way to get here in those days. He was also the first man to take a barge loaded with wood over the rapids at what is now Cascade Locks. His name has been mentioned in several books dealing with the early history of the Columbia river. He came to this area in 1843.

Cliff was educated in Latourell and Portland. Later on he worked in Portland for a number of years. After that, he worked and lived for three years in Buffalo, New York before deciding to return to Oregon.

Cliff is married to the former Mildred Jerome. His wife is an accomplished sculptress, and is working on a pioneer family group which is nearing completion.

Cliff still has an uncle and two aunts living in Latourell Falls. His Uncle Henry and wife, who are 98 and 99 years young respectively, recently

Rips and Trims

Mr. and Mrs. **Willis Bowen** were recent guests of Mr. and Mrs. Neal Woolf of Portland.

At a dinner honoring **Beulah Choate** on her birthday, guests included son Tom and his wife, Fred Luscher and Gretchen Fraser, and husband, Tom.

Harry Densmore flew to Lincoln, Nebraska, recently to visit his mother, who is ill and in the hospital.

————42————

March Birthdays
Many Happy Returns of the Day!

Martha Jones	Paul Dooley
Dale Emmons	Noah Atchley
Walter Stolin	Elden Gross
Ed Harnam	

————42————

Disabled Children

Under the Social Security law children of retired or deceased workers are entitled to benefits as long as they are under 18 and unmarried. But under a 1956 amendment to the law, a disabled child whose disability began before age 18 can continue to receive benefits after age 18 for as long as he remains disabled and single, if his father or mother is receiving retirement benefits or if he has lost the support of a deceased parent insured for survivor's benefits.

————42————

A Texas millionaire decided to bestow a modest gift of $500,000 upon a university near Houston. One newspaper, however, made a slight mistake in its report of the bequest. It said that the gift was five million.

Fortunately, however, the millionaire and the owner of the paper are friends. So there was not too much anger in the voice of the millionaire when he phoned.

"I don't suppose I can make a liar out of that sheet of yours," he grumbled. "Since you said so, I'll make the gift five million this time. But confound it: don't let this happen again.

observed their 75th wedding anniversary.

When time permits, Cliff enjoys both fishing and hunting. He also likes to work around their home.

BRIDAL VEIL LUMBER & BOX CO.

News Letter

Volume II, Number 8   BRIDAL VEIL, OREGON   APRIL, 1957

New Business

One of the well known national magazines, in an article on the prospects of the residential building industry for the year 1957, reports that housing starts probably hit the low point in February 1957 at a seasonally adjusted rate of about 900,000 starts per year. The article goes on to predict that from now on activity will gather momentum until a rate of 1,090,000 is achieved late this year, with actual starts for the year totalling 1,060,000.

It appears that the housing business has a built-in advantage which exists by way of a constantly expanding demand for its products. New family formations are currently running around 900,000 per year. On top of this we have a couple hundred thousand housing units retired each year by reason of fire, obsolescense, etc., which means a constant demand for some 1,100,000 new homes each year. Population shifts also add to the demand for new homes, since people moving to rapidly expanding areas cannot offset a shortage even a few hundred miles away.

While much has been written about the short supply of money and the need for government subsidy to help our industry supply the demand, there is probably nothing wrong with the industry that a reduction in cost wouldn't cure. The simple fact is that in many areas the product costs too much. One large item of cost that seems to have gotten out of hand is land values. Around the larger metropolitan areas of the East, builders try to find land within 90 minutes transportation time from employment centers. As the quality of land is limited, it has been bid up in price. Many other factors are involved, and all are complex and difficult to meet.

Our Board of Directors, in its annual meeting held at Bridal Veil Wednesday March 27 has expressed its confidence that answers to the problems of the housing industry, one of America's basic industries, can and will be met and solved. To help accomplish this goal the Board has endorsed a program of continuing to increase our productivity through the use of improved tools and methods, and to achieve full employment for all of our people through expanded markets and new products.

To demonstrate that these are not idle words and flowery phrases, the Board has directed the Management to procede without delay in providing the necessary equipment to produce K. D. Sash. It is contemplated that this move will result in broader markets, better service, better utilization of raw material, bigger volume, steadier employment, and consequently be a concrete step at the local level toward the industry goal—Maximum efficiency in production and marketing to the end that our product will come within the reach of more and more home buyers.

Len Kraft

————19————

New Employees

A hearty welcome is extended to the following new employees.

Rodney Jacobson
Bob Fitzgerald
Richard Jacobson

————19————

The present housing boom (about 1,100,000 new houses in 1956) is down from its peak mainly because there were fewer births in the 30's, and consequently fewer young people of the marriage ages in these days. This slack-off is likely to continue for 2 or 3 years, apart from factor of tight money, just because of the slack-off in marriages, new families.

NEWS LETTER

Published on the 10th of each month by
Bridal Veil Lumber & Box Co.
Bridal Veil, Oregon

Editor . . . . . Don West

10th Anniversary

April 21th will be the tenth anniversary at Bridal Veil for George Murray, nailer operator.

George was born in Whitehaven — Cumberland, England, one of six children. George's father was a district manager for a life insurance company. George remained in England for twenty-one years. He came to this country and landed in New York on Saint Patrick's day. He thought that possibly the annual Saint Patrick's day parade might have been in his honor.

He went directly to Great Falls, Montana, where two of his brothers were living. George's ambition was to be a doctor but the depression came along about that time and the boys decided they could not afford to all go to college, so they flipped a coin to see who it would be and it turned out to be brother Tom. George and brother Joe worked to put Tom through school and he is now a college professor in California.

George worked for the Anaconda Copper Co. in Great Falls for awhile

Pictured above is Patsy Smith, successor to Eleanor Taylor, payroll clerk.

Patsy was born in Julesburg, Colorado. The family moved to the west coast and Patsy attended school in Klamath Falls and Santa Rosa, California.

Patsy was married in October 1953 to Gerald Smith. They have one daughter, Linda Marie. Mr. Smith is employed at the Albers Milling Co. in Portland.

They are members of the Reorganzed Church of Jesus Christ of Latter Day Saints. Patsy is a member of the choir.

and later as a male nurse for several years.

He and the former Marilla E. Powell were married August 10, 1938 in Great Falls. They have two daughters, Jean and Doris, both students at Corbett. The Murrays' left Montana in 1942 for Portland and moved to their present home near Corbett in 1945.

One of George's hobbies is raising dahlias. He says he presently has over forty varieties. With over thirteen acres of land he also raises all the vegetables and meat for the family. Sounds like he manages to keep busy, at least part of the time.

—19—

A batchelor is a fellow who comes to work every morning from a different direction.

20th Anniversary

April 8th will be the twentieth anniversary at Bridal Veil Lumber & Box Co. for Marvin Jackson, truck driver.

He has actually lived in Bridal Veil for some thirty-five years, and worked for the company preceeding the present one.

Marv was born in Fairfield, California and the family also lived in Dixon and Stockton. Then the family moved to Prescott, Arizona by horse and wagon, a trip which took thirty days to complete.

Marv's father ran a horse drawn freight line from Kingman, Arizona to Gold Roads, a distance of sixty-five miles, and a round trip took eight days. Marv worked in grocery stores in Kingman, Prescott, Cedar Glade, Arizona. Later on Marv moved to Salt Lake City where he worked in a sugar beet factory. Then he moved to Emmett, Idaho and worked as a truck driver for a produce company. Then he bought his own truck and contracted hauling produce.

Marv was married in Parma, Idaho to the former Myrtle Wilson. His wife passed away in 1943. They have one son, Stan, who is office manager for the Russell Towboat and Moorage Co. in Vancouver, Wash.

Marvin's hobby is baseball. He has been managing semi-pro teams for thirty - seven years. He played ball himself until 1942. In that year his son pitched and Marv was the catcher.

15th Anniversary

The fifteenth anniversary at Bridal Veil for Eldon Nielson, rip sawyer, will be April 21st.

Eldon was born at Springdale, Oregon but spent most of his early years at Herman Creek, near Cascade Locks. The family lived there for eighteen years altogether. His father was employed by the Oregon State Game Commission. They also lived at Maupin for a while before returning to Springdale. Eldon worked in a service station and a garage for a year before coming to work at Bridal Veil.

Eldon and the former Donzella Newman of Jay, Oklahoma were married in January 1943 in Vancouver, Washington. They now have three children, Ronnie 12, Lanny 7, and Taria Lyn 5.

During the war Eldon was a member of the Sheriff's reserve and the Oregon State Guard. His hobbies are model railroading and music. He has had a dance band for eleven years and they play at various dances around this area.

Eldon built his own trailer house a couple of years ago and is now planning on building a home near Springdale. In fact, he has already begun clearing the land, which totals three acres.

He is a member of the Portland Baseball Association. Another hobby is bird hunting.

Rips and Trims

Chyrl Bowen, daughter of former employee James Bowen, returned home from Providence Hospital March 31st, after a siege of pneumonia.

Anna and Willis Bowen attended the home show in Portland Saturday evening.

Merrill and Dorothy Hartshorn are planning a new home, and expect to build on a five acre tract on Salzman Road, next to the Fay Davis property at Corbett. They hope to get started in April.

Martha Jones has a new Plymouth Belvedere. The family tried it out last weekend on a trip to Pendleton, where they visited Martha's sister.

Ted Hansen has something new in home heating, an automatic thermostatically controlled wood burning circulating heater. He hopes to get good results with it.

Mira Nielson is entering Portland Sanitarium on Monday, April 18, for an observation and checkup. It may take a week to complete the tests. All hope they find nothing serious.

Beulah Choate returned to work April 2nd, after being off work since March 20th with a bad case of the flu, combined with sinus infection. We are all glad to see you back on the job, Beulah.

Eldon Nielson and family accompanied Marvin Jackson on a weekend trip to Heppner, where they visited Marvin's sister, whose home was completely destroyed by fire last week.

John H. Van Orsow completed his last day of work for Bridal Veil Lumber & Box Company Friday March 29th. John is retiring and will concentrate mostly on fishing and hunting, along with "take it easy program" for a while. John started in Bridal Veil originally in June 1941, and worked all during the war, then left and came back in January 1951 until the present time. His friends and fellow employees wish him happy hunting and fishing and lots of rest.

———19———

Health and Welfare

The following employees worked the required number of hours in February to become eligible for Health and Welfare coverage and will be covered on the first day of April, 1957. Employees who did not work the required number of hours will become ineligible the same day. Additions: Wesley Adams, Louis W. Bissell, Paul D. Dooley, Leon Dunlap, Charles N. Gaymon, Clem Hancock, Roland B. Morgan, Orien Pitts, Leslie D. Polzel, Ed L. Wendler, Donald Westlake. Deletions: Ralph L. Sanders, Edward J. Steele.

———19———

April Birthdays
Many Happy Returns of the Day!

Jim Eversull	Joe Van Orsow
Wilbur Houchin'	Dorothy Hartshorn
Ted Hanson	John Willms
Fred Long	Clarence Noble

———19———

The households being formed today represent, for the most part, people who were born about twenty years ago. That was in the depths of the depression when the birth rate was low. New household formations will go up in numbers more and more rapidly as the bumper baby crops of the war and post-war periods come of age. age.

———19———

Patient: "Tremendous, Doctor! Simply tremendous! Would you call that therapy a transverse adjustment of the sacroiliac?"

Doctor: "Naw. Your suspenders were twisted."

1957 SAFETY CHART

Month	Tot. Hourly Pd. Man Hrs.	Lost Time Accidents	Accident Freq.	Days Lost	Accident Severity
January	14,288	1	70.0	3	210
February	15,318	0	0	0	0
TOTAL	29,606	1	33.8	3	101

BRIDAL VEIL LUMBER & BOX CO.

News Letter

Volume II, Number 9   BRIDAL VEIL, OREGON   MAY, 1957

Injustice

So far as I know, no one has popped up to explain the high standard of living enjoyed in our country on any basis other than the high degree of personal liberty we have attained plus our tradition of respect for private property and our market economy. Personal liberty is probably the greatest single difference between Western civilization and the social organizations existing in African and Oriental countries. These ideas are as old as the ancient Grecian civilizations which first conceived them. In the West these ideas have slowly developed over the intervening centuries, in the East, these ideas never caught on in spite of centuries of exposure. The social organization of Saudi Arabia has remained unchanged for centuries and possibly a millennium or two.

There are those, however, who seem to feel a sense of guilt because our country is so prosperous while our Eastern and African neighbors are still scratching the ground with sticks. The World Council of Churches, for example, declared in 1948: "Justice demands that the inhabitants of Asia and Africa should have the benefit of more machine production." This makes sense only if one implies that God presented mankind with a fixed quantity of machines and expected that these contrivances would be equally distributed among the various nations of the world. Yet the capitalistic countries, through greed and trickery, were bad enough to take possession of much more of this stock of tools that "justice" would have assigned to them and thus to deprive the inhabitants of Asia and Africa of their fair portion.

The truth is that the accumulation of capital and its investment in machines is the source of the comparatively greater wealth of the Western

peoples. It is no fault of the capitalists that the Asiatics and Africans did not adopt those ideologies and policies which would have made the evolution of a similar standard of living possible.

Neither is it the fault of the capitalists that the policies of these nations thwarted the attempts of foreign investors to give them "the benefit of more machine production." No one contests that what makes hundreds of millions in Asia and Africa destitute is that they cling to primitive methods of production and miss the benefits which the employment of better tools and up-to-date technological designs could bring them.

There is only one means to relieve their distress. What they need is private enterprise and the accumulation of new capital plus a few capitalists. It is nonsensical to blame capitalism and the capitalistic nations for the plight the backward peoples have brought on themselves. The remedy indicated is not "justice" but the substitution of sound policies for unsound policies.

Capital is not a free gift of God or nature. It is the outcome of a provident restriction on consumption on the part of man. It is created and increased by saving. Men, cooperating under the system of the division of labor, have created all the wealth which the daydreamers consider as the free gift of nature.

Mexico, following a period of stagnation arising from a misgided whirl of expropriation, is now inviting foreign investment again, and the economy of Mexico is making rapid strides toward raising its people out of poverty. Venezuela and Brazil are also examples of states making progress by creating a climate favorable to
(Continued on Page 3)

NEWS LETTER

Published on the 10th of each month by
Bridal Veil Lumber & Box Co.
Bridal Veil, Oregon

Editor . . . . . Don West

10th Anniversary

May 14th will be the tenth anniversary at Bridal Veil for Martha Jones, box factory.

Martha was born in Elkhorn, Iowa, one of six children. While still a small girl, the family moved to Audabon, Iowa, where Martha attended school. After graduating from school, she spent a year in California and then returned to Iowa to work for her father. Her father was in the livestock brokerage business, and Martha helped by driving truck, buying livestock and keeping books. She worked for her father for five years.

On July 23, 1943, Martha and Floyd Jones were married in Omaha, Nebraska. Shortly after their marriage they came out west to visit relatives and, like so many people, decided to stay. They both worked at Bridal Veil for a while. Floyd is now employed by the Oregon State Fish Commission.

The Jones's have one daughter, Marilyn, who attends Roecker private
(Continued on Page 3)

15th Anniversary

The fifteenth anniversary at Bridal Veil for Bertha Davis, band saw feeder, will be May 6th.

Bertha was born near Latourell Falls, where her grandfather homesteaded. She was one of five children. Her grandfather was also in on the gold rush in California but was not too successful.

Bertha's father was in the logging business until an accident resulted in the loss of an arm. After that he turned to farming and concentrated on raising cattle, which he exhibited at fairs and livestock shows.

Bertha lived all her life at the same place until she and Fay were married on May 7th, 1925. She attended school at Brower, which is now consolidated with Corbett. They have one son, Robert, and one grandson.

For hobbies, Bertha lists reading as her favorite, especially historical novels.

Bertha has never had an accident in the fifteen years she has been at Bridal Veil. That is an outstanding record, in view of the high accident rate for the industry.

——— 49 ———

Another trouble with Socialism is that it soon runs out of rich people and has to fall back on folks like you and me.

Pictured above, in the center of the picture, is an old lumber cart, wagon, or what have you. It is isolated about fifteen feet above Bridal Veil creek. As near as we can find out, it has probably been there for at least fifteen years, as it has been that long since the bridge was in use. We can see no way of getting it down or why anyone would want to and can only wonder how long it will be before Mother Nature takes charge and dumps it unceremoniously into the creek.

10th Anniversary

(Continued from Page 2)

day school in Portland. She spends the weekends with her parents.

Martha is interested in sports and was active in sports while in school. She and her husband attend quite a few baseball and football games.

Martha lives at Moffett Creek about eight miles east of Bridal Veil at the present time but plans on moving to Bonneville dam so that her husband will be near the fish hatchery.

———— 49 ————

New Employees

A hearty welcome is extended to the following new employees:

David L. Wilks   Robert A. Haley
Carl A. Smith   Wesley L. Horner
Manuel P. Kelley   Walter S. Cheek
Lawrence B. Gowens

Injustice

(Continued from Page 1)

capital. No country has ever helped its people by creating a climate favorable to communism.

It appears that the best export we have for helping backward countries is not dollars. Our best export is ideas—the principles that have made America great.

Len Kraft
———— 49 ————

"Why did you let the other Pastor go?" the visitor asked.

"Oh, he always preached that if we didn't mend our ways we would go straight to hell."

"But that's just what this minister said today!"

"Yes," replied the member, "but the other one acted as if he was glad!"

Rips and Trims

Earl Hutchison spent five days at Long Beach, Washington, digging clams. Earl said he had good luck.

Paul Dooley came to work Friday, May third, all smiles because he had just become the father of a 6 pound, 11 ounce baby boy. He has been named **Mickel Wayne. Mrs. Dooley** is the daughter of **Mr. and Mrs. Eugene Potter,** so we have a new father as well as a grandfather among our fellow workers.

Gerald Roberts, John and **Marvin Van Orsow** spent opening day of trout season at Devil's lake but were very unlucky.

Inez Houchin is on the sick list and doesn't know when she will be able to return to work. Everyone hopes for a speedy recovery.

Carol Ayles won a R o y a l portable typewriter for selling subscriptions to the Gresham Outlook.

Eldon Nielson and family visited with old friends, the Francis Berry family of Tigard, over the weekend.

Durward Litton, Marvin Stolin, Ed Kinonen and **Ralph Lamke** went salmon fishing May first but came home empty handed.

Clarence Noble and **Einar Mickelson** are busy tearing down one of the old Bridal Veil houses, when the weather permits. They plan to build a double garage with the lumber. Clarence says that Einar's new Mercury is too big for his present garage.

Martha Jones and family attended church in Portland Easter Sunday, then took a long drive through Hood River valley and across to the Washington side of the river. Ended the day by having dinner in Hood River.

Merrill and **Dorothy Hartshorn** have the basement dug for their new home and hope to have a carpenter on the job very shortly.

Bertha and **Fay Davis** entertained their grandson, Gordon Timothy, over the weekend, while son Bob and wife enjoyed a trip to the coast.

It is rumored that **Delbert Dunken** went on a fishing trip on opening weekend. Delbert isn't talking so it can be assumed that his luck was terrible.

Connie Meyer has purchased about three quarters of an acre at Corbett on the Benfield road. He hopes to start building a home in the near future.

The list of new car owners include **Einar Mickelson** with a Mercury, **Bob Layton** with an Oldsmobile, and **Dale Emmons** with a Ford.

——— 49 ———

Health and Welfare

The following employees worked the required number of hours in March to become eligible for Health and Welfare coverage and will be covered on the first day of May, 1957. Employees who did not work the required number of hours will become ineligible the same day. Additions: Robert K. Bird, Robert J. Fitzgerald Jr., James L. Hargrove, Richard Jacobson, Rodney Jacobson, Raymond W. Kreman, Charles Long, Patsy R. Smith. Deletions: Max Bissell and John W. Hancock.

——— 49 ———

May Birthdays
Many Happy Returns of the Day!

Leo Hageman	Frank Bowen
Lawrence Peterson	Inez Houchin
Lloyd DeMain	David Rees
Leon Dunlap	Stanley Hills
Homer Walker	Ralph Taylor
Cliff Latourell	Fred Bailey
Marvin Stolin	Anna Bowen
Leslie Polzel	

1957 SAFETY CHART

Month	Tot. Pd. Man Hrs.	Hourly Accidents	Lost Time Freq.	Accident Days Lost	Accident Severity
January	14,288	1	70.0	3	210
February	15,318	0	0	0	0
March	17,182	2	116.4	2	116
FIRST QUARTER	46,788	3	63.9	5	107

BRIDAL VEIL LUMBER & BOX CO.
News Letter

Volume II, Number 10   BRIDAL VEIL, OREGON   JUNE, 1957

Building Costs

Recently a national magazine said the average 1956 house cost 41% more than the 1950 house. Offhand this statement seems to bear out the oft-repeated criticism that residential housing has been priced out of the market. While it is fortunate that in many cases housing connotes lumber, in this case it seems there is an unpopular inference that lumber and lumber products are the culprit, and that the increase in costs are due to unreasonable increases in (the cost of) forest products.

There is no question but that there are many faults to be found in home building industry. A. B. Segur says, for example, "We believe that the next big fundamental fortune will be made in putting up homes. When the builder has succeeded in making this big fortune, it will be discovered that he did so by holding the measurements to within 1/64" instead of to 1½" as is now too many times the case. When he does so, we believe the total cost of building will be reduced around 50%."

The National Association of Home Builders points out that the cost of the typical 1956 house was actually 45% more than the average 1950 house, but that lumber products were not the culprit. In the first place, they are not the same house. The cost of producing the 1950 house in 1956 was only 20.7% more.

The typical 1956 house is 26% larger; it contains 1230 square feet compared to 983 square feet for the 1950 house.

Over half the 1950 houses had neither carport nor garage; only 30% of the 1956 houses had neither.

About 92% of the 1950 houses had only one bathroom; this is true of only 49% of the 1956 houses.

Two-thirds of the 1950 houses had two bedrooms or less; 78% of the 1956 houses had three or more bedrooms.

Official data of the Bureau of Labor

Statistics show the following changes since 1950 in building materials, labor and construction costs:

Construction costs (Boechk Index) up 20.7%.

Building materials price index up 21.4%.

Average hourly earnings in building construction up 43.5%.

Average hourly earnings paid by building contractors rose from $2.00 in June, 1950, to $2.87 in November of 1956.

The Boechk Index, used by the Government, weighs in selected wage rates and materials used in home building, and some items such as local taxes. It does not include land, selling costs, architect's fees and other non-construction costs.

A survey of NAHB in early 1956 indicated that land costs accounted for only 10% of the sales price of the 1950 house, whereas in 1956 land costs accounted for more than 17% of the sales price. A more recent survey by NAHB indicates a further 14% increase in land during 1956.

Here is how the index on prices of individual housing materials went up between June, 1950, and December, 1956:

All building materials	21.4%
Lumber	7.8
Millwork	15.9
Plywood (down)	7.0
Prepared paint	26.6
Hardware (finish)	44.1
Window glass	33.9
Plumbing equipment	29.7
Heating equipment	19.7
Asphalt roofing	15.7
Portland cement	32.5
Concrete products	19.9
Structural clay products	36.1
Gypsum products	24.2

Data on average hourly wages and wholesale prices are from the Bureau of Labor Statistics.

Len Kraft

· Bridal Veil Wins Award!

Thursday, the sixteenth of May, was a day which everyone at Bridal Veil should remember, for on that day, we were presented an award of merit in recognition of our safety record for 1956.

The award was presented to Len Kraft, who accepted in on behalf of the employees and management of the company in recognition of the employees' compiling a significantly outstanding safety record last year. The presentation was made at the two-day Governor's Seventh Annual Industrial Safety Conference, held in Portland, by William A. Callahan, Chairman of the State Industrial Accident Commission, and who presided at the opening session.

As was explained in the February issue of the News Letter, our accident frequency in 1956 was 17.6, which was 5.5 points below the 1955 national industrial average of 21.4, and we ended the year with 243 consecutive days without a time-lost accident.

Representing Bridal Veil at the conference was Marv Jackson, chairman of the plant safety committee.

It was emphasized at the conference that labor, with its tremendous organizing power, can provide a great force for the enactment of a dynamic accident prevention program. It was further emphasized that both labor and management have a great stake in an effective accident prevention program. Stephen J. Hall, vice-president of the Simpson Timber Company of Seattle, pointed out that the management which cannot afford a safety program cannot afford to stay in business. He went on to say that labor should be the most important force in the safety movement, for labor's basic interest is in the health and welfare of the working man.

Governor Robert D. Holmes, principal speaker at the evening banquet, stated that safety consciousness must be learned, and he stressed the importance of safety education. "There is no way we can legislate common sense or prudence," he said.

It is probably an understatement to say that we are off to a good start on our safety program at Bridal Veil. All of us can well be proud of our record of reducing our accident frequency figure from 58.1 in 1955 (two and one-half times the national industrial average), to 17.6 in 1956. The record looks very good (it must to have been recognized by the State Industrial Accident Commission) and it can be made even better. The record shows four time-lost accidents in 1956, but we can be hopeful that this year will show that figure very much reduced. The credit for our present achievement goes to you, the employees, and upon you rests the responsibility for further lowering the incidence of time-lost accidents.

Our congratulations and a hearty well done. Keep up the excellent record!

———— 80 ————

It's Later Than You Think

Everything is farther than it used to be. It's twice as far from my house to the station now, and they've added a hill that I've just noticed. The trains leave sooner, too, but I've given up running for them because they go faster than they used to.

Seems to me they are making staircases steeper than in the old days. The risers are higher and there are more of them because I've noticed it's harder to make two at a time. It's all one can do to make one step at a time.

Have you noticed the small print they are using lately? Newspapers are getting farther away when I hold them I have to squint to make out the news. Now it's ridiculous to suggest that a person of my age needs glasses, but it's the only way I can find out what's going on without someone reading aloud to me, and that isn't much help because everyone seems to speak in such a low voice I can scarcely hear them.

Times sure are changing. The barber doesn't hold a mirror behind me when he's finished so I can see the back of my head. The material in my clothes, I notice, shrinks in certain places, (you know, like around the waist, or in the seat). Shoe laces are so short they are next to impossible to reach.

Even the weather is changing. It's getting colder in winter, and the summers are hotter than in the good old days. Snow is much heavier when I attempt to shovel it, and rain is so much wetter that I have to wear rubbers. I guess the way they build windows now makes drafts more severe.

People are changing, too. For one thing they are younger than they used to be when I was their age. On the

Repeat Performance

Einar Mickelson and Clarence Noble stand triumphant over a house they tore down, the lumber from which they are using to build a double garage. Einar built a garage several years ago, but now with the cars getting longer, it is too small to accommodate his new Mercury. We wonder how long it will be before this one is too small.

———— 80 ————

New Employees

A hearty welcome is extended to Donald E. Flanagn, a new employee.

other hand, people my own age are so much older than I am. I realize that my own generation is approaching middle age (to me, that is roughly between 20 and 101), but there is no reason for my classmates tottering blissfully into senility.

I ran into my roommate the other night and he had changed so much that he didn't recognize me. "You've put on a little weight, Bob," I said. "It's this modern food," Bob replied. "It seems to be more fattening."

I got to thinking about poor Bob this morning while I was shaving. Stopping a moment, I looked at my own reflection in the mirror. They don't use the same kind of glass in mirrors anymore.

State Industrial (

of

Accident P

is please

Employees

BRIDAL VEIL L

AWARI

.....in recognition of outstanding eff

Industrial Accident Commission

Wm J Callahan
CHAIRMAN

T. Morris Dunne

L. O. Arens.

cident Commission

n

ation Division

resent the

Management

ER & BOX CO.

MERIT

achievement in the interest of safety.

Accident Prevention Division

G. S. Kallenbaugh

DIRECTOR

Date— *January 3, 1957*

NEWS LETTER

Published on the 10th of each month by
Bridal Veil Lumber & Box Co.
Bridal Veil, Oregon

Editor . . . . . Don West

Bridal Veil Visitors

John Chase has been a frequent visitor to Bridal Veil in recent years, but this time he appeared in a new role. Formerly sales manager for Dant and Russell, John has formed his own wholesale lumber company, the Chase Lumber and Millwork Company, with offices in the Terminal Sales Building in Portland. We extend to John our best wishes for success in his new venture.

———— 80 ————

A young soldier lost his rifle. Brought before the colonel, he was told he would have to pay for it.

"Suppose I lost a tank, sir," protested the soldier. "Surely I wouldn't have to pay for that.

"Yes," replied the colonel. "Even if it took the rest of your career to do it."

"Gosh," said the soldier. "Now I know why a captain goes down with his ship."

———— 80 ————

A woman will look into a mirror any time except when she's about to pull out of a parking place.

New Equipment

Pictured above is a new Holland Chisel Mortiser, to be used in the manufacture of window sash stock, a recent addition to Bridal Veil's line of products. In offering sash stock, our customers may now take advantage of buying mixed cars of sash, door frames and window frames. This will, to some extent at least, eliminate the necessity of our customers ordering straight carloads of each item and should aid them in their inventory control, which in these times, is very important. Also, the addition of sash will provide us with broader markets, more employee man hours, and more complete usage of our raw material.

———— 80 ————

June Birthdays

Many Happy Returns of the Day!

Rodney Jacobson	Jerald Roberts
Ray Schneringer	Roland Morgan
Durward Litton	Jim Kendricks
Harold Jacobson	Earl Hutchison

———— 80 ————

To a woman the perfect husband is the one who thinks he has a perfect wife.

Fisherman's Luck

Good fishing was responsible for the pleased expressions on the faces of the fishermen pictured above. The steelhead salmon were taken on flies, from the Bogachiel river on the Olympic Peninsula in Washington early last April. We have not questioned any of the fishermen, but we are inclined to believe they caught more fish on the trip than are shown in the picture. Left to right: Gerry Kraft, Earl Jeans, Emmy Abbott, Doug Walwyn and Len Kraft.

Rips and Trims

Danny Hills, son of **Mable and Stanley Hills,** met with an unfortunate accident on May 21st. He slipped and fell as he was jumping over a fence and broke two bones in his left wrist. Danny will have his arm in a cast for some time. Have a speedy recovery, Danny .

Clarence and **Gert Noble** drove to Vancouver, B. C., over Memorial weekend and visited with friends and relatives. While there, they attended the wedding of Gert's grandniece on Saturday, June 1st.

——— 80 ———

A Missourian reports no luck with a lockjaw serum given his wife after an accident. "She still talks," he says.

Health and Welfare

The following employees worked the required number of hours in April to become eligible for Health and Welfare coverage and will be covered on the first day of June, 1957. Employees who did not work the required number of hours will become ineligible the same day. Additions: Lawrence B. Gowens. Deletions: Robert K. Bird, James L. Hargrove, Raymond W. Kreman, Charles Long, and John H. Van Orsow.

——— 80 ———

In the old days a person who missed a stagecoach was resigned to waiting a day or two for the next one. Now, you often see a man annoyed if he misses one section of a revolving door.

Rips and Trims

Marvin Stolin, Ed Kinonen and two of Ed's brothers went up to Tanner Creek. Among the four of them, they caught nine jack salmon.

Ralph Lamke, however, went to the same place and caught five by himself. No specifications, though, as to size. How about it, Ralph?

Ted Van Hee caught some youngsters robbing his crawfish traps recently. Ted, we understand, was pretty unhappy. What we want to know is, what is there in a crawfish trap that would attract youngsters as well as crawfish?

Dean Davis figures on taking his vacation starting June 11. He says he's getting married while he's gone. Is he getting married so he can take a vacation, or is he taking a vacation so he can get married?

Lillie Yerion has been absent from work the last four weeks. It seems she was called for jury duty. She says it was quite an interesting experience.

Chuck Kraft, now out of college, is killing time waiting for his orders to active duty in the navy by helping **Don West** prepare the News Letter.

Mr. and Mrs. Fred Harp spent three days of the Memorial weekend in Yakima, Wash., visiting relatives.

Wesley Adams is the proud father of a 7 lb. 15 oz. baby boy, born the 16th of May. They have named him Earl Lloyd. Congratulations, Wesley.

Mr. and Mrs. John Van Orsow and son **Marvin** spent four days in Eastern Oregon on a fishing trip. We hear they brought home their limit. Their catch ranged from 10 to 22 inches in length. On the way home, they also visited with **Clarence Van Orsow** and family in Madras.

Martha Jones starts her vacation June 10. She and her family will drive to Iowa to visit her mother. They plan to return by way of Montana and Yellowstone Park to visit her sister.

Their daughter **Marilyn,** celebrated her 14th birthday Saturday, June 1st.

The **Ray Hartshorn** family, the **Merrill Hartshorn** family, **Mrs. Charlotte Muse** and family, and **Mr. and Mrs. Jerald Roberts** spent Mother's Day visiting Mrs. H. Hartshorn in Portland at the J. M. Van Orsow home.

Merrill Hartshorn is taking a week of his vacation beginning June 3rd. He did a little fishing over the long Memorial weekend with undisclosed luck, and he expects to be busy around their new home the balance of the time.

At last we have pictorial proof that all the tales we hear aren't tall ones. Walt Norgard is shown with a limit of clams taken in the Long Beach, Wash-

ington, area recently. The thing behind the clams that looks like a pump of some kind is Walt's clam "gun," which Walt says is very effective in aiding in the capture of the critters.

Willis and **Anna Bowen,** with son **Jimmy** and his wife **Peggy,** visited at Burlington Saturday evening, June 1st, with Anna's brother, Mr. Ralph Crowe, and his family.

Mira Nielson has returned to work after being off quite some time with a major operation. We're happy to have you back, Mira.

Kenneth Meyer and family are taking their last year's vacation. He has not yet reported where they are going or what they will do.

Clarence reported that he saw what is said to be the oldest automobile on the North American continent today. It is an 1896 model Woolsey, made in England and shipped around the Horn. According to Clarence's information, it arrived in Vancouver, B. C., five years later, the original purchaser taking delivery there in 1901.

The Nobles returned with a friend, Mrs. Tupper, who will be a visitor for about two weeks.

BRIDAL VEIL LUMBER & BOX CO.

News Letter

Volume III, No. 1　　　BRIDAL VEIL, OREGON　　　JULY, 1957

The Safety Factor

From the volume of literature included in the laws, directives, suggestions and ideas concerning industrial safety which have from time to time come to Bridal Veil, it would seem that the subject of safety is one. which someone, apparently feels is pretty important. The qustion is, who? Oregon has an industrial accident commission, which is concerned with making safe all places of employment in the state, but the heart of the matter really lies much closer to the industry itself.

I know of very few employers who are unwilling to be bothered with the subject. In the first place, the law requires them to be concerned with it, to the point where they must do something about making their plants safer places in which to work. In the second place, it's just plain uneconomical; no employer can afford to maintain an unsafe place of business, simply because, apart from the legal angle, an employer would find himself paying for his lack of safety consciousness in lost time, high turnover, numerous medical bills and lost production. The prohibitive cost of all these factors would put an employer in a poor place to maintain a satisfactory competitive position.

Time was, however, when employers didn't have to be bothered with safety in their plants, because they never had to worry about paying medical bills for injured employees. If the injured worker took the employer into court to try to collect compensation for his injury, the employer could nearly always wiggle out of it by pleading one or more of the old common law defenses. One, and the most often used defense of managements was that the accident was caused by the worker's own negligence. If this wasn't enough, or would not stand up, an employer would of-

fer the "assumption of risk" defense, wherein he admitted the job was unsafe and dangerous, but held that the employee realized this and went ahead and took the job anyway. This was probably the most convincing defense under the old common law. But employers could plead still another defense, which was called the "fellow servant" defense, the employer maintaining that although the job may not have been hazardous nor the injured worker negligent, the one who was at fault was one of the worker's fellow employees (servants) and so it was the latter who was to blame; therefore the suit should be dismissed since the wrong party (the employer) was being sued.

By using one or a combination of these defenses, an employer was generally able to get off the hook, but this practice of employers refusing to claim responsibility for what happened in their plants grew to be so abusive and unjust that a reform in safety and in accident compensation became a must. So, in order to make plants safe and accident compensation just, it was necessary to legislate the burden of accident compensaton and the responsibility for making plants safe onto the employer. A few farsighted employers had already taken steps in this direction, but around the turn of the century, the number of enlightened managements actively safety conscious was disappointingly few.

When this burden was shifted by law onto management, employers set up a great wail of protest, claiming that such a practice would be ruinous and that the added cost of remodeling a plant to make it safe could never be justified from a profit standpoint (ignoring, it seems, the human factor involved). This, of

(Continued on Page 6)

NEWS LETTER

Published on the 10th of each month by
Bridal Veil Lumber & Box Co.
Bridal Veil, Oregon

Editor . . . . . Don West

Seniors Graduate

Thirty-seven seniors of the class of 1957 were graduated from Corbett High School Tuesday night, June 4. Nine of those thirty-seven were sons or daughters of Bridal Veil employees and include:

Donald Bowen, son of Mr. and Mrs. Frank Bowen. Donald won the University of Oregon Dads' Award in recognition of his scholarship record and his qualities of character and leadership. He was recognized as a University of Oregon honors scholar and has received honors at entry to the University.

Mary Emmons, sister of Dale Emmons

Wayne Kilness, son of Mr. and Mrs. Jarvis Kilness. Wayne will be playing in this year's class "B" Shrine football game in Pendleton.

Mary Jo Long, daughter of Mr. and Mrs. Fred Long.

Carol Meyer, daughter of Mr. and Mrs. Kenneth Meyer.

Nancy Mickelson, daughter of Mr. and Mrs. Einar Mickelson.

Jean Murray, daughter of Mr. and Mrs. George Murray.

Mary Lee Taylor Kreman, daughter of Mr. and Mrs. Ralph Taylor. On, June 27, Mary Lee and Mr. Wayne Kreman were married in St. Luke's Episcopal Church in Gresham. They will make their home in Inglewood, California where Wayne will attend Northrup Aeronautical School.

Jack Westlake, son of Mr. and Mrs. Donald Westlake.

We extend our congratulations to all of the Class of 1957 from Corbett High School, and wish you the very best of everything in the years ahead!

———— 11 ————

Metal is used for frying pans and ice cube trays because it is an excellent conductor of heat and cold. Wood is the preferred material for framing windows because it is a very poor conductor of heat and cold.

15th Anniversary

July 14 will mark Dorothy Hartshorn's 15th anniversary at Bridal Veil. Dorothy, who works in the box factory, has never had a lost time accident, nor has she missed a paycheck.

She was born and raised on Larch Mountain and went to grade school and high school at Corbett. Her parents now live in Pleasant Home. Her father, Harry Burkholder, now retired, is a former employee at Bridal Veil.

Dorothy lived in Portland for a year, selling her residence there to Marvin Van Orsow and moving to Bridal Veil. Before coming here, she worked in a restaurant for two years.

She was married to Merrill Hartshorn on June 26, 1944 in Vancouver Washington. They have two children, Sharon, 12, and Rebecca, 22 months. Currently they are living in Bridal Veil, but they are building a home on a five-acre spread they own east of Corbett near Larch Mountain. It is going to be a three bedroom place with full basement. Carpenters have put up the frame of the house and aside from the wiring and plumbing, Merrill will finish the job himself.

When she has time for hobbies, she enjoys sewing, knitting, crocheting and fancy needlework. She is also an ardent baseball and basketball fan, and she enjoys fishing and camping.

Bridal Veil Visitors

Clifford R. Lafferty   Charley Bamford   Doug Walwyn

Lafferty Gets Bid

Pictured above (left) is Mr. Clifford R. Lafferty, district supervisor of the accident prevention division of the state Industrial Accident Commission. Mr. Lafferty was in Bridal Veil on June 6th at the invitation of the safety committee to discuss the injury record of Bridal Veil as compared with other plants in the state in the same industrial classification. The nature and location of such accidents was discussed. Mr. Lafferty pointed out that in Bridal Veil's industrial classification, injuries to the fingers are the greatest single kind of accidents, and together with injuries to hands and wrists, account for one-third of all lost-time accidents. Injuries to eyes, he added, were the next highest group.

Mr. Lafferty and the safety committee discussed means of accident prevention, especially for eye protection and the prevention and care of injuries resulting from punctures by splinters and slivers.

The accident prevention division is responsible for the enforcement of the safety laws and codes of Oregon. It also seeks to educate the public to become more safety conscious, and to appreciate its necessity and realize the benefits accruing from a conscientious concern for safety in all places of employment.

Hammes, Dewey Seek to Sell

On June 12th, Mr. F. E. Hammes, Vice-President of the Edward Hines Lunmber Co. of Chicago, and Jay Dewey of the Portland office of that company, came by to investigate the possibilities of selling lumber to Bridal Veil from Hines, Oregon.

Howard Picks Up Orders

Also on June 12, Mr. Charles W. Howard of the Tallman Machinery Co., Inc., of Seattle was in Bridal Veil to pick up two orders for new machinery. One order was on the Ames Manufacturing Co. of Tacoma for two 5,000 lb. capacity scissor lifts (at $1050 each), to be installed at the band rips. They will be used at the head of the band rips to keep loads at table height. The other order was on the Mattison Machine Works of Rockford, Illinois, for a grooving unit (at a cost of $1195) for the Mattison No. 274 moulder with which to score sash for weather stripping.

Bamford to Design Machinery

A Bridal Veil visitor on June 18th was Charley Bamford (center) of Bamford Special Machinery, Inc., of Portland. Charley has designed and built specialty machinery for a number of well-known organizations as Crown-Zellerbach (two lathes), Kraft Foods (two color printers) and International Wood Products of Cathlamet, Wn. (a predecessor of Bridal Veil). He is currently building machinery for U.S. Plywood Corp's. new plant in Roseburg. Charley's field is in the woodworking industry and he has de-

(Continued on Page 6)

The first of the sash stock is shown here coming thru the Greenley No. 542 tennoner. Cliff Latourell is off-bearing and preparing to add the stock to a load.

In this shot w
man whose experi
have facilitated th
initial sash run. H
Mattison moulder.

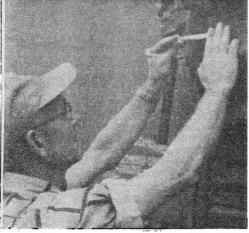

Everything's finished now; the first car containing sash is loaded and ready to go. Willie Bowen, shipping clerk, is seen here attaching the seal on the car. Soon it will be on its way to Kansas City.

Here is the first run of sash stock being hopper-fed into the moulder by Eugene "Shorty" Potter.

A Milesto

First Sash Order Here

Another milestone has be
we received our first order f
of Kansas City, Missouri.
course of the production of
with our camera looking fo
story is the result.

This shot shows Norma
low chisel mortiser. Just to
small chip flying away. In
being used to bore away th

e, our key set-up
tention to detail
production of this
his set-up on the

Ted Van Hee, partially obscured at right, is seen in this view operating the Powermatic No. 41 chain mortiser, mortising bottom rails of the sash stock.

Bridal Veil

ation of New Product

r Bridal Veil. On May 6th,
Martin Material Company
ly shipped, and during the
e roamed around the plant
ut it. The following picture

Thelma Rowe is shown here tailing the stock off the moulder.

iting the Powermatic hol-
chisel bit, one can see a
hollow chisel mortiser is

In this shot we see Homer Walker at the dip tank treating the sash with preservative to ensure longer effective usage. From the dip tank, the sash will go to the car waiting at left over that set of rollers at the left side of the picture.

Bridal Veil Visitors

(Continued from Page 3)

signed and built machinery for twenty-six wood working plants of all kinds.

As far as Bridal Veil is concerned, Charley's job will be to act upon the suggestions of George Esch (see News Letter, February, 1957) to design and create machinery for the plant which will bring a saving of money to the company in general as well as savings in time necessary for production and effort on the part of those working at the machines. Charley emphasised that no machine he would design for Bridal Veil would cause anyone to be thrown out of work; but should result in expanded production and greater employment.

The project, Charley added, will not bear fruit in the form of new machines around the plant overnight. The planning stage will necessarily be a long one, but the first machine he hopes to have in the plant will be a feeder-equalizer for the band line in the box factory.

Walwyn Checks Liability

In Bridal Veil on June 20th was Doug Walwyn, (right) Vice-President and Insurance counsellor of Smith & Crakes of Eugene. Doug is well known at Bridal Veil as he periodically runs an inspection of the reservoir to check on its adequacy (some call it fishing). This time, his visit was for the purpose of checking on the state of our liability coverage and to review existing hazards (the insurance boys call it exposure) arising out of the business and the management of dwellings in Bridal Veil. He also wanted to find out if any new hazards had cropped up recently for

course, proved to be untrue, to the purpose of perparing an annual statement regarding such hazards and their liability coverage.

Doug is in his ninth year as an insurance counsellor for Bridal Veil.

——— 11 ———

The Safety Factor

(Continued from Page 1)

management's surprise and labor's great benefit.

The evolution of plant safety and of accident compensation programs, however, was only one of the great forward strides in American industry, but it was, perhaps, one of the most important. Making plants safe has paid off in ten ways that I know of, and also in a great many more:

1. Fewer deaths
2. Fewer injuries
3. Less grief and suffering
4. Less expense
5. Less worry
6. Less property damage
7. Less lost time
9. More peace of mind
10. More useful years.

Legislation alone cannot do the job, however. Nor are machine guards and safety clothes the complete solution. Safety still remains, as it always has, the concern and responsibility of every man and woman employed in industry everywhere. Without the co-operation and active participation of every employee, the most ambitious and praiseworthy safety program can accomplish little. With this co-operation and support, however, there is no plant, no job which cannot be made abundantly safer and thus more productive, and perhaps more pleasant.

Chuck Kraft

1957 SAFETY CHART

Month	Tot. Hourly Pd. Man Hrs.	Lost Time Accidents	Accident Freq.	Days Lost	Accident Severity
January	14,288	1	70.0	3	210
February	15,318	0	0	0	0
March	17,182	2	116.4	2	116
FIRST QUARTER	46,788	3	63.9	5	107
April	17,055	0	0	0	0
May	18,924	0	0	0	0
TOTAL	82,767	3	36.2	5	60

My Impressions

After hearing complaints about business being slow from retail dealers, brokers and mill men, I was surprised at the optimistic attitude prevailing among the jobbers in the midwest and eastern sections of the country. Of the several jobbers I visited, they all said that business is near or slightly ahead of last year. They were speaking of total dollar volume, not of millwork alone, as most of them handle many different types of inventory.

One detrimental factor this year has been the weather. Of course people blame everything on the weather, thereby avoiding rebuttal. But though I didn't actually encounter any rain on my trip, nearly every place where there was a low spot, there was water. Several jobbers stated that they couldn't take their trucks off the pavement for fear of getting stuck, which some of them did, so they are unable to make deliveries. I got the impression that order files were in pretty good shape, and as soon as the ground dries out, business should pick up considerably.

Apparently no one seems to be concerned with what some people call a tight money market. At least I heard no complaints along that line. Naturally, the people or companies that have excess funds to invest are looking for short term investments which yield a high return, but even so, there seem to be mortgage funds available.

Another factor which seems to be pretty universal is that the houses that are being built are larger than they were in past years and, that of course, means they cost more. That leads to more complications, including a larger down payment and larger monthly payments. The people who invest in mortgages may be shying away from the small, two bedroom homes in fear that they might become a drug on the market, if the current trend toward bigger houses continues. So even though you solve a problem or eliminate a bottleneck in one place, by doing so you create another to take its place.

Everyone seems to be agreed that consumers are becoming more particular, whether the purchase is a five dollar one or a twenty thousand dollar one. There are lots of people shopping for homes but they are taking all the time they need, instead of buying blind as was the case in the few years following the war. Prefabricators say that standard, ready built homes are almost a thing of the past, so when they get an order for one, it is quite an occasion. So in a sense, the prefab people are building custom houses, making changes in the original plan to suit the customer.

Whenever business falls off, competition becomes keener (I'd lke to know who created that problem!) To stimulate customer interest, suppliers are resorting to all sorts of gimmicks, devises and services. In order to keep from going over the edge, you have to follow suit. I believe that the addition of sash stock to our line of products will help us immensely. It will enable our customers to order more mixed cars, thereby holding down their inventories. It will also afford us the opportunity of obtaining new customers, and may increase our volume.

Also, in connection with keener competition, is the fact that customers, even the good ones like we have, demand, and rightly so, the finest in quality and workmanship. So we must always remember that we are not indispensable. Our very jobs depend on our customers.

Don West

———— 11 ————

Health and Welfare

All employees who worked the required number of hours in May will become eligible for health and welfare coverage and will be covered on the first day of July, 1957. Additions: Lewis E. Apitz, Edward J. Arenz, Alfred E. Barnes, Donald E. Flanagin, Robert A. Haley, Wesley L. Horner, Marion E. Jones, James J. Lvingston and Merlin O. Schnoor. Employees who did not work the required number of hours will become ineligible on the same day. Deletions: Richard A. Caffrey, Inez M. Houchin, Wilbur O. Houchin, Richard Jacobson, Lillie P. Yerion.

———— 11 ————

Our country needs more of every kind of building there is—homes, churches, penitentiaries. Just name them; we need them.

Rips and Trims

Norman Van Buskirk is the proud papa of a baby girl, Kathy Rose Van Buskirk, born at 1:52 on the morning of June 6 at Portland Sanatarium. She weighed in at 8 pounds 6½ ounces.

We were sorry to learn of the death of James Eversull in a fire at his Coopey Falls home on the 15th of June. He was employed as a car loader. He is survived by a brother in Seattle and his father in Gernsey, Wyoming. The body was returned to Wheatland, Wyoming for burial.

Patsy Smith, payroll clerk since March, quit on June 5th. We are all sorry to see her leave. Eleanor Taylor came in to pinch-hit for a few days until the office could get adjusted to one less person on the staff.

Mira Neilson was ordered by her doctor to stay home in bed for a week. Mira has been back to work only a short time after a major throat operation, and the doctor's orders are to prevent possible pheumonia. We hope to see you back on the job again soon, Mira.

Connie Meyer says he took a short vacation trip to the beach, but spent most of the time clearing land recently purchased as a homesite. Connie says he is glad to be back to work again, in order to rest up.

Master Sergeant Bob Lollar and wife Gwen were recent visitors of the Durward Littons. Gwen is Durward's sister. Most of us remember Bob as a former employee at Bridal Veil shortly after World War II. They have been enjoying an 18-day furlough from Camp Mathews, California, near San Diego. They returned there Monday, June 24th.

Eldon Nielson and family will be vacationing July 1st. They intend to drive back to Oklahoma to visit relatives. Young Jackie will accompany them on the trip.

Bert and Fay Davis report that they finished getting in their new lawn recently, also that they will start their vacation July 8th.

Merrill and Dorothy Hartshorn will be taking a week's vacation starting July 1st. Merrill says that he will probably be working on their new home. He says they have all the framing and sheathing on.

Willis and Anna Bowen are leaving July 1st for a California vacation.

They will stop at Yreka, California, to visit the Alton Taylor family, then on to San Diego to see son Kenny and family. On the way back they will stop over in Los Angeles to visit daughter Betty and family.

Fred Crouser is spending his two weeks vacation at home working on his place in Latourell Falls.

Tech. Sergeant Charles Roberts and family from Cheyenne have been spending the last two weeks visiting relatives around the Portland and Gresham area. Charles used to be an employee at Bridal Veil before the war years.

Charles and Gerald Roberts and Jackie Ball spent two days on the Deschutes river and Timothy Lake fishing. They report poor results. Better luck next time.

John Williams has a new car ordered. If it's the color he wanted, he should have it by now. If not, he won't be able to get it until the end of July. It is a white Plymouth with blue trim.

Laurel Macy from Springfield spent Fathers' Day with her folks, Mr and Mrs. Howard Hunt of Corbett.

Mr. and Mrs. Ed L. Wendler during June had their son, Ed H. Wendler and his family and Mr. and Mrs. Brandenberg from Denver as visitors. While they were here they spent some time at the coast. They also went steelhead fishing and Ed H., Jr. (age eight years), hooked four of them while the rest came back with none.

House number five in Bridal Veil is available for renting. Anyone who is interested may contact Ade Jones for particulars.

——— 11 ———

July Birthdays

Many Happy Returns of the Day !

Harold Vogel	Paul Detrick
Wesley Horner	T. Van Hee, Sr.
James Livingston	Bob Layton
Lillie Yerion	Jim Cowling
Willie Bowen	Orien Pitts
Lester Anderson	

——— 11 ———

Throughout our nation, 9 million families move every year. To the extent that they move to previously undeveloped areas, it means a need for new houses.

BRIDAL VEIL LUMBER & BOX CO.

News Letter

Volume III., No. 2   BRIDAL VEIL, OREGON   AUGUST, 1957

Halfway

I was very much interested in a report made by Oregon's four referees in bankruptcy covering the fiscal year ended June 30, 1957. It appears that bankruptcies in the State of Oregon reached an all time high of 2,170 cases last year—an increase of 343 cases over the previous year. The report goes on to forecast an even greater number of bankruptcies during the present year if the current trend continues.

The greatest single factor in the steady flow of bankruptcy petitions, according to the four referees in bankruptcy, is the decline of the lumber business, upon which a great number of other businesses depend.

Without getting into the "whys and wherefors" too deeply, it is safe to say that a bankruptcy occurs when a company cannot manufature its product at a price which the customers are willing to pay. In periods of low business volume and falling prices, it is always the weaker and less efficient companies that are shaken out first.

Now the word is out from the sundry reporting services to which we subscribe that from all indications the bottom has been reached in the slump in the housing business. None of the services forcast anything like a rapid pick-up, but rather a gradual and steady increase over the next few years. The remedies adopted by the Congress and other governmental agencies are not expected to cause a rapid about face in housing starts. The point is, however, that the bottom has been reached, and from now on out, for the foreseeable future, business should slowly improve.

What does all this mean so far as we at Bridal Veil are concerned? It means that while our industry has gone through the wringer, the product of our efforts has been measured in the market place, and has passed the test. It means that our continuing efforts to improve our equipment and methods to further better our competitive position are paying off and that the broadening of our product line will result in expanding markets and new opportunities to be of service to our trade.

With the first half of 1957 now in the record books it seems to me that we can face the future with renewed confidence based on the firm foundation of the marketability of our past performance. We can all take a measure of personal pride in our past accomplishments, and we can all have a hand in the future success of our venture.

Len Kraft

———— 42 ————

Why the Customer Is Our Real Boss

There's certainly nothing new about the fact that it's the customer—the customer who buys the products we make—who is our real boss!

Competition is keener today that it has been for many years and it is steadily getting keener!

That's what makes the customer so important to every one of us. The more we are able to please our customers with our products, the more production we are going to have.

When we decide to buy an article, we want the kind of quality built into it that will give us good service. We want to have delivery when we need it—and we are certainly interested in the price we have to pay.

That's what we want when we are customers—and that's exactly what our customers want from us.

Every one of us in the entire company—whatever our individual jobs may be—plays a part in building the product to the customer's satisfaction.

NEWS LETTER

Published on the 10th of each month by
Bridal Veil Lumber & Box Co.
Bridal Veil, Oregon

Editor . . . . . Don West

Tragedy at Coopey Falls

Graphically protrayed in the photograph above is the fire at Coopey Falls on July 15th which took the life of Jimmy Eversull and destroyed the homes of Jimmy and of Hiram Layton. The picture, taken by Eldon Nielson, was received too late for inclusion in the July News Letter.

———— 42 ————

DEVELOPING THE SAFETY HABIT

Do every single part of every job the safe way. Not just once —not just when there's time—but every time—all the time.

The safety habit won't be built in an hour or a day. But, like increasing the number of threads in making a rope, there will come a time—sooner than you think—when your safety habit will be so strong that it will be almost second nature for you to do every job the safe way.

———— 42 ————

"What is life?" Mr. Marconi once asked. Well, about eleven years in this country, our parole commissions being what they are.

20th Anniversary

August 30 will mark the twentieth anniversary at Bridal Veil for Fred Crouser, cutter. Fred was born and raised in Summeville, Oregon, which is somewhere north of La Grande on the way to Wallowa Lake. He received his education in Imbler, 12 miles north of La Grande. His parents were Kentuckians, but they mover to Oregon in 1908, two years before Fred was born, returned to Kentucky and then came back to stay. He was one of eight children, neither the youngest nor the oldest. A brother is now living in Gresham and a sister in Portland.

Fred worked a while for the old Timber Company in Bridal Veil, a year or two before it ceased operations, then he went to Toledo to work for the C. D. Johnson Lumber Company before returning to Bridal Veil in 1937. Before becoming a cutter, about six years ago, Fred used to unload cars and work on the green chain.

Since 1938, he has lived in Latourell Falls, where he is presently in the process of building a house. That and gardening, Fred explained, are his chief hobbies.

In 1935, Fred and the former Evelyn Robbs, also of Summerville, were married in Stevenson, Washington. They have two sons, Lyn, a senior at Linfield College, and Bruce, a sophomore at Corbett high school.

20th Anniversary

August 19th will be anniversary number 20 for Frank Bowen, jitney driver. Prior to becoming jitney driver

Frank worked in the lumber department and in the old boiler room which was torn down a few years ago. Frank has never had a lost-time accident nor has he ever missed a paycheck.

He was born in Vancouver, Washington in 1908. After five years there, the family moved to Camas. He received his education in Camas and Vernonia. Before moving to Bridal Veil, Frank lived two years in Corbett, and returned there in 1946, where he has lived since.

Frank and the former Evelyn Hines of Hillsboro were married in Vancouver, Washington, on October 9, 1937. They have three children: Donald, 18, who will enroll in the University of Oregon in the fall, Richard, 16, a student at Corbett High School, and Dorothy, 11, who is in Corbett Grade School.

They live some two miles east of Corbett, where they own their own home on 1 1/3 acres of ground where Frank does some vegetable gardening and berry growing.

Prior to working at Bridal Veil, Frank worked for four years as a commercial fisherman. He has also been in dairying and he has worked

Seniority List

Following is a list of those employees still here who were on the seniority list for October, 1939, the earliest list we have a record of, and their positions on the list, then and now.

Oct. 1939	July 1957	
4	1	Noah Atchley
13		A. D. Jones
16	2	Ward Dull
20		Clyde Hambrick
29	3	Clarence Noble
24	4	Ralph McCredie
40	5	Fay Davis
42	6	Marvin Jackson
52	7	Walter Stolin
67	8	Frank Bowen
71	9	Fred Crouser
86	10	Verl Bird
80	11	Ralph Taylor
84		Willis Bowen
95	12	Ted Hanson
96	13	Joseph M. Van Orsow
101		Jim Cowling
105	14	Delbert Dunken
129		K. D. Burkholder

As the seniority list applies only to hourly paid employees, those now paid monthly do not appear in the 1957 listings.

---

for the Ridge Lumber Company south of Corbett.

The event in Frank's life which he recalls most vividly was the time his cousin drove a car over him; we assume it was all accidental. According to Frank, the front bumper of the car caught on his pants and whipped him under the car, front and rear wheels passing over his legs. Somehow, he came away only slightly bruised, but somewhat shaken up, no doubt, by the experience.

Frank has a brother, Alfred, and a sister, Pearl living in Portland, and brother Willie, whose anniversary appears in this month's issue, is shipping clerk at Bridal Veil.

Frank's chief hobby is gardening, which keeps him pretty busy around the home. He is a member of the Corbett grange and belongs to the Multnomah County Sheriff's Reserve. He and Evelyn are members of the Corbett Christian Church.

——— 42 ———

Every two years we gain a population equal to all metropolitan Chicago including its suburbs.

Bridal Veil Visitors

John Couch, above, Oregon Moulding & Lumber Co., spent the better part of a day trying to convince us why one type of bundling was better than another. We can't remember whether he succeeded or not but come to think of it, we'll probably change to his method anyway.

Mr. J. O. Burgess, above, representative for the Hy-Test Safety Shoe Co. was in Bridal Veil, July 18th, in con-nection with our safety program. We are going to stock safety shoes in the office for sale to employees, at our cost. Purchases may be made for cash or on payroll deductions. Interested persons should see Mel Mallinson, who is handling the program.

Pictured above is Jim Roberts of Knapp Lumber Sales. Jim was out to see us in connection with a large order for boxes which we successfully

——— 42 ———

WHY OUR REPUTATION IS IMPORTANT

Our company's reputation — what outsiders think of us—is extremely important to all of us.

The "outsiders" may be customers, possible customers for the future, friends or neighbors, or any other residents of our community.

How they feel about our company can have a definite effect on the success of our business and, in turn, on the jobs of all of us.

——— 42 ———

Have you ever pondered over the significance of the little numbers used to separate News Letter stories, you know, the things that look like:

——— 42 ———

It's really quite simple. They are reminders of the number of lost-time accident-free days we have had as of the first of the current month.

Bridal Veil Visitors

Very welcome visitors in the month of July included Mr. Leonard Martin, right, of Martin Material Co., Kansas City; Mr. Neal Clark, center, of Kansas City; and Mr. Clarence Jewett of Portland, Oregon. Martin Material Co., as you will recall, was our first sash customer.

———— 42 ————

Summer Replacements

Lyn Crouser, who has one more year at Linfield College, is back for his fourth summer at Bridal Veil. He is presently working on the cut-off line.

Tom Cowling, a sophomore at the University of Oregon, and Jim Yerion, a sophomore at Oregon College of Education, are back for their third summer. Both are on the cutter line.

Gerry Kraft, back for his second summer, is working as a clerk in the office. He will be a senior at Lincoln High School in Portland.

———— 42 ————

We are forming new non-farm households at a rate of about 800,000 a year.

Health and Welfare

All employees who worked the required number of hours in June will become eligible for health and welfare coverage and will be covered on the first day of August, 1957. Additions: Tom Cowling, Lynfred Crouser, Jim Yerion, Lillie P. Yerion, Charles E. Kraft, and Gerald Kraft. Employees who did not work the required number of hours will become ineligible on the same day. Deletions: Lewis Apitz, Edward Arenz, Robert Haley, Wesley Horner, Marion E. Jones. Merlin Schnoor, and Patsy R. Smith.

———— 42 ————

Flower Fund

Following is a report on the employees' flower fund since last reported in the News Letter of December, 1956:

Balance brought forward	...........$ 1.77
Flowers—V. Bird (Dad)	......$7.50
Phone call for same	.... .30
Collections (12-11-56)	.......................32.55
Collections (12-11-56)	.... 7.50
Collections (12-14-56)	.... .50
Flowers—D. West (Dad)	.... 7.50
Phone call for same	.... .45
Flowers—Lampke (Dad)	.... 7.50
Phone call for same	.... .30
Flowers—J. Eversull	.... 7.50
Phone and telegram	.... 1.25
Total collections	.... 42.32
Paid out	.....................................32.30
Balance on hand (6-21-57)	...........$10.02

We are sorry if anyone has been missed.

Jim Cowling

———— 42 ————

Our country's population is increasing at the rate of 2,800.000 persons annually.

1957 SAFETY CHART

Month	Tot. Hourly Pd. Man Hrs.	Lost Time Accidents	Accident Freq.	Days Lost	Accident Severity
January	14,288	1	70.0	3	210
February	15,318	0	0	0	0
March	17,182	2	116.4	2	116
FIRST QUARTER	46,788	3	63.9	5	107
April	17,055	0	0	0	0
May	18,924	0	0	0	0
June	16,317	1	61.3	4	245
SECOND QUARTER	52,296	1	19.1	4	76
TOTAL	99,084	4	40.4	9	91

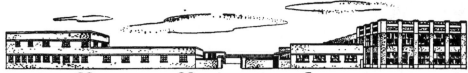

MARTIN MATERIAL COMPANY
ASBESTOS AND ASPHALT ROOFING ★ CELOTEX PRODUCTS

5301 East Ninth Street
KANSAS CITY, MISSOURI
Telephone HU. 3-9500-1-2-3

Fourth and Messanie
ST. JOSEPH, MISSOURI
TELEPHONE 3-1449

July 25, 1957

Bridal Veil Lbr. & Box Co.
Bridal Veil, Oregon

     Att: Mr. Don West

Dear Don:

With reference to our Order 5545, your M-100

This order covers our first car of sash from Bridal
Veil, and we know that you will be interested in our
reaction.

In view of the many sash problems we have experienced
in the past, we inspected this car with extreme
thoroughness and are happy to report that we found
both the quality of material and machining of sash to
be excellent.

Once again you have demonstrated to us the thoroughness you employ in producing millwork.

       Yours, truly,

       Logan Mason
       MARTIN MATERIAL COMPANY

LM:ms

RECEIVED
JUL 29 1957
BRIDAL VEIL LBR. & BOX CO.
BRIDAL VEIL, OREGON

20th Anniversary

August 19th will see Willie Bowen's twentieth anniversary at Bridal Veil. Willie is the shipping clerk and since 1945 he has occupied that little cubby hole at the east end of the moulding department.

Not the least bit bashful about such things, Willie told us he was born July 9th, 1902, in Durand, Wisconsin. At the tender age of 5, he moved west to Vancouver, Washington. He claims he still remembers seeing Indian wigwams and cattle skulls from the train as he crossed the plains.

He received his education in such places as Vancouver, Madras, McMinnville and Corbett, where he finished school. He lived in Lower Corbett until the war came along when he moved to Bridal Veil where he has lived ever since.

He worked as a commercial fisherman at Lower Corbett from 1918 to 1934. Then he worked three years at the Ridge Lumber Company, in the Gordon Creek area south of Corbett before coming to Bridal Veil. He recalls a story of his commercial fishing days, that had to do with that terrible winter of 1919 (you will remember it, no doubt). He says that in December of that year the temperature got down to 12 below and stayed there for three days, long enough to freeze the river solid enough to drive a team of horses from one side

to the other. After a terrific storm which accompanied the freeze, trains were stalled at Bridal Veil and before the thaw came, some time later, passangers and crew has just about cleaned the store out of rations. It was the kind of storm that lands suddenly and then just as suddenly, moves on. Willie called it a "quick storm", but at 12 below, even a quick storm can seem to last a pretty long time.

On May 25th, 1924, Willie and the former Anna Crowe were married in Sandy. Mrs. Bowen was originally from Roseburg. They have four children: Betty, now in Los Angeles, Willie Jr., who works for the Multnomah County road department and lives in Portland, Kenneth who works for Convair in San Diego, and Jimmy, who now lives in Springdale and is custodian of the national guard armory in Gresham. Willie Jr., Kenneth and Jimmy are former Bridal Veil employees. The Bowens have eight grandchildren.

Willie has two sisters, one living in Portland and the other in Toledo, Oregon, and two brothers, Alfred, who lives in Portland and Frank, jitney driver, who came to work at Bridal Veil with Willie on the same day twenty years ago.

Although he has lived in Bridal Veil since the start of the war, Willie still owns the place where he lived in Lower Corbett. He says that he wouldn't want to go back to it to live though, as it is too hard to get in and out in the winter.

His chief hobby is hunting. When asked about fishing (which usually seems to accompanying hunting), he said that sixteen years of commercial fishing had pretty well taken the glamour out of fishing of any kind.

Before becoming shipping clerk, Willie had worked everywhere in the plant except the box factory and with the maintenance gang. As near as he can remember, he has never had a lost-time accident nor has he ever missed a paycheck. That is a pretty enviable record for twenty years of work.

———— 42 ————

"For 20 years," mused the man at the bar, "my wife and I were ecstatically happy."

"Then what happened?" asked the bartender.

"We met."

Rips and Trims

Eugene Potter has bought a home in Wood Village and expects to move within a month or six weeks.

Stanley Hills and family plan to spend their vacation in California visiting relatives and attending the Arabian Horse Show at the Cow Palace in San Francisco.

Don Westlake is back at work after a long seige of back trouble.

David DeMain outfished his dad the other day. He caught two steelhead and the only assistance David required was a firm arm around his waist while bringing them in.

Ray Schneringer has added a 14' boat to his fishing equipment. Now if he can keep his son-in-law from knocking the fish off his hook, he should bring home plenty of fish.

Pete Ellis is planning his annual vacation trip to Wisconsin to visit relatives.

Mary Woodard is afoot while her car is being repaired; the result of an accident. No damage to Mary and very little to the car.

Ralph Taylor took one week of his vacation the latter part of July. Most of the time was spent working around his home

Delbert Dunken spent a pleasant week on his vacation entertaining his sister and brother-in-law, Mr. and Mrs. Walter Gibson of Watsonville, Calif.

Leon Dunlap and wife attended the S.D.A. camp meeting at Gladstone, the weekend of August 3 and 4.

Martha Jones and f a m i l y, **Eldon Nielson** and family and the **L a r r y Smazal** family attended the union picnic at Oaks Park.

Bert and **Fay Davis** enjoyed a vacation trip to Reno and Virginia City. Bert says they took quite a few pictures with their two new cameras.

Charlie Gaymon and family are planning a trip to Tacoma this coming weekend to visit friends.

A quick trip to Missouri during a recent heat wave made **Ralph Lamke** happy to be back in Oregon's cool climate.

Martha Jones and family have moved from their old residence on Moffet Creek, near Bonneville, to Cascade Locks.

Walt and **Lillian Norgard** vacationed at Sun Lake State Park in Eastern Washington. Walt's 'tan' proves the park lives up to its name. Since their return Lillian has been busy packing, preparatory to their move to an apartment in Portland.

Fred Harp is planning on visiting Lassen Volcano State Park, Reno, Yosemite Park, and the Redwood forest on his vacation. He will be coming home via highway 101.

Jerry and **Vera Nell Roberts** spent their vacation in Reno, Virginia City, Carson City, Sacremento and San Francisco. They also visited Jim Hartshorn in Port Orford, Oregon. Jim is a former employee of Bridal Veil. **Jerry** a n d **Vera Nell** also spent a couple of days fishing in eastern Oregon without success.

Mr. and Mrs. Marv Van Orsow are going to spend a few days on the Washington coast, then are going to eastern Oregon for a few days of fishing.

Mr. and Mrs. Marvin Van Orsow and daughter Linda, and Mrs. H. Hartshorn went to Battleground, Washington to pick up son Donald, who spent four days at summer camp.

Bob Fitzgerald reported the theft of two rifles and some fishing gear from his home recently.

––––––– 42 –––––––

August Birthdays

Many Happy Returns of the Day!

Ralph Ellis	Theophille Van Hee, Jr.
Archie Davies	Robert Fitzgerald
Lester Howell	Vera Nell Roberts
Ann Keller	Theodore Van Hee
Jarvis Kilness	Dean Burkholder
Ralph Lamke	Harry Densmore
Fred Long	Donald Westlake

––––––– 42 –––––––

President Eisenhower favors golf as a playing sport and baseball as a game to watch. One day at Washington's Burning Tree Country Club, he lined a 225 yard drive down the middle of the fairway, then watched his partner top a little bunt like dribbler off the tee. "Go on," Ike shouted, "run it out."

––––––– 42 –––––––

More than one fourth of the softwood lumber output of t h e United States, about 46 per cent of all plywood and about 25 per cent of all hardboard produced in the nation comes from Oregon.

BRIDAL VEIL LUMBER & BOX CO.
News Letter

Volume III, No. 3   BRIDAL VEIL, OREGON   AUGUST, 1957

How to Beat the Car Salesman

When you see a young couple zip past you in a shiny new car, do you ever stop to wonder what kind of a home they live in? They are probably paying high rent on a rundown house, plus high payments on an automobile whose value will soon be virtually nil because of depreciation.

Don't blame the young people. Blame the lumber industry for not going after the consumer dollar as tenaciously as the automobile industry has.

Take a young couple who put $1,000.00 down on a beautiful new car three years ago. What do they have today? Nothing. They are still paying high rent on a rundown house, which has depreciated to practically nothing in value — and what are they thinking about today? Not the mistake they made. They are eagerly scanning through the new car brochures, wondering what model they are going to get this year.

Better merchandising by lumber could have sold the young couple an $18,000 house, instead of an automobile. They could have kept their 1954 car and had a brand new home to show off. And they would have been money ahead. Following is a comparison showing the savings.

Price of 1957 model	$3,000.00
Trade-in value of 1954 model	1,000.00

Additional cost (usually borrowed)	2,000.00

And between now and 1960 his cost will be:

Interest on car loan	300.00
Insurance and licenses	330.00
Repairs	225.00
Depreciation (per above)	2,000.00

Total	$2,855.00
Less tax savings on interest if in 25% bracket	75.00

Bringing the total three year expense of new car to	2,780.00
Plus rent for three years	3,600.00

Total expense for 1957 car and rent for three years	$6,380.00

But now let us show what the other and best choice is. They buy a new house and hang onto the old car for another three years, and between now and 1960 the cost will be:

*Expense on 1954 model (1957 to 1960)	$ 210.00
Insurance and licenses	200.00
Depreciation	625.00

Total three year expense	$1,035.00
Down payment on $18,000 house	2,000.00
Interest at 5½% for three years on balance	2,640.00
Property taxes	600.00
Insurance on house	100.00

Total	$6,375.00
Less tax savings on interest and taxes	810.00

Total net cost for 1954 car and new $18,000 home including $2,000 down payment	$5,565.00

To summarize:

If he buys a 1957 car and rents the house, his expense for three years is $6,380.00. If he keeps his 1954 car and buys an $18,000 home, his net expense for three years is $5,565.00

Less down payment $2,000.00	$3,565.00
He saves	$2,815.00

The $2,815.00 saved will pay back the $2,000 down payment with $815.00 left over.

*Including gas, oil, lubrication and tires.

Russ Fryberg,
Sales Manager of Timberlane
Lumber Co., Eugene, Oregon.

NEWS LETTER

Published on the 10th of each month by
Bridal Veil Lumber & Box Co.
Bridal Veil, Oregon

Editor . . . . . Don West

Welcome Back

After a three year stay in Seattle,
Fred Damerell, knife grinder and
set-up man in the moulding depart-

ment, has returned to Bridal Veil.
Fred said his wife likes it so well
here in the Gorge they decided to return. Their daughter-in-law is with
them while their son, Ray is finishing
his hitch in the Air Force. He is presently stationed in France.

Fred and his family are living at
Coopey Falls. Welcome back, Fred.

———— 16 ————

New Employees

A hearty welcome is extended to the
following new employees:

Cyril Lang	Marvin Dhone
Ronald Catlin	Junior McMorran
Bill North, Jr.	Arthur Johnson
Delbert Cloe	Bill Moon
Alfred Barnes	Jack Westlake
Kenneth Catlin	Arthur Howell
David Gullickson	John Matson
Jack Dempsey	

15th Anniversary

September 30th will be Mrs. Willis
(Anna) Bowen's fifteenth anniversary
at Bridal Veil, just slightly more than

a month after her husband's twentieth anniversary. Anna works as a
circle resaw feeder in the box factory.

Anna was born at Roseburg, Oregon. Her father was a farmer and they
lived on the same farm where her
father was born. They remained in
Roseburg until Anna was eleven years
old, then the family moved to Portland. From Portland, Anna's family
moved to Corbett and Anna also lived
in Sandy. She went to school in Roseburg, Portland, Corbett, and Sandy.
She worked in a grocery store in
Sandy while attending high school.

On May 25th, 1924, Anna and Willis
were married. They have four children and eight grandchildren. Their
daughter lives in Los Angeles; one
son lives in San Diego; one son in
Portland, and one son in Springdale.

Anna has two sisters and three
brothers in Portland; a sister in Eugene, and a brother in Seattle.

Her favorite hobby is cooking which
she says she thoroughly enjoys.

Like her husband, Anna has never
had a lost time accident since she has
worked at Bridal Veil. Between them
they have a total of thirty-five years
of accident free time, an extremely
enviable record.

20th Anniversary

September 20th will mark the passing of twenty years at Bridal Veil for Verl Bird, band sawyer. For twelve

of those years Verl has been running the band saw line in the box factory.

Verl was born in Baker, Oregon. The family lived in Portland for a time and Verl went to school in Portland as well as in Baker. Verl's father and mother were from New York City. His father was an iron worker. There were four other boys in the family besides Verl, but no girls.

Verl first worked in the lumber industry in Lewiston, Idaho. Later on he worked in Klamath Falls, Baker and Portland. Afterwards he was a salesman for the Portland Box and Lumber Co. for a period of three years. After that he worked for the Ford Motor Co. for seven years as an inspector. He resigned from the Ford Co. when the firm moved the plant from Portland to Long Beach, California.

Verl and the former Evelyn Willey were married in Baker, Oregon. They have two children. Son Bob is an apprentice sheet metal worker at Willamette Iron & Steel Co., in Portland and daughter Darlene is employed by the Farmer's Insurance Co., in Portland. Both the children are living at home.

Verl's hobbies are woodworking and

New Discovery

If no one knew anything about wood, and someone announced that he had just discovered it, he would soon be acclaimed as one of the leading benefactors of humanity.

Here is a material, he could say, that is plentiful, useful and available in several hundred strengths, hardnesses, grains, and weights. It can easily be cut or shaped to fit many needs. It lasts a long time, readily accepts many different kinds of decorative or protective finishes, and can be worked with relatively simple tools. It can be used by a child to make a crude box for a turtle, and it is perfectly satisfactory for either of these purposes.

The discoverer could point o u t that the new material can be carved for fun or for artistic expression; and that it burns, it smells good, it floats. It will stand around in good condition, in the form of trees, until you need it — and all the time will be increasing its volume, and providing a handsome part of the landscape as well.

The makers of plastics, bricks, and metals would turn pale to the announcement of this new wonder-substance — if it hadn't been discovered yet. As it is, they have known about wood all their lives, just as we have, and share the universal admiration for the dependence on this superb and common material.

———— 16 ————

From Out of the Past

Very welcome visitors to Bridal Veil were Walter Horton, his brother and sister, and his sister's husband. The Horton's father worked at Bridal Veil around 1890 to 1900. He helped build the flume from Palmer to Bridal Veil. Walter Horton was a young boy of twelve or thirteen at the time and remembers it very well. They were unable to stay very long but promised to return and tell us more of the early history of Bridal Veil.

———— 16 ————

Corsets have been declared non-essential by the British Board of Trade —a pretty compliment to the girls, and very subtly put.

sports of all kinds. He is a member of the Masonic lodge, and the Bridal Veil Community Church.

10th Anniversary

September 9th will be the tenth anniversary at Bridal Veil for Theodore Van Hee, set-up man in the moulding department.

Ted was born in Gresham, Oregon, August 28, 1926, just twenty minutes before his younger brother, Theophile. Ted says he has lived at Corbett most of his life, except for three or four years when the family lived at Aberdeen, Washington. He received his education at Corbett, Oregon, where he still lives.

In 1943 Ted enlisted in the Navy for four years. He received his boot training at Farragut, Idaho. Most if not all his Navy hitch was spent in the Submarine service. He was a Torpedoman and spent considerable time on the eastern seaboard where they tested torpedoes. He also spent about two years on a submarine tender both at San Diego, California and at Midway Island, in the Pacific.

Ted says he prefers fishing for relaxation. He is a member of the Elks Lodge.

Up until the time this was written, Ted has remained a batchelor. Also, though we are sure it has no connection, Ted has never had a lost time accident since he has been at Bridal Veil.

Remember When?

The editors of the News Letter are conducting a search for old photographs, taken in the Bridal Veil area, of people and scenes which might be of interest to our readers. We are prepared to offer $2.50 for each photograph printed in the News Letter accompanied by a suitable story telling something about it.

Pictures 20 years old and older are preferred since the object of this search is to find pictures showing people, places and scenes of bygone days. Please be sure to identify adequately any photos submitted, and don't fail to let us know who is submitting them. We'd hate to print a photo and then not know who should receive the $2.50.

If you find a photo you wish to submit, pass it along to Don West or your foreman who will see that the editors get it. We will keep the photo strictly on a loan basis (unless you have a negative from which we can make copies).

All pictures that will not be printed will be returned immediately. Those which will be printed will be returned as soon as we can get the plates made up. We guarantee to take excellent care of all pictures submitted while in our hands. The $2.50 will be payable when your picture is printed.

———— 16 ————

Sept. Birthdays

Many Happy Returns of the Day!

Marion Jones	Steve Kuzmesky
Leonard Kraft	Joe Cote
Merrill Hartshorn	Roley Zumwalt
Howard Hunt	Edsel Kinonen
Ade Jones	Lloyd Frazier
Lawrence Smazal	Lula Cowling

———— 16 ————

Rips and Trims

Mr. and Mrs. Art Haley of Tacoma, were weekend guests of Mr. and Mrs. Charles Gaymon of Gresham.

Martha Jones reports her niece, Jill Medwick, of Anacortes, Washington, was seriously injured but is recovering nicely.

———— 16 ————

There are two dwelling units and several garages for sale by the company for moving or demolishing. Persons interested should contact Ade Jones.

Ten Thoughts on Safety

1. Lifting: No one should attempt to do a two-man lifting job by himself. Always get someone to lend a hand.

2. Loading and piling: Storage and moving stock should be periodically checked, and unsafe piling or loading should be corrected.

3. Menor injuries: All minor cuts, scratches, abrasions, etc. should be reported promptly. A minor injury which becomes infected or otherwise complicated can lead to time-lost just as can a major injury. Employees should also report all protruding nails, splinters, rough objects, etc. in order that such sources of minor injury may be eliminated.

4. Rolling conveyances: Wherever pushed, not pulled. Exceptions: Where possible, rolling conveyances must be one must pull away from a wall or where a high load creates a blind area and the conveyance may run into someone. Employees operating such conveyances should wear safety shoes. Keep hands away from sides of racks, troughs, trucks, etc. Injury may be caused by having the hand caught between the conveyance and racks, posts, or other objects.

5. Falling objects: (heavy objects such as skids, trays, ramps, receptacles, etc.) Too great a hurry, slippery hands, nervousness, etc. can cause imporper handling which may lead to the object's being dropped.

6. Tools: All tools must be made safe, maintained in good condition and used properly. They should be checked regularly. Defective equipment should be quickly repaired or replaced.

7. Floor maintenance: Holes, loose boards, and other tripping hazards should be reported promptly for immediate repair.

8. Tripping: Always observe closely for possible tripping hazards. Keeping aisles and stairs free of obstructions is a definate part of routine jobs. Where hazards occur, they should be removed immediately.

9. Running: For safety — walk don't run. Wear shoes that give firm support and protection from injury. Many falls are due to high heels, worn soles, too loose footwear, lack of laces, etc.

10. Cleaning and adjusting of machinery: Machinery should always be stopped before cleaning, adjusting or removing ANY material. The machine must be FULLY stopped.

No one should ever operate any equipment unless it is a part of one's duties to do so.

———— 16 ————

Health and Welfare

All employees who worked the required number of hours in July will become eligible for health and welfare coverage and will be covered on the first day of September, 1957. Additions: Lewis E. Apitz, Frederick C. Bailey, Jr., Donald Bowen, Ronald E. Catlin, Robert L. Cowling, Fred Damerell, Donald Hageman, Marion Earl Jones, Larry L. Lamke, Cyril Lang, Bill North Jr., and Paul Watts. Employees who did not work the required number of hours will become ineligible the same day. Deletions: Alfred L. Barnes and Robert E. Polzel.

1957 SAFETY CHART

Month	Tot. Hourly Pd. Man Hrs.	Lost Time Accidents	Accident Freq.	Days Accident Lost	Accident Severity
January	14,288	1	70.0	3	210
February	15,318	0	0	0	0
March	17,182	2	116.4	2	116
FIRST QUARTER	46,788	3	63.9	5	107
April	17,055	0	0	0	0
May	18,924	0	0	0	0
June	16,317	1	61.3	4	245
SECOND QUARTER	52,296	1	19.1	4	76
July	19,880	0	0	0	0
TOTAL	118,964	4	33.6	9	76

Rips and Trims

Eldon Gross is going to take his vacation the latter part of September and is going to go deer hunting in the Paulina Lake area. If he has any time left, he is going to do some steelhead fishing.

Mr. and Mrs. Fred Harp and **Mr. and Mrs. Clarence Noble** report a very nice vacation trip. They went to Reno, Nevada, Virginia City, also in Nevada, and came back through the Redwoods and along the Oregon coast. While in Virginia City they were very pleasantly surprised to meet Mr. and Mrs. John Van Orsow and Mr. and Mrs. Richard Kerslake and family. From the way they talked, they didn't win much money in Reno.

Jerry Roberts is driving a new Mercury. He also has a new pair of glasses. Wonder if his eyesight had anything to do with his needing a new car.

Mr. and Mrs. John Van Orsow and **Marvin** spent Labor day weekend fishing in eastern Oregon but reported only fair luck, which evidently isn't very good.

Mrs. Fred Harp is entering the hospital on September 5th, for an operation. We all wish her a speedy recovery.

Paul Dooley is planning on spending his vacation just taking it easy, which is what a vacation is for.

Mr. and Mrs. Howard Hunt spent the Labor day weekend in eastern Oregon fishing with fair success. They found what they believe to be a lead ball from a muzzle loading shotgun, which they turned over to the Corbett high school for their collection.

Mr. and Mrs. Noah Atchley spent their vacation visiting Mr. and Mrs. Anderson, Mr. and Mrs. Wring, and Mr. and Mrs. Gilley, who all live in the North Bend-Coos Bay area.

The Bowen family enjoyed a picnic Thursday evening, August 29th, at Dabney State Park, on the Sandy river. Present were **Mr. and Mrs. Willis Bowen, Mr. and Mrs. Frank Bowen** and family, Mr. and Mrs. Jimmy Bowen and family, and Mr. and Mrs. Willis Bowen, Jr., and family.

Tom Cowling will be returning to the University of Oregon about the middle of September. Tom bought a 1937 Dodge, to take back to school with him. He kind of figured if he got an older car no one would want to borrow it but he might be wrong this time because the car is good looking.

The Ralph Taylor family and the **Jim Cowling** family spent a weekend camping at Clear Lake, on the McKenzie pass.

The weather was beautiful, and the fishing great, as the picture of **Durward Litton** and his prize attests, but

Durward, Don and **Riley West** probably didn't appreciate it as much as they should have. They were the guests of John Chase, of Chase Lumber & Millwork Co., Portland, on a deep sea fishing trip Saturday, August 24th. About one hour out of Ilwaco, Washington, Durward, Don, and Riley put on a masterful exhibition of seasickness but in spite of that came home with three salmon. Seven people on the boat brought in ten fish, which isn't bad for three hours, especially when five of the people were seasick.

During his vacation, **Einar Mickelson** and family spent two days at Lost Lake and also took in the Shrine football game at Pendleton. Einar's mother is visiting here for the summer and was with them on their vacation. She is from Iowa.

Phil Van Hee is back on the job after a serious illness. Phil says the fact that the nurses were good looking at Portland Sanitarium contributed to his recovery.

BRIDAL VEIL LUMBER & BOX CO
News Letter

Volume III, No. 4   BRIDAL VEIL, OREGON   OCTOBER, 1957

We Win

During the balance of 1957 and on through 1958 we all are being treated to ringside seat at a dramatic illustration of how the market economy system operates in the Unites States. The Ford Motor Company has poured an estimated $250,000,000.00 into the launching of the new Edsel in one of the big gambles of the century.

Not only do we get free tickets to watch the show, but also, and far more important, we get to sit in as judge and jury when the awards are passed out.

There has long been a tendency to presume·that wealth begets wealth automatically and that all that is necessary to the making of a fortune is sufficient money to go into business. This is only true in the sense that a well-heeled outfit can take longer to get established than a poorly financed outfit, but even a well financed company cannot go on forever in a losing venture. The basic ingredient in the success of any manufacturing enterprise is customers, not money.

It is doubtful that any company is big simply because someone or some group put a lot of money into it. It is much more likely that our biggest companies got that way because they were able to give their customers more value for their money and consequently had more customers than they could handle. Expansion and bigness follow, then, as a result of satisfied customers and not as a result of investment of huge sums of money. The automobile industry furnishes us with a clear-cut example of the failure of big money vs. the success of many customers.

Not too many years ago, Henry Kaiser, in the full flush of success during the war years, decided to show the automobile industry how to make automobiles. There can be no question as to Mr. Kaiser's ability to run a business, as he has been successful in a wide variety of industries including steel, cement, aluminum, chemicals and others. His reputation made it easy for h i m to get financing in breath-taking quantities. He even got an extra boost from a temporary shortage of cars.

However, in spite of all these advantages, the Kaiser automobile has disappeared from the American scene. The one ingredient necessary to success—customers—was missing. Automobile buyers, shopping carefully for the best value for their hard-earned money, decided that they could do better elsewhere, and refrained from buying Mr. Kaiser's product in sufficient quantities to permit him to continue the business.

The Ford Motor Company probably has a better chance for success in that they have an established reputation, and they have other cars to help carry the load while developing their markets. One thing is sure, however —the American customer is boss and the American customer will determine the degree of success to be accorded the Ford Motor Company in this big gamble.

That's where we come in. Just as the sum total of our ballots in a national election decides who is going to run the government, so also will the sum total of our ballots (purchases) in the market place decide who is going to make our automobiles, and woe to the manufacturer who fails to gather sufficient votes. No amount of money will help him. The mere thought of not being able to please us strikes terror in the hearts of American's biggest executives.

This is the Battle of the Giants as Ford, Chrysler and General Motors vie for our favor. While it is a foregone conclusion that the one that gives the best value will come out on top, it is fun to know that the decision is ours. On our decision rides the future of thousands upon thousands of workers, executives and shareholders.

Len Kraft

The Payoff

Doug Walwyn (right) of Smith and Crakes, Eugene, is shown on a recent trip to Bridal Veil presenting Len Kraft with Smith and Crakes check representing $6018.49 in premium refunds arising as a direct result of the co-operation of Bridal Veil Lumber & Box Co. with Smith and Crakes engineering staff in complying with the recommendations in the installation of fire prevention and safety facilities.

It would be interesting to all that Bridal Veil Lumber & Box Co. has suffered no losses of any kind since the fire protection program was instigated with the help of Smith and Crakes.

1957 SAFETY CHART

Month	Tot. Pd. Man Hrs.	Hourly Accidents	Lost Time Accident Freq.	Days Lost	Accident Severity
January	14,288	1	70.0	3	210
February	15,318	0	0	0	0
March	17,182	2	116.4	2	116
FIRST QUARTER	46,788	3	63.9	5	107
April	17,055	0	0	0	0
May	18,924	0	0	0	0
June	16,317	1	61.3	4	245
SECOND QUARTER	52,296	1	19.1	4	76
July	19,880	0	0	0	0
August	21,330	1	46.9	11	516
TOTAL—8 Months	140,294	5	35.6	20	143

NEWS LETTER

Published on the 10th of each month by
Bridal Veil Lumber & Box Co.
Bridal Veil, Oregon

Editor . . . . . Don West

October Birthdays

Many Happy Returns of the Day!

Wesley Adams   Charles N. Gaymon
Ward Dull   Jacob Van Orsow
Charles L. Long   Einar Mickelson
———— 21 ————

Just Around the Corner

Now is the time to prepare for winter, when it is not too cold. The Company has material available for

Health and Welfare

All employees who worked the required number of hours in August will become eligible for health and welfare coverage and will be covered on the first day of October, 1957. Additions: Alfred L. Barnes, Kenneth Catlin, Delbert P. Cloe, Jack L. Dempsey, Marvin N. Dhone, David Gullickson, Arthur R. Johnson, Junior D. McMorran, William L. Moon, Philip Schneringer. Employees who did not work the required number of hours will become ineligible the same day. Deletions: Glenn Willoughby, Lawrence B. Gowens, and Charles E. Kraft.

boxing in water pipes to protect them from freezing. It might be a good idea to do it early.

Seniority List

1. Atchley, Noah 3-23-36	42. Layton, Hiram 11-13-46	81. Wilson, Louis A. 9-20-54
2. Dull, Ward E. 5-18-36	43. Lofstedt, Clarence 1-16-47	82. Rees, David 9-23-54
3. Noble, Clarence 7-27-36	44. Murray, George 4-21-47	83. Morgan, Roland B. 12-14-54
4. McCredie, Ralph H. 8-27-36	45. Jones, Martha A. 5-14-47	84. Polzel, Leslie D. 1-5-55
5. Davis, D. Fay 3-22-37	46. Van Hee, Theodore V. 9-9-47	85. Gaymon, Charles N. 3-29-55
6. Jackson, Marvin T. 4-8-37	47. Rowe, Thelma Y. 11-12-47	86. Pitts, Orien 4-13-55
7. Stolin, Walter F. 5-11-37	48. Hills, Mabel M. 1-14-48	87. Adams, Wesley A. 5-9-55
8. Bowen, Franklin M. 8-19-37	49. Dunken, William L. 9-15-48	88. Dooley, Paul D. 5-9-55
9. Crouser, Fred 8-30-37	50. Hills, Stanley B. 1-15-51	89. Hageman, Leo C. 6-1-55
10. Bird, Verl W. 9-20-37	51. Roberts, Vera Nell 1-15-51	90. Dunlap, Leon C. 7-5-55
11. Taylor, Ralph L. 11-22-37	52. Van Treeck, Paul 2-20-51	91 Hancock, Clem A. 8-15-55
12. Hanson, Theodore N. 4-18-38	53. Van Hee, Theo. Sr. 2-27-51	92. Wendler, Ed L. 9-6-55
13. Van Orsow, Jos. M. 4-22-38	54. Schneringer, Ray 10-8-51	93. Westlake, Donald 10-17-55
14. Dunken, J. Delbert 7-18-39	55. Walker, Homer F. 10-9-51	94. Jacobson, Rodney 3-11-57
15. Meyer, Kenneth L. 9-16-40	56. Frazier, Lloyd 10-9-51	95. Fitzgerald, Robt. Jr. 3-15-57
16. Hartshorn, Merrill 1-8-41	57. Eveland, Roy D. 10-15-51	96. Livingston, James J. 5-1-57
17. Harp, Fred 5-21-41	58. Anderson, Lester W. 5-19-52	97. Jones, Marion E. 5-6-57
18. Mickelson, Einar E. 7-1-41	59. Emmons, Dale 5-20-52	98. Flangin, Donald 5-8-57
19. Roberts, Jerald G. 9-8-41	60. Zumwalt, Wayne 5-26-52	99. Apitz, Lewis E. 5-8-57
20. Ellis, Ralph 10-9-41	61. Howell, Lester B. 6-23-52	100. Watts, Paul A. 6-26-57
21. Latourell, Cllifford 3-23-42	62. Hutchison, Earl 6-23-52	101. Damerell, Fred 7-2-57
22. Vogel, Harold A. 3-25-42	63. Van Buskirk, Norm. 7-28-52	102. Catlin, Ronald E. 7-2-57
23. Nielson, Eldon F. 4-21-42	64. Hancock, Loren 9-2-52	103. Lang, Cyril 7-9-57
24. Davis, Bertha M. 5-6-42	65. Long, Fred M. 9-9-52	104. Cloe, Delbert P. 7-22-57
25. Hartshorn, Dorothy 7-14-42	66. Cote, Joseph 9-10-52	105. Barnes, Alfred 7-22-57
26. Bowen, Anna 9-30-42	67. Adolph, Harry 9-22-52	106. Catlin, Kenneth V. 7-22-57
27. Hageman, Leo F. 7-14-43	68. Willms, John G. 9-29-52	107. Dempsey, Jack L. 8-9-57
28. Yerion, Lillie P. 7-19-43	69. Potter, Eugene H. 10-28-52	108. Dhone, Marvin N. 8-12-57
29. Cloe, Pearl P. 11-12-43	70. Davies, Archie L. 4-1-53	109. McMorran, Junior D. 8-12-57
30. Britton, Thomas C. 12-20-43	71. Bissell, Louis W. 5-1-53	110. Johnson, Arthur 8-19-57
31. Nielson, Mira J. 1-23-44	72. Layton, Bob 5-28-53	111. Westlake, Jack V. 8-23-57
32. Litton, Durward 5-9-44	73. Ayles, Elmer L. 8-4-53	112. Matson, John E. 8-29-57
33. Peterson, Lawrence 9-24-45	74. Gross, Elden 8-27-53	113. Howell, Arthur V. 8-30-57
34. Hunt, Howard G. 10-1-45	75. Kuzmesky, Steven 9-15-53	114. Howell, Allen G. 9-5-57
35. Smazal, Lawrence A. 10-2-45	76. Burkholder, Harold 5-4-54	115. Nicks, Shelby W. 9-5-57
36. Stolin, Marvin J. 3-28-46	77. Kinonen, Edsel 5-4-54	116. Mershon, John 9-9-57
37. Van Hee, Theophile 4-17-46	78. Long, Frederick H. 6-2-54	117. Ahlstedt, Thomas L. 9-10-57
38. Kendrick, James B. 5-13-46	79. Kilness, Jarvis 6-2-54	118. Murphy, Charles H. 9-10-57
39. Woodard, Mary R. 6-3-46	80. Zumwalt, Roley 9-7-54	119. Reiter, Norman F. 9-10-57
40. Jacobson, Harold R. 9-16-46		120. Blaine, Roger A. 9-12-57
41. Choate, Beaulah 10-7-46		121. Craig, Kenneth O. 9-13-57

Rips and Trims

Martha Jones has received a report of the murder of an uncle, Thomas R. Jessen, near Boone Springs, Nevada. Mr. Jessen was a driver for North American Van Lines, and was reported to have been carrying $1350. in cash, which has not been found. A truck driver's helper is being sought by authorities in connection with the case.

Martha and Vera Nell Roberts attended a fashion show Monday evening September 30th, at the Glendoveer Country Club.

Anna Bowen had two of her grandchildren, **Jack and Jean Bowen**, as house guests over the weekend, while **Willie** was opening the deer season in eastern Oregon. Willie failed to bring home any evidence of the hunt.

According to reports, **Mira Nielson** is recovering nicely from a leg injury sustained August 16th and will be back to work in a week or so.

Eldon Nielson has six pups, of Fox Terrier and Chihuahua descent, which he will give to anyone who will give them a good home. Eldon also has four Persian kittens he is hoping someone will adopt. We take it that one per family is sufficient and that you need not take all of them.

Verl Bird and wife **Evelyn**, spent a week at her sisters' home in Baker, Oregon. Verl said they visited the new dam in Hells Canyon. We also happen to know that Verl spent some of his time visiting a woodworking plant. Just like a sailor who takes his girl for a ride in a canoe.

The following students are newly elected members of the National Honor Society, which recognized outstanding students: **Marsha Howell, Bob Cowling, Bob Long,** and **Patty Westlake.**

Dewayne Kilness was one of the stars in the annual high school shrine football game played at Pendleton. Dewayne scored a touchdown but his team came out on the short end of the score.

Eleanor Taylor was a recent house guest of Mrs. Jim Tanner.

Fred Harp is the proud owner of a new camping trailer. Looks like Fay and Fred are planning a few trips in the future.

Noah Atchley spent the last week of his vacation driving back and forth to the hospital where his wife was convalescing from an operation. She is home now and reported to be getting along fine.

Mr. and Mrs. Wayne Zumwalt hunted near Mitchell on opening weekend of the deer season with no success.

Ed Wendler also spent the weekend near Mitchell hunting without luck.

Jerry Roberts and **Marv Van Orsow** hunted out of Mitchell and came home empty handed, or very nearly. Marv got one shot at a deer which he missed by a country mile and then shot at a coyote and hit him. The coyote turned on Marv and got within five feet of Marv before he fell dead. Marv says if was five or ten minutes before he was able to resume hunting. Must have been quite a scare at that. Marv says it was about the size of a large lion.

Jim Cowling also flunked out on deer hunting. We haven't heard of anyone bringing one home this year. The boys must be going to the wrong places to hunt.

Proof of a successful fishing trip may be seen above. **Riley West** is holding two silver salmon taken out of Ilwaco, Washington. The fish run around eleven and twelve pounds. Not a bad days work!

BRIDAL VEIL LUMBER & BOX CO.
News Letter

Volume III, No. 5   BRIDAL VEIL, OREGON   NOVEMBER, 1957

Limitations

Many thousands of lines have been written over the past twenty years about the new industries to be drawn to the Northwest by cheap power from the Bonneville grid. This story has been repeated so often that it is pretty generally accepted as being a fact.

It would be fair to say that if all other factors are equal, then cheap power might well determine the location of an industry. Transportation, for example, is a major factor which far outweighs cheap power. Even free power wouldn't help the operator of a rock crushing plant in Portland to compete for the Seattle and San Francisco crushed rock markets. The transportation costs would be more than the rock is worth. In a similar fashion, cheap power would not have much effect upon the location of a sawmill since these plants must be near the raw material for the most efficient use of transportation.

Taxes are another major consideration which determines the location of an industry. I once heard that in the beer business, taxes are the raw material, and the trick is to make beer out of taxes.

Personal property taxes, real property taxes and income taxes far outweigh power costs in most businesses. Personal property taxes cause a kind of a "button, button, who has the button" game at the end of each year as manufacturers, wholesalers and retailers each try to keep from getting stuck with an inventory at December 31, and this situation is the major cause of the stagnation of our own business along towards the end of each year.

Down Los Angeles way, where the commercial power rates are twice those of the Portland area, new industries swarm in by the dozen. In Portland, it is big news when an out-of-state manufacturer builds a warehouse, and the warehouse doesn't use power.

There is even some reason to believe that cheap power has a kind of reverse spin so far as the attraction of new industries and the creation of new jobs are concerned. The industry most likely to be attracted by cheap power is the industry in which power is, in a sense, the raw material. The aluminum reduction industry is a case in point, and the paradox is that such an industry uses relatively few man hours when related to the power consumption. The rolling mills and fabricating plants are all located elsewhere, where persumably the power rates are higher, but are also a relatively minor factor.

The state of Michigan has succeeded in adopting a set of rules and regulations affecting business which has created a climate unfavorable to business to the extent that General Motors contemplates locating its new facilities in other areas. Maybe there is a lesson here for the state of Oregon. Cheap power alone will not do the trick.

Len Kraft

——— 52 ———

New Employees

A hearty welcome is extended to the following new employees.

Allen Howell	Kenneth Craig
Shelby Nicks	Floyd Oden
John Mershon	James Belcher
Charles Murphy	Robert Roberson
Roger Blaine	

——— 52 ———

Remember — tight money doesn't stem from a declining economy but from a record economic expansion which has resulted in a highly competitive demand for investment capital.

Seven Economic Fallacies

1. That government has something to give the people which it does not first have to take away from them.

Government is never a source of goods. Everything produced is produced by the people, and everything that government gives the people it must first take from the people. Government benefits are raised through taxes and, as Franklin D. Roosevelt said in 1932, "taxes are paid in the sweat of every man who labors."

2. That job security can be guaranteed by management.

In our modern exchange economy, all payroll and employment comes from customers, and the only worth-while job security is customer security: if there are no customers, there can be no payroll and no jobs.

3. That the workers of any nation can improve their welfare by increasing their pay without increasing their production.

Because wages are the principal cost of everything, wage increases (without corresponding increases in production) simply increase prices and do not improve the welfare of the worker.

4. That labor-union pressures are primarily responsible for the workers' rising standard of living.

Ninety-five percent of man's ability to increase production is due to the use of better tools. Organized labor has played a very small part in the accumulation of these all-important tools.

5. That any system other than a free production-and-exchange system can provide the greatest good for the greatest number.

The greatest good for the greatest number means, in its material sense, the greatest productivity per worker. And the greatest productivity per worker is reached when production, as well as markets, operate under the stimulus of free competition, as shown by the history of American industry.

6. That the law of supply and demand can be repealed.

The more scarce an article (goods or service), the higher the price of it becomes. The more plentiful the article, the lower the price of it. This law of supply and demand is a law of nature and cannot be repealed by man. Government efforts to suspend or ignore it have always had disastrous results.

7. That the owners of industry get the lion's share of the product and the workers get only the crumbs.

The amount of the product of all industry that goes to workers is about 90 percent. The amount that accrues to the owners of the tools (investors) is about ten percent. Yet the tools do more than 95 percent of the work.

———— 52 ————

Burns accounted for about 5,200 home accident fatalities last year. Falls killed about 13,800 persons.

1957 SAFETY CHART

Month	Tot. Pd. Man Hrs.	Hourly Accidents	Lost Time Freq.	Accident Days Lost	Accident Severity
January	14,288	1	70.0	3	210
February	15,318	0	0	0	0
March	17,182	2	116.4	2	116
FIRST QUARTER	46,788	3	63.9	5	107
April	17,055	0	0	0	0
May	18,924	0	0	0	0
June	16,317	1	61.3	4	245
SECOND QUARTER	52,296	1	19.1	4	76
July	19,880	0	0	0	0
August	21,330	1	46.9	11	516
September	20,706	2	96.6	29	1401
THIRD QUARTER	61,916	3	48.5	40	646
TOTAL	161,000	7	43.5	49	304

NEWS LETTER

Published on the 10th of each month by
Bridal Veil Lumber & Box Co.
Bridal Veil, Oregon

Editor . . . . . Don West

Health and Welfare

All employees who worked the required number of hours in September will become eligible for health and welfare coverage and will be covered on the first day of November 1957. Additions: Thomas L. Ahlstedt, Roger A. Blaine, Kenneth O. Craig, Allen G. Howell, Arthur V. Howell, John E. Matson, John Mershon, Charles H. Murphy, Shelby W. Nicks, Norman F. Reiter, Jack V. Westlake, Eleanor Taylor. Employees who did not work the required number of hours will become ineligible the same day. Deletions: Gerald Kraft, Mira J. Nielson, Frederick C. Bailey Jr., Robert L. Cowling, Lynfred Crouser, D e a n Davis, David Gullickson, Donald Hageman, Vyrtle Kuntz, Larry L. Lamke, Phillip Schneringer.

——— 52 ———

Nov. Birthdays

Many Happy Returns of the Day!

Clem Hancock	Fred Harp
Harry Adolph	E. W. Norgard
Harold Burkholder	Kenneth Meyer
Verl Bird	Louis Bissell
Fay Davis	Bill Dunken

——— 52 ———

Safety Shoes

Since the start of the safety shoe program early in September, twenty-eight employees have taken advantage of the opportunity to purchase safety shoes at factory cost.

Anyone interested in this low cost protective plan should see either Jim Cowling or Mel Mallinson for details.

——— 52 ———

As Samuel Gompers, the "grand old man" of labor, said forty years ago: "There has never yet come down from any government any substantial improvement in the condition of the masses of the people unless it found its own initiative in the mind, the heart and the courage of the people."

20th Anniversary

Ralph Taylor, saw filer, will observe his twentieth anniversary at Bridal Veil on November 22, 1957.

Ralph was born and raised, on a farm, near Vienna, Illinois. In 1932 he joined the CCC (Civilian Conservation Corps) and spent the next two years stationed in Illinois. In January 1935 he was transferred to Washington. In June of the same year he left the CCC and went to work for the Crown Zellerbach Corp. Later on he worked for Long-Bell Lumber Company and International Wood Products Co. in Cathlamet, Washington.

Ralph and the former Eleanor Akers were married in Chehalis, Washington on December 9, 1936. They have two children. Mary Lee Kreman who lives in Englewood, California a n d Diana, an eighth grade student at Corbett. Eleanor was payroll clerk at Bridal Veil for five years and still helps out part time.

Ralph, Eleanor and the girls built their own home at Corbett several years ago. They did an excellent job.

Ralph's hobbies are woodworking and gardening. He also enjoys fishing and bird hunting. Ralph is a member (active) of the Masonic Lodge.

Ralph has a sister, Beulah Choate, who is also employed at Bridal Veil.

Rips and Trims

Marvin Stolin, Jerry Roberts, and Walt Stolin went bird hunting n e a r Stanf'eld over the weekend and came home with six pheasants and five ducks.

Danny Hills, son of Mr. and Mrs. Stanley Hills got his first deer near Prineville.

Ralph Lamke says bird hunting is good down in the valley. Only trouble is he didn t say what valley.

Willis Bowen, Jim Bowen, Max Bissell, Larry Granberg, Lloyd and Ed Kogel all went Elk hunting on the Grand Ronde river near Starkey, Oregon over the weekend. No one got an elk but one scared Larry Granberg out of a little growth. Larry and Max Bissell were former employees.

Mrs. James Bowen and daughter spent the weekend with Mrs. Willis Bowen. Both the mother and the daughter had the flu, unfortunately.

Eldon Gross and his wife spent the weekend fishing down on the coast with no luck. They don't bite every weekend Eldon.

Harry Adolph started his vacation the first of November and plans on going elk hunting, at least part of the time.

Bob Bird, former employee, brought home a nice four point buck from the area around Kinzua. Now you fellows know where to go.

Merrill Hartshorn is back on the job after a week battling the flu.

Martha Jones is at home with the flu but it is hoped she will be able to return to work shortly.

Mr. and Mrs. Robert Fitzgerald are journeying to Miami, Oklahoma. Mrs. Fitzgerald's parents are both going to undergo surgery.

Mrs. Noah Atchley is recovering rapidly from her recent operation.

Mr. and Mrs. Roy Eveland spent a weekend visiting relatives in Sunnyside, Washington.

A very extensive and impressive list of fellows failed to bring home a deer during the season just past, even though some of them apparently tried several times. You can probably tell who the unlucky ones were by whether they have any bragging to do.

Roley Zumwalt and his father went Elk hunting and Mr. Zumwalt got a spike elk.

Donald Flanagin was killed in an automobile accident near Springdale Sunday night. Don was an employee at Bridal Veil.

Ray Schneringer was seriously injured in an automobile accident below Crown Point last Monday afternoon. Ray is improving slowly.

All Bridal Veil employees were saddened by the sudden death of Lloyd Frazier last Friday. Mr. Frazier died just after coming to work in the morning, apparently from a heart attack.

Len and Jerry Kraft went deer hunting around Izee and didn't come home with anything but the flu. They were both immobilized for a week.

We understand Ted Hanson has found a new way to hunt deer, or at least to bring them to bay or whatever you do to a deer. It was too confusing to us but we are pretty sure that Ted said something about throwing rocks at one and finally coming home with it. Better ask him.

———— 52 ————

Back to School

Under a company sponsored program, Marv VanOrsow and Ralph McCredie are taking a course entitled,

Marv Van Orsow   Ralph McCredie

"The Leadership Development Program" at the University of Portland. The class is attended by representatives of various industries throughout the area. The course is restricted to two students from a single company so that no one company might monopolize the discussions. It is expected that the course will be available every year so that eventually all the foremen will have attended. The course began in late September and runs through December.

BRIDAL VEIL LUMBER & BOX CO.

News Letter

Volume III, No. 6   BRIDAL VEIL, OREGON   DECEMBER, 1957

Who Do You Think You Are?

During the last few years, we've gotten the habit of pinning labels on ourselves and on others. We call one man a "Worker", another a "Consumer," another a "Capitalist", and so on. The only trouble with this system is that it won't work. People in America just do not fit nicely into rigid classes or classifications. And anybody who says they do is peddling pure, unadulterated hokum.

Take yourself as an example. You have a job and you work at it. So some people will classify you as a "Worker" or "Laborer". Sure you work, but let's look farther. You and your family have to eat, buy clothes, pay rent, spend money for entertainment, furniture, appliances, etc., don't you? And that makes you a "Consumer", doesn't it?

So now you fall into two classifications. You probably have a savings account, an insurance policy, some war bonds or maybe a share or two of stock, don't you? O.K. When you put money into insurance, or savings accounts, or bonds, or stock, you're supplying capital for some business to operate. So that makes you a "Capitalist". Of course you don't have any millions like Rockefeller or Morgan— but even if you have only ten bucks in a savings account, its just as important to you as a million to Morgan. Your money is being rented by some business man and being used to buy raw materials and pay wages. In other words you're a "Boss" —a "Capitalist". Yes, you!

So here's you — worker, consumer, capitalist, just like the boss and just like all the rest of us. The interests of labor are your interests. The interests of the consumer are your interests.

The interests of capital are your interests too. You cannot hurt any one class without hurting yourself.

When wages go up too high, the cost of the finished product goes up high, too. This hurts you in the pocketbook as a consumer. And it lowers the value of the savings which make you a capitalist. When production goes down, most of the things you buy go up - and that reduces the value of your savings. It brings inflation which is equally the foe of worker, consumer or capitalist.

What's the answer? You - Mr. Worker - Consumer - Capitalist - you have the answer. If all of us produce more, if we give more work for each dollar we earn, if we produce more of the goods so badly needed, we get more through lower prices when we ourselves buy the things we need. And, by thus preventing inflation, we protect our savings, our bonds and our insurance. And if we realize that you can't label people - even ourselves - or divide them arbitrarily into classes - we'll discover we can't war on another so called "Class" without hurting ourselves. We - each of us - at some point or other are members of all classes—not just one. So in the end our best interests lie in what's best for all. It's as simple as that.

———— 30 ————

Dec. Birthdays

Many Happy Returns of the Day!

Clyde Hambrick	Charles Murphy
Walter Keller	Hiram Layton
Eugene Potter	

———— 30 ————

We are losing housing at a rate of 300,000 to 400,000 units a year (demolition, conversion, floods, etc.)

Accidents Just Don't Happen

"Accidents' kill nearly 100,000 people in this country every year, but a lot of them didn't have to happen. As Dr. John E. Eichenlaub puts it, "At least a fifth of the victims were 'accident prone' — and might have lived if they had recognized they were setups for the morgue ahead of time". And that's on the basis of the record; a lot more were in that category but the record didn't show it.

One thing is certain: A big share of the "accidents" can be traced to a relatively small part of the population. And they aren't made up of wild youngsters or roaring drunks, either. A lot of them are ordinary sober citizens like yourself.

But they are "accident-prone".

It's customary to write off somebody who has a series of accidents as "having a streak of bad luck". However, it is said that luck stops when the accident run gets up to three - and that's regardless of whether the record shows that they were "somebody else's fault".

Dr. Eichenlaub, writing in an AMA publication, found "accident prone" people fall into three general groups:

Those who unconsciously are like the small boy who tells his folks he'll run away and freeze to death and "then you'll be sorry." When they're angry at something they deliberately take chances - like racing around the countryside in a car. It's not a sure road to destruction, but they take tremendous risks.

Those who are insecure or dissatisfied. They can't win as much success as they think they need and they make up for it by "taking a chance" or defying the laws of nature. It doesn't have to be as obvious as "Russian Roulette", but it's the same idea - thrill - hunting and taking risks by impulse or deliberately flouting safety rules. It gives them a feeling of "success", but it can kill them or somebody else.

Those who may be usually calm and efficient, but react to an emergency -large or small - by flying off in all directions. They let their emotions dictate actions and literally act without thinking. They are the kind that let go of the wheel and cover their faces when the car goes into a skid.

Take a good look at yourself. If you fall into any of these categories, look out because unless you recognize it and put a curb on your reactions, you are an "accident looking for a place to happen".

Your Health, April 1957

———— 30 ————

In 1949, more than half of our families had a total of $3000 per year income. Today, only about one-third are in this bracket.

1957 SAFETY CHART

Month	Tot. Pd. Man Hrs.	Hourly Lost Time Accidents	Accident Freq.	Days Lost	Accident Severity
January	14,288	1	70.0	3	210
February	15,318	0	0	0	0
March	17,182	2	116.4	2	116
FIRST QUARTER	46,788	3	63.9	5	107
April	17,055	0	0	0	0
May	18,924	0	0	0	0
June	16,317	1	61.3	4	245
SECOND QUARTER	52,296	1	19.1	4	76
July	19,880	0	0	0	0
August	21,330	1	46.9	11	516
September	20,706	2	96.6	29	1401
THIRD QUARTER	61,916	3	48.5	40	646
October	21,394	1	46.7	23	1075
TOTAL	182,394	8	43.9	72	395

NEWS LETTER

Published on the 10th of each month by
Bridal Veil Lumber & Box Co.
Bridal Veil, Oregon

Editor . . . . . Don West

Taxes Are Paid in Hours of Work

Let's see if we can bring you and your job a little closer to the way things are shaping up on the American economic scene.

First, let's look at the tax picture, because it is of such great and growing importance to all of us who work for a living. Here, the basic fact to remember is that Government produces no goods or other forms of material wealth. Before the Government can have anything to give out, it must take in.

That is why you are taxed. The more the Government gives out, the more it must take in from you, because you produce goods and wealth.

Today 37,817,000 citizens are receiving direct payments from the Treasury of the Federal Government. Considering the dependents of these individuals, it may be that fully half of our population is on the receiving end in some degree. The other half necessarily is on the paying end. You are in the group that pays.

Maybe you had not thought of it this way, but it is a fact: You pay your taxes in hours, days and weeks of working time on your job. You can figure it out for yourself. Just take the total amount of your own 1956 tax payments and divide that figure by your hourly pay rate. The result will be the actual number of hours you worked to produce your share of Federal Government payouts.

Would you think that you had to work as much as six full weeks out of each working year and see every penny of your earnings for that period diverted to the Federal Government? With some it's more, with others it's less. You work a full year and wind up with approximately ten months' pay to show for it.

Whether that's too much, too little, or just about right is something you can decide for yourself. But it's your

At This Point .. I Must Have Lost My Presence of Mind

"Comes now the story to end all stories on the topic of safety in construction work.

The following is vouched for as gospel by the distinguished British newspaper, the Manchester Guardian, which published a letter from a bricklayer in Barbados, in the West Indies, to the firm in England which has employed him:

"Respected Sir, when I got to the building, I found that the hurricane had knocked some bricks off the top. So I rigged up a beam with a pulley at the top of the building and hoisted up a couple of barrels full of bricks. When I had fixed the building, there was a lot of bricks left over.

"I hoisted the barrel back up again and secured the line at the bottom, and then went up and filled the barrel with extra bricks. Then I went to the bottom and cast off the line.

"Unfortunately, the barrel of bricks was heavier than I was and before I knew what was happening the barrel started down, jerking me off the ground. I decided to hang on and halfway up I met the barrel coming down and received a severe blow on the shoulder.

"I then continued to the top, banging my head against the beam and getting my finger jammed in the pulley. When the barrel hit the ground, it bursted its bottom, allowing all the bricks to spill out.

"I was now heavier than the barrel and so started down again at high speed. Half-way down, I met the barrel coming up and received severe injuries to my shins. When I hit the ground I landed on the bricks, getting several painful cuts from the sharp edges.

"At this point I must have lost my presence of mind, because I let go of the line. The barrel then came down giving me another heavy blow on the head and putting me in the hospital.

"I respectfully request sick leave."

personal labor and sacrifice that provides a 72 billion dollar budget.

Since your own take-home pay is so directly affected, you have a natural right to your own say in Government spending.

That's where you come in.

Rips and Trims

The **Eldon Nielson** family s p e n t Thanksgiving at the **Jerry Roberts** home in Gresham.

John Matson spent Thanksgiving at the home of his parents in Battleground, Washington. He then went Elk hunting in the Yakima area for three days but the hunt was in vain.

Marv Van Orsow and party went Elk hunting near the Idaho- Washington border, but failed to score. Wait till next time.

Mr. and Mrs. John Van Orsow spent Thanksgiving at the **Marv Van Orsows** home in Portland.

Mr. and Mrs. Clarence Van Orsow and family spent the holiday weekend visiting friends and relatives in the Corbett and Portland area.

Harry Densmore is sporting a new Chevrolet. Wish he would bring it out so we could see it.

Clyde Hambrick and Jim Cowling are driving Buicks this season. How about next.

The **Harry Densmore** family recently enjoyed a short vacation trip to Canada. Vancouver and Victoria were among the places visited.

A surprise birthday party was held on November 15th for **Fay D a v i s** at the Davis home in Corbett. An enjoyable time was had by all.

Ralph and Eleanor Taylor, a n d daughter **Diana** spent a week in Los Angeles visiting their daughter and son-in-law, Mr. and Mrs. Wayne Kreman. While there, they went sightseeing which included a trip to Disneyland.

Bertha and **Fay Davis** entertained their grandson, Gordon Timothy, over Thanksgiving weekend.

Mr. and Mrs. Shelby Nicks a n d family are going to spend Christmas in St. Joseph, Missouri, visiting Mrs. Nicks parents. From there they are going to visit Mr. Nicks parents in Iowa.

David Rees visited Mr. and Mrs. Van Orsow in Madras on his way back from Reno and Disneyland. Didn't say how he made out in Reno.

Mr. and Mrs. Fred Harp and the Einar Mickelson family, spent Thanksgiving with Mr. and Mrs. Frank Jeffers in St. Johns.

Mr. and Mrs. Fred Crouser spent Thanksgiving in Portland.

Mr. and Mrs. William Dunken and family spent Thanksgiving at the Robert Dunken home.

Mr. and Mrs. Lester Anderson had Mrs. Anderson's parents and son Arlyn as guests for Thanksgiving.

Mr. and Mrs. Roy Eveland's daughter and four grandsons from Seattle spent four days during Thanksgiving holidays at the Eveland home.

——— 30 ———

Overpass to Handle Traffic in Both Directions

Following is a quotation from a letter received from the State Highway Department which we believe will be of interest to many of us, especially those living in the Corbett area.

"In reply to your recent inquiry about access to Corbett Station on the Columbia River Highway, I am happy to inform you that we have obtained the necessary approval so that our interchange area at Corbett Station will permit traffic to and from the Freeway in any direction. T h i s will permit traffic from Corbett Station to have direct access to the Freeway eastbound to Bridal Veil, or from the Bridal Veil area direct access into Corbett Station."

This, of course, means that those of us living at Corbett will be able to come to work over the new road instead of having to use the old highway.

——— 30 ———

Homebuilding to Show Spring Build-Up

According to the people who know, home building should show a faster spring pick-up than was originally anticipated. It is now predicted t h a t housing starts in 1958 will total 1,100,-000, and increase of 10 percent over 1957. We hope, by faster pick - up, they mean an earlier pick-up.

Although our December order file leaves something to be desired, we have hopes that the month of January will show a considerable increase. From what our customers tell us we can expect January to be somewhere around 70 percent of a normal month. We have been disillusioned before but we believe that the "slack' period this winter will be somewhat shorter than usual.

BRIDAL VEIL LUMBER & BOX CO.

News Letter

Volume III, No. 7   BRIDAL VEIL, OREGON   JANUARY, 1958

At Random

The year end is the traditional time for statistics. Here is a look see at a few figures on the last couple of years.

The year at Bridal Veil has always ended on November 30 instead of December 31. I suppose there was a good reason for that back in 1935 when the company was organized, but I don't remember now what the reason was. Anyway, all the figures I use are for years ending on November 30 in the year mentioned.

In 1957 we sold 6,751,169 FBM of products. This was 1,440,384 FBM or seventeen and a half percent less than the 8,191,553 FBM sold in 1956. As a matter of curiosity, our sales in 1955 were 10,632,248 FBM — fifty seven and one half percent more than in 1957.

With such a drop in sales, we experienced a substantial reduction in the number of people required to get our work done. During 1957 we had an average of 133 names on the payroll each month. During 1956 we had an average of 160 and in 1955 the figure was 175.

The only good thing we can say about the drop in employment is that while the number of employees dropped twenty and one-half percent, the man hours worked only dropped twelve and one-half percent. On paper that works out to increased earnings for the average employee of $464.00 during 1957.

Increased earnings per employee were also affected by wage rate increases negotiated early in 1957 and effective March 1. The average hourly rate for all employees rose from $2.10¾ to $2.18½.

During the year just past our average sale price dropped approximately 8 percent. When we relate the increase in wages to the decrease in sales we find that our payroll required 35¼ cents of every dollar of net sales. In 1956 the payroll requirement was 29 ¾ cents out of every dollar of net sales.

If it weren't for the lessons to be learned, 1957 would best be forgotten from a safety standpoint. Lost time accidents jumped from 4 in 1956 to 9 in 1957. The number of days lost because of accidents jumped from 19 in 1956 to 103 in 1957. At our average hourly rate of $2.18½, those 103 days represent $1800.44 in lost earnings. Safety is not due to luck. Here is a fertile field for improvement in 1958.

In November of 1957 we had 145 people on the payroll. It is interesting to note that almost half of our people have been with us ten years or longer. This, in a decade characterized by full employment, can only mean that these people chose to work here because they found Bridal Veil a good place to work. We now have fifteen 20 year employees representing 307 years of service to the company:

Noah Atchley	Marvin Jackson
Verl Bird	Ade Jones
Frank Bowen	Len Kraft
Willie Bowen	Ralph McCredie
Fred Crouser	Clarence Noble
Fay Davis	Walt Stolin
Ward Dull	Ralph Taylor
Clyde Hambrick	

Competition, we are told, is going to be rougher during the coming year. The firms getting the business will be the ones who are able to supply the customer with the best service, quality and price. Our problem in 1958 is to beat the competition. We have the men, materials and machinery to do it.

Len Kraft

A traveling man had a very pretty wife and took her on one of his trips. The porter looked the lady over and said, "You sho' picked a good looker this time, Mr. Jones."

Money! Money! Money!

A topic of general interest—the piece reprinted here by permission of Arizona Progress (in whose pages we first saw it) and its publishers, the Valley National Bank (who should know whereof they speak).

"Money, of itself, is not very amusing. In fact most people take it quite seriously although they sometimes do funny things with it. Recently there has been a lot of loose talk about tight money, indicating that some confusion exists. So, if you will gather round, kiddies, and be very attentive, we shall brief you on this complicated subject.

"Theoretically money is a medium of exchange but we mention this only to show that we know what we are talking about. Actually business is now conducted largely with I.O.U's, thus rendering money superfluous if not obsolete. However, from sheer force of habit people persist in trying to make money anyway. It is hardly worth the trouble. Money is not only difficult to come by, but to keep. It is here today and gone tomorrow.

"Money is something which, if you haven't any, worries you and, if you have any, worries you. It can be tight or loose (viz. loose change) hard or soft, hot or cold (viz. cold cash), easy or uneasy, saved or squandered. When money loses value, this is Inflation. When it increases in value, that is Deflation. When it stays put, that is a miracle. When it evaporates, that is a calamity.

"Love of money is supposed to be the root of all evil, which sounds interesting, but you can get into plenty of trouble by loving other things. Women, for example, or cucumbers, or race horses. They also say that money talks, but it has a language all its own, including the Scandinavian. Some people understand it better than others, which isn't fair. All we have learned in our lifetime, and all anyone needs to know, is this: you can't eat money. That is, unless you are a goat. Goats don't appreciate the value of money.

"Bankers still consider money quite important. They say it with Music. Bankers are known as money — changers, not a complimentary term, but someone must do it. Banks also store money, rent money, hire money and, at times, create money. But that is another subject—and even more complicated. The main thing to remember about money is this: MONEY CAN BE MANUFACTURED, BUT CAPITAL MUST BE SAVED."

———— 27 ————

Economical family size package: One that holds five times as much as you'll ever use.

1957 SAFETY CHART

Month	Tot. Pd. Man Hrs.	Hourly Lost Time Accidents	Accident Freq.	Days Lost	Accident Severity
January	14,288	1	70.0	3	210
February	15,318	0	0	0	0
March	17,182	2	116.4	2	116
FIRST QUARTER	46,788	3	63.9	5	107
April	17,055	0	0	0	0
May	18,924	0	0	0	0
June	16,317	1	61.3	4	245
SECOND QUARTER	52,296	1	19.1	4	76
July	19,880	0	0	0	0
August	21,330	1	46.9	11	516
September	20,706	2	96.6	29	1401
THIRD QUARTER	61,916	3	48.5	40	646
October	21,394	1	46.7	23	1075
November	17,905	0	0	25	140
TOTAL	200,299	8	39.9	97	484

NEWS LETTER

Published on the 10th of each month by
Bridal Veil Lumber & Box Co.
Bridal Veil, Oregon

Editor   .   .   .   .   Don West

Health and Welfare Coverage

All employees who worked the required number of hours in November will become eligible for health and welfare coverage and will be covered on the first day of January 1, 1958. Additions: Leroy Brenneke, Gerald Carver, James Dawes, Joseph Gerke, Robert D. Godat, Allen Hornaday, Walton Jones, Robert Reischel, Robert Roberson. Employees who did not work the required number of hours will become ineligible the same day. Deletions: Robert J. Fitzgerald Jr., Arthur Johnson, Martha Jones, Cyril Lang, Frederick H. Long, Raymond Schneringer.

———— 27 ————

The Order File

The order file has finally begun to show signs of life. A couple of weeks ago it looked pretty sick but has come out of it in pretty good shape. We have enough orders on hand and promised to carry us well into the month of February. On the surface that appears to be a fairly healthy situation but it might be well to remember that February and March are traditionally slow months. But as stated in the boss' column, if we can meet the competition, and we're sure we will, this might turn out to be a pretty good year.

———— 27 ————

Wood Windows Preferred

Because they are quiet, wood windows are preferred in the home. The resiliency and shock-absorbing qualities of wood windows reduce or eliminate the vibration of glass and deaden the sound of window operation. Wood windows are easily cleaned. Wood sash and frames do not stain rain water or cleaning water. When metal windows are rusted or corroded, they are likely to stain the building surface below them.

———— 27 ————

If your wife wants to learn to drive don't stand in her way.

The General Outlook

HOUSING STARTS Figures just released for the month of October show private housing starts as 87,000 or down slightly from the 88,000 in September. The October total works out to a seasonally adjusted rate of 1 million per year; however, an estimate based on the total number of starts for the first 10 months (846,800) points to a yearly total of 980,000, considerably less than last year's 1.09 million.

Both sets of figures are important. The estimate based on 10 months is, of course, more accurate in forecasting the 1957 total. But the 1 million annual rate derived from the number of starts in October is a more accurate gauge to the future. If that rate continues, as it has for three of the last four months, the housing slump may really be ended. For many lumber and plywood producers, a million housing starts next year won't be enough to sustain production; but there are many who, having adjusted to a lower rate, will welcome the slight change for the better.

———— 27 ————

You cannot bring about prosperity by discouraging thrift. You cannot strengthen the weak by weakening the strong. You cannot help the wage earner by pulling down the wage payer. You cannot further the brotherhood of man by encouraging c l a s s hatred. You cannot help the poor by discouraging the rich. You cannot establish sound security on borrowed money. You cannot keep out of trouble by spending more than you earn. You cannot build character and courage by taking away man's initiative and independence. You cannot help m e n permanently by doing for them what they could and should do for themselves.

ABRAHAM LINCOLN

———— 27 ————

January Birthdays

Many Happy Returns of the Day!

Tom Britton	Roy Eveland
Ralph McCredie	Eldon Nielson
Bertha Davis	John Mershon
Pearl Cloe	Loren Hancock
Clarence Lofstedt	Thelma Rowe
George Murray	Mira Nielson
Marvin Jackson	Mel Mallinson

Rips and Trims

Mr. and Mrs. Paul Dooley spent Christmas day at the home of **Mr. and Mrs. Eugene Potter,** in Wood Village.

Mr. and Mrs. Loren Hancock and **David Rees** spent a day in Seattle visiting **Mr. and Mrs. Dean Davis and family.** Dean is a former employee.

Harry Adolph is sporting a new black and white Ford station wagon.

Mrs. Ed Wendler is in the hospital recovering from an operation. Ed says she is getting along fine.

Mr. and Mrs. John Willms spent Christmas week in eastern Washington visiting his relatives.

Mr. and Mrs. Bud Hunt spent Christmas at the home of **Mr. and Mrs. Howard Hunt** in Corbett.

Howard Hunt's father, who is 89 years old, suffered a slight stroke recently. Everyone wishes him a speedy recovery.

Fred Harp got a new fishing outfit for Christmas and he is open for suggestions on how fish are caught. Anyone here know how?

Mr. and Mrs. John Van Orsow, Mr. and Mrs. Richard Kerslake and family, Mr. and Mrs. Donald Over-guard of Vancouver Wash., Mr. and Mrs. Clarence Van Orsow of Madras, Oregon, were all guests of **Mr. and Mrs. Marvin Van Orsow** of Portland on Christmas day. Got room for any more Marv?

Eugene Potter and family spent New Years week at Donner Lake Lodge, California, visiting his niece, Jo Conley. They spent about four hours in Reno on the trip down but say they did not help the expense situation any.

Vera Nell Roberts is recovered from a bout with the flu and is back on the job.

Connie Meyer and family moved into their new home at Corbett on December 30th.

Eldon Nielson's band played for a dance at Mosier on New Years eve.

Willis and Anna Bowen entertained Anna's brother and sister-in-law, Mr. and Mrs. Everett Clymer of Seattle, over the Christmas holidays.

Beverly Hills of Stanwood, Washington was a holiday visitor at the home of her parents, **Mr. and Mrs. Stanley Hills** of Coopey Falls.

Building Outlook for 1958

Estimates By U.S. Departments of Commerce and Labor.

The November issue of "Construction Review" published by the Commerce and Labor departments has the following to say on page 4:

"A strong advance in total residential building is anticipated for the next year (8 percent, from $17.0 billion to $18.4 billion). This represents an expected 6 percent, $675 million increase in new private nonfarm dwelling units—and, in addition, rapidly rising expenditures for addition and alterations to existing housing (up $335 million) and for construction of new public residential buildings (up $345 million)."

They estimate a total of 1,100,000 new nonfarm dwelling units will be started in 1958, of which 1,050,000 will be privately financed.

F. W. Dodge Estimates

New nonfarm dwelling units will increase 6 percent over 1957 in the opinion of the F. W. Dodge Corporation, for a total of 1,075,000 homes in 1958.

Housing and Home Finance Administration Predictions

Albert Cole, H&HFA administrator, predicts that more than a million new homes will be built in 1958 and cites the easing of mortgage money as the principal basis for his estimate.

Home Financing Outlook

The Wall Street Journal for December 11 quoted financers and builders as reporting easier mortgage financing in Chicago, Philadelphia, Houston and San Francisco. No change yet in Boston and Cleveland but improvement is expected.

The National Savings and Loan League forcasts an increase of about 80 percent in the availability of mortgage money in 1958 as compared with 1957.

BRIDAL VEIL LUMBER & BOX CO.
News Letter

Volume III, No. 8   BRIDAL VEIL, OREGON   FEBRUARY, 1958

Fringe Mathematics

FRINGE: An ornamental border. . .
. . . . . . .N. Webster.

Perhaps it is a little unfortunate that we use the word "fringe" to describe the various forms of compensation not paid directly to employees. The word seems to imply that these forms of pay serve no useful purpose — being of a decorative nature, they are added for appearances' sake only.

Because we use the word "fringe", we tend to belittle the items covered, and thus to lose sight of the cost. For quick figures we can divide the cost of any manufactured product into three main parts — materials, labor and overhead. It makes little practical difference to the manufacturer whether he pays the labor item to his employees or whether he with-holds part and pays it elsewhere at the employees' direction. In this sense, the "fringe' is not something taken out of the employer's pocket.

The logical question at this point is, "How much does the fringe cost?" Let's get it down to pennies per hour so we can see it, understand it, and know what we are doing.

A good round figure for a year's work would be 1920 hours. Starting with 365 days, we knock off the Saturdays and Sundays, the paid vacations, the paid holidays and an average figure for absence, and we come up with 240 working days. Any fringe item can then be divided by 1920 to get the hourly cost.

For example, twelve month's payments for Health and Welfare of $11.00 per month adds up to $132.00. The $132 divided by 1920 hours gives us a cost of 6.9 cents per hour. And this is on the low side. For those who work less than a full year the payment per hour is more.

Based on our average wage of $2.185

per hour, the company pays 2¼ percent or 4.9 cents per hour for social security. The employee matches that with 4.9 cents of his own, making the cost of social security 9.8 cents per hour.

The comapny pays 2.1 percent of the payroll to the State Unemployment Compensation Commission. That works out to 4.6 cents per hour.

The State Industrial Accident Commission comes in for 1.04 percent to pay the cost of accidents past, present and future. Per hour the cost is 2.3 cents per hour.

Here are a couple of items that the employee gets back during the course of a year. To meet the cost of paid vacations and paid holidays and to have the money ready when it is due requires 13.3 cents per hour.

The point here is not that these forms of pay are either "good" or "bad". The real point is that these items total 36.9 cents per hour. And knowing the cost we are better able to decide how much of this type of compensation we want.

L. Kraft

—————— 58 ——————

Construction men prefer wood for windows because when used with modern weather stripping, the combination forms the most efficient method for keeping out cold, heat and dust. It is more difficult to weatherstip metal sash effectively. Also, all buildings, especially when new, settle slightly, often enough to throw windows out of line and cause sticking. Readjustment of wood windows to operate smoothly again is done quickly and economically by simple carpentry. Pre-assembled wood window units—sash, frame, glass, weatherstip, and hardware—can be easily and quickly installed in the wall opening with a minimum of fitting and adjustment.

Record Continues in Maintenance Department

The faces may change but the record goes on. It has been over two years since there has been a lost time accident in the maintenance department. Some of the men responsible for the outstanding achievement are pictured above. From left to right they are: Elmer Ayles; Paul Detrick, foreman; Marvin Jackson, Ralph Taylor, Fay Davis, and Louis Wilson.

Missing when this picture was taken were: Tom Britton, Fred Long and Pearl Cloe.

———— 58 ————

A Texas GI was playing poker with some English soldiers. He drew four aces. 'One pound," ventured the Englishman on his right, "Ah don't know how you'all count your money," said the Texan, "but ah'll raise you a ton."

1957 SAFETY CHART

Month	Tot. Hourly Pd. Man Hrs.	Lost Time Accidents	Accident Freq.	Days Lost	Accident Severity
January	14,288	1	70.0	3	210
February	15,318	0	0	0	0
March	17,182	2	116.4	2	116
FIRST QUARTER	46,788	3	63.9	5	107
April	17,055	0	0	0	0
May	18,924	0	0	0	0
June	16,317	1	61.3	4	245
SECOND QUARTER	52,296	1	19.1	4	76
July	19,880	0	0	0	0
August	21,330	1	46.9	11	516
September	20,706	2	96.6	29	1401
THIRD QUARTER	61,916	3	48.5	40	646
October	21,394	1	46.7	23	1075
November	17,905	0	0	25	140
December	10,926	1	91.5	27	2471
FOURTH QUARTER	50,225	2	39.8	75	1049
TOTAL YEAR	211,225	9	42.6	124	587

NEWS LETTER

Published on the 10th of each month by
Bridal Veil Lumber & Box Co.
Bridal Veil, Oregon

Editor . . . . Don West

20th Anniversary

F e b r u a r y fifteenth will be the twentieth anniversary at Bridal Veil for Paul Detrick, maintenance superintendent.

Paul was born and raised in St. Joseph, Missouri. Later on, the family moved to Montana. While in Montana, on November 11, 1918, Paul was inducted into the army. On the same day, of course, the war ended so the army released him.

In a short while, Paul migrated in a westerly direction and wound up working as a carpenter in Berkeley, California. A little later, Paul and the former Florence Leash were married in Santa Rosa, California. Mrs. Detrick is the daughter of George Leash, a former employee.

After working in Berkeley and Medford, Oregon, Paul went north to work

Health and Welfare Coverage

All employees who worked the required number of hours in December will become eligible for health and welfare coverage and will be covered on the first day of February, 1958. Additions: Robert J. Fitzgerald Jr., Raymond Schneringer. Employees who did not work the required number of hours will become ineligible the same day. Deletions: James C. Belcher, Roger A. Blaine, Leroy H. Brenneke, Gerald G. Carver, Kenneth Catlin, Delbert P. Cloe, Kenneth O. Craig, James E. Dwaes, Jack L. Dempsey, Marvin N. Dhone, Dale Emmons, Joseph E. Gerke, Robert Godat, Stanley B. Hills, Allen D. Hornaday, Allen G. Howell, Walton G. Jones, Edsel E. Kinonen, John E. Matson, Junior D. McMorran, John Mershon, Charles H. Murphy, Shelby W. Nicks, Floyd F. Oden, Orien Pitts, Robert W. Reischel, Robert E. Roberson, Vera Nell Roberts, Jack V. Westlake, Wayne Zumwalt.

for International Wood Products in New Westminster, British Columbia. He worked there for eight years and then to Cathlamet, Washington, where he stayed for five years. Then he came to Bridal Veil.

A number of years ago, P a u l bought a farm near Corbett. He has spent many hours working to improve it and the Detrick's have a very nice home. Paul lists a few of his hobbies as farming, photography, and w o o d-working.

Paul is also fond of pets and has quite an imposing array. He has a Mexican burro called Chester; and a black Labrador dog called Ink. He did have a pet skunk he named Archie but Archie decided to strike out on his own one day.

An amusing incident occurred one evening after Archie had left home. Paul was out milking the cow when he noticed a skunk approaching. Since all skunks look pretty much alike P a u l couldn't tell whether it was Archie or a stranger. In a desperation move to try and decide whether to retreat or hold his ground, Paul blurted out, "Is that you Arch?"

——— 58 ———

A home town is a place w h e r e people wonder how you got as far as you have.

Rips and Trims

Eldon Nielson and his band played for a dance at the Powell Valley Grange Hall January 18th.

Willis Bowen Jr. and family were dinner guests of **Mr. and Mrs. Willis Bowen** on January 26th, in celebration of the fifth birthday of granddaughter, Joyce.

Bob Bird, son of **Mr. and Mrs. Verl Bird,** and former employee, will be married February 7th, to Miss Betty Jo Fast of Dobson. Bob is a machinist apprentice at the Willamette Iron and Steel Co. in Portland. The couple plan on living in Portland.

Connie Meyers' daughter, Carol, who is in nurses training at Providence hospital, received her training cap on Sunday, February 2nd.

February Birthdays

Many Happy Returns of the Day!

Elmer Ayles	Norman Van Buskirk
Mabel Hills	Paul Van Treeck
Beulah Choate	Delbert Dunken
Fred Crouser	Louis Wilson
Ed Wendler	Mary Woodard

Ward Dull is sporting a new French built Renault automobile.

Bob Cowling and Donald Hageman have been selected to play at the Shrine football game in Pendleton this year.

——— 58 ———

Wood Windows Are Still Better

Six companies have been named in a superior court suit seeking $540,-000 damages for alleged inferior workmanship and materials used in construction of additions to St. Cyprians Catholic Church, River Grove, Ill. (a suburb of Chicago).

The complaint was filed by attorney James Muench in behalf of the Rev. Arthur Douaire, and the Catholic Bishop of Chicago. The suit contends defective weathering materials and workmanship in aluminum windows and sashes caused leaks which ruined plaster, ceilings, drapes, rugs, and other furnishings.

The complaint adds that because of the faulty work, the church will have to replace the weathering materials.

The smiles on the faces above would seem to indicate that school can't be as bad as we used to think it was.

Pictured are Marv Van Orsow (left) and Ralph McCredie, attending one of the classes for foremen at the University of Portland.

BRIDAL VEIL LUMBER & BOX CO.
News Letter

Volume III, No. 9   BRIDAL VEIL, OREGON   MARCH, 1958

Safety in 1958

Thursday afternoon February 27th, we held a Safety Committee meeting — the first meeting since August 15, 1957. Making a fresh start after so long a period, we appointed a new safety committee made up of: Marvin Jackson, Chairman; Mel Mallinson, Secretary; Leo Hageman, Jim Kendrick, Eldon Nielson.

Also in attendance at the meeting were Bill Bohlender, Field Representative and W. G. Thorsell, Safety Representative of the State Industrial Accident Commission. At the suggestion of Mr. Thorsell it was agreed that the committee should serve for a period of one year.

The Safety Committee has a serious job to do. The nature of the problem can best be illustrated by our record for the past five years. The following figures express our accident experience in terms of the number of lost time accidents per million man hours worked:

Year	Accidents per Million Man Hours
1953	45.9
1954	52.6
1955	58.1
1956	17.6
1957	42.6

According to the United States Department of Labor figures, our industry averages around twenty accidents per million man hours. After several bad years from 1953 through 1955, we hung up an enviable record in 1956 — the only year in the last five in which we were able to beat the industry average. In 1957 we again fell off the wagon and again had more than twice as many accidents as our industry, and almost two and one half times as many accidents as in 1956.

Lest we get the idea that the campaign against accidents is occasioned only by our desire to reduce our premiums to the State Industrial Accident Commission, we must point out that a reduction in accidents will not result in a reduction in premiums. We already pay the lowest possible rate under the Accident Commission's schedule.

Every lost time accident is a personal problem to someone through loss of earning power and physical suffering. Physical suffering cannot be evaluated, but we can show that lost time accidents caused a loss of $1,800.44 in wages last year. Such a loss is unnecessary — accidents do not have to happen.

Of course, it is one thing to decide that we have had "too many" accidents, and quite another thing to figure out what to do about it.

Over the past couple of years our Safety Committees and the representatives of the State Industrial Accident Commission have turned in almost two hundred suggestions relating to unsafe physical conditions existing in our plant. Ninety-five percent of these dangerous conditions have been corrected. The various Safety Committees have been hard pressed to find additional recommendations. The answer seems to lie in another direction.

The most fertile field now seems to be in the area of unsafe practices. Now we must be alert to the dangers in performing a job in an unsafe way.

In answer to the question, "Am I my brothers' keeper?" The answer is a flat "yes". In addition to looking out for ourselves we are obligated to conduct ourselves so that we do not create a hazard for those around us. And even further, we cannot stand by and watch another pursue a dangerous course, with a shrug of the

(Continued on page 3)

School Days

The first recruits liked school so well three more foremen have signed up for the class on Leadership Development at the University of Portland. As a matter of fact, they are nearly half way through now. This time instead of two men they have allowed three men to take the course together. The happy students this time are Clyde Hambrick, Dean Burkholder, and Einar Mickelson.

1958 Vacations

JANUARY:
1 Fred Crouser 10
8 Merrill Hartshorn 10
23 Mira Nielson 10
26 Clem Hancock 6

FEBRUARY:
7 Roland Morgan 7

MARCH:
1 Ralph Taylor 10
1 Leslie Polzel 7
11 Rodney Jacobson 5
15 Robert Fitzgerald Jr. 5
15 Stanley Hills 10
22 Edward Wendler 6
22 Fay Davis 10
23 Noah Atchley 10
23 Clifford Latourell 10
25 Harold Vogel 10
28 Marvin Stolin 10

APRIL:
1 Archie Davies 10
15 Vera Nell Roberts 10
17 Theophile V. Van Hee 10
18 Theodore Hansen 10
21 Eldon Nielson 10
22 Joseph Van Orsow 10

MAY:
1 Louis Bissell 10
5 Donald Westlake 6
6 Marion Jones 5
6 Bertha Davis 10
6 Harold Burkholder 8
6 Edsel Kinonen 8
8 Lewis Apitz 5
9 Durward Litton 10
11 Walter Stolin 10
13 James Kendrick 10
13 Hiram Layton 10
18 Ward Dull 10

19 Lester Anderson 10
21 Fred Harp 10
27 Theophile V. Van Hee Sr. .. 10
27 Charles N. Gaymon 7

JUNE:
3 Mary Woodward 10
8 Jarvis Kilness 8
13 Orien Pitts 7
20 Paul Van Treeck 10
23 Lester B. Howell 10
28 Bob Layton 10
30 Anna Bowen 10

JULY:
1 Einar Mickelson 10
2 William Dunken 10
2 Fred Damerell 5
2 Ronald Catlin 5
8 Wesley Adams 7
10 Paul Dooley 7
14 Leo F. Hageman 10
18 J. Delbert Dunken 10
19 Lillie Yerion 10
22 Delbert Cloe 5
22 Alfred Barnes 5
22 Kenneth Catlin 5
28 Norman Van Buskirk 10

AUGUST:
9 Theodore V. Van Hee 10
12 Marvin Dhone 5
12 Junior McMorran 5
19 Franklin Bowen 10
21 George Murray 10
23 Jack V. Westlake 5
27 Ralph McCredie 10
29 John Matson 5
30 Arthur Howell 5

SEPTEMBER:
2 Loren Hancock 10
4 Elmer Ayles 10

5 Allen G. Howell 5
8 Jerald G. Roberts 10
9 Fred M. Long 10
10 Joseph Cote 10
11 Roley Zumwalt 8
16 Kenneth Meyer 10
16 Shelby Nicks 5
20 Verl W. Bird 10
20 John Mershon 5
22 Harry Adolph 10
24 Lawrence Peterson 10
27 Kenneth Craig 5
27 Charles Murphy 5
27 Elden Gross 10
29 John Willms 10
29 Roger Blaine 5

OCTOBER:
1 Howard Hunt 10
2 Lawrence Smazal 10
4 Marvin Jackson 10
9 Ralph Ellis 10
9 Homer Walker 10
10 Louis Wilson 8
13 David Rees 8
14 Mabel Hills 10
28 E. H. Potter 10

NOVEMBER:
8 Raymond Schneringer 10
8 Lean Dunlap 7
12 Pearl P. Cloe 10
15 Roy Eveland 10
16 Harold Jacobson 10
23 Earl Hutchison 10
24 Clarence Lofstedt 10

DECEMBER:
7 Beulah Choate 10
12 Thelma Rowe 10
14 Dorothy Hartshorn 10
20 Thomas Britton 10

NEWS LETTER

Published on the 10th of each month by
Bridal Veil Lumber & Box Co.
Bridal Veil, Oregon

Editor . . . . . Don West

Safety in 1958

(Continued from page 1)

shoulders and an "its his funeral" attitude. It may be just that.

Some cne must accept responsibility for every accident in 1957 — who among us will accept responsibility for the accidents of 1958?

Len Kraft

Health and Welfare Coverage

All employees who worked the required number of hours in January will become eligible for health and welfare coverage and will be covered on the first day of March, 1958. Additions: Eleanor Taylor, Kenneth Catlin, Delbert Cloe, Marvin Dhone, Leo C. Hageman, Stanley B. Hills, Allen G. Howell, Arthur V. Howell, Edsel Kinonen, John E. Matson, Junior D. McMorran, John Mershon, Orien Pitts, Vera Nell Roberts, and Jack Westlake. Employees who did not work the required number of hours will become ineligible the same day. Deletions: Lewis E. Apitz, James J. Livingston, and Norman Van Buskirk.

Forecast on New Residential Construction for 1958

Private new residential construction will go up about 6 percent this year.

For this segment of the market, particularly, the year will get better as it goes on.

Biggest disappointment in the first half of the year: although encouraged by the new housing act, home builders will not be able to build as much as they're now planning at least not until money eases and they get commitments.

Another sad fact (though more expected): lower profits, as the squeeze of rising cost continues.

But — and economists make a big point of this — the rate of increase in costs (and other inflationary trends) has slowed down. One result: the median price house has probably reached a plateau at just over $15,000. (NAHB surveys show the median price went up only 3 percent in 1957, compared with 8 percent in '56. No hike is seen in '58.

What this adds up to is a slowly but definitely improving housing market in '58, with starts and dollar volume going up 5-6 percent over '57.

Here's a capsule outlook for '58:

Price tags. Trend toward lower price houses (12,000 to $14,000).

Interest rates. Mortgages, now at peak, will taper off.

Mortgage money. Easier, less competition for it from industry.

Costs. Less climb. More stable price indexes — both wholesale and consumer.

Starts. Up 5-6 percent (ditto dollar volume). Total at least 1,050,000, rock bottom. Estimates range from 1 million to 1.2 million. Figure it this way: a net gain of 800,000 families. Plus 300,000 houses removed from the market. That's a basic need of 1.1 million new houses just to keep afloat.

Rental and cooperative housing. Bigger share of market in '58. Rate of investment return will be more attractive.

Farm housing. Continued drop, creat ing demand for more nonfarm houses.

Housing for elderly. Heavy emphasis in '58.

In short, a very healthy growth year for private housing.

———— 8 ————

New Employees

A hearty welcome is extended to the following new employees:

Melvin Mier   John H. Henigin
Anthony Angelo   Charles D. Jacobson

1958 SAFETY CHART

Month	Tot. Pd. Man Hrs.	Hourly Accidents	Lost Time Accidents Freq.	Accident Days Lost	Accident Severity
January - - - - - - - - -	13,534	0	0	22	1626

Rips and Trims

Charles Gaymon and family visited with friends in Hood River Sunday, February 23rd.

Bert and Fay Davis entertained their grandson, Gordon Timothy, the weekend of March 1st.

Connie Meyers is taking the balance of his vacation during the first week of March. Connie says he is just going to take it easy.

Eugene Potter is back on the job after recovering from an arm injury suffered while playing with a neighbors young son. He found out the younger generation is pretty rugged.

Hiram Layton has three fractured ribs, as the result of a fall, which occurred Saturday, February 22nd.

Delbert Dunken, son Bob, and their families, attended the "Gay Nineties" celebration at Forest Grove the past weekend. It is rumored that Delbert took a prize.

Bob Bird suffered third degree burns on one hand while at work at the Willamette Iron and Steel Co. He is continuing on the job, however. Bob is the son of Mr. and Mrs. Verl Bird.

Its a baby boy for the Edsel Kinonen's. Born February 15th at Portland Osteopathic Hospital. Congratulations.

Eldon Nielson and family visited the Leroy Newman family in Shelton, Washington, the weekend of February 22nd.

———— 8 ————

We were steaming up the Mississippi river in our Navy destroyer last month when we became enveloped in a dense fog. Lookouts were posted, and the man on the bow of the ship was ordered to keep a very sharp watch —particularly for floating debris that might foul up our propellers.

As we eased through the strange, opaque atmosphere, the captain nervously paced around the bridge. Suddenly the sailor on the bow watch boomed out: "Large tree — dead ahead!"

"Which way is she floating?" yelled back the captain.

"Floating, hell! It's growing!" roared back the man on the bow as we splintered into the tree and went aground on a mud bank.

March Birthdays

Many Happy Returns of the Day!

Martha Jones	Noah Atchley
Walter Stolin	Elden Gross
Paul Dooley	

New Safety Committee

Let's get acquainted with the new safety committee, which, under a new system worked out at the last safety meeting, will be in office for an entire year. Left to right are: Eldon Nielson, Mel Mallinson, secretary; Jim Kendricks, Marvin Jackson, chairman; and Leo Hageman.

BRIDAL VEIL LUMBER & BOX CO.
News Letter

Volume III, No. 10   BRIDAL VEIL, OREGON   APRIL, 1958

Now You Know

Some months ago, someone handed me a magazine with an article in it about a fellow named Gumperson. Gumperson's claim to fame is that he was the father of the now famous Gumperson's Law. The law, simply stated, is that the contradictory of a welcome probability will assert itself whenever such an eventuality is likely to be most frustrating. People familiar with these matters will perhaps recognize another version of the law: The outcome of a given desired probability will be inverse to the degree of desirability.

Dr. R. F. Gumperson, internationally famous divisist, began serious work in 1938 on a phenomenon long known to scientists but up until then considered as a mere curiosity. This was the fact that the forecasting record of the weather bureau, despite its use of the most advanced equipment and highly trained personnel, was not as good as that of "The Old Farmers' Almanac". After four years of research, Dr. Gumperson ennunciated his law and was able to make a series of predictions later confirmed by other scientists in the field. The following are included in his better known predictions:

1. That the girl at the race track who bets according to the color of the jockey's shirt will pick more winners than the man who has studied the past performance of every horse on the program.

2. That the person who buys the most raffle tickets has the least chance of winning.

3. That good parking places are always on the other side of the street.

Dr. Gumperson also served as a consultant to the armed services during World War II and evolved the procedure whereby the more a recruit knew about a given subject, the better chance he had of receiving an assignment involving some other subject.

I have been fascinated by the wide applications we can make of Gumperson's Law of Perverse Opposites in our daily lives. Here, for example, is the explanation of why, after years of pampering and fertilizing, I have never been able to harvest over a half a dozen spears of asparagus from my asparagus bed while I have to tear the stuff up like crazy from among my shrubs and flower beds.

Everybody bumps up against the inexorable workings of Gumperson's Law at one time or another. The kids get measles during vacation. What kid ever had his own school house burn down? How many mothers have knocked themselves out preparing a special meal only to have the kids pick at it with the comment, "I'm not hungry"? All examples of the operation of Gumperson's Law.

This thing lops over into the business world, too. Now we know why the switcher comes at 9:00 a.m. to pick up a car that will be ready at 2:00 p m.: Gumperson's Law.

How come the luggage orders never fit the stock that has been cut? Gumperson's Law. Which days do the truckers carefully cover the lumber—sunny days or rainy days? Is the banker more apt to loan you money when you need it or when you don't?

You can work up your own examples by the dozens. But I thought you'd ought to know about Gumperson's Law.

Len Kraft.

———— 33 ————

The Bridal Veil Trucks are wearing "Spring finery" in the way of identifying signs in accordance with P. U. C. regulations.

20th Anniversary

Joe Van Orsow, Tenoner operator, will observe his twentieth anniversary at Bridal Veil on April 22, 1958. Need-

less to say, Joe was quite young when he came to work here.

Joe was born in Fairbault, Minnesota, the son of a farmer. He received his education in Fairbault. When Joe was fifteen years old the family moved to Multnomah, Oregon. After a while Joe got a job at a dairy and stayed there until he could get on at Bridal Veil.

In September, 1941, Joe joined the Army where he was to remain until September, 1945. He served in the Coastal Artillery in the Aleutian Islands, and also in the Chemical Warfare Service in Germany.

Joe and Mary Britton were married at Vancouver, Washington, on October 9, 1948. Mary is the daughter of Tom Britton, who is pretty well known here at Bridal Veil. Joe and Mary have four children: Mary 7, Terry 6, Walter 4 and little Tommy, aged 2.

Goin' Fishin'

After twenty-two years at Bridal Veil, Noah Atchley, above, has retired. Noah says he is going to do a lot of fishing, something he enjoys. We hope you catch all you want, Noah.

Joe says Tommy looks just like the fellow he is named after.

Joe and Mary have their home at 1212 S. E. 175th Place in Portland. They are members of St. Anne s church near Rockwood.

Besides being related to Tom Britton, Joe is a first cousin of Marvin Van Orsow, cutter foreman.

Joe has never had a lost time accident in the twenty years he has been here. A very enviable record. Keep it up Joe.

———— 33 ————

"If you can spare me five minutes, sir," announced the door to door canvasser, "I can show you how to earn twice as much money as you are now getting."

"Don't bother," said the man sadly, "I do that now."

1958 SAFETY CHART

Month	Tot. Hourly Pd. Man Hrs.	Lost Time Accidents	Accident Freq.	Days Lost	Accident Severity
January	13,534	0	0	22	1626
February	14,089	2	141.9	21	1491
Total	27,623	2	72.4	43	1557

NEWS LETTER

Published on the 10th of each month by
Bridal Veil Lumber & Box Co.
Bridal Veil, Oregon

Editor . . . . . Don **West**

20th Anniversary

April 18, 1958, will be the twentieth anniversary at Bridal Veil for Ted Hanson, crossworking department.

One of eight children, Ted was born in Clarrissa, Minnesota. His father was a farmer. Ted went to school in Clarrissa.

Ted worked in St. Paul, Minnesota, for two years and then came out to Portland. He worked at a dairy for a year and then came to Bridal Veil in the fall of 1927. Yes, Ted has actually been working at Bridal Veil for thirty years, but of course not all of that time for the present company.

He worked for the Bridal Veil Timber Company until the mill burned down, either in 1935 or 1936. Then he moved to Springfield and worked in a mill there until he came back to Bridal Veil to work for the present company on April 18, 1938.

On July 3, 1942, Ted and the former Euleta Wheeler of Walla Walla, Washington, were married in Vancouver, Washington. They have three children, Dale, 15, a student at Laurelwood Academy near Gaston, Oregon; Dick,

Health and Welfare

All employees who worked the required number of hours in February will become eligible for health and welfare coverage and will be covered on the first day of April, 1958. Additions: Roger A. Blaine, Kenneth O. Craig, Robert D. Godat, Charles H. Murphy, Shelby W. Nicks, Mira J. Nielson, Robert W. Reischel and Norman Van Buskirk. Employees who did not work the required number of hours will become ineligible the same day. Deletions: Thomas C. Britton, George Murray and Eleanor Taylor.

——— 33 ———

April Birthdays

Many Happy Returns of the Day!

Dorothy Hartshorn   Ted Hanson
Joe Van Orscw   Fred Long
John Willms

——— 33 ———

The drunk started ringing the hotel operator at 5 a.m. and demanded to know when the bar opened.

She told him it did not open until 11 a.m. He called again at 6 a.m. and again at 7. Finally she had the night clerk answer the phone.

"Good morning," said the clerk to the drunk, "and listen to me. We don't care to have your kind of business. And we don't care if you never get into our bar."

"Shay, you," was the angry reply. "I'm already in the bar, I'm trying to get out."

——— 33 ———

You're getting old when the gleam in your eye is from the sun hitting your bifocals.

When it takes twice as long to rest and only half as long to get tired.

When you don't care where you go, just so you're home by 9 p.m.

13, and Cheryl, 10. The Hansons live right here in Bridal Veil.

Ted has an aunt and a sister in Portland and two brothers and a sister in Springfield, Oregon.

Ted's hobby is leathercraft. He turns out some mighty nice billfolds and purses.

Ted has only one lost time accident since he has been at Bridal Veil and it was only a minor one. Wish we all had a record like that.

Rips and Trims

Walt and Ann Keller are off on a two week vacation to Canada. **Ruth Litton** and **Trinnie Bailey** are "minding" the store while Kellers are away.

Walt Norgard is driving a new Buick. **The Norgards** went "C l a m ming" down at Long Beach, Washington over Easter weekend. As ususal, they got their limit of clams.

Jim and Lou Cowling motored to Eugene to visit Lou's parents and then on to Oakridge to see Jim's brother and sister-in-law.

Robert Fitzgerald spent his vacation going to school to learn to be a service station operator. He plans on working at it part time.

Rodney Jacobson has to report for induction into the Army on the 21st of April. Good luck Rodney.

William Dunken's son cut his finger quite badly in a fall last week but Bill says it is healing rapidly now.

Mr. and Mrs. Marv Van Orsow and family spent a recent weekend at the home of Clarence Van Orsow in Culvert, Oregon.

Bert Cowling and Jim Tuiekes were guests of the **Jim Cowlings'** recently, as were Mr. and Mrs. J. J. Kennedy of Medford.

Eldon Nielson has five pups which ie will give away in about three weeks, as soon as they are six weeks old. Anyone interested in aquiring a puppy should get in touch with Eldon for particulars.

Roy Eveland had a surprise visit from a niece and a sister-in-law during his lunch hour last week. T h e y were on their way to Tygh Valley to visit relatives.

Mr. and Mrs. Marv Van Orsow and family spent Easter Sunday at the home of Mr. and Mrs. Don Overguard in Vancouver.

Durward and Ruth Litton entertained Ruth's sister, Ethel Matheson, of Hermiston, the past weekend.

Frank Bowen reports that his son, **Donald,** has left the University of Oregon and enrolled at Benke - Walker Business College in Portland.

Fred Harp went fishing on Easter Sunday. Fred says fishing was terrible but that he did manage to lose a couple of lures. Stay with it Fred.

Lawrence Peterson visited a brother at Cottage Grove during his vacation; and also took in two basketball games at Eugene during the state high school tournament.

Bridal Veil Visitors

Visiting Bridal Veil on April 3 were Dominic Santerelli and Walter Mann, both from Aurora, Illinois. They were accompanied by E. W. Ruddick of Western Tree Products, Inc., of Tacoma, Washington. Mr. Mann, center, and Mr. Ruddick, on the right, purchase window frames at Bridal Veil.

BRIDAL VEIL LUMBER & BOX CO.
News Letter

Volume III, No. 11   BRIDAL VEIL, OREGON   MAY, 1958

'Take Out'

The credit reference book used by the lumber trade is known as the Lumbermen's Red Book. Twice a week we receive a supplement to the Red Book listing changes in credit ratings. The supplement covering the four days from April 26 to April 29, which include a Saturday and a Sunday carries a total of fifty entries labelled "take out". The fateful words "take out" incidate that the firm listed is no longer in business, and we are being instructed to remove its name from the book. The thought never occurred to me before, but the color of the book might be considered especially well chosen, considering the condition of the industry.

The fifty "take out" entries include a wide range of sawmills, retail yards, millwork houses, furniture makers, wholesalers, jobbers and other types of customers of the lumber industry. There are a lot of reasons why a name should be dropped from the Red Book. Maybe an outfit isn't making money, and decides to quit before the sheriff takes over. Maybe the sheriff has already taken over. Another outfit may be closing unprofitable branches.

The heat is on competitively speaking. And those who can't stand the heat, paraphrasing "Engine Charley" will have to get out of the kitchen. That is another way of saying that a company that cannot maintain efficiency won't remain competitive very long. And a long line of tough and vigorous competitors are always ready, able and anxious to move in and take over.

Now if all we had to worry about in the lumber business was competition among ourselves, that wouldn't be so bad. But those fateful words in the Red Book "take out" may have another and far more sinister meaning. It may mean that the firm taken out is no longer using wood products. They may have found a serviceable substitute for less money. We in the millwork business can understand the seriousness of the threat of competing products. Almost every road we travel leads past houses in which metal sash has replaced our product. Most particularly we notice that practically all industrial and commercial properties have switched to metal. We know from personal observation that we must furnish high quality, low cost merchandise or we will lose our markets to those who do.

Getting down to specific examples, Bridal Veil Lumber and Box Co. can say, "This is where we came in." During the late thirties Bridal Veil employed up to two hundred people making wooden cheese boxes. The volume of business was so big that even then the fibre boys were nipping at our heels. The post war explosion of rising costs of materials and labor caught us with our competitive pants down, and the cheese box business slipped away to the more efficient fibre box manufacturers. It is significant that we do not have a single employee with us today whose employment dates from 1949 or 1950, the period of conversion from boxes to millwork. We just plain weren't hiring. There was no business — for us.

The implication is clear. Competition is not just something for the boss to worry about. Although he bumps into competition every day, the sales manager alone can't solve the problem. Our competitive position will be assured at the individual work station where quality and cost, concern for the customer, and elimination of waste and scrap originate.

The hard facts of layoffs, shorter

(Continued on Page 4)

O. and K. Revamps Backyard

All the activity between the dry kiln and the dip tank has been prompted by the fact that the company is planning to move the dry lumber shed to a new location. It is to be placed just east of the dip tank along the railroad track.

In later editions we plan to do a story on how the building is to be used in its new location.

When it was decided to move the building, it was found that it would not leave any place for the larger trucks

to unload and turn around. O and K construction company of Gresham has undertaken to provide such a place between the tank for the toxic treating material and the dry kilns. At the same time they are making three fills which were badly needed. In that way they are not only making a turnaround, but they have a place to put the dirt and rocks. By the time the next issue of the Newsletter is out the project should be completed.

At a dinner party one evening, a lady was introduced to a tall, rangy Texan.

"Oh, are you one of those rich Texans I've heard so much about?" gushed the lady.

"Well, I reckon I have about 36 acres."

"That doesn't sound like much," the lady said dubiously.

"Mebbe not," the Texan said slowly, "but my 36 acres are called downtown Dallas."—Manage Magazine

A human being is a guy who'll laugh himself silly over a family album, then look in a mirror and never crack a smile.

———— 63 ————

The boss met the tardy employee at the door.

"Do you know what time we start work?" the boss asked.

"I think it's 8:30," the employee said, "but I'll find out for sure and let you know."—Phoenix Flame

NEWS LETTER

Published on the 10th of each month by
Bridal Veil Lumber & Box Co.
Bridal Veil, Oregon

Editor . . . . . Don West

Things Are Looking Up

Having just returned from week's trip to the Middle West (back east to me), I feel much better about business conditions.

It's amazing how much territory one can cover in a week's time.

We left Portland at nine-thirty on a Sunday morning. At 6 o'clock that evening I had dinner with Howard Dekker of Dekker-Brish Millwork Co. and later on that night I traveled on to Cincinnati, Ohio.

While in Cincinnati, I called on Pease Woodwork Co. and the Cincinnati Sash and Door Co. I left Cincinnati Monday night and went to St. Louis, Missouri. There I rented a car and called on a customer in East St. Louis and a former customer up north in Mattoon, Illinois.

Wednesday night I left St. Louis and traveled to Kansas City. There I called on our regular customers as well as a few new prospects. From there I came home.

The thing that pleased me so much about business conditions was the fact that all the companies I visited seemed to be very busy. Some of them even stated that they could not set up window frame units as fast as they were selling them. Needless to say, things have taken a decided turn for the better in the past month. The way it looks now, business should hold up fairly well for the balance of the year.

Don West

——— 63 ———

May Birthdays

Many Happy Returns of the Day !

Cliff Latourell	Anna Bowen
Homer Walker	Fred Bailey
Leon Dunlap	Ralph Taylor
Junior McMorran	Stanley Hills
Lloyd DeMain	David Rees
Lawrence Peterson	Frank Bowen
Leo Hageman	Leslie Polzel
Marvin Stolin	

Retiring

Leon Dunlap, employed at Bridal Veil since July 1955, is retiring on May 16th. Leon says he is going to do a lot of salmon fishing, something he really enjoys. We hope you catch lots of them Leon.

——— 63 ———

Health and Welfare

All employees who worked the required number of hours in March will become eligible for health and welfare coverage and will be covered on the first day of May, 1958. Additions: Anthony Angelo, Lewis Apitz, Arthur Baker, Lercy Brenneke, Tom Britton, Raymond Coté, James E. Dawes, John H. Henigin, Charles D. Jacobson, Walton G. Jones, Steven Kuzmesky, Melvin Mier, and George Murray. Employees who did not work the required number of hours will become ineligible the same day. Deletions: Shelby Nicks, and Louis Wilson.

——— 63 ———

Safety is not a contest between different companies. It is a contest waged by each of us against the ambulance, the hospitals and the funeral.

——— 63 ———

Drunk: What's that crawling up the wall?

Bartender: A ladybug.

Drunk: Gad! What eyesight.

Rips and Trims

Robert Fitzgerald's son has returned home after a week in the hospital battling pneumonia.

Rodney Jacobson, who recently was called up by the Army, is now stationed at Ford Ord in California and reportedly likes what he has seen in the Army so far.

Gerald Roberts spent opening weekend of trout season on the Deschutes but didn't have very good luck. Wonder if that means he got skunked?

Harry Adolph recently visited with his sister in eastern Oregon for several days. While there he got in a little fishing, and claims he did quite well.

Roy Eveland hooked into a big Sturgeon over the weekend. Roy didn't get to find out how big the fish was because after he was hooked, the fish just took off down the river and didn't stop for anything.

Fred Harp has been fishing a couple of times already but has had little success. Stay with it Fred.

Robert Godat and Robert Fitzgerald have both had automobile accidents within the last month. They were both very lucky as they were unhurt.

Paul Dooley and family are now living at Springdale.

Mr. and Mrs. Roy Eveland recently spent a few days in Seattle visiting with their daughter.

John Matson was employed for two weeks in a mill at Shelton, Washington while he was laid off.

David Rees came back to work with a good tan after his vacation.

Allen Howell and Junior McMorran are both reported to be working on a dam near Pasco, Washington.

The Charles Gaymon family recently enjoyed an outing at Ocean Lake, Delake, and Depoe Bay.

Mr. and Mrs. Willis Bowen and Mr. and Mrs. Jimmy Bowen and family were recent guests of **Mr. and Mrs. Delbert Dunken.**

Verl Bird received word that his brother Howard, Superintendent of Kinzua Pine Mills, is confined to a hospital in Heppner, Ore., after suffering a light heart attack Friday, May 2nd, at Kinzua. He is reported to be recovering nicely.

Mr. and Mrs. Willis Bowen were guests of the Jimmy Bowen family at a potluck dinner held at the Gresham Elks Club.

Ed Kinonen landed a twenty - two pound chinook salmon at the Bonneville fishing grounds, while off the job recently.

Mabel and Stanley Hills attended the wedding of their daughter Beverly, on April 26th, at the Immaculate Conception Church in Arlington, Washington. The groom is Mr. William Steffan of Camano Island, Washington. Mr. Steffan is a salesman for the Corona Coffee Co. of Tacoma, Wash. The couple will be at home with their friends, in Tacoma, after a short honeymoon in Canada.

——— 63 ———

'Take Out'

(Continued from Page 1)

work weeks, plant closings and declining profits are all about us. The answer lies in efficient operation — the ability to meet and beat all comers in the competition of the market place. There is no other way. That is the way our market economy works.

Len Kraft

——— 63 ———

One out of every 40 Oregon teenagers who accept industrial jobs is liable to injury, a ten-year state bureau of labor study has shown.

1958 SAFETY CHART

Month	Tot. Pd. Man Hrs.	Hourly Lost Time Accidents	Accident Freq.	Days Lost	Accident Severity
January	13,534	0	0	22	1626
February	14,089	2	141.9	21	1491
March	19,340	0	0	21	1086
First Quarter	46,963	2	42.6	64	1363
First Quarter 1957	46,788	3	63.9	5	107

BRIDAL VEIL LUMBER & BOX CO.

News Letter

Volume III, No. 12   BRIDAL VEIL, OREGON   JUNE, 1958

NWMA

Some months ago Bridal Veil Lumber and Box Co. joined the National Woodwork Manufacturers Association, Inc. The roster of members reads like the Blue Book of millwork manufacturers in America. Forty-one firms including the largest and best known in the country are members.

Our attention was first drawn to NWMA when we were called upon by the United States Department of Commerce to record our opinion of Stock Millwork Standards being worked up by NWMA. This project is but one of several being conducted by NWMA. Another is working up minimum standards for toxic and water repellant treatment of Ponderosa Pine millwork. Still another project involves work on the design of a wood combination door to compete with the presently popular product of the aluminum industry.

Of particular interest to us is the statistical information collected from the members and made available to all those who participate. For example, twenty-six companies supply the Association with information on orders received, production and shipments of exterior frames. The Association totals the figures from the individual companies and reports back to the membership.

By comparing orders received, production and shipment figures of Bridal Veil with the industry totals, we are able to tell where we stand — are we maintaining our position in the industry, bettering our position, or losing ground?

In new orders were placed equally between all the twenty-six mills reporting, each mill would have roughly 4 percent of the total. In 1956 Bridal Veil received 3.8 percent of the exterior frame orders reported to the Association. In 1957, although our volume fell substantially below 1956, our share of the industry total inched upward to 3.9 percent. In both years, ours was slightly less than an "average" share.

All of which is interesting as a matter of past history. The important question is—how are we doing today? During the first four months of 1958, orders for window frames and exterior door frames received at Bridal Veil have moved forward to 5.1 percent of the industry total.

Stated another way, orders received at Bridal Veil during the first four months of 1958 are running ahead of last year by 5.4 percent. The industry as a whole, however, has received 3.5 percent fewer orders this year than last year.

The conclusion that we can readily draw from all these figures is that not only are we increasing our share of the business, but also we are bucking the industry trend.

And this is as it should be. At least from our standpoint. So long as we remain enterprising and vigorous, we can wrest an even larger share of the market from our competitors. In this direction lies steady employment and job security.

But, lest we get too cocky, let's remember that our markets are nationwide, and that there are twenty-five other outfits that we know about that are more than anxious to knock us off. The winner will be the ones who can produce the best product at the best price.

Len Kraft

———— 4 ————

Arguments and quarrels at home are many times behind the rage expressed by reckless driving on the highway. Many a husband who cannot control his home has tried to prove his manhood by overcontrolling his car and has thus become a traffic hazard.   Billy Graham

Coming Events

Paul Detrick and his maintenance crew, with an assist from the Troutdale Sand and Gravel Company, are shown pouring the foundation for the lumber shed, which is to be moved from its present location. Although we were unable to get them into the picture, there were several sidewalk superintendents giving invaluable aid to the project.

Health and Welfare Coverage

All employees who worked the required number of hours in April will become eligible for health and welfare coverage and will be covered on the first day of June 1958. Additions: None. Employees who did not work the required number of hours will become ineligible the same day. Deletions: Wesley A. Adams, Harry Adolph, Lester Anderson, Anthony Angelo, Lewis Apitz, Noah Atchley, Arthur Baker, Alfred Barnes, Louis Bissell, Roger Blaine, Leroy Brenneke, Kenneth Catlin, Ronald Catlin, Delbert Cloe, Joseph Cote, Ray Cote, Kenneth Craig, James Dawes, Marvin Dhone, Paul Dooley, William Dunken, Leon Dunlap, Roy Eveland, Charles Gaymon, Robert Godat, Eldon Gross, Leo Hageman, Clem Hancock, Loren Hancock, John Henigin, Mabel Hills.

Stanley Hills, Allen Howell, Arthur Howell, Lester B. Howell, Earl Hutchison, Charles Jacobson, Marion Jones, Walton Jones, Edsel Kinonen, Steven Kuzmesky, John Matson, Junior McMorran, John Mershon, Melvin Mier, Roland Morgan, Charles Murphy, Orien Pitts, Leslie Polzel, E. H. Potter, David Rees, Robert Reischel, Vera Nell Roberts, Thelma Rowe, Raymond Schneringer, Norman Van Buskirk, Theophile Van Hee Sr., Homer Walker, Edward Wendler, Donald Westlake, Jack Westlake, John G. Willms, and Roley Zumwalt.

——— 4 ———

My buddy won top honors last Saturday for the best advice to a woman driver. We pulled up alongside a female at an intersection who kept gunning her motor wildly, but appeared unable to get the car moving. After watching her for a few minutes, my buddy shouted above the roar of her engine: "Let the clutch out, lady. The fan won't pull it."

——— 4 ———

If an armload of boxes
Your vision impairs,
You take a chance
On falling downstairs.

Safety Monitor

NEWS LETTER

Published on the 10th of each month by
Bridal Veil Lumber & Box Co.
Bridal Veil, Oregon

Editor . . . . Don West

Bridal Veil Visitor

Pictured above is Mr. H. C. Nielsen of Hardwood Products Corporation of Neenah, Wisconsin, for whom we supply core blocks. Mr. Nielsen made a one month tour of the western part of the country, calling on core block suppliers.

———— 4 ————

Summer Replacements

Bob Cowling and Don Hageman are working in the mill during school vacations, filling in for regular employees on vacation.

Home Building Gains Sharply

Reports from FHA for April indicate increased activity in new home building. Here are the figures.

April applications for new h o m e mortgages were 26 percent ahead of March, and 89 percent above April 1957.

Starts for new FHA insured homes during April were 33 percent above March and 82 percent above April 1957, the highest monthly volume since April, 1955.

These are encouraging signs a n d should forecast increased demand for woodwork products within the n e a r future.

———— 4 ————

June Birthdays

Many Happy Returns of the Day!

Rodney Jacobson	Jerry Roberts
Earl Hutchison	Harold Jacobson
Jim Kendrick	James Dawes
Roland Morgan	Durward Litton
Ray Cote	Ray Schneringer

———— 4 ————

Today, through scientific treatment with chemical preservative, wood windows are more durable, more lasting than ever before. Wood windows treated with a water repellent preservative are highly resistant to decay and dimensional change such as swelling, shrinking and warping. Wood windows do not rust or corrode. Wood windows withstand the salt air of seaside locations and even the concentration of acid fumes which occur in many industrial areas.

———— 4 ————

"Good morning madam. I'm from the gas company. I understand there's somthing in the house that won't work."

"Yes, he's upstairs."

1958 SAFETY CHART

Month	Tot. Pd. Man Hrs.	Hourly Accidents	Lost Time Accident Freq.	Accident Days Lost	Accident Severity
January	13,534	0	0	22	1626
February	14,089	2	141.9	21	1491
March	19,340	0	0	21	1086
First Quarter	46,963	2	42.6	64	1363
April	9,312	0	0	22	2368
Total	56,275	2	35.5	86	1528

Rips and Trims

Ed Wendler and party spent Memorial day weekend at Wickiup Reservoir and Crane Prairie. They had little luck at Wickiup but did rather well at Crane Prairie.

Edsel Kinonen and party of six fished at Cove state park over the weekend and came home with eighty-six trout. Not too bad.

Mr. and Mrs. Fred Harp spent the holidays at Long Beach, Washington digging clams and came home with the limit. Fred's mother will be with the Harps for a two week visit.

T/Sgt. and Mrs. Calvin Roberts and family arrived in Gresham on June 4th where they will visit relatives. Calvin is a former employee.

Mrs. Marvin Dhone is spending a week in Washington visiting her mother and sister.

Fred Crouser says he is going to take it easy on his vacation. He will probably have plenty of work to do at home.

Howard Hunt and a party of three spent the holidays fishing on the White River but reported scant success.

John Van Orsow, Richard Kerslake, and **Marvin Van Orsow** spent a recent weekend fishing at Wickiup but like the others, didn't do too well. We hope, before the season is over, that someone comes up with a real good fish story. We need at least one a year.

Jerry Roberts and Bernard Anderson fished the Deschutes on the 31st of May and came home with a limit of trout.

Sons and daughters of Bridal Veil employees who graduate from either grade or high school this year include: **Rose Howell, Sharon Hartshorn, Marjorie Stolin, Diana Taylor, Archie Westlake, Don Hageman, Phillip Schneringer, Bob Cowling, Marsha Howell, Gerald Kraft, Val Rae Dull,** and **Judy Jones.**

Walt and Lillian Norgard have just returned from a vacation trip which took them to Madison, Wisconsin, for a visit with son David and family.

Mary Lee Kreman (Taylor) was a recent visitor at the home of her parents, **Mr. and Mrs. Ralph Taylor.**

Mr. and Mrs. Willis Bowen and Mr. and Mrs. Neal Woolf drove to Aberdeen, Washington over Memorial day weekend and dug clams at Copalis Beach. Anna says the clams were big and plentiful.

Martha Jones, and family have moved from Cascade Locks to Bonneville.

Marilyn Jones, daughter of **Mr. and Mrs. Floyd Jones** celebrated her 15th birthday June first.

Jerry and Vera Nell Roberts are taking a three weeks vacation, beginning Friday June 6th, just after work. They are going to Jay, Oklahoma, to visit relatives and will return by way of Mexico and California.

Eldon Nielson and family will accompany them as far as Oklahoma, but will return by a different route through Texas and Utah. They also plan to visit relatives in Colorado.

Durward and Ruth Litton have completed moving to their new home on the lower Bridal Veil road. Now for a little rest.

Robert Crooke, one of our newer employees, says his daughter **Wendy** is entered in the Multnomah County district "baby contest" to be held June 28th. Good luck Wendy.

Merrill and Dorothy Hartshorn are taking two weeks vacation beginning Saturday, June 7th. Merrill is going to do some fishing but Dorothy says she is going to stay home.

Beulah Choate enjoyed a two weeks vacation recently, staying home and getting rested up to come back to work.

Charles Gaymon and family took a trip to Madras and The Dalles over the weekend.

Gerry Kraft will attend summer school at Lewis and Clark college this year.

———— 4 ————

New Employees

A hearty welcome is extended to the following new employees:

Arthur R. Johnson   Donald Bowen
Leonard Volkman   Harold Powell
Ronald Jackson   Floyd Jacobs
Peter Graymer   Don Barnes
Wayne Owens   Ray Gregor
Robert Crooke   Gerald Dull
David Johnson

BRIDAL VEIL LUMBER & BOX CO.

News Letter

Volume III, No. 12   BRIDAL VEIL, OREGON   JULY, 1958

Ruether vs. Economics

Walter Ruether has been in the news quite a bit of late. He says that General Motors Corporation isn't being run right—a point which G. M.'s 171,-746 shareholders would probably dispute which him. Anyway, Mr. R. says G. M. makes too much money, charges too much for cars, and doesn't pay high enough wages.

About a hundred years ago a very brilliant and highly educated man named Karl Marx wrote a document which he called a "Communist Manifesto." Briefly, Marx argued that workers would never be free until they themselves owned the facilities of production. But in developing this theory, Marx made one fatal mistake which has spread misery and suffering all over the world. He thought that public ownership and government ownership were one and the same thing. And of course, they aren't. They are p o l e s apart, as millions of wretched people have discovered to their sorrow.

The workers in Russia had their revolution, but they did not end up owning the tools of production. T h e State owns the tools and the workers own nothing — not even the right to protest through their labor unions.

Then the workers in England had their revolution too — with ballots instead of bullets. The government — acting in the name of labor — t o o k over virtually all of the key industries in Britain; but still the men who worked in the mines, in the steel mills and on the railroads did not own the tools of production. The government owned them — the men themselves soon found out they had merely traded one set of bosses for another.

Instead of taking orders from the former owners of these enterprises, the workers now took their orders from the bureaucrats; and the very first thing these bureaucrats tried to

do was to show a profit on these state-owned operations. To that end they raised prices substantially and repeatedly; and they resisted wage increases with a determination and force that government alone can command.

In his thirst for revolution, Marx overlooked completely the only economic system on earth under which it is possible for the workers themselves to own, to control and to manage directly the facilities for production. And shocking as the news may be to the disciples of Karl Marx, that system is Capitalism.

Here in America we have real and direct public ownership of our biggest and most important industries. That ownership is sold daily, in little pieces, on the stock market. If the workers of this country truly wish to own the tools of production, they can do so very simply. All in the world they have to do is to buy, in the open market the capital stock of the corporation they want to own -- just as millions of other Americans have been doing for decades.

Which brings us back to W a l t e r Reuther. The 588,160 employees of General Motors could buy, in the market, working control of G. M. in ten years for something like $16.00 per week. Then they could elect W a l t e r Reuther president of the company, and straighten things out.

Along about the time each worker ended up with some $8,000 or $9,000 invested in the business, some interesting problems would arise. The workers would still not be their own bosses, for the true bosses of every American business are its customers, and unless those customers are satisfied as to the quality and price of the product, there will be no business and there will be no jobs. Wage policies that used up the

(Continued on Page 4)

20th Anniversary

Out of his life, Jim Cowling has spent twenty years as saw filer at Bridal Veil, first as second filer and then as head filer, his present position.

Jim was born at Sweet Home, Oregon, one of six children. Jim's father came to this country from England at the age of twenty-one. Jim received his education at Brush Creek and Mohawk, Oregon.

Jim spent five years as saw filer at Westfir, Oregon; one year filing at Coquille, and several months filing at Linnton before coming to Bridal Veil.

Jim and the former Lula M. Drew were married in Vancouver, Washington on July 5, 1935. Lou is the present Postmaster at Bridal Veil. The Cowlings have three children: Thomas J., Robert L., and Patricia Lou. Tom will be a junior at the University of Oregon this fall and Bob will be a freshman at the same school. Patty will be in the eighth grade at Corbett. The Cowlings live in Bridal Veil.

Hunting and fishing are Jim's hobbies. It has been said that he is fairly proficient at both. Jim likes sports of any kind and has been known to drive as far as two hundred miles to see a high school football game.

Jim is a member and Past Master of the Bridal Veil Lodge of the Ancient Free and Accepted Masons. He is a member of the Order of Eastern Star,

15th Anniversary

July 14th will be the fifteenth anniversary at Bridal Veil for Leo Hageman, tenoner operator. Since coming

to Bridal Veil, Leo has worked in nearly all departments of the plant.

Leo was born on a farm near Carroll, Iowa, one of eleven children. He remained on the farm until he got married. Leo was educated in a country school which was also near Carroll.

Leo and the former Edna Jones of Audubon, Iowa, were married on February 7, 1933 in Carroll, Iowa. After their marriage, Leo worked in Gray, Iowa, as a school custodian and bus driver. They have two sons, Leo and Donald, both of whom are presently working in the plant.

The Hageman family came to Oregon in early July 1943 and Leo came to work at Bridal Veil two weeks later as a result of a talk with George Leash, who lived near where Leo was staying at the time.

Leo has a sister living in Portland and a brother in Vancouver. His mother lives in Seattle. Leo enjoys gardening as a hobby. He is a member of the Eagles lodge.

Troutdale Chapter 80. He is a thirty year member of the M.W.A. The Cowlings are members of St. Luke's Episcopal Church of Gresham.

NEWS LETTER

Published on the 10th of each month by
Bridal Veil Lumber & Box Co.
Bridal Veil, Oregon

Editor . . . . . Don **West**

20th Anniversary

July 18th will mark the twentieth anniversary at Bridal Veil for Delbert Dunken, circular resaw set-up man.

Delbert was born in Nelson, Nebraska. His father was a farmer. Delbert was educated in Nelson and after he finished school he too became a farmer. When he decided to give up farming he went to work for Menasha Woodenware Corporation making butter tubs. He also worked for a company that manufactured serum. In 1937 the Dunkens' moved to Oregon.

Delbert is one of six children. He

Health and Welfare Coverage

All employees who worked the required number of hours in May will become eligible for health and welfare coverage and will be covered on the first day of July 1958. Additions: Ole K. Barto, Earl J. Chaussee, Robert C. Crooke, Gerald V. Dull, Ray N. Gregor, Ronald D. Jackson, Floyd F. Oden, Wayne Owens, Leonard F. Volkman, Wesley A. Adams, Harry Adolph, Lester Anderson, Alfred L. Barnes, Louis W. Bissell, Roger A. Blaine, Leroy H. Brenneke, Kenneth Catlin, Delbert P. Cloe, Joseph Cote, Raymond Cote, Kenneth O. Craig, James E. Dawes, Marvin N. Dhone, Paul D. Dooley, William Dunken, Leon Dunlap, Roy D. Eveland, Charles N. Gaymon, Robert D. Godat, Eldon Gross, Leo C. Hageman, Clem A. Hancock, Loren Hancock, Mabel M. Hills, Stanley B. Hills.

Employes who did not work the required number of hours will be come ineligible the same day. Deletions: Rodney. Jacobson.

has four sisters and one brother. Burton. Burton (Mick) is a former employee. He presently operates the Larch Mountain Label Co. Del has two sisters in California and two in Nebraska.

On March 22, 1926, Del and the former Nellie Wilde of Superior, Nebraska, were married in Mankato, Kansas. They have two sons, Bob and Bill. Bob works for Multnomah County and Bill is employed by Tektronix. There a r e four grandchildren in the Dunken family, two boys and two girls.

The Dunken's own their home, which is located one mile south of Corbett. Del built the house by himself. In his spare time, when he isn't fishing, he manages to find plenty of work at home to keep him busy.

1958 SAFETY CHART

Month	Tot. Pd. Man Hrs.	Hourly Accidents	Lost Time Accident Freq.	Days Lost	Accident Severity
January	13,534	0	0	22	1626
February	14,089	2	141.9	21	1491
March	19,340	0	0	21	1086
First Quarter	46,963	2	42.6	64	1363
April	9,312	0	0	22	2368
May	20,657	4	193.6	42	
Total	76,932	6	78.0	128	1664

Rips and Trims

Don Barnes is back on the job after two weeks at National Guard camp at Ft. Lewis, Washington.

Fred Harp, Frank Jeffers and son, spent a weekend at Barview on the Oregon coast recently. Mr. and Mrs. Jacob Van Orsow and family and Mrs. Don Overguard and son Larry also spent the weekend in the same vicinity. On Sunday the men went deep sea fishing. There were two boats and included in the party were **Fred Harp, Don Harp, Tom Cowling, John, and Jacob Van Orsow.** They caught a variety of fish including Ling Cod, Sea Bass, and Red Snapper. Only a couple of the boys got seasick but a couple more didn't look to healthy. Fred Harp caught the biggest fish. Not bad for a beginner.

Phil Van Hee Sr. is vacationing the first half of July. Phil plans on a trip to Crater Lake and the Oregon Caves, with a possible trip to Victoria, British Columbia. Any spare time will be spent at the Van Hee cottage at Seaside, Oregon.

Mrs. Jimmy Bowen and daughter, Cheryl, have spent the last two weeks with **Mr. and Mrs. Willis Bowen,** while Jimmy was attending National Guard camp.

Miss Lucille Morrow of Chicago has been visiting at the home of her brother, **Peter Graymer,** the past two weeks.

Martha Jones and family will be spending the holidays at Bremerton, Washington, as the start of her vacation. They also plan to spend a week at Brookings, Oregon visiting a sister. The rest of the vacation will be spent at home just taking it easy.

Merrill Hartshorn has a new Chevrolet pick-up. It is the brightest yellow you ever saw.

Bertha and Fay Davis report the birth of a new grandson, **Richard Scott Davis.** Weighing in at seven pounds, five ounces, he was born June 19th, and is the son of **Mr. and Mrs. Robert Davis** of Portland.

Mira Nielson is also vacation bound, but isn't just sure how she is going to spend it.

Mary Vogel is in Salem Memorial Hospital undergoing surgery as a result of an automobile accident suffered several months ago. We all wish Mary a speedy recovery. Harold's mother is taking care of the family in Mary's absence.

Eldon Nielson reports that son **Ronnie** will be the new Oregon Journal carrier for the Bridal Veil district, beginning July 1.

Diana Taylor, daughter of **Mr. and Mrs. Ralph Taylor,** is spending three weeks in the Los Angeles area visiting her sister, Mary Lee Kreman.

Nancy Mickelson, daughter of **Mr. and Mrs. Einar E. Mickelson** and **Dewayne Kilness,** son of **Mr. and Mrs. Jarvis Kilness,** were married June 26th at St. Luke's church in Gresham. Barbara Mickelson was maid of honor and Jack Dempsey was best man.

———— 6 ————

Ruether vs. Economics

(Continued from Page 1)

usual provision for research and new product development would cause the company to run out of gas in a few years, and the investment would be lost.

Most important however, is that Mr. R. would soon discover some rather hard economic facts. One is that the customer pays the wages. Continued increases in wages without at least comparable increases in productivity must either be added to the sales price, or the company goes bankrupt. Continued raising of prices without a comparable increase in value received by the customer generally results in the customers refusal to buy. Either way the result is fewer jobs.

It would certainly be interesting to know if the new owners could forebear killing the company for an immediate wage raise.

Len Kraft

———— 6 ————

July Birthdays
Many Happy Returns of the Day!

Leonard Volkman	Lillie Yerion
Lester Anderson	Willis Bowen
Harold Powell	Gerald Dull
Arthur Howell	Bob Layton
T. Van Hee Sr.	Orien Pitts
Harold Vogel	Jim Cowling
John Matson	Paul Detrick

BRIDAL VEIL LUMBER & BOX CO.
News Letter

Vol. IV, No. 2   BRIDAL VEIL, OREGON   AUGUST, 1958

Nine Eggs, Please

After several weeks of rather left-handed effort, car No. NYC 46768 rolled July 26, 1958, consigned to Lumber Dealers Service Company in Kansas City, Missouri. The noteworthy feature of this particular shipment is that it was unit loaded.

So far as we have been able to tell, this is the first time a car of stock millwork has ever been shipped in packages that could be loaded and unloaded with a finger-lift. Two major strapping companies were consulted on how to procede. While both were quick to admit that they knew all about package loading, when the chips were down, it developed that neither had ever participated in organizing a similar shipment.

Signode Steel Strapping Company, through its representative, Mr. Gerald Smith, finally came up with a loading diagram for the car and a schedule of package sizes that did the trick. Mr. Smith also spent four days at Bridal Veil supervising the whole show.

As of now, we obviously didn't cut our handling costs on this initial car. We are not even sure that the car will arrive in Kansas City in good shape. The question naturally comes to mind. "Why bother with such an expensive program that on the surface, at least, is a losing game?"

The best reason we can think of is that the customer asked for it. When you get right down to it, it is the customer who meets the payroll — the best way to insure continuing payrolls is to give the customer the service he requires. By way of reinforcing this thought, the customer in this case has said that the mill who can solve the problems of finger-lift loading and unloading can have all of his millwork business.

We have several other customers who have expressed an interest in palletized shipments. Up to this point, we have always replied, "It isn't practical," or "it can't be done." We are indebted to Lumber Dealers Service Company for supplying the burr that got action.

This is one of the newest and most interesting problems we have bumped into. Obviously, perfection has not been reached. Nobody claims that we can start packaging millwork tomorrow and save money. Nobody claims that a customer can reduce costs automatically just by ordering packaged millwork. There is good evidence however, that the mill which has proper facilities, adequately engineered, can lower its loading costs. And the customer who is properly equipped can save money on unloading. Nobody is going to ship, or order, packaged millwork just for the fun of it. But when the customer finds that he **can** save money, he's going to demand packaged millwork. The laws of economics and good merchandising will call the shots.

The mill which anticipates it's customers' needs, instead of waiting to be forced to do so by its competition, is going to reap the greatest benefits. Those who fail to recognize this fact are going to wake up some day and wonder what hit them. Packaging has been a standard practice in other industries for years. And it has paid off.

Who would think of going into a market today and asking for nine eggs?

—Len Kraft

———— 37 ————

REMEMBER—running in the mill is dangerous as well as being a violation of Safety Rules.

NEWS LETTER

Published on the 10th of each month by
Bridal Veil Lumber & Box Co.
Bridal Veil, Oregon

Editor . . . . . . Sara Mahn

Social Security In the Red

Tax Foundation, Inc. research shows that a man earning $85 a week, works all day Monday and slightly more than half of Tuesday to pay taxes to his federal, state and local governments.

Where Is the End?

Recent annual report of the Federal Old-Age and Survivors Insurance Trust Fund, paints a dismal picture as to future financing of social security benefits. 1958 deficit will amount to $428 million. 1959 deficit is expected to be over $1 billion. This does not consider the increases that is before Congress now. It looks like an added tax burden is the answer. That has a familiar ring, doesn't it.

SENIORITY LIST

1. Dull, Ward E.........5-18-36	49. Van Hee, Theop. Sr. 2-27-51	97. Murphy, Charles H. 9-10-57
2. McCredie, Ralph H. 8-27-36	50. Schneringer, Ray ...10-8-51	98. Blaine, Roger A. 9-12-57
3. Davis, D. Fay 3-22-37	51. Walker, Homer F. 10-9-51	99. Craig, Kenneth O. 9-10-57
4. Jackson, Marvin T. 4-8-37	52. Eveland, Roy D. ...10-15-51	100. Reischel, Robert W. 5-1-58
5. Stolin, Walter F.....5-11-37	53. Anderson, Lester W. 5-19-52	101. Cote, Raymond 5-1-58
6. Bowen, Franklin M. 8-19-37	54. Howell, Lester B. ...6-23-52	100. Reischel, Robert W. 5-1-58
7. Crouser, Fred 8-30-37	55. Hutchison, Earl 6-23-52	101. Cote, Raymond 5-1-58
8. Bird, Vrl W...........9-20-37	56. Van Buskirk, Norm 7-28-52	102. Godat, Robert D......5-2-58
9. Taylor, Ralph L. ...11-22-37	57. Hancock, Loren 9-2-52	103. Brenneke, Leroy H. 5-2-58
10. Hanson, Theodore N. 4-18-38	58. Long, Fred M..........9-9-52	104. Oden, Floyd F. 5-5-58
11. Van Orsow, Joseph 4-22-38	59. Cote, Joseph 9-10-52	105. Jacobson, Charels D. 5-6-58
12. Dunken, J. Delbert 7-18-38	60. Adolph, Harry 9-22-52	106. Jones, Walton G. ...5-6-58
13. Meyer, Kenneth L. 9-16-40	61. Willms, John G. 9-29-52	107. Mier, Melvin 5-7-58
14. Hartshorn, Merrill 1-8-41	62. Potter, Eugene H. 10-28-52	108. Dawes, James E. ...5-7-58
15. Harp, Fred 5-21-41	63. Davies, Archie L. 4-1-53	109. Kuzmesky, Steven 5-8-58
16. Mickelson, Einar E. 7-1-41	64. Bissell, Louis W. 5-1-53	110. Dull, Gerald V. 5-8-58
17. Roberts, Jerald G. ...9-8-41	65. Layton, Bob 5-28-53	111. Barto, Ole K. 5-14-58
18. Ellis, Ralph 10-9-41	66. Ayles, Elmer L. 8-4-53	112. Crooke, Robert C. 5-15-58
19. Latourell, Clifford 3-23-42	67. Gross, Elden 8-27-53	113. Jackson, Ronald D. 5-15-58
20. Vogel, Harold A. ...3-25-42	68. Burkholder, Harold 5-4-54	114. Bowen, Donald ...5-19-58
21. Nielson, Eldon F. 4-21-42	69. Kinonen, Edsel 5-4-54	115. Volkman, Leonard 5-19-58
22. Davis, Bertha M..... 5-6-42	70. Kilness, Jarvis 6-2-54	116. Graymer, Peter J. 5-19-58
23. Hartshorn, Dorothy 7-14-42	71. Zumwalt, Roley 9-7-54	117. Barnes, Don B. 5-21-58
24. Bowen, Anna 9-30-42	72. Wilson, Louis A. 9-20-54	118. Jacobs, Floyd 5-22-58
25. Hageman, Leo F. 7-14-43	73. Rees, David 9-23-54	119. Layton, James 6-2-58
26. Yerion, Lillie P. 7-19-43	74. Morgan, Roland B. 12-14-54	120. Cowling, Robert 6-2-58
27. Cloe, Pearl P. 11-12-43	75. Polzel, Leslie D. 1-5-55	121. Hageman, Donald 6-3-58
28. Britton, Thomas C. 12-30-43	76. Gaymon, Charles N. 3-29-55	122. Bailey, Fred. C. Jr. 6-9-58
29. Nielson, Mira J.....1-23-44	77. Pitts, Orien 4-13-55	123. Cowling, Thomas J. 6-16-58
30. Litton, Durward 5-9-44	78. Adams, Wesley A. ...5-9-55	124. Yerion, James M. 6-16-58
31. Peterson, Lawrence 9-24-45	79. Dooley, Paul D. 5-9-55	125. Schneringer, Phil. 6-17-58
32. Hunt, Howard G. 10-1-45	80. Hageman, Leo C. ...6-1-55	126. Cook, Francis 6-26-58
33. Smazal, Lawrence A. 10-2-45	81. Hancock, Clem A. ...8-15-55	127. Lamke, Larry L. 6-24-58
34. Stolin, Marvin J......3-28-46	82. Wendler, Ed L..........9-6-55	128. Mickelson, Fred 6-26-58
35. Van Hee, Theophile 4-17-46	83. Westlake, Donald 10-17-55	129. Watts, Paul ...:....6-30-58
36. Kendrick, James B. 5-13-46	84. Jacobson, Rodney ...3-11-57	130. Howell, Keith 7-1-58
37. Woodard, Mary R. ...6-3-46	85. Fitzgerald, Robt. Jr. 3-15-57	131. Smith, Curtis R......7-1-58
38. Jacobson, Harold R. 9-16-46	86. Jones, Marion E. 5-6-57	132. Sprague, LeRoy 7-3-58
39. Choate, Beulah 10-7-46	87. Damerell, Fred 7-2-57	133. Dempsey, Jack L. 7-8-58
40. Layton, Hiram 11-13-46	88. Catlin, Ronald E. 7-2-57	134. Bowen, Richard L. 7-8-58
41. Lofstedt, Clarence....1-16-47	89. Cloe, Delbert P. 7-22-57	135. Howell, Marvin 7-8-58
42. Murray, George 4-21-47	90. Barnes, Alfred 7-22-57	136. Bartlett, Albert E. 7-11-58
43. Jones, Martha A. ...5-14-47	91. Catlin, Kenneth V. 7-22-57	137. Post, Geo. Wesley 7-14-58
44. Van Hee, Theodore V. 9-9-47	92. Dhone, Marvin N. ...8-12-57	138. Baker, Jeffrey J. 7-15-58
45. Rowe, Thelma Y....11-12-47	93. Westlake, Jack V. 8-23-57	139. Kilness, Dewayne 7-17-58
46. Hills, Mabel M. 1-14-48	94. Matson, John E. ...8-29-57	140. Bedford, Leon Sr. 7-17-58
47. Hills, Stanley B. ...1-15-51	95. Howell, Arthur V. 8-30-57	141. Bird, Robert K. 7-24-58
48. Roberts, Vera Nell 1-15-51	96. Mershon, John 9-9-57	

Mallinson Replaces West

It was with regret that we bid "farewell" to Don West, above right, our former Sales Manager, who has moved to Oroville, California, to begin his new job with High Sierra Pine Mills. Mel Mallinson, left, who has been with our company since 1947 and is now Draftsman, will take over duties of Sales Manager.

New Secretary

Her name is Sara Mahn, and she is the new secretary in the office. Sara was born in Rocky Point, North Carolina, a few miles from Wilmington,

where she has spent most of her young life. She completed high school at Collegedale Academy at Collegedale, Tennessee and graduated from Secretarial Science Course at Southern Missionary College, which is also in Collegedale.

After graduating, Sara returned to Wilmington where she lived with her father, until moving to Portland in May of this year. In Wilmington Sara was employed as secretary to the Manager of the Becker Builders Supply Company for the past three years.

Sara has two sisters living in Wilmington, and she has four brothers, one in Wilmington, one in Charlottesville, Virginia, one at Travis Air Force Base, California, and one at Fairbanks, Alaska.

Sara is a member of the Seventh-Day Adventist Church. Her hobbies are golfing, deep sea fishing, and hi-fi music.

———— 37 ————

"Yes, I'll give you a job. First I want you to sweep out the store".

"But I'm a college graduate."

"Okay, I'll show you how."

The actual building of the pallet of window frames is being done by Gerald Smith and Clem Hancock.

The steel stra
bottom, leaving
under the pallet

This is the first pallet of window frames loaded in the car of the first shipment of palletized millwork.

New E

Bridal Veil Lumber an
mile stone. July, 1958, m
palletized millwork. The
Dealers Service Company i

This could very easily
future be the only acceptab

Gerald Smith, repre
Company in Portland, s
the palletizing and loadi

Van Hee inspects the pallets
in the partially loaded car
to determine where the
next units will fit to
the best advantage.

x 2's on the
k lift to go

ɔping

any has reached another
ginning of shipments of
s consigned to Lumber
ty, Missouri.

ining of what may in the
if shipping millwork.

le Steel Strapping
r plant supervising
and door frames.

Some of the long picture window parts had to be manually loaded because of the length.

Theophile Van Hee operates the fork lift which transported the pallets from the dip tank shed directly into the car.

After the loading is completed, the shipping clerk, Willie Bowen, seals the first car of palletized millwork in history.

Better Leadership

Above are the graduates of the "Leadership Development Program" which was completed on April 30, 1958, at the University of Portland. Our company is represented by three of our foremen. They are Kenneth D. Burkholder, extreme right on the front row; Einar E. Mickelson, extreme left on the back row, and Clyde H. Hambrick, extreme right on the back row. We are proud of these men who represented our company so well.

Health and Welfare Coverage

All employees who worked the required number of hours in June will become eligible for health and welfare coverage and will be covered on the first day of August, 1958. Additions: Fredrick C. Bailey, Jr., Don Barnes, Donald Bowen, Robert L. Cowling, Thomas J. Cowling, Peter J. Graymer, Donald Hageman, Floyd Jacobs, Arthur Ross Johnson, David Johnson, James M. Layton, Harold L. Powell, Phillip Schneringer, Louis Wilson, James M. Yerion.

Employees who did not work the required number of hours will become ineligible the same day. Deletions: Earl J. Chaussee, William Dunken, Leon C. Dunlap, Stanley B. Hills, Wayne Owens, Paul Van Treeck.

1958 SAFETY CHART

Month	Tot. Hourly Pd. Man Hrs.	Lost Time Accidents	Accident Freq.	Days Lost	Accident Severity
January	13,534	0	0	22	1626
February	14,089	2	141.9	21	1491
March	19,340	0	0	21	1086
First Quarter	46,963	2	42.6	64	1363
April	9,312	0	0	22	2368
May	20,657	4	193.6	42	2033
June	21,017	1	47.6	24	1142
Second Quarter	50,986	5	98.1	88	1726
Total	97,949	7	71.5	152	1552

Attractive?

This is one of the lovely homes built by Pease Woodworking Company, Hamilton, Ohio. The millwork for these homes is manufactured by you, the employees of the Bridal Veil Lumber and Box Company.

Rips and Trims

Martha Jones and family recently entertained with a barbecue at their home in Bonneville. Guests were Mr. and Mrs. Merrill Richmond and Mr. and Mrs. Ray Soderholm. In the evening they attended a softball game at Bonneville and the Greyhound race. She wasn't very lucky at the race.

Larry Smazal, band rip saw operator, is driving a different pick-up truck. He is baching while wife Irene and daughter Bobbi, together with Vickie Vogel, are spending some time with relatives in Chili, Wisconsin.

Floyd Oden and family have moved into their new h o m e recently purchased at 18233 SE Oak in Portland. They formerly lived in Corbett.

A speedy recovery to **Kenny Catlin's** daughter, who dislocated her shoulder while vacationing at Lost Lake. Also to **Jeffery Baker** after his accident on the motorcycle. Hurry back to work Jeff.

Sympathy also to Mr. and Mrs. **Melvin Mier** on the death of her mother in Greenbay, Wisconsin.

———— 37 ————

August Birthdays

Many Happy Returns of the Day!

Robert Fitzgerald, Jr.	Ralph Ellis
Theodore Van Hee	Ann Keller
Theophile Van Hee	David Johnson
Harry Densmore	Marvin Dhone
Ralph Lamke	Archie Davies
Vera Nell Roberts	Jarvis Kilness
Donald Westlake	Lester Howell
Kenneth Burkholder	

———— 37 ————

"Little known fact—smoking breaks add ten days a year to our paid time off."

Rips and Trims

Our sincere sympathy to **James Kendrick,** band rip saw operator, on the death of his mother. He and Mrs. Kendrick spent two weeks with her in Houston, Texas before she passed away.

Congratulations to Mr. and Mrs. Paul Heller who were married on Saturday, July 26. Mrs. Heller is the youngest daughter of **Jarvis Killness.**

Paul Dooley was scheduled for a routine physical on July 30 as a member of the Inactive Army Reserve.

The Fourth of July weekend was enjoyed by all. **Mr. and Mrs. Marvin Van Orsow** and family fished at the Wickiup Reservoir and Timothy lake. **Mr. and Mrs. Howard Hunt,** Barbara Wilson and Mitze Howell camped on Barlow Creek. **John Matson** went home to Battleground, Washington. **Mr. and Mrs. Fred Harp** camped at Tollgate on Mt. Hood.

Other weekends during July were filled with activity. **Bert and Fay Davis** entertained grandson Gordon Timothy. **Mr. and Mrs. Connie Meyers** attended the "Country Fair and Barbecue" given by St. Luke's Episcopal Church of Gresham on Saturday, July 26. They enjoyed it enough to plan to attend again next year. **Charles Gaymon** and family had to fight the traffic Sunday, July 27, returning from the Local 1120 picnic at Jantzen Beach. **Ed Kinonen** returned from his fishing trip with two steelheads and one chinook. No such good luck for **Leslie Polzel,** and **Eldon Gross,** who said fishing was good, but didn't bring back any fish. **Mr. and Mrs. Howard Hunt** welcomed home their daughter and her children from Eugene, Oregon, July 26 and 27. The same weekend, visitors at **Fred Harp's** home were his sister and her husband from Iowa. Eleven nice trout were the reward for **Mr. and Mrs. Roy Eveland** at Badger Creek in Tygh Valley, while **Jerry Roberts** and Jackie Ball caught the limit of trout on the Deschutes River in Warm Springs. **Don Hageman, Bob Cowling** and **John Matson** tried navigating on air mattresses from Coopy Falls across the Columbia to Rooster Rock. **John** was deflated by a wire he hit, so they ended at Bridal Veil. Better luck next time.

Hageman   Cowling

Don Hageman and **Bob Cowling** are getting back in the school routine early with football practice starting August 10. They will be playing in the Shrine All Star game at Pendleton on August 23.

Mrs. Harold Jacobson arrived in French Lick, Indiana, after a nice plane trip, to attend a three-day Niagara Convention.

Vacation time!! **George Murray** and daughter went to Montana, while **Joe Van Orsow's** choice was to spend a peaceful vacation at home. Pearl Cloe and family spent a few days at Seaside and also visited relatives and friends at St. Helens and Washougal, Washington. Don't mention rain to **Marvin Stolin,** as it rained every day he vacationed in North Dakota. Forty trout all over ten inches long — the catch for **Ed Kinonen** and family for the three days of his vacation spent at Cove State Park near Madras. **Mr. and Mrs. Ed Wendler** went to Denver and Colorado Springs, Colorado and Shawnee, Oklahoma visiting relatives —including her 90 year old mother. A visit to Tillamook Cheese plant was included in the vacation of **Mira Neilson** while she was at Oceanlake and Seaside. **Donald Westlake,** together with his wife, spent his vacation entertaining his mother from Iowa. They visited some scenic spots of Oregon — Mt. Hood, Seaside and Astoria. Now all these lucky people who have enjoyed their vacations in July can get the rest always needed after a vacation.

That '55 Ford Crown Victoria is owned by **Don Bowen.** He is as pleased a sa kid with a new red wagon.

BRIDAL VEIL LUMBER & BOX CO.
News Letter

Vol. IV, No. 3　　　BRIDAL VEIL, OREGON　　　SEPTEMBER, 1958

The New Capitalism

A most important change has taken place in American capitalism during the lifetime of many yet living. The past seventy-five years have seen the development of a new role of corporate citizenship. Corporations n o w recognize their social and economic responsibility to the whole community.

Before the turn of the current century, businesses were largely owned by single individuals. While generalizations are dangerous, it is probably fair to say that these individual owners had little difficulty resolving any conflicts between their own interests and the best interests of society. They were czars in their field. They could operate or shut down—raise wages or lower them—be stubborn, arbitrary—and generally disregard any toes that might be stepped on along the way. It may be that some of todays remaining public attitudes and fears of "big business" stem from the remembrances of such situations.

However, in the sixty odd years since the Sherman Anti-trust Act first warned business that it was in real and deserved political trouble, many changes and improvements have been made. In recent years we have had a new concept of capitalism in America. In 1956 the Stock Exchange pointed out that American industry had 8,600,000 o w n e r s — three-fourths of whom have incomes of less than $7,500 per year—in 4,600 companies with over $350 billion of assets. Even the flow of capital funds has changed. Today the financial markets are turning largely to the thrift and savings accumulations of millions of people rather than to the odd-style capitalists.

Comparing the capitalism of 1958 with the capitalism of 1875 is like comparing horse-and-buggy travel w i t h todays jet plane travel. Likewise, it is just as ridiculous to condemn 1958 business for the excuses of 1875, as it would be to condemn air travel today because people whipped t h e i r horses in 1875.

It is indeed unfortunate for all society that politicians have been able to mislead a majority of their fellow citizens by hammering home the misgotten "fact" that the public is being abused by "wicked business" — that the few are punishing the many in this country. It is particularly ironical that this clamor should be taken up by labor leaders—when there is some evidence that the public has a far greater need for protection f r o m greedy labor leaders than from rampant businessmen.

One fact should be recognized by all segments of society—labor, management, owners, customers, teachers, clergy—that big business is labor's best friend. Research in new products, new techniques and new tools have been paid off for big business and enabled big business to pay the world's highest wages, supply the greatest social benefits for its employees, and furnish Americans with the best living conditions the world has ever known.

And the best part of it is that if we are willing to save a portion of our income and invest in American industry, we can all own a share of the New Capitalism.

—Len Kraft

————— 68 —————

The first plastic material was created in 1868, when a prize was offered for a substitute for ivory in making billard balls.

NEWS LETTER

Published on the 10th of each month by
Bridal Veil Lumber & Box Co.
Bridal Veil, Oregon

Editor . . . . . Sara Mahn

Who Decides Our Profit?

Do company officials decree our profit every year?

Some people think they do.

Actually, it doesn't work this way at all.

You can't decree profit. For profit is the **end**-result of business, not the beginning.

First, management estimates how much it will cost to make and sell our products. They get this figure by tallying all the wages, taxes, material costs, rent, repairs, and other costs of production.

This **is** the least they can charge and still **break** even.

But **you** can't stay in business or grow, just breaking even. So they add to the cost a profit that will give them money to plow back into company growth and also give shareholders a fair return for use of their money. That's the price they'd like to charge.

But competition has to be considered. The customer will buy the best product he can get for his money and often a company can't charge the price it would like to charge.

So engineering and manufacturing must continually look for ways to cut production costs so we can give customers more and more for their money and keep them buying our products. If our costs in the end prove to be higher than our sales, our end-result is a "loss" rather than a profit and we go into debt to keep in business.

Management **never** decreed a profit in our free enterprise system. Customers, competition, and the efficiency of operation determine profit.

———— 68 ————

WHAT IS SUCCESS?

It is being able to carry money without spending it; being able to bear an injustice without retaliating; being able to do one's duty even when one is not watched; being able to keep on the job until it is finished; being able to accept criticism without letting it whip you.

Safety Minded

As you have read your News Letter from month to month, have you stopped to think what the numbers that separate the articles mean, or don't they have a meaning to you?

This is the number of days that have passed since the last "Lost-Time" accident occurred in the mill. This month we have climbed a little—68 is our number. Think "Safety" so this number will continue to grow.

———— 68 ————

Special Notice

Effective immediately, all requests for extended vacations must be made to the management in writing.

———— 68 ————

She's Yours

Maybe you have heard the story of the two Irishmen who were on shipboard. One rushed up to the other and shouted, "The ship is sinking!" The other said, "Let 'er go. She ain't ours!"

His reasoning was more tragic than funny. He forgot a great and fundamental truth: all those engaged in a particular enterprise are in the same boat. And you can't sink half a ship.

You can't sink the officers and let the crew continue on as if nothing had happened. You can't sink the crew and let the officers continue to cruise undisturbed.

It's the very same thing in business — ours or any other.

You can't sink half, or a third, or a fourth of a business and let the rest of it stay on top of the stream. So, between us — whether employees, management, stockholders or customers— we have one common denominator. That's our mutual interest in keeping the ship afloat — BECAUSE WE'RE ALL ON IT!

———— 37 ————

Sept. Birthdays

Many Happy Returns of the Day!

Marion Jones

Leonard Kraft

Merrill Hartshorn

Howard Hunt

Robert Godat

A. D. Jones

Lawrence Smazal

Steven Kuzmesky

Joseph Cote

Floyd Oden

Roley Zumwalt

Edsel Kinonen

Lula Cowling

A New Lift

The load seems to lift much easier with this new Hyster Fork Lift. Don Westlake operates this machine which is another piece of the new equipment recently purchased to keep our operations up to date.

——— 68 ———

Health and Welfare Coverage

All employees who worked the required number of hours in July will become eligible for health and welfare coverage and will be covered on the first day of September, 1958. Additions: Sara Mahn, Albert E. Barlett, Leon M. Bedford, Sr., Richard L. Bowen, Francis P. Cook, Jack L. Dempsey, Keith Howell, Marvin Howell, Dewayne Kilness, Larry L. Lamke, Einar Fred Mickelson, George W. Post, Curtis R. Smith, LeRoy V. Sprague, Paul Watts.

Employees who did not work the required number of hours will become ineligible the same day. Deletions: Ray N. Gregor, Arthur R. Johnson, David Johnson, Harold L. Powell.

——— 68 ———

Wood windows do not require any special provisions for the attachment of shades, curtains or venetian blinds. Wood windows allow mounting brackets to be placed wherever desired and changed at will.

"You Might Be Next"

What's all this talk of accidents
And Safety Signs I see
It's just to warn the other men
It was not meant for me.
I am a very clever guy
To caution I'm a snob,
I've worked for over twenty years
On every kind of job.
I never had an accident
And as far as I can see
Bearded Old Man Accident
Won't catch up to me.
That Safety stuff's a lot of bunk
Said I, the great 'I AM'.
Just then something hit me
Not a tap — a 'wham'!
Now I'm in the hospital
Stretched out on a bed
Thinking about accidents
And foolish things I've said.
I've learned I'm not so clever
Now I can plainly see
By the laws of average
The next guy hurt was me.
You may have worked a long, long time
Without an injury,
But before you take to bragging
Take a look at me.
—From Safety In Logging

——— 68 ———

Machines perform more than 93 percent of the hard work in our country's amazing industrial production, and a great deal of the light work in factory and home.

WALK DON'T RUN FALLS AREN'T FUN!

Car No. N
Kansas

The first car of palletize
Bridal Veil in August has re
rough handling, the bulkh
places; however none of th
broken. The shipment was

Although we did not c
car, Lumber Dealers Servic
a saving of approximately

"The inspection was mad
with the cooperation of M
Frank Stewart, Yard Supe
intendent. He was kind en
parisons:

Old Method
    2.5 to 3 days   2 men @
Packaged Method
    Doorway   1.25 hrs.
    Both Ends   4 hrs.

"The equipment used fo
Ross lift truck and a 2,000
"The customer's satisfac
cost comparisons which he
We are pleased with ou

8 Arrives
ssouri

vhich was shipped from
stination. Through much
broken in a number of
ping on the pallets was
very good condition.

ling costs on this initial
was able to unload it at
their usual cost. Below
quote part of the in-
tion report from Sig-
e Steel Strapping Co.

me the following com-

Cost — $82.00 to $98.00

.05/hr.   Cost — 7.70
.05/hr.   Cost — 16.40
  TOTAL $24.10
was a 15,000-lb. Clark-
truck inside the car.
vident on the time and

t at palletized shipping.

Toys in the Making

The new splitter which was put into operation in May of this year has cut the production cost in making the roof slats which are an important part of a set of Lincoln Logs. A single block of wood is fed into the machine and comes out 10, 15 or 20 roof slats.

Business is like an automobile—the only way it will run by itself is downhill!

A joint checking account is n e v e r overdrawn by the wife—it's just under-deposited by her husband.

1958 SAFETY CHART

Month	Tot. Hourly Pd. Man Hrs.	Lost Time Accidents	Accident Freq.	Days Lost	Accident Severity
January	13,534	0	0	22	1626
February	14,089	2	141.9	21	1491
March	19,340	0	0	21	1086
First Quarter	46,963	2	42.6	64	1363
April	9,312	0	0	22	2368
May	20,657	4	193.6	42	2033
June	21,017	1	47.6	24	1142
Second Quarter	50,986	5	98.1	88	1726
July	25,291	0	0	22	870
Total	76,277	5	65.6	110	1442

Rips and Trims

Frank Bowen, Mabel Hills, C l i f f Latourell, and Lester Howell have all been on vacation from the Millwork Department. However, t h e y didn't say what their plans were. We hope you all had a very enjoyable vacation.

Is it lonesome at home Walton Jones while your wife is spending a month with relatives in North Dakota? Or are you finding time now to do the things you haven't had time for with your family home? Mr. and Mrs. Roy Eveland spent a weekend with her mother and sister at Sunny Side, Washington.

While many travelled, some were entertaining at home. Among these were Ted Hanson who had as his guest his brother-in-law from Walla Walla, Washington. Ed Farrell of Washougal, who served with Pearl Cloe during World War One was a welcome visitor. From British Columbia came Mr. and Mrs. Bud Mattock to visit Fred Damarell.

Ruth and Durward Litton entertained her sister and brother-in-law, Mr. and Mrs. Marvin Matheson of Hermiston. Mr. and Mrs. James Butzin and Mr. and Mrs. Morris Baum of Hood River came down to visit Charles Gaymon and family.

Mr. and Mrs. Floyd Oden were in Everett, Washington, over Monday, August 11. He is very happy about the adoption and custody of Ronald, a son of Mrs. Oden from a former marriage.

Floyd Jacobs won't have to drive so far now that he has moved to Coopey Falls and is nearer his work.

Back home again is Marvin Jackson after a brief stay at Providence hospital. We hope you are feeling fine by now, Marvin.

Dorothy Hartshorn has also returned home after a few days of observation at a Portland hospital. We hope Marylin, daughter of Martha Jones, will soon be over the measles and ready for her operation which had to be postponed when she broke out with all those little red bumps.

Wedding bells will soon be ringing for Jack Dempsey and Jo Ann Ball of Corbett. The date is set for September 12. They will also ring at the Corbett Christian Church on September 20 for Marsha Howell, daughter of

Arthur Howell, and Robert Correll of Dodson. Rev. Guy Armstrong is to officiate. Congratulations and B e s t Wishes to both couples.

A baby boy was born to Mr. and Mrs. Theodore Hanson on Wednesday, August 20, and Anna and Willis Bowen have a new grandson weighing 8 lbs. and 12 ozs. He was born on August 23 at Emmanual Hospital in Portland, the second child of Jimmy and P e g g y Bowen.

Have you ever taken 5 grade school boys to a football game? Clarence Lofstedt tried it, but hasn't said if he will be willing to do so again.

The dedication of the new International Airport in Portland on August 24 was attended by Charles Gaymon and his family. He said it was very interesting, but the weather was hot.

All reports are that the Shrine All-Star Game at Pendleton was v e r y good. Don Hageman broke an upper front tooth while playing and Bob Cowling was hurt during practice, but was able to play in the game. A number of Bridal Veil people attended the game, including the Cowlings, Hagemans, DeWayne Kilness, and Wesley Post.

A sad "Farewell" to Vera Nell Roberts, employed here since 1951, w h o has left our ranks to accept a position as a doctor's receptionist. We wish you the best of luck in your new job, Vera Nell.

———— 68 ————

PRACTICE SAFETY AND LIVE
———— 68 ————

According to the December, 1956, issue of the Ohio Monitor, a tool and supply house in Baltimore, Maryland, displayed the following safety advertisement:

"The following items are not in our stock and cannot be purchased f o r any amount:

Fingers — hands — toes — arms — feet — legs — skull — brains — eyes (right or left, sight of either).

"While the hospital workshop w i l l attempt to repair any of the above if damaged, it cannot guarantee the results.

"Should science succeed in developing any of these items, you will be advised."

Rips and Trims

Bridal Veil has been rather deserted during the weekends of August as vacations and fishing trips have taken many out into nature's wonderlands. **Jim** and **Robert Cowling** spent Saturday the third on Tanner Creek and came back with their limit of trout. **Donald Barnes** and his father spent a Friday and Saturday on the Ochocho Reservoir where they caught their limit of trout averaging ten inches in length. Another lucky fisherman up to Ochocho Reservoir was **Harry Adolph.** Bonneville Dam was the fishing spot for **Fred Harp,** but he didn't catch any. Maybe you could try the Hatchery next time, Fred. **Vogel** says his son can catch more and bigger fish than he can. Is he bragging or complaining?

Driving to and from fishing took much of **Harry Adolph's** time, but he still had time to catch two salmon. **Mr. and Mrs. Howard Hunt** caught enough fish to eat on the Barlow Trail.

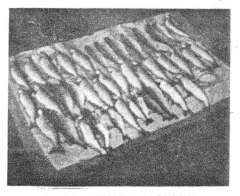

NICE CATCH, MARVIN

To prove his fishing ability, **Marvin Van Orsow** snapped a picture of his catch while on vacation. You did a very fine job, Marvin, at the Crane Prairie Reservoir. Clamming was the pastime of **Larry Lamke** and his guests and family at Long Beach, Washington. **Clyde Hambrick** and family also did some clamming at Long Beach, as well as swimming. Mr. and Mrs. Eugene Potter with their daughter, **Mrs. Paul Dooley,** and her family were also there. The clams at Long Beach had better hide before the long Labor Day weekend, or there won't be any left.

Summer days are not complete without picnics. **Mac** and **Mrs. McCredie** enjoyed an outing with friends on the Sandy river. **Charles Gaymon** and family visited the beaches and particularly enjoyed Short Sands beach. Clams were plentiful was the report from **Delbert** and **Nellie Dunken** after their trip to Long beach with Mr. and Mrs. Roy Much. **John Matson** hasn't given up air mattress navigation. He and **Phil Schneringer** crossed the Columbia to take a half-mile walk on the Washington shore, and of course, to improve their navigation.

Fairs can be fascinating when you bring back an armful of prizes like **Danny Hills** did. **George Murray** attended the State Fair at Great Falls, Montana. He witnessed a half-million dollar crop destroyed by hail and rain. However, he still enjoyed his trip.

Mr. and Mrs. Floyd Jacobs attended the fair at Tillamook while spending a weekend there.

How was the Rodeo at Prineville, **Jim Yerion?**

Mr. and Mrs. Jacob Van Orsow and Linda drove up to Battle Ground, Washington, to pick up Donald from summer camp. **Wesley Adams** visited the Baptist Church in Haines, Oregon on August 10, to get acquainted with the people and make himself available as future pastor of the church.

Old Mexico was the destination of **Fred Harp** and his wife when they started their vacation on August 15. They picked up her brother and his wife, Mr. and Mrs. Ray Jeffers, in Los Angeles to accompany them.

Ward and **Thelma Dull** were also traveling on their summer vacation and giving their Renault a real tryout —38.5 miles per gallon. Their itinerary included Glacier National Park; Canada; Helena, Montana; Yellowstone National Park; Eli, Nevada; and San Leandro, California. He is still peeved at the California cop who fined him $21.00 for speeding. He says he was in second gear passing a truck that he had followed for 25 miles.

Willie and Anna Bowen spent a nice quiet vacation at their home in Bridal Veil.

BRIDAL VEIL LUMBER & BOX CO.
News Letter

Vol. IV, No. 4   BRIDAL VEIL, OREGON   OCTOBER, 1958

True or False

Americans seem to have a rough time explaining America to o t h e r countries. The reason is s i m p l e enough. We don't understand out-selves.

Sometime ago one of the public opinion survey outfits went out to talk to the man in the street.

The results were remarkable.

On the average, people in New York, Chicago and San Francisco believe that the average U.S. corporation makes a profit of 35 percent of the sell-ing price of its merchandise.

Similar surveys were conducted in several European countries. These sur-veys revealed that the average Euro-pean had an even higher estimate of profits of American Corporations. In Vienna the estimate of profit ran up to 50 percent. In West Berlin 47 per-cent. In Paris and Amsterdam 40 per-cent.

With this kind of an idea g o i n g around, it is easy to see why m a n y Americans are somewhat apologetic over American economics. If you think the profits of American business aver-age 35 percent, you are much more-inclined to agree with the economic free-wheelers who charge that the profit system is bad because it is founded on greed and avarice.

What are the facts?

How much do representative Ameri-can corporations really make? The last year that I have figures for is 1956. Neither the top year nor the worst. Mr. Reuther says the automo-bile companies make too much profit. Is he right? Let's look. The results for 1956 look like this:

Company	Per Cent of Profit
General Motors	7.9%
Ford	5.1%
Chrysler	.8%
American Motors	Loss
Studebaker-Packard	Loss

These companies are all listed on the New York Stock Exchange. They are subject to the regulations of the Securities and Exchange Commission. The above figures are from their au-dited and published reports.

How about food companies? T h e y come in for a good share of abuse. Over-charging the customer and under paying the farmer is the complaint. Here is how a few representative food companies stack up:

Company	Per Cent of Profit
General Foods	4.2%
National Dairies	3.1%
Borden	2.7%
Armour	.7%
Swift	.6%

Steel companies? We will be hearing from Mr. MacDonald about excessive profits in the steel business when his contracts expire next year. And re-member that these figures are for 1956—not 1958 when the steel business fell on evil days.

Company	Per Cent of Profit
United States Steel	8.2%
National Steel	7.9%
Republic Steel	7.3%
Inland Steel	7.3%
Bethlehem Steel	6.9%
Youngstown Sheet & Tube	6.4%
Jones & Loughlin	6.1%

Let's try an industry with its feet in the public trough—the aviation com-panies:

Company	Per Cent of Profit
Boeing	3.2%
Douglas	3.1%
Martin	3.0%
Lockheed	1.9%

All of the above companies repre-sent the cream of American industry. These are the "Big Boys" who are in the roughest and toughest competitive market in the world. When you try to

(Continued on Page 2)

NEWS LETTER

Published on the 10th of each month by
Bridal Veil Lumber & Box Co.
Bridal Veil, Oregon

Editor . . . . . . Sara Mahn

Waste and Abundance

Waste takes a terrible toll of American industry. Usually we think of the cost of waste in terms of dollars—but although there are no available statistics on the subject, waste must have cost many jobs too, as businesses failed to keep pace in highly competitive markets due to excessive costs, including the cost of waste. Layoffs, even complete business failures, were the inevitable result.

Sometimes we wonder if the amazingly abundant production of the American economy is not, to some extent, a psychological factor in the waste situation. Do employees feel, subconsciously perhaps, that our industrial capacity is so high that it is not especially important to conserve time and materials to the maximum? Whatever the answer, no economy can produce so abundantly as to afford waste.

———— 99 ————

IT'S TODAY THAT COUNTS

If someone could guarantee that you would not get hurt on or off the job, it would be the most valuable guarantee you could ever receive.

Such a guarantee is of course impossible. But there is a way to keep yourself safe that's the next best thing to a guarantee.

The secret of staying safe is summed up in these four words:

"It's today that counts!"

———— 99 ————

"The only full blooded American is— The Mosquito."

———— 99 ————

Health and Welfare Coverage

All employees who worked the required number of hours in August will become eligible for health and welfare coverage and will be covered on the first day of October, 1958. Additions: Robert K. Bird, Elvin D. Smith.

Employees who did not work the required number of hours will become ineligible the same day. Deletions: Albert E. Barlett, Leon M. Bedford, Sr., Donald Hageman, Dorothy M. Hartshorn, D. W. West.

A Miraculous Machine, the Hand

The hand is one of the most perfect mechanisms ever contrived, as well as being one of the most useful. Even in an age of electronic devices that dazzle the imagination, the hand is still one of the most intricate and delicate.

Before a person is entrusted to operate one of these complicated and expensive electronic devices he must very often complete years of instruction and education. However, every person is entrusted with the use of his hands at birth and far too many times proves that he is not competent to use such important and valuable tools wisely and safely.

Anything so important and necessary as the hand deserves the best of care—a care much better than most of us give it. The hand, however, is like a machine in that it only does what it is told to do. It functions according to the plans of the brain.

To give the hand the care it deserves we must think in terms of its value and protect it against injury and damage. To do this we must be constantly safety conscious and alert and protect it against injury and damage. To do this we must be constantly safety conscious and alert to possible hazards that can destroy or impair the function of this mechanism.

—Goodyear Safety News

———— 99 ————

A Russian lecturer who insisted that democracy worked only for a few was asked to explain a photo of an American parking lot filled with cars.

"Aha, look at the hubcaps," he said, "most of them are owned by one man — Ford!"

———— 99 ————

True or False

(Continued from Page 1)

satisfy the toughest customers in the world—Americans—you would do well to make 10 percent profit, let a l o n e 35 percent.

Tight competition and low profit margins add up to benefits for the American consumers. At the same time, these companies pay the highest wages in the world. Their employees are the best-clad, best-fed and best-housed in the world.

In short, it looks like we have the best economic system in the world.

—Len Kraft

Rips and Trims

(Continued from Page 8)

Marylin Jones, daughter of **Martha** and **Floyd**, had an appendectomy at Good Samaritan Hospital. **Kenneth Calin's** wife is much improved and is home again. A speedy recovery to each of you.

Ralph Lamke and son, **Larry**, were in Corbett area one Saturday hunting pigeons. They got four pigeons, got wet, and had lots of fun.

Les Anderson has purchased the Dimitt place at Crown Point.

Vernon Bettendorf has been called back to the Coast Guard Reserve for six months and is to report to New York City.

College has taken a number f r o m our ranks. Among these are **Tom and Bob Cowling, Paul Watts, L e r o y Brenneke and Gerry Kraft** who are attending the University of Oregon at Eugene. **Wesley Post and Don Hageman** are at Oregon State College at Corvallis. **Jim Yerion** is at Oregon College of Education at Monmouth. And **Phillip Schneringer, Curtis Smith and Marshall Howell** are at Portland State College in Portland.

———— 99 ————

October Birthdays

Many Happy Returns of the Day!

Wesley Adams	Charles Gaymon
Roger Blaine	Peter Graymer
Kenneth Craig	Sara Mahn
Ramon Damerell	Einar Mickelson
Ward Dull	Jacob Van Orsow

Visitor Welcomed

Mr. R. F. (Bob) Steele, one of the partners in the firm of Schultz, Snyder and Steele of Lansing, Michigan,

with his son Ted (left) and J i m Schultz (right), was a recent visitor at Bridal Veil. His firm is the buyer of millwork for Capitol City Lumber Company of Lansing.

Ted and Jim, while enroute to Portland, were passengers on the plane that crashed near Minneapolis. There were no fatalities in that crash.

———— 99 ————

Special Notice

Effective October 13 there will be an increase in price of some Safety Shoes. Place your order now for winter shoes.

1958 SAFETY CHART

Month	Tot. Hourly Pd. Man Hrs.	Lost Time Accidents	Accident Freq.	Days Lost	Accident Severity
January	13,534	0	0	22	1626
February	14,089	2	141.9	21	1491
March	19,340	0	0	21	1086
First Quarter	46,963	2	42.6	64	1363
April	9,312	0	0	22	2368
May	20,657	4	193.6	42	2033
June	21,017	1	47.6	24	1142
Second Quarter	50,986	5	98.1	88	1726
July	25,291	0	0	22	870
August	22,808	0	0	21	921
Total	146,048	7	47.9	195	1335

A M

The lumber shed pic
moved forward is aga
This building measuring
moved 300 feet so tha
cated in order that part
as a shop for the man
Sash.

The new location is n
be Toxic Treated as the
ping. The rest of the b
millwork which will eli
it is Toxic Treated.

Lebeck & Son, Movin
proximately a month p
to its new location. Pai
the new foundation.

ward

arious stages of being
d for lumber storage.
g by 60 feet wide, was
more conveniently lo-
e near future, be used
ocked Down Window

nk where the sash will
into the cars for ship-
be used for storage of
g the track again after

of Portland, spent ap-
building and moving it
laintenance Crew built

Before Disaster Strikes

Each day we hear and read of disasters in all parts of the world. Some are in the form of floods, hurricanes, tornadoes, etc. You may recall the Vanport Flood in 1948 and the explosion of the Fireworks Warehouse in Portland on July 5 of this year. These were near enough that we could see the destruction; yet, we were not among those who lost homes and possessions. The Salvation Army and The American Red Cross were on the spot almost immediately to care for the injured, and provide shelter, food and clothing to those who needed their help. We were fortunate enough not to be among those who needed help in these two emergencies; however, in case of war, we could be among those who are left homeless and need the aid of these agencies.

Where do these organizations obtain their money for such operations? They are both non-profit; therefore, the funds they use are private contributions. These are two of the 71 agencies which are members of the United Fund.

Each Fall the United Fund campaigns for contributions to continue the work of these 71 agencies. The goal for this year has been set at $3,203,200 for the Tri-county area, which consists of Multnomah, Clackamas and Washington counties. The goal looks high, but when each person in the three counties does his share, the goal can be reached easily.

We have not been asked to give several hundred dollars, which is often required by the Government in taxes, but only one hour's pay per month throughout the year. This is not very much to give, but just think what the amount would mean to you if you were homeless and without food and a job. Then it would seem like a very large sum.

Disasters are not the only times that United Fund Agencies help. There are many other organizations who are receiving their funds through this combined fund-raising campaign. Among these are the Boy and Girl Scouts and other clubs which are doing so much for youth in preparing them for the future as good citizens. Some of these boys and girls that are helped by your contribution will no doubt be the Leaders of Tomorrow in our country. Don't you want leaders who have had the right training in their youth?

There are many other ways we may benefit from the United Fund, too numerous to mention. Just to name a few—there are Community Centers Child Services, Aid Societies, Family Services, Rehabilitation Centers, Health Services, Convalescent Homes and many others. Each of the 71 agencies are doing a good job to make life more pleasant for many who need the help they can give.

We should feel very proud that we are able to give our share and are not on the receiving end where we must depend on someone else for our food and shelter. Those who are unable to work only wish they could give their share. Won't you do your share to keep these 71 agencies operating by giving at least one hour's pay per month to the **United Fund**.

MEETINGS ARE HELD SECOND MONDAY EVENING & FOURTH SATURDAY MORNING, LABOR TEMPLE, S. W. FOURTH AVENUE & JEFFERSON STREET
PORTLAND 1, OREGON

Phone CApitol 8-0171 - Ext. 286 - 287
315 Labor Temple

PETER BEACH, *Bus. Rep.*
HENRY GERLACH, *Asst. Bus. Rep.*

MILLMEN'S LOCAL UNION
No. 1120
U. B. of C. and J. of A.
AFL-CIO

Affiliated with the Carpenters' District Council, Oregon State Council of Carpenters.
Building Trades Council and the Central Labor Council of
Portland and Vicinity

September 19, 1958

To the members of Millmen's Local Union #1120 working at
Bridal Veil Lumber & Box Company:

For several years Labor has supported the United Fund, however, this
year Labor is going all out to do everything they can to make this
campaign a success. Labor has five members on the United Fund Board;
they are Glen Blake, President of the Multnomah County Labor Council,
O.J. Falkenberg of the Chemical Workers, Mel Lienard of the Streetcar-
mens Union, Lew Cornelius of the Teamsters Union, and Al Zimmerman of
the Railroad Brotherhood.

There are 72 agencies in the United Fund; some of them are very close
to our hearts, such as the Albertina Kerr Nursery, the Boys and Girls
Aid Society, the Family Counciling Service, the Waverly Baby Home,
the Pal Club for boys, and many others.

The United Fund campaign is a once-a-year giving plan; organized
Labor fought hard for the formation of the United Fund so that we
could abolish the many bothersome fund-raising campaigns that
formerly plagued the community.

Your cooperation in this matter will be greatly appreciated.

Millmen's Local Union No. 1120

Peter Beach
Peter Beach, Business Representative

Rips and Trims

Maybe you don't think of Bridal Veil as being such a pretty place, but the surroundings really don't make a lot of difference as long as it is home. **Fred and Fay Harp** realized this while on their recent vacation to Mexico and Los Angeles. They spent three weeks living in their new house trailer seeing the country and visiting friends. They tell of seeing signs on the highway saying "¼ mile to litter can." When they reached the litter can, that's all it was sitting under one lone tree and perhaps three or four cars that had arrived there first all trying to park in the shade of that one small tree. They should appreciate our beautiful trees here now. They stopped at Knotts Berry Farm and Capistrano. They missed seeing the swallows at Capistrano but the doves swarmed over them as they entered the gates. Fred did get to fish a little at Florence and Wilson River on the way home. They seem to be happy to be home after a nice vacation.

Others who have returned from vacations are **Louis Bissell, Mary Woodard, Ralph Ellis** and **Lloyd DeMain. Ralph Lamke** spent part of his vacation at Long Beach clamming and at Alsea Bay fishing for Salmon. **Art Howell** also planned to spend some time on the coast fishing after visiting relatives in Pasco, Washington. **Buck Howell** brought back something with him to remember his vacation. How is your poison oak by now, Buck?

Many of the Bridal Veil fishermen have been rather busy recently. Coos Bay is minus three nice Chinook salmon—weights 16, 19 and 21 pounds — caught by **Pete Graymer. Ed Kinonen, Marv Stolin** and two of Ed's brothers fished out of Ilwaco and caught 8 Salmon each weighing approximately 30 pounds. **Eldon Gross** wasn't very lucky this time, but at least he tried. **Mr. and Mrs. Howard Hunt** with Mr. and Mrs. Burnham of Corbett spent Labor Day weekend camping on the Barlow Trail and also did some fishing. Twenty-three rainbow trout were the catch of **John, Marvin** and **Donald Van Orsow** at Timothy Lake.

Jim and Lou Cowling, Tom, Bob and **Pat** with guests **Janet Larson** and **Wesley Pont,** drove to Long Beach one Friday evening to take advantage of some good clam tides over the weekend. They had good luck clamming and a very enjoyable weekend. Tom, Bob and Wesley had to cut their weekend at the beach short in order to be back for a wedding on Saturday night and then joined Gerry Kraft on Sunday at a fraternity ski party at Lake Oswego.

Others who have been roaming about are **Charles Gaymon** and family who visited his aunt and uncle near Springfield, Oregon. **Delbert** and **Nellie Dunken** with Everett and Mildred Evans attended the "Pendleton Round-up" and shot three rolls of movies. **Eldon Nielson** and his wife spent the Labor Day weekend at Burns, Oregon and saw **Marvin Jackson's** Blue Lake Baseball team take two out of three games from the Burns Elk team. **Mr. and Mrs. Bobby Layton** visited former Bridal Veil employee Jack Kreman and his wife in St. Helens, Oregon. **Mr. and Mrs. Roy Eveland** spent a day at the Oregon State Fair **Ray and John Matson** spent a weekend at Seattle, Washington, visiting Tommy Christophore. John has given up air mattress navigation for water skiing. There are more spills and also more fun. He also spent a weekend visiting a cousin at Coquille and stopped at Sea Lion Caves enroute home.

Among those entertaining at home this month were **Mr. and Mrs. Ed Wendler** with visitors from Colorado Springs. **Ward Dull's** cousins were here from Wyoming, and his father came here for his vacation. **Mabel Hills'** daughter, Mrs. Bill Steffen, was here from Tacoma. **Mira Nielson** and her husband entertained their grandchildren, Ronnie and Carla. **Martha Jones** recently entertained Mr. and Mrs. Peter M. Olsen at her home in Bonneville and also the **James Kendrick** family. Guests of **Mr. and Mrs. John Willms** for a week were Mr. and Mrs. Al Willms. Al, John's brother, attended a school of refrigeration at Tigard.

On our Sick List this month are: Bruce Crouser, son of **Fred Crouser,** who was thrown from a horse and injured his knee. He was a patient at Portland Sanitarium and hospital.

(Continued on Page 3)

BRIDAL VEIL LUMBER & BOX CO.
News Letter

Vol. IV, No. 5   BRIDAL VEIL, OREGON   NOVEMBER, 1958

Definition

Here is another difficulty we bump into in trying to explain our way of life to other nations. We use words and phrases that don't mean much to us.

Consider that good old expression "Free Enterprise." It is used in hundreds of editorials every day. What does it mean?

When the Gallup Pole asked people what it meant, only 30 percent had any clear idea. The other 70 percent either couldn't define it at all, or else thought that it meant freedom to put over a fast one in a business deal.

Now, oddly enough, there is some historical basis for this kind of thinking. The wandering peddler of wooden nutmegs is an American legend. He must have gotten along fine as long as he only traveled the same road once.

Abe Lincoln, so the story goes, gained something of a reputation as a horse-trader. One wise fellow, determined to beat Abe in a horse trade, offered to swap horses sight-unseen. At the appointed hour he appeared leading as sad a looking bag of bones as ever was foisted off as a horse.

And quite a crowd gathered to join in the fun. Abe was going to take a beating for sure this time.

However, the joke soured when Abe finally showed up carrying a saw horse.

A good example of free enterprise, you might say. Certainly it is in the tradition that we have come to associate with the phrase "Yankee Trader."

The only trouble is that this sort of monkey-shines won't work in the business world of today. Successful business can only be built on satisfied customers. The business that cheats soon runs out of customers. Payrolls, profits and jobs can only result from a good reputation for sound value and fair price.

What then is free enterprise? What does it involve? What does it mean to us?

For one thing it means a great deal more than just the right to open a filling station if we should take the notion.

It means the right to move from Illinois or Iowa or Oklahoma and make a new start in Oregon without asking the government for permission. Many of us have done just that—including me.

It means the right to buy a piece of ground and build a home of your own. Sweden has been controlled by the Socialists for over 25 years. Housing is rigidly controlled. And in Stockholm alone over 110,000 couples are on the waiting lists for housing yet to be built by the Socialist planners.

It means the right to raise a few daffodil bulbs or cultivate a few raspberries in your spare time. If you were a Swede in Stockholm and wanted to buy a little plot of farmland and putter around raising things, nine chances out of ten the government wouldn't permit it. You would have to prove you knew a great deal about farming —or you couldn't buy the land.

Free enterprise even involves Walter Reuther's right to organize a labor union of multi-million dollar proportions and to dicker with the boss on wages, hours, and working conditions. About the only suggestions acceptable from a Russian labor union are that work quotas be raised and wages be cut.

So, contrary to popular opinion, free enterprise has nothing to do with turning a fast buck in a shady deal. If it did, there is reason to think that the Russian bureaucrats have us outclassed.

No, free enterprise involves all the
(Continued on Page 2)

NEWS LETTER

Published on the 10th of each month by
Bridal Veil Lumber & Box Co.
Bridal Veil, Oregon

Editor . . . . . . Sara Mahn

How to Get Wet

Everyone of us ought to know
That recessions are bound to come and go,
But, instead, each dip is a great surprise,
As if such a contingency couldn't arise.
When things go well in the business field,
As history so often has revealed,
He who cries, "Caution — beware the boom",
Is just laughed off as a "prophet of doom".
When earnings are high it is "fun" to spend,
As if prosperity never would end.
And when rivers of cash flow across the nation,
Who gives a thought to the threat of inflation?
The fashionable thing is to live for the day,
As if there won't be a piper to pay.
And the fact that the world's in a horrible mess
Is simply a matter of "couldn't care less".
That is the policy tried and true
Of those now eating recession stew,
And that is the way it always will be
All the way down through history.
An ancient formula still applies
To governments, businesses, gals and guys:
Spend more than you get as you go on your way,
And you'll be all wet — come t h e rainey day.

By Richard E. Snyder

(With p r o f o u n d apologies to all legitimate poets, living or dead, even including Edgar A. Guest.)

——— 21 ———

Definition

(Continued from Page 1)

rights and privileges that we, as citizens, have taken so much for granted that we have forgotten them.

It is time we got up on our soap box and let the world know.

Len Kraft

YOU

Personal success and happiness will be ours when we acquire:

Skill—Complete mastery of our tools, techniques and equipment.

A Sense of Purpose — Without a goal to strive for, our efforts are meaningless.

Friendliness—No man succeeds alone —be sincere and friendly to all.

Self-Control — Respect cannot be demanded — it must be deserved.

Profit by Failures — Finding out what we did wrong and starting over.

Confidence — Belief in ourselves, our company, and country.

Diligence— A realization that nothing h o n e s t and worthy was ever accomplished without enthusiasm— and hard work.

Education — Living without learning is like eating without digesting. Everyone can be educated by reading good books.

"Success is a ladder which cannot be climbed with our hands in our pockets."

——— 21 ———

An old country doctor parked his Model T on the street. When he came back a number of youths were standing around laughing at the old bus. The doctor climbed into the seat and said mildly, "The car's paid for, boys." He looked deliberately from one boy to another. "You're not — — and you're not."

WAGE EARNERS

PROTECT THE...!

Trip Proves Profitable

On my recent trip East, I visited with a few of our customers in Chicago, St. Louis and Kansas City and also met with a sales representative in St. Louis who represents several manufacturers including our company.

I visited the Ill-Mo Sash and Door Company in East St. Louis, Illinois, and a new customer, The Morgan-Wightman Company in St. Louis, Missouri, who gave me their first order for window and door frames.

In Chicago I visited with Howard Dekker and Chuck Brish of the Dekker-Brish Millwork Company. They were unloading two carloads of our millwork, one of which had caught on fire in route. While there was considerable damage from smoke and water, they were able to salvage over half of the car.

In Kansas City, Missouri, I visited with the Martin Material Company, Luce Manufacturing Company (where I also obtained an order), and with Lumber Dealers Company of Kansas City, Kansas.

It was a pleasure to meet these customers whom I had previously dealt with only by phone. I received a very cordial welcome at each firm and feel that we will continue to receive nice orders from these customers.

Mel Mallinson

What? A Blower?

The first half of the new blowing system for the Moulding Department has been installed as pictured above. It will be completed as soon as the Moulding Department can be shut down for approximately a week. This new system will give us more blowing capacity which should result in more efficient operation of equipment.

——— 21 ———

For the first time in many years our forests are growing more wood than we are using.

1958 SAFETY CHART

Month	Tot. Hourly Pd. Man Hrs.	Lost Time Accidents	Accident Freq.	Days Lost	Accident Severity
January	13,534	0	0	22	1626
February	14,089	2	141.9	21	1491
March	19,340	0	0	21	1086
First Quarter	46,963	2	42.6	64	1363
April	9,312	0	0	22	2368
May	20,657	4	193.6	42	2033
June	21,017	1	47.6	24	1142
Second Quarter	50,986	5	98.1	88	1726
July	25,291	0	0	22	870
August	22,808	0	0	21	921
September	23,096	1	43.3	11	476
Third Quarter	71,195	1	14.1	54	758
Total	169,144	8	47.3	206	1218

Millmen's Federal Credit Union

315 Labor Temple
Portland 1, Oregon

Balance Sheet as of September 30, 1958

ASSETS

Current Assets		
Cash on hand and in banks	$1,285.83	
Loans Outstanding	9,699.11	
Total Current Assets		**$10,984.94**
Other Assets		
Furniture and Fixtures	$ 66.70	
Prepaid Insurance	74.59	
Misc. Assets	28.25	
Total Other Assets		**169.54**
TOTAL ASSETS		**$11,154.48**

LIABILITIES AND NET WORTH

Current Liabilities		
None		— 0 —
Net Worth		
Shares	$9,878.98	
Regular Reserve	241.98	
Reserve for Delinquent Loans	544.03	
1958 Profit	489.49	
Total Net Worth		**$11,154.48**
TOTAL LIABILITIES AND NET WORTH		**$11,154.48**

The Millme
established to
men's Local Un
June 29, 1955
J. E. Delgard, H
Emery Thomps
officers. Progre
years this Unio
tell by the Bala

The purpose
you a better pla
it is insured an
— and an easi
make a loan.

All investme
sured and then
no additional co
your Credit Uni
death, your wi
$1,000 you inv
surance. Divi
your investment

Loans are als
from the Credit
your loan will
without your fa

KE
ME

Today---No Worries Tomorrow

...edit Union has been ...he members of Mill- ...20. It was founded ...rter No. 10380 with ...mirk, Henry Gerlack, ...ster Ford as original ...n made in the three ...operating as you can ...or September.

...edit Union is to give ... your money—where ...good rate of interest ... expensive place to

... Credit Union are in- ...vith life insurance, at ...f you have $1,000 in ... at the time of your ...ceive $2,000 — the ... the $1,000 life in- ...% may be paid on

When you borrow ...e unpaid balance of ... the event of death, ...ig to worry about it.

The interest rate on loans is never more than 1% per month on the unpaid balance, or one cent per month on each dollar not repaid.

To make an investment or a loan, you must be a member of the Credit Union. In order to become a member, you must make a deposit of at least $5.00 (which is your first savings in the Union) and 25 cents for membership fee. Deposits can be made at the Union Office, by mail, directly to Leo F. Hageman or can be deducted from your pay check. The payroll deduction plan is very simple. Just see Leo and he will have you sign a card giving the amount you wish deducted each month. Then your savings begin to grow and you won't even miss it after the first month.

Applications for loans can be made at the Union Office or to Leslie Polzel. Liberal loans can be made without co-signers or chattel mortgages.

Every member of the Millmen's Local Union can join the Credit Union. Also your wife and children under the age of 21.

Make your family's future secure by opening your account today with your Millmen's Federal Credit Union.

Leslie Polzel
Member
Loan Committee

Leo F. Hageman
Secretary
Board of Directors

Rips and Trims

The trees have put on their new colors of red, yellow and brown and the days are getting shorter. The East wind is beginning to blow harder and the air is a little cooler. It is easy to tell that it is Fall and Winter will soon be here.

We have enjoyed a beautiful Fall and it has been a pleasure to get out and enjoy the hunting season which always accompanies Fall. Each one who got his deer and birds without an accident has much to be truly thankful for as this Thanksgiving approaches.

Many from Bridal Veil were among those hunting during the past few weeks. John and **Marvin Van Orsow** with Richard Kerslake spent the opening weekend of Pheasant season in the Madras area. They had some success. **Marvin and Walt Stolin** went to Stamfield and got seven pheasants. The **Cowling** family enjoyed their hunting trips and brought back ducks, quail and pheasants. **Lou** also brought back the tail feathers of a pheasant without the bird. It was very interesting to hear her tell about reaching in the pocket across the back of **Jim**'s coat to take out the dead (?) pheasant. She grabbed the tail

Fine birds, Tom

feathers and was bringing them out on one side when the pheasant had a different idea and flew out the other side minus the feathers that Lou was holding so tightly. That was the lucky one that got away. Did you keep those feathers, Lou? They say their dog did a magnificent job of retrieving the birds and Tom looks as proud of Rusty, in the picture, as he is of the birds.

Jim also got his deer early in the season. It was delicious, Jim. **Ed Wendler** got his at Goblers Knob in the Tillamook Burns. **Stanley Hills** and son, Danny, **Marvin and Mae Stolin** also returned with a deer each. **Floyd Jacobs** was hunting when someone broke a window in his car and took about $250 worth of tools and threw his keys away. He didn't even get his deer there in the Mt. Hood area. **Einar and Fred Mickelson** were with a party on the first day of deer season down in the Tillamook Burns section when a beautiful buck was spotted. Someone fired and the shot hit the antlers, then ricochetted back and went in the front and out the side of Fred's leg. After several weeks in the hospital, he is now recuperating at home.

Now that Elk season has opened many will have their elk before this is published. **Howard Hunt** plans to be with a party at Pilot Rock in the Ukiah district, **Fred Bailey** in Eastern Oregon, and **Roley Zumwalt** didn't say which direction he was going. **Ed Kinonen** didn't get his deer, but perhaps he had better luck with elk.

The visitor's list this month includes **Roy Eveland's** brother and sister-in-law from Sunny Side, Washington; **Leo Hageman's** mother from Seattle, Washington; Mr. and Mrs. E. A. Hageman and small daughter of Wathena, Kansas at the home of **Martha Jones**; Mr. and Mrs. Bob Gear of Denver, Colorado, visiting the **Charles Gaymans**; and Mr. and Mrs. Ralph Redmann of Everett, Washington, who were with the **Clyde Hambrick** family.

Those visiting elsewhere were Ruth and **Durward Litton** who went to see Barbara and Don West (former Sales Manager at Bridal Veil) in Oroville, California; the **McCredies** visited

(Continued on Page 7)

Rips and Trims

(Continued from Page 8)

with friends and relatives in California while on vacation; **Fred Damerell** went to Spokane to see his son and enjoyed a good Hockey game while there over a weekend. He also enjoyed his recent vacation in Canada. **Paul Dooley's** vacation trip to Idaho was interrupted at Boise after the camping equipment was all set up, by the illness of his 17 month old son, Michael, who had to be rushed back home. Paul spent the remainder of his vacation at home after Michael was better.

Mabel Hills, who has just celebrated her 29th wedding anniversary, is very proud of her new granddaughter. It was also a daughter, Laurel Lee, born on October 4 at Sandy, weighing 8 lbs. 13 oz., to **Mr. and Mrs. Charles Murphy.**

Bert Davis enjoyed having her daughter-in-law, Carol stay with her while **Fay** and son, Bob, went hunting.

Anna and Willis Bowen were guests on October 6 at a dinner in honor of granddaughter, Jean Ann's tenth birthday.

That blue and white '55 Plymouth Hardtop r e c e n t l y making an appearance at Bridal Veil belongs to **Bob Bird.**

Marylin Jones, daughter of **Martha,** is now attending the "Roecker Private Day School" in Portland.

Eldon Gross spent a recent weekend overhauling his car. It should run much better now.

Pat Link, daughter of **Archie Davies,** is real happy that her husband is home again after serving sixteen months in Korea.

Harry Densmore suffered a heart attack on October 22 and is a patient at Providence hospital in Portland. We wish you a very speedy recovery, Harry.

———— 21 ————

Nov. Birthdays

Many Happy Returns of the Day!

Harry Adolph	Fay Davis
Alfred Barnes	Clem Hancock
Verl Bird	Harold Burkholder
Fred Harp	Kenneth Meyer
Louis Bissell	E. W. Norgard
Ronald Catlin	Ronald Snyder

60th Wedding Anniversary

Mr. and Mrs. George M. Leash celebrated 60 years of wedded bliss at their home in Northeast Portland on November 1. They were married in Wisconsin in 1898. Mrs. Leash is the former Anna Mutter.

George retired in November, 1956 after 19 years of service with Bridal Veil Lumber and Box Company and is now enjoying his hobby of inlaid woodwork. His lamps and chess boards are truly a work of art.

His life presents a very interesting picture. He was born in South Bend, Indiana, on July 14, 1874. A number of years were spent working in various machine shops before he joined the Kraft family in 1922. Since that time he has worked in a number of Kraft plants and built the Cheese Box Plant at New West Minister, Canada. He came to Bridal Veil on October 1, 1938 and remained here until his retirement. He has also invented several machines in his spare time.

The Leashes have three children, Mrs. Paul Detrick of Bridal Veil, Mrs. C. C. Robinson of Portland and Noble W. Leash of Santa Rosa, California. They also have four grandchildren and five great-grandchildren.

When asked the secret of their many years of happy marriage he replied, "I just kept my dirty tricks from my wife."

Mr. and Mrs. G. M. Leash

15th Anniversary

Pearl Cloe will have completed 15 years of service at Bridal Veil Lumber and Box Company on November 12. At present he is a strapper, but in his time at Bridal Veil he has worked as night watchman and on the band re-saw, cleat saw, and power rip saw. There has been only one lost time accident recorded against him and that was when he fell and broke his leg.

January 4, 1897 in Marysville, Iowa, marked the beginning of his life. At the age of four his parents moved to a Timber Homestead in Northern Minnesota, and when he was 13 they moved West. The rest of his life has been spent in Washington and Oregon.

On February 3, 1922, Pearl married Ethel Beatty in Washougal, Washington, which was her home at that time. They have five children: two daughters, Mrs. Marie Bowen and Mrs. Marjorie Taylor living in Portland, two sons, Delbert (who is also employed here) and Harvey living in Bridal Veil, and Carol is still living at home and is a student at Corbett high school. The Cloes have seven grandchildren.

Pearl has two sisters, Mrs. Velta Hansen living in Portland and Mrs. Hattie Gerrard in St. Helens.

His hobby is fishing; however, he says he isn't an expert at it. He also enjoys watching a good baseball

The Spelling of Safety

S is for the Signs put there to protect you and help you protect others.

A is for your Attitude which after all is a big part in being careful.

F is for your Family—so dependent upon you and your health.

E is for the Effort you make to keep yourself all in one piece and able to support them.

T is for the Team you w o r k on. Whether it's the basketball 5 or the 2 men working together on the pond, one man's injury affects the others too.

Y is for You. The most important part of safety. Remember the life you save may be YOUR own.

—By Mrs. Dorothea Yantis
Coos Bay Toastmistress Club

——— 21 ———

Protect Your Pipes

Don't wait until the weatherman says "It will freeze tonight" to check your water pipes. Take advantage of the material the Company has available for you to box up those pipes. Don't delay, do it now.

——— 21 ———

Health and Welfare Coverage

All employees who worked the required number of hours in September will become eligible for health and welfare coverage and will be covered on the first day of November, 1958. Additions: Vernon J. Bettendorf, Kenneth R. Crooke, Ramon A. Damerell, Donald Hageman, Stanley B. Hills, Robert S. Russell, John W. Smith, Ronald A. Snyder.

Employees who did not work the required number of hours will become ineligible the same day. Deletions: Fredrick C. Bailey, Jr., Richard Lee Bowen, Leroy H. Brenneke, Raymond Cote, Keith Howell, Marvin Howell, Larry L. Lamke, James M. Layton, Einar Fred Mickelson, Vera Nell Roberts.

game.

During World War I he spent about 8 months in the service of his country at Camp Grand, Illinois and a short time at Fort Lewis, Washington, where he received his discharge.

Pearl and his family are members of the Protestant church in Portland.

BRIDAL VEIL LUMBER & BOX CO.

News Letter

Vol. IV, No. 6   BRIDAL VEIL, OREGON   DECEMBER, 1958

Erosion

Since 1940 the purchasing power of the dollar has been reduced by 52 cents.

Aside from the fact that the government has consistently failed to live within its income, what causes this?

Let's look at one basic economic truth. Production is the source of wealth. Improved efficiency in production is the accelerator of economic progress.

Who says so?

At the height of the economic "recession" of 1949, the Executive Council of the American Federation of Labor presented a report to the 68th convention of the A. F. of L. This report stated: "We have consistantly recognized that living standards rise as production per man-hour increases and efficiency improves."

Visualize, just for fun, the output of United States industry as a pie. To increase wages without increasing the size of the pie merely increases the price of the slices. No gain there.

If, on the other hand, we are able to increase the size of the pie and to increase wages in proportion, everyone is better off.

And it cannot be otherwise. Our friends in Red China could increase wages until the cows come home and it wouldn't do any good. There just hasn't been enough pie produced to go around.

The situation in China best illustrates the futility of basing the economy on anything other than productivity. And productivity is based on the quality of the tools men use in production. Tools in turn are stored up effort in the form of capital.

Mao can't get around economic fact by passing a minimum wage law or he'd have done it long ago.

And in a similar fashion, Walter Reuther does his people a disservice when he uses the cart-before-the-horse theory of economics which holds that in the economic equation purchasing power comes ahead of production in importance.

Double everyone's wages for the same amount of production and everything costs twice as much.

Up to this point inflation doesn't mean much to the man with a job. Sure, prices are up, but so are wages. Yet he is better off than twenty years ago. In most cases — particularly in industrial employment — "real" income has more than kept pace with inflation.

Hardest hit have been people on fixed incomes such as pensions and insurance annuities. Inflation is a very serious threat to all who hope to retire and live on Federal Old Age Benefits (Social Security).

In twenty years our money supply has been increased 275 percent. The rate of industrial production has increased 119 percent. The population has increased 35 percent.

And the buying power of the dollar has been more than cut in half.

What does the next twenty years hold for us?

—Len Kraft

——— 52 ———

Kindness

Kindness is an investment which pays dividends in personal satisfaction and the enrichment of our lives. Cultivating a cheerful, kindly disposition is one of the best things we can do to have peace of mind. When we stoop to lighten another's load, we lighten our own. Who can estimate the power of kindness?

—Carl Holmes

NEWS LETTER

Published on the 10th of each month by
Bridal Veil Lumber & Box Co.
Bridal Veil, Oregon

Editor . . . . . Sara Mahn

The Difference

The essential difference between a starving coolie and a prosperous American worker, with his own home and car, **is tools,** it is pointed out by the **GE Fort Wayne News.** The coolie works much harder, physically, but tools make it possible for the American to produce and enjoy more than 50 times as much.

So the conflict which some people try to stir up between wages and profits is an utterly false one. Both depend upon productivity. Increased productivity alone prepares the path for higher wages and profits—and "the key to higher productivity is teamwork between employees and management to make machines, systems, procedures and techniques as efficient and economical as possible; being constantly on the alert for the 'better way' that has made America the marvel of the world."

————— 52 —————

Health and Welfare Coverage

All employees who worked the required number of hours in October will become eligible for health and welfare coverage and will be covered on the first day of December, 1958. Additions: Anthony Angelo, John Estep, Harold Fuller, John Monjay, Joe Sazama.

Employees who did not work the required number of hours will become ineligible the same day. Deletions: Don Barnes, Vern Bettendorf, Robert L. Cowling, Thomas J. Cowling, Ramon Damerell, Jack Dempsey, Donald Hageman, John Matson, George W. Post, Philip Schneringer, Curtis Smith, Elvin D. Smith, Paul Watts, James M. Yerion.

————— 52 —————

Saving Through Payroll Deduction

Thirty-two employees have joined the Millmen's Federal Credit Union up to the present time. A total of $360 was deposited with the C r e d i t Union through the payroll deduction plan this month. If you haven't joined yet, see Leo Hageman real soon and he will be glad to help you open your account.

Advantages of Wood Windows

Wood excells aluminum by its ease of repair. Damaged wood sash is easily repaired and reglazed with ordinary labor and ordinary tools. New parts can easily and quickly be made by nearby wood working plants. Consequently, wood sash and frames never become "orphans" and repair or replacement is always possible.

Standard wood window frames will accommodate wood storm sash and screens without additional framing expense. Storm windows are important fuel savers — storm sash on 20 windows (3' 4" x 4' 6") are estimated to save 2,750 pounds of coal, 220 gallons of oil, or 270 therms of gas per year (according to Small Homes Council Bulletin F11.2). One therm is t h e supply of heat needed to lift a gram of water at maximum density one degree centigrade.

In fire, wood windows will provide a means of exit whereas aluminum windows will often twist and buckle, preventing their opening. After a fire, wood sash and frames can frequently be repaired at less cost than metal sash. Portions of a partly damaged wood sash can be replaced, or the entire sash and frame can be completely removed without difficulty. Metal windows that buckle or twist are either a total loss, or must be removed from their anchorages with considerable trouble and expense.

————— 52 —————

How Much?

Congress thinks nothing of spending billions of our hard-paid tax dollars these days. How much is a billion dollars?

Well, it's a pile of $1,000 bills reaching 111 feet higher than the Washington Monument! If you had been able to borrow a billion dollars, interest free, and had paid it back at the rate of $1,000 per day, with the last payment made sometime this year, your original loan would have been made in the year 784 B.C.

————— 52 —————

Dec. Birthdays

Many Happy Returns of the Day!

Clyde H. Hambrick	Francis Cook
Eugene H. Potter	Walter Keller
Charles Murphy	Hiram Layton
Jack Westlake	

Ernie Subs	Visitor Welcomed

Ernie Farrari is back in the filing room substituting for Jim Cowling, who is recuperating from a hunting accident. Ernie spent a number of years with our company as head filer. He is now working as a trouble-shooter in the machinery field. Welcome back, Ernie.

———— 52 ————

"The boss is mean," the man told his wife, "but he's fair."

"What do you mean by that?"

"Well, he's mean to everybody."

Frank Wheeler, a former employee in the Maintenance Department, was a recent visitor at the mill. He is now retired and lives in Anchorage, Alaska, where he spends his extra time in the garden. While here he is visiting his daughter, Mrs. Ted Hanson. He also plans to visit his brother and sisters before he returns to Alaska in the Spring. ———— 52 ————

The only people you should want to get even with are those who have helped you.

1958 SAFETY CHART

Month	Tot. Hourly Pd. Man Hrs.	Lost Time Accidents	Accident Freq.	Days Lost	Accident Severity
January	13,534	0	0	22	1626
February	14,089	2	141.9	21	1491
March	19,340	0	0	21	1086
First Quarter	46,963	2	42.6	64	1363
April	9,312	0	0	22	2368
May	20,657	4	193.6	42	2033
June	21,017	1	47.6	24	1142
Second Quarter	50,986	5	98.1	88	1726
July	25,291	0	0	22	870
August	22,808	0	0	21	921
September	23,096	1	43.3	11	476
Third Quarter	71,195	1	14.1	54	758
October	24,771	0	0	0	0
Total	193,915	8	41.3	206	1062

Alone in the

No . . . we have plenty of company in the millwork business. Just look at a few of the names of the prominent people in the field. Do you know what we call them? They are more aptly known as "competitors."

"So what!" might be the retort from the average Bridal Veil employee. "Competition isn't my headache. That's a worry for the big boys up in the office. I've got enough to do tending my machine. Let the salesmen or the top brass worry about competition.

Besides, that's out of my bailiwick. What could I do about it, anyhow?"

Lots could be done by you. But first, do you have any idea just how dangerously your job hangs on the string of competition?

Everytime an order is placed—single residence, large project, apartment or hotel—the Bridal Veil salesman isn't the only man with his hand out. Many hands, those of men representing reliable, able competitors also reach for that order.

. . . Never

Sales can be created, profits induced, and wages assured by each of us whether we operate a machine, punch a typewriter or whatever. Each bit of waste—of material, of set-up, or time—add to our costs and cut the quality of our product.

Everytime a customer is disappointed, either by poor quality or consistently high prices . . . or both . . . a competitor is waiting to take away that business. Now, if we want to keep the plant running with paychecks coming

in 12 months a year, we just have to have orders. And we can't get orders unless our product is superior and our price based on reasonable cost.

We can take home the much needed weekly package if we all do our level best on the job. And not "just part of the time." By doing your part on the job you will have contributed to the successful operations of the company and will have made one more turn on the nut toward greater job security.

15th Anniversary

Thomas Cecil Britton joined the Bridal Veil Lumber and Box Company family on December 20, 1943 as a Hikeaway for the Edger Chain. Since that time he has spent twelve years at his present job as Watchman and three years as a general laborer on the rip saws, band saws and sticker. In his fifteen years with the Company he has had only one lost time accident and was out just one day due to eye infection caused by a sliver.

Tom was born in Crawford, Nebraska, one of eleven children. He met and married Alice Coil while in Crawford. They have ten children: Charles in Idaho, Irene Demmon in Kansas, Nina Chamberlain in Ohio, Arlene Ashcroft in California, Ray in Powers, Oregon, Mary Van Orsow (wife of Joe who is Tenoner Operator here) in Portland, Reva O'Neil in Bly, Oregon, Pauline Stutezman in Logsdon, Anna Selby in Wyoming and Carol, a seventh grader in Fairview grade school, still living at home.

Before coming to Oregon, Tom spent 24 years with the Colorado Fuel and Iron Company in Sun Rise, Wyoming.

Tom is now living in Wood Village where he owns his home. His hobby is gardening, both vegetables and flowers, and he also enjoys hunting and fishing. Baseball and horse racing are very interesting to him, but he doesn't

Social Security Tax Increase

Starting January 1, 1959, the new Social Security law requires an increase in your Social Security deduction from the old 2¼ percent to the new 2½ percent of your pay. The tax will be deducted at this rate each pay day until your total wages reach $4,800 during the year, instead of $4,200 as in the past.

As you know, the company will increase its contribution to match yours, dollar for dollar. This means the company will pay another 2½ percent of your wages to your Social Security account.

In addition the company will continue to pay the unemployment insurance tax of 2.7 percent up to $3,600 per year for each employee, as well as the benefits you now receive.

———— 52 ————

It costs more now to amuse a child than it used to cost to educate his father.

———— 52 ————

Rips and Trims

(Continued from Page 8)

Did you get warm, **Fred Damerell?** There are easier ways than lighting the whole book of matches. Perhaps you were just too excited about your son getting home from the service.

Speaking of the service, **John Mershon** was called for his physical examination last month. He expects to receive orders soon after January first.

Among good hostesses **Martha Jones** should rate high. She and her husband entertained Mr. and Mrs. John Nelson and their daughter Bonnie one weekend and Mrs. Al Wood Knapp another weekend at their home in Bonneville. Mr. and Mrs. Jim Butzin of Hood River were guests at the home of **Charles Gaymon** in Gresham. **Stanley and Mabel Hills** enjoyed the visit of their daughter and her husband, Mr. and Mrs. Steffen of Mount Vernon, Washington. The **Eugene Potters** had a niece visiting with them from Missouri.

care for dog racing.

His military service was spent at Camp Grand, Illinois and McArthur, Texas. He received his discharge from World War I at Fort Riley, Kansas.

a Christmas Prayer...

May the true meaning of Christmas be with us now as on the night of the Christ Child's birth. May the Christmas story live anew in every heart. May all of us keep Christmas as He would have us do, with good will toward men. And may all the blessings of Christmas be yours.

Rips and Trims

Thanksgiving is past and Christmas is almost here. This year will soon end and the new year begin. So time marches on. We have not been standing still as many exciting things have been happening to the employees.

First, congratulations go to **Mr. and Mrs. Bob Bird** on the birth of their son, Randal Duane. Randy was born on November 9 at 3:30 p.m. at Emanuel Hospital and weighed 7 pounds 4 ounces. He is the grandson of **Verl Bird**.

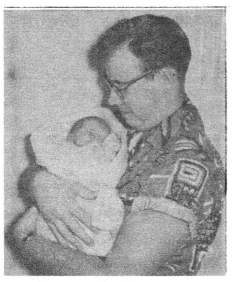

Congratulations, Pop

It was also a son for **Mr. and Mrs Wesley Adams**. Roy Hue was born on November 7 and weighed 7 pounds, 14½ ounces.

Still on the sick list are: **Harry Densmore**, who is still at Providence hospital, but seems much improved. **Jim Cowling** is relaxing at home after spending a couple of weeks at Emanuel Hospital. W h i l e hunting, Jim found that his dog has a lighter step than he does. The dog crossed the nice green meadow nicely, but Jim's weight was too much and he fell in a ditch that was partly covered with grass. **Joseph Cote** is also recuperating at home following his surgery. **Ed Kinonen** seems to be doing f i n e since his stay in the hospital, but has not returned to work as yet.

It's nice to have **Dorothy Hartshorn** back again after her extended illness.

Delbert Dunken has returned to work after spending his vacation working on his place. Also back from vacation is **Roger Blaine** and his wife after spending a weekend at Seattle and a week in San Francisco visiting an uncle. **Ray Schneringer,** also on vacation, went to Nebraska.

Elk season is over and the "elk hunting widows" will have their husbands back home again. **Anna Bowen** spent a recent weekend with her daughter-in-law Peggy while **Willis** a n d Jimmy were hunting in Eastern Oregon. **Fred Bailey** brought back his Elk from the Tollgate area, but **Roley Zumwalt** wasn't that lucky. Neither was **Marvin Stolin** who went to Desolation area and said it was really desolate.

Sergeant and Mrs. Bob Lolbar have returned to Camp Mathews, California, after a three week visit with the **Durward Littons**. Mrs. Lolbar is Durward's sister.

Ralph Lamke, with his son Larry, did very well to bring back 8 ducks from their hunting trip.

The office employees helped **Mr. Norgard** celebrate his 65th birthday with a delicious cake baked by **Eleanor Taylor**. We wish you many more happy birthdays, Mr. Norgard.

Happy Birthday, Mr. Norgard

1959

1959 will not lack for problems.

We still have with us those perennial favorites: t h e unbalanced budget — farm subsidies—integration—public vs. private enterprise—inflation — protective tariffs—urban redevelopment and many others. You can make your own list.

And there are a few items tending to become problems of 1959. Increased imports of foreign manufacturers for example. Many new items will be produced in newer and more' modern foreign factories than ours and at wage rates lower than ours. The competition from the continent on light cars and from Japan on camera equipment will be rough.

But probably the most dramatic problem of 1959 lies in Berlin. Here, some one hundred and fifty miles within the Russian occupation zone of East Germany, sits a small island of freedom—West Berlin.

Berlin—split between East and West —has become a showcase in which the merchandise of capitalism can be compared with the merchandise of socialism—communism.

And the Reds come off a poor second.

What kind of a product has the East to put on display? Only oppression, misery and poverty. On every hand the rubble of destruction from World War II. Grim-faced and underfed, the population drudges out an existence. And in their spare time they can listen to harangues outlining the glories of the workers paradise. And mayhap they may be given an "opportunity" to worship at the shrines of Marx, Engels, Lenin and Stalin.

In the Western zone the product is unbelievable by comparison. The destruction of World War II has long since been cleaned up. The people are well fed, well clothed and housed, and busy at occupations of their own choosing. The stores are full and people are able to buy. And they are free to travel, change jobs and to worship as they please.

Here, for all the world to see with sparkling clarity, are the results of the two systems.

And the people of East Germany have seen.

Every day hundreds of highly skilled and professional people from the Eastern zone are "voting with their feet." These are the people that must be kept behind the Iron Curtain at all costs if the situation in the East is not to get worse.

Probably many more would leave if a way could be found that did not involve the abandonment of families. That desperate men and women should risk their very lives to escape the "workers paradise" is shocking testimony of the evils of the Soviet system.

The Russians can't stand the comparison. We will be subjected to all kinds of pressures to knock us out of West Berlin, but we will hold fast.

And here is an interesting question. While the peoples of the East are risking their lives to escape the socialistic utopia, how many of our freedoms will we throw away in chasing the mirage of security?

—Len Kraft

———— 5 ————

Relative Cost

The Model T. Ford, first produced in 1908, had a price tag of $850—but the average American had to work 86 weeks to earn enough to buy one. Today, Ford economists say, the price of a 1959 model can be earned in only 26 weeks.

NEWS LETTER

Published on the 10th of each month by
Bridal Veil Lumber & Box Co.
Bridal Veil, Oregon

Editor . . . . . Sara Mahn

Steak $3 a Pound?

How would you like to have to pay $7,000 for a medium-priced car; ordinary pair of shoes, $40; modest suit, $200, and $3 a pound for sirloin steak?

Unless the wage-price spiral is checked, we may see a 30-cent dollar and prices like these in ten years, according to industrialist Lansing P. Shield, president of Grand Union Co. He points out that productivity is declining when measured against wages and says that this trend is "the greatest single internal threat to our domestic economy."

In 1956 wage increases outran increases in output per man-hour by four percent. Then, in 1957, inflation got well under way, with wages up by 8.4 percent while productivity increased by only 1.6 percent. By the end of 1957, the dollar saved in 1946 was worth only 67 cents.

———— 5 ————

Luxuries

What is a luxury? In Berlin it may be a door knob. In Italy it is likely to be an unfrayed shirt, or an electric light. What about our country? You would have to look close to find an American who thinks that a radio or even an automatic refrigerator is a "luxury". And only in the biggest cities is an automobile ever classed as such.

———— 5 ————

Health and Welfare Coverage

All employees who worked the required number of hours in November will become eligible for health and welfare coverage and will be covered on the first day of January, 1959. Additions: Dorothy Hartshorn, Eleanor Taylor.

Employees who did not work the required number of hours will become ineligible the same day. Deletions: Anthony Angelo, Robert Bird, Francis Cook, Joseph Cote, Kenneth Crooke, John Estep, Harold E. Fuller, Dewayne Kilness, John D. Monjay, Robert S. Russell, Joe Sazama, John W. Smith, Ronald Snyder, LeRoy Sprague, J. W. Cowling.

Wood Preferred

Wood windows are preferable to aluminum because wood has a beautiful natural texture, grain figure and color. Sash, frame and trim of wood can be painted or stained to harmonize with any decorative treatment. The many styles of wood windows assure correct architectural beauty and design for any home.

Wood is more suited for use in window frames because wood is nature's own insulator while metal readily conducts heat and cold. Wood as an insulator is 1800 times more effective than aluminum. Because wood is a good insulator, it is generally free from frosting or condensation. Metal sash and frames are as subject to condensation as glass itself; are often damp and frosty during the winter months. Wood windows prevent costly damage to curtains and interior wall finishes often caused by condensation on metal windows.

Fashion designers find wood superior to aluminum because stock wood windows may be had in a variety of sizes, designs and types — awning, casement, double - hung, projected, horizontal sliding and picture sash. They are adapted to all types of construction and architectural design, and by varied methods of installation and arrangement, may be used to produce a special effect at a minimum of cost. Wood windows readily take any decorative finish—paint, enamel, stain or natural finish — and can be refinished from time to time. Wood windows require less frequent painting than steel sash and deteriorate less rapidly when not painted. Wood holds paint longer than steel because paint penatrates the wood while it only adheres to the surface of steel.

———— 5 ————

The only ideas that will work for you are the ones you put to work.

———— 5 ————

January Birthdays

Many Happy Returns of the Day!

Thomas Britton   Mel Mallinson
Bertha Davis   John Mershon
Loren Hancock   Eldon Nielson
Marvin Jackson   Mira Nielson
Charles Jacobson   Thelma Rowe
Dewayne Kilness   LeRoy Sprague
Clarence Lofstedt

Annual Audit

The two new faces pictured above are the auditors from Haskins and Sells who have spent many hours in our office checking our records for the annual audit. Mr. W. E. Offord, right, is a Certified Public Accountant, and his assistant is Mr. George Neidhart.

Born Too Soon

When Columbus started out, he didn't know where he was going. When he got there he didn't know where he was. When he got back, he didn't know where he had been. And he did it all on other people's money.

What a politician Columbus would have made today!

1958 SAFETY CHART

Month	Tot. Hourly Pd. Man Hrs.	Lost Time Accidents	Accident Freq.	Days Lost	Accident Severity
January	13,534	0	0	22	1626
February	14,089	2	141.9	21	1491
March	19,340	0	0	21	1086
First Quarter	46,963	2	42.6	.64	1363
April	9,312	0	0	22	2368
May	20,657	4	193.6	42	2033
June	21,017	1	47.6	24	1142
Second Quarter	50,986	5	98.1	88	1726
July	25,291	0	0	22	870
August	22,808	0	0	21	921
September	23,096	1	43.3	11	476
Third Quarter	71,195	1	14.1	54	758
October	24,771	0	0	0	0
November	17,806	1	56.2	3	1685
Total	113,772	9	79.2	209	1837

Wha

"I just couldn't stand at the same machine all day on a production job. Doing the same thing over and over would drive me balmy." This could be any number of a dozen people speaking. Their occupations could cover the range from construction worker to salesman. This is a common reaction of many people who visit factories. All they get a glimpse of is what appears to be the monotonous rhythm of picking up a piece of wood and feeding it into a hungry machine — the same thing over and over all day long.

The point, of course, is that no one does put in "a couple of bolts or something eight hours a day—any more than a construction worker pounds nails in a roof all day"—But a five minute stop on the construction job might give a visitor that impression.

We spent some time recently watching Eldon Nielson in the Moulding Department. Eldon is a rip saw feeder—what might be mistakenly termed as one of those repetitive and dull production jobs. Eldon has been doing this job for nearly 17 years. What does he say about it? "There's

Job?

What the Visitor sees of a so-called monotonous job. Can judgment be based on a passing glance? In the box factory thousands of mouse traps are processed every day.

Eldon Nielson, 17 years a rip saw feeder: "There's nothing dull in my job."

nothing dull about my job," he says proudly. For a man like Eldon who likes machinery a n d people and takes a satisfaction and pride in his work, a job like his offers interest and variety that would surprise the casual factory visitor. His day is full and bustling in an atmosphere of activity and diversity.

The man on the big planer can glory a bit in the drama of power and noise that surrounds him — plenty of ear-splitting noise that smooths the surface of the lumber used in building window and door frames. But what about the guy who works on the softer-spoken machine. A guy like Eldon Nielson?" My rip saw doesn't make much noise," says Eldon, "but it speaks for itself at the end of the day in the amount of work turned out."

Eldon's job might seem repititive; he picks up a piece of wood, pushes it through the saw. Then another piece — and another — and so on.

To Eldon Nielson a big part of his day is wrapped up in the people he works with — the buddies who share his work-day. They'll be the first to tell you that he is a very hard worker.

15th Anniversary

Mira J. Nielson passes another milestone in her life with the completion of 15 years at Bridal Veil Lumber and Box Company. Mira started working for the Company on January 23, 1944, as tail off for the saws and tie up, which she has continued to do up to the present.

Mira's anniversary date is the same month and day as her birth, with the year of her birth being 1901. She was born at Troutdale and liked it well enough to continue to live there. She and her husband, George, who is now retired, own their farm at Troutdale.

Aside from her job here, Mira finds time to do all her house work and cooking and also time for crocheting, which is her hobby. She also enjoys sitting down and telling h e r three grandchildren the stories her mother and father told her of their crossing the plains in a covered wagon many years ago.

Before coming to Bridal Veil, she worked about eight months at the Gresham Cannery, but most of her working days have been spent here.

Mira's favorite spectator sport is wrestling and she is always in front of her TV when it comes on. She also enjoys watching baseball if there is not a wrestling match to watch.

Her son Eldon is also employed at Bridal Veil and is pictured in the cen-

More for Taxes Than Food

The American people pay more for taxes than they do for food, according to the Grocery Manufacturers of America, Inc. Total food consumption expenditures last year were estimated at $79 billion by GMA. By comparison, last year's tax bill is expected to be about $108 billion.

The Grocery Manufacturers found also that Americans spend about 25 percent of their disposable income for food. However, if they were satisfied to buy the same "market basket" they bought just before World War II, they could get it for only 16 percent of their disposable income.

Products which did not exist 10 years ago now account for about one-third of all food store sales. Grocery manufacturers spend about $100 million a year on product and market research.

————— 5 —————

Rips and Trims
(Continued from Page 8)

During the Christmas and New Year holidays, much time was spent repairing and improving the mill. Above are some of the employees of American Sheet Metal Company who were putting up blower pipes.

ter spread this month.

She attends the Seventh-Day Adventist Church in Gresham.

1959 ... UNLIMITED

**To meet the challenges of the space age . . .
to make ever greater advances for mankind
. . . it's 1959, unlimited!**

**After a year of increasing success in probing the mysteries of
space, a New Year of further exploration lies ahead. May
these scientific ventures lead the world to an era of unpara-
lelled achievement, ever beneficial to human welfare.**

Rips and Trims

Christmas is over and a New Year has begun. Many resolutions have been made and some already broken. What will 1959 hold in store for you? This is the question which we would all like to know the answer.

Let's look back for just a moment to at few of the happenings of December. **Marvin Van Orsow** won't soon forget the two spikes and a forked horn that he and his party brought back from the Chesmus Area on the Joseph River. He probably won't forget the weather the morning they started home, either. The temperature was 12 degrees below zero and the ground was covered with 16 inches of snow.

Floyd Jacobs will remember the elk he finally got on the last week end of the season in the Heppner area. **Howard Hunt** was with a party in the Ukiah area around Pilot Rock, but didn't get his elk.

Eldon Gross was proud of the five pound steelhead he caught on the Wilson River.

Leo Hageman, Jr. got his deer out of season by hitting it with his car.

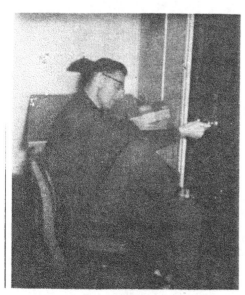

A Safe Cracker

In the absence of both Mr. Norgard and Harry Densmore, it was necessary for **Mr. Kraft** to obtain the combination and open the vault in the office.

It took several tries before he finally opened it.

Other memorable events of this past month were: The engagement of Marilla Jean Murray was announced by her parents, **Mr. and Mrs. George Murray**, to Patrick Kenneth Wagner. The wedding is planned for April 4. The purchase of a home with approximately one-half acre of land at Springdale by **Paul Dooley. John Monjay's** purchase of two race horses. His father-in-law brought them up from the track at Santa Anita, California, and will train them for the coming season. John plans to race them at Portland, Salem and Gresham this year. **Harold Jacobson's** two weeks vacation spent in Denver, Colorado, visiting relatives. The time spent nursing a pulled muscle in **Ed Wendler's** right leg. And many other things too numerous to mention.

Also not to be forgotten in November are those Thanksgiving dinners enjoyed by all. Mr. and Mrs. Clarence Van Orsow and family of Culver, Oregon, Mr. and Mrs. Don Overguard and family of Vancouver, Washington, Mr. and Mrs. John Van Orsow and Mr. and Mrs. **Marvin Van Orsow** were all guests of Mr. and Mrs. Richard Kerslake. **Mira Nielson** had as guests at her home in Springdale, her son **Eldon** and his family and **Marvin Jackson. Martha Jones** and her family were guests at Hood River with Mr. and Mrs. John Nelson.

Harry Densmore is recuperating at home after his long stay in the hospital. He seems much improved. **Jim Cowling** is back on the job after his accident, almost as good as new.

Our sincere sympathy to the family of Mr. **E. W. Norgard.** He will truly be missed in our office.

Don West, former sales manager, returned to visit us over the holidays. Don and Barbara moved to Oroville at the end of August where Don works for High Sierra Pine Mills.

———— 5 ————

Dog tired at night? Maybe you growl too much during the day.

———— 5 ————

If you want to leave your footprints in the sands of time, wear your work shoes.

BRIDAL VEIL LUMBER & BOX CO.

News Letter

Vol. IV, No. 8   BRIDAL VEIL, OREGON   FEBRUARY, 1959

Point of Agreement

Walter Reuther, it says here, along with four other American union leaders, gave a luncheon for Anastas I. Mikoyan. And as things turned out, they didn't get along too well. They couldn't understand each other.

Mr. Mikoyan, the No. 2 man of The Workers' Paradise, said he had some difficulty understanding why American labor leaders are so much more vitriolic than American capitalists in condemning Communism.

Mr. Ruther, the No. 2 man of the AFL-CIO, took offense at having the American union man referred to as "exploited" and as a "wage slave."

There is no doubt in my mind but that Mr. Reuther's hatred of Communism comes from experience. He knows that it is far easier to deal with an American business man than to do business with any government. He knows that the Russian labor leader is a mere funnel through which orders are passed from the government to the workers. He knows that a strike in Russia is impossible.

He knows that his stake and the American union man's stake in capitalism is just as big and just as vital as any business man's.

One difficulty with Communist though, is that they still judge capitalism in terms of conditions fifty or a hundred years ago. Once upon a time huge American enterprises were owned by one man. More often than not the single owner may have been greedy and ruthless.

But let's look at today.

General Motors has 629,000 stockholders and 599,243 employees, counting all hands and the cook.

American Telephone and Telegraph Company has 1,492,297 stockholders and 766,174 employees.

The Bank of America has 200,000 stockholders and 22,833 employees.

And so it goes on through the list. Manufacturing, Utilities, Banking — all with more owners than employees. With owners and employees so mixed and scattered that it is impossible to sort them out into distinct groups.

The owners of American business come from all walks of life. This might well be one of the things Mr. Reuther had in mind in his hassle with Mr. Mikoyan.

I disagree with Walter Reuther on many points of economies. But we have one common meeting ground. Neither one of us has any respect for Communism.

—Len Kraft

———— 28 ————

A Russian Lecturer who insisted that democracy worked only for a few was asked to explain a photo of an American parking lot filled with cars.

"Aha, look at the hubcaps," he said, "most of them are owned by one man, Ford!"

———— 28 ————

Standard Time Is Only 41 Years Old

Strange as it seems, up until 41 years ago Americans couldn't say for sure what time it was. Each community set its clocks at noon when the sun passed directly overhead, which meant that the time was seldom the same in any two communities.

This really didn't matter much until railroads started carrying passengers long distances. Then to straighten out the confusion in schedules, the railroads got together and established the standard time system in 1883.

It wasn't until March 19, 1918, however, that Congress officially synchronized the watches of the nation by adopting the Standard Time act.

NEWS LETTER

Published on the 10th of each month by
Bridal Veil Lumber & Box Co.
Bridal Veil, Oregon

Editor . . . . . Sara Mahn

Recession Provides a Few Lessons

The recession has been a painful experience for almost everybody, especially for those who have been laid off their jobs because of a drop in sales and a consequent curtailment of production in many industries.

If experience teaches us anything, then there may be some value in the lessons the recession has set forth in pretty plain terms.

For instance, while the boom was hot it was easy for our federal government to ignore the warnings of business groups and economists that income tax rates were dangerously high. Taxes drained away the savings of both individuals and businesses and prevented adequate investment in industry—investment which was necessary for expansion, improvement, the creation of jobs and the general economic growth which among o t h e r things would have increased the federal government's revenues.

There should be a lesson for our government in the fact that fiscal 1958 tax receipts were about $2 billion less than the previous year's. And this year's receipts, it is estimated, will be down another $2.2 billion.

The downturn in business has made most of us more appreciative of our jobs and has made us realize that our jobs deserve more care and effort and enthusiasm than we may have been giving them—and that no matter what we do, we are always in competition with somebody else, somewhere.

Finally, the recession has provided a sharp lesson to union leaders: that repeated rounds of wage increases going far beyond gains in productivity can only result in forcing costs and prices so high that people will stop buying. When people stop buying, other people stop working.

This has been a recession born of inflation. Maybe all of us, including union leaders, have learned something from it.

Below Zero Weather

That there is a wide variation of temperatures throughout the country, was very much in evidence to me on my recent trip east. When I left Portland, the temperature was in the low 50's. When I arrived in Detroit it was 7 degrees below Zero.

Although the construction business in Detroit and Cincinnati is at a stand still now due to bad weather conditions, all of our customers in this area anticipate a good business year.

—Ade Jones

———— 28 ————

Times Change—Like It or Not

In 1912, Mr. Olds of the Oldsmobile Manufacturing Company wrote: "The car I now bring out is regarded by me as pretty close to finality. . .I do not believe that a car materially better will ever be built."

In 1912 there were no such things as television, streamline trains, synthetic rubber, flourescent lighting, colored home movies, polarized glass, synthetic hosiery, antibiotic drugs.

Also in 1912 there were no such things in America as these taxes: income, estate, excess profits, capital gift, excise and sales.

———— 28 ————

Accuracy Demanded

With the wide spread use of Automatic Nailers (most of our customers have them) it becomes more and more necessary to check and double check on our cross workings.

On cross members or head members that cut in between, 1-32 of an inch long or short is **NOT** acceptable.

—Ade Jones

———— 28 ————

The Safest Way is Frightening!

What's the safest form of transportation?

The answer given by Ned H. Dearborn, president of the National Safety Council, may surprise you. And here are some other answers you may or may not know.

According to national statistics the safest place to be is on the job, the most dangerous in your home. The most common types of industrial accidents are falls and sprains. The same is true in the home.

What causes most accidents? People. They don't think, or they think wrong.

And the safest form of transportation? It's the roller coaster.

Hatfield New Office Manager

Richard R. Hatfield, a Licensed Public Accountant, has joined our firm to fill the vacancy left by the death of Mr. E. W. Norgard.

After eight years working with his father and brother in their firm, R. H. Hatfield and Company, Certified Public Accountants, as Staff Accountant, Dick felt he would like to get into private accounting. We are fortunate to get a young man with this much experience.

Dick was born on May 21, 1928 in Portland and is still at home on the East Side with his parents.

He is a graduate of Grant High School and studied Business Administration at the University of Oregon. Upon leaving college, he went to work with his father.

To fulfill his military obligation, Dick spent five years in the Oregon National Guards working in the Finance Office.

As hobbies, he has listed fishing and photography.

Dick doesn't claim any relationship to Mark, our Governor.

———— 28 ————

Rip Van Winkle is the only man who became famous while asleep.

1958 SAFETY CHART

Month	Tot. Hourly Pd. Man Hrs.	Lost Time Accidents	Accident Freq.	Days Lost	Accident Severity
January	13,534	0	0	22	1626
February	14,089	2	141.9	21	1491
March	19,340	0	0	21	1086
First Quarter	46,963	2	42.6	64	1363
April	9,312	0	0	22	2368
May	20,657	4	193.6	42	2033
June	21,017	1	47.6	24	1142
Second Quarter	50,986	5	98.1	88	1726
July	25,291	0	0	22	870
August	22,808	0	0	21	921
September	23,096	1	43.3	11	476
Third Quarter	71,195	1	14.1	54	758
October	24,771	0	0	0	0
November	17,806	1	56.2	3	169
December	17,628	1	56.7	0	0
Fourth Quarter	60,205	2	33.2	3	50
1958 Total	229,349	10	43.6	209	911
1957 Total	211,225	9	42.6	124	587
1956 Total	226,656	4	17.6	19	84

Jim has a right to feel real proud of his invention.

Looking at the fro
which hold the slats

On the back (belo
arms that adjust the
material.

To insure a perfect job, Jim tightens
a screw.

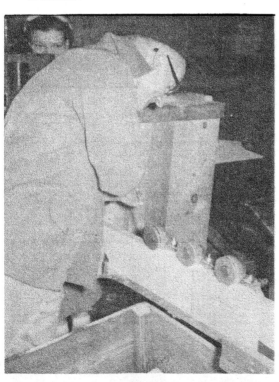

Effort, Abili

A new idea becomes a
Filer, saw the need for a bette
is discarded when mouse trap
material. In the past, either th
cline that was not satisfactor
material was cut in four equ
weight which was also costly.

Jim realized the problem
tion. After talking with Mr. Kr
assistant in the Filing Room, R

This device with the thre
action arms, holds the four pie
them in so they will hug the
the slab drops into a box and
the end of the machine wher

By using this invention,
on an average car of shook wi

Congratulations, Jim, on

:e the three wheels

Ralph Taylor helped Jim with the construction.

two scissor action
her wide or narrow

d to Success

on! Jim Cowling, Head Saw
handling the extra slab which
s and slats are cut from 7/4
routed to one side on an in-
equired more labor, or 7/4
hich resulted in unnecessary

idea which he put into ac-
ng his approval, Jim and his
made the gadget pictured.

hich are mounted on scissor
irm to the bottom and directs
f the machine. At this point
maining pieces follow on to
acked by a tail-off.

d that the savings in freight
approximately $70.00.
done.

We see the slab drop into the box
while the rollers hold the other four
pieces in place.

Completes One Score Years

Kenneth Dean Burkholder will celebrate 20 years of service with Bridal Veil Lumber and Box Company on February 22.

Dean has been yard foreman for the past four years. He previously operated the carrier and has also worked in the Moulding Department on a number of different machines.

He has never had a lost-time accident. However, while he was operating the carrier he had an unusual accident. The switch (the locomotive that switches the cars on the track) came in a little faster than usual one day and didn't give any signals. Dean had taken a load of material over to the Moulding Department and was going back down the ramp when he saw the switch. He didn't have time to stop before he was on the track and the switch hit the carrier, turned it over and threw Dean out. He was lucky that he only got a little shook up.

It was August 19, 1915 that Dean was born in Portland. His father came to the West while just a boy. He did some farming and later worked here at Bridal Veil until his retirement.

Dean attended Corbett Grade School and Graduated from Corbett H i g h School. He worked for approximately two and one-half years as gardner for ex-governor Meiers Estate at the summer home, before coming to

Wages Make Up 75% of Price

How do wages compare with profits in industry?

If you added the price tags on all the products made in America, upwards of three-quarters of their total value would represent the employment costs incurred all along the line of production.

Out of the remaining quarter must come the cost of all raw material, rental on property, interest on debt, and individuals to pay for use of the tools of production. The profit part of the price of a product is insignificant in comparison with wage costs.

———— 28 ————

The salesman had managed to get into the house, and he was putting on a big personality act for the lady of the house. "My, what a lovely home you have," he gushed. "And what a beautiful vase on the mantel."

"Yes," sighed the woman, "that contains my husband's ashes."

"Oh, I'm so sorry. How long has he been dead?"

"He's not. He's just too lazy to find an ashtray."

———— 28 ————

February Birthdays
Many Happy Returns of the Day!

Elmer Ayles	Mabel Hills
Kenneth Catlin	Melvin Mier
Beulah Choate	Norman Van Buskirk
Delbert Cloe	Ed Wendler
Robert Crooke	Louis Wilson
Fred Crouser	Mary Woodard
James Dunken	

Bridal Veil.

On July 16, 1938, he married Zola E. Dayton in Portland. They live near Corbett in the home they built on their 12 acres. They have six children, all still at home. Linda is 17 and a senior at Corbett High School, Darlene is 15 and a freshman, Kenneth D. Jr., is 13 and Dennis is 10 and both are students at Corbett Grade School. The latest addition to the family are twin boys, Dale and Darryl just two years old.

Harold Burkholder, carrier operator is Dean's brother.

Hunting and gardening take up the most of Dean's spare time. He also enjoys watching Basketball and Baseball.

Recent Visitor

Mr. R. A. Holmes, one of the partners of Firpine Products, Inc., visited our mill recently.

He is in the local Oswego office and handles the buying of Paxton Window Frames for Des Moines.

———— 28 ————

Health and Welfare Coverage

SPECIAL NOTICE: The report that appeared in the News Letter last month was incorrect. Therefore, we are correcting the coverage policy this month.

All employees who worked the required number of hours in November and December will become eligible for health and welfare coverage and will be covered on the first day of February, 1959. They must have worked the required hours in both months. Additions are: Dorothy Hartshorn, Eleanor Taylor.

Employees who did not work the required number of hours will become ineligible the same day. Deletions: Anthony Angelo, Robert Bird, Francis Cook, Joseph Cote, Kenneth Crooke, John Estep, Harold E. Fuller, Dewayne Kilness, John D. Monjay, Robert S. Russell, Joe Sazama, John W. Smith, Ronald Snyder, LeRoy Sprague, J. W. Cowling.

Rips and Trims

(Continued from Page 8)

With the first month of the new year also came some new cars at the mill. **Gerald Roberts** has a new black Ford Galaxie with white sidewalls and red, black and white upholstery. The Pontiac nine passenger station wagon in yellow and white belongs to **Dean Burkholder.** He says he can take the whole family in just one load now. He really likes the power brakes and power steering. **Delbert Dunken** has the white Ford with the blue upholstery. The new blue and white Chevrolet pickup is the **Harold Burkholders. Bob Godat** has a medium blue Renault which he likes very much.

Several employees were on vacation during the holidays. **John Willms** went over to Central and Eastern Washington. He seemed happy to get back out of the snow and ice. He was just 17 miles from the Canadian border at one place on his trip. **Roy Eveland** spent the holidays in Seattle. **Earl Hutchison** planned to just take life easy while entertaining guests from Nebraska. However, his wife had other plans for him. The last day he worked before starting his vacation, his wife met him at the door ,as he came home and handed him a paint brush. Did you get all the painting done, Earl?

There have been several employees on the sick list during the past month. **Durward Litton** had the flue, **Joe Cote** had a foot operation, **Fred Bailey** also had an operation, **Mary Woodard** fell and broke a bone in her knee, and **Phil Van Hee, Sr.,** is on leave of absence due to the illness of his wife.

Charles Gaymon and family recently drove up to Larch Mountain, but reported very little snow. Mr. and Mrs. **Charles Murphy** have purchased a home in North Bonneville, Washington.

Howard Hunt has been trying his hand at batching for the two weeks his wife spent visiting a daughter-in-law at Oakland, California.

Rips and Trims

Partly Cloudy with scattered showers—seems to be the usual forecast for this season of the year. Of course, their definition of scattered is not always the same as ours. However, now that one month of rain is over, we know that in another couple of months spring will be arriving. So it gives us something to look forward to.

In the mean time, let's turn the pages of time back a little and l o o k again at the first month of 1959. **Mira Nielson** probably remembers m o s t vividly the Friday morning, January 16 when the Fire Department had to be summoned at 6:20 to put out a fire at her home. Luckily, it was only a chimney fire and Mira was able to be at work on time.

There were a number of employees laid off during the holidays and some were called back to work during January. However, there are still approximately 25 men to be called back after the lumber shortage eases enough for us to get in more lumber.

Mr. and Mrs. Leon Dunlap of Portland and Mr. and Mrs. John Johnson of Gresham, were dinner guests at the home of **Mira Nielson** in Springdale. The big occasion was Mira's birthday. **Martha Jones** and family were visitors at the John Nelson's home in H o o d River and at the Irvine French's home in Portland. They also had Martha's sister, Mrs. Arden Wedwick, of Brookings, Oregon, and Mr. and Mrs. Charles Hanson of Corvallis at their home in Bonneville, before daughter, Marilyn returned to Roecker Private Day School in Portland.

Bert and Fay Davis were recent dinner guests at the home of their son, Bob.

Mrs. Beth Curtiss has returned to Nevada after a visit with **Ward and Thelma Dull**. They drove up to Bonneville Dam and showed her the water falls along the Scenic Highway. There should be some good reports on the Columbia River Gorge when she returns home.

Owners of '59 Cars

Shown with Robert Godat's Renault are, left to right, Delbert Dunken, Gerald Roberts, Dean Burkholder, Godat and Harold Burkholder.

Bridal Veil
NEWS LETTER

Vol. IV, No. 9   BRIDAL VEIL, OREGON   MARCH, 1959

NEWS LETTER

Published on the 10th of each month by
Bridal Veil Lumber & Box Co.
Bridal Veil, Oregon

Editor . . . . Sara Mahn

Not Only Quantity

The word "Productivity" is being tossed around more and more these days, in discussions of wages, the cost-of-living, and future economic progress —yet there is much confusion over just what the term means. The usual way of getting a productivity figure is to divide output by man-hours of labor.

This is simple—too simple. Because it indicates that the one important factor in productivity is man-hours. Which, when you think of it, simply cannot be so.

Imput takes in many things besides man-hours. Output isn't merely quantity, it is quality, too. Along with man-hours, making a product requires materials of high standards, the best machines, equipment and methods, based on the latest technological developments. And the man-hours we do put in must include skill and cooperativeness—not just minutes.

——————— 8 ———————

One of the most difficult things to give away is kindness, for it usually is returned.

Pay Attention to the Job at Hand!

Quiet — Do Not Disturb

Leo C. Hageman has buckled down to studies at the American Institute for Foreign Trade which is located approximately sixteen miles out of Phoenix, Arizona.

On a leave of absence from Bridal Veil, he is pursuing a course of study including F r e n c h, Foreign Trade, Marketing, International Law and Area Study—to prepare him for a job in Foreign Trade in the Far East. He has been interested in a job of this type since spending some time in Japan during his tour of duty in the Air Force.

He seems very well pleased with the school, but doesn't particularly care for the hot weather there.

We all wish you much success, Leo.

——————— 8 ———————

It Doesn't Change

Even in our rapidly changing times the road to success seems to remain pretty much the same.

Shortly after Stanley C. Hope was elected president of the National Association of Manufacturers, a reporter asked him "how does a man get to the top these days?"

Mr. Hope, who climbed from a salesman's job to the presidency of three corporations, replied:

"I don't believe the ingredients for success have changed very much. They still consist of ambition, hard work, persistency and a willingness to work with others."

Lumber

Every winter about this time, we experience a shortage of lumber. The present winter of 1958-59 is no exception. Why this should be is no mystery.

I have heard it suggested in some quarters that the coincidence of the annual lumber shortage and of the anniversary date of our contract with Millmen's Local No. 1120 was more by design than by accident. This version generally makes the rounds when we are running up the phone bill trying to find lumber.

Right off the bat, if all other things were equal, there would be less kiln dried ponderosa pine shop lumber available in winter than at any other time of year. This is true because cold weather affects the operation of dry kilns. First, there is a greater heat loss in unloading and loading a kiln in winter than in summer. The result is that it takes longer to get the kiln back up to drying temperature after the doors have been closed on the n e w charge.

Again, the lumber loaded into a kiln in winter is generally colder than in summer. Indeed, it may even be frozen. In these cases it takes longer to heat the lumber up to the point where drying may start.

Another point, though not so serious, is the heat loss through the walls and doors of a kiln. Obviously, the heat loss would be greater in the winter than in the summer. In any event, the various factors mentioned all have a restricting effect on the volume of kiln dried lumber available in the winter.

There is another good operating reason why there is less shop lumber produced in the winter than in the summer. This has to do with the decking of logs for the winter run. The big fat shop logs are harder to deck than the smaller common logs. There is, therefore, a tendency to saw the shop logs as they develop rather than to deck them for winter use.

In the p i n e country the allied species—douglas fir, larch, spruce, etc. have a tendency to be smaller in size than a good shop log. Hence, they too tend to find their way into the deck while the shop logs are being sawn up as developed during the fall.

A few years ago we didn't have the problem of pine mills cutting anything but pine. So, while the number of mills in the pine region stays relatively stable, an ever increasing percentage of production is diverted from pine into the so-called allied species.

Comes the day of reckoning, the mills have to saw up their decks. Then the mills report long runs on fir and larch. Or the story is that "our pine logs just haven't developed much shop lately." And they are telling the truth. Shop is just plain scarce in the wintertime.

Some mills shut down for repairs in the winter, and many mills take off for a week or two at Christmas and New Years. So, under the best of circumstances, the actual production of shop lumber goes down in the winter

While all this is going on, we at Bridal Veil have one eye on the tax collector. So we let our inventories run down at December 31 to save a tax dollar.

One way to beat the game would be to build sheds adequate to hold a couple of million feet of shop lumber. Of course, in addition to the cost of the buildings we would be stuck for the tax on a quarter of a million dollars worth of inventory.

All of which is more money than we can handle.

A better solution from our standpoint would be for the lumber companies to carry adequate inventories to t a k e care of their customers. Not too many years ago our suppliers volunteered to stock pile lumber for us for winter and spring shipment. For the most part however, the lumber companies now have taken the attitude that their customers must buy when the lumber is available. Lumber is one of the few industries where this type of an operating philosophy can be made to stick. It doesn't work that way in the millwork business.

Anyway, there is the story. We cut inventories to save taxes. The mills do the same thing. After personal property taxes are assessed December 31, normal winter scarcities make it hard to build up a good reserve supply again.

—Len Kraft

Time passes rapidly and people change. This picture was taken in 1948—just 11 years ago. Front row: Theophile V. Van Hee, Clyde Hambrick, Jim McDonough, Warren Thorpe, Lloyd DeMain, Verl Bird, Jim Cowling, Ted Hanson, Fred Harp, Ernie Clink, Mick (Burton) Dunken, Gerald Roberts, Merrill Hartshorn, Mervin Hartshorn (deceased), Ray Britton. Second Row, standing: Eldon Neilson, Bertha Davis, Louise Rhodes, Anna Bowen, Dave Vincinzi, Einar Mickelson, Marvin Van Orsow, Howard Bohlae, Marvin Jackson, Fred Crouser, Walter Stolin. Third Row, seated: Dwain Whitney,

This?

Roy Anderson (deceased), Steve Crane, Fay Davis, Willis Bowen, Jr., Frank Wheeler, John Dobing, Jim Rhodes, Clarence Noble (deceased), Bill Wilson, Ted Butler, Willis Bowen, Frank Stolin (deceased), Bill Ball. Fourth Row, standing: Paul Detrick, Ralph Taylor, Norman Elliott (deceased), Durward Litton, George Leash, Harry Burkholder, Noah Atchley, Bob Davis, Bob Polzel, Pearl Cloe, Harold Jacobson, William F. Marschheuser, Dean Burkholder, Bill Uddey, Ernie Farrari.

Board of Directors

The annual meeting of the Board of Directors of Bridal Veil Lumber & Box Company was held at the office on February 27.

The Directors are Mr. C. W. Kraft of Niles, California; Mr. Leonard Kraft; Mr. A. D. Jones; Mr. H. W. Winfree of Portland, and Mrs. E. P. Snyder of Chicago, Illinois.

Tax on Company Bites Employees

Where do taxes hit the wage earner hardest?

Although an employee may not feel it as directly, studies indicate that the tax bite on his company may be more damaging to his security than the bite on his pay.

The employee can't work efficiently without efficient tools. Heavy taxes are making it difficult for companies to replace outmoded machinery and equipment. And unless the company can meet competition successfully, it can't pay high wages.

That is why employees have a bigger stake than they think in efforts to spur government economy and tax reform.

———— 8 ————

Wife: "I didn't like that new secretary of yours, so I discharged her this morning."

Husband: "Before giving her a chance?"

Wife: "Before giving you a chance."

One of the hardest secrets for a man to keep is his opinion of himself.

———— 8 ————

Rips and Trims

(Continued from Page 8)

Lillie Landreth spent the weekend of February 22nd with her son Jimmy (a former employee) at Monmouth. They attended the college play "Oedipus Rex."

Congratulations to the proud father, **Leslie Polzel**. It was a girl, Nora Gina weighing 8 pounds and 3 ounces born on Sunday morning, February 15 at 3:15 a.m.

Mr. and Mrs. Pearl Cloe celebrated their 37th wedding anniversary on February 3 with all their children at home.

Mr. and Mrs. Leonard Kraft attended the 32nd annual meeting of the National Woodwork Manufacturers Association, Inc., in Chicago February 9 and 10. He was made a member of the Board of Directors after being a member of the Association for only one year.

Visits Bridal Veil

Mr. Vincent L. Pickens, millwork sales representative of Herbert A. Templeton Lumber Corporation in Spokane, Washington, was recently in our office. They are manufacturers of ponderosa pine products and purchase cut stock from us.

——— 8 ———

An American has more food to eat than a man of any other country, and more diets to keep him from eating it.

——— 8 ———

Health and Welfare Coverage

All employees who worked the required number of hours in December and January will become eligible for health and welfare coverage and will be covered on the first day of March, 1959. They must have worked the required hours in both months. Additions: J. W. Cowling.

Employees who did not work the required number of hours will become ineligible the same day. Deletions: Edsel Kinonen, Theophile Van Hee, Sr.

——— 8 ———

There are bigger things than money. For instance, bills.

Able Assistance

Mason Nolan, a Principal in the Accounting firm of Haskins and Sell, recently spent several days in our office assisting with the preparation of the financial statements.

Mr. Nolan has been with Haskins and Sells for ten years and audited our company books from 1950 through 1954.

He is now in management advisory service which includes consultation, cost accounting, budgeting, system procedures — which is an application of electronic computers to business data processing.

——— 8 ———

Money may not buy happiness but it sure helps you to look for it in more interesting places.

——— 8 ———

March Birthdays

Many Happy Returns of the Day!

Kenneth Crooke	Floyd Jacobs
Fred Damerell	Martha Jones
Paul Dooley	Walton Jones
Elden Gross	Walter Stolin

1959 SAFETY CHART

Month	Tot. Hourly Pd. Man Hrs.	Lost Time Accidents	Accident Freq.	Days Lost	Accident Severity
January - - - - -	18,468	1	54.1	1	541

Rips and Trims

February started with a couple of beautiful days after January's snow. During the month we had all types of weather, from snow to lovely spring-like days. Along with February came accidents and illnesses. **Mary Woodard** fell and broke her leg the end of January and is still in Providence Hospital. She hopes to get home about the middle of March. **Delbert Duncan** spent several days in the same hospital as a result of surgery. **Don Westlake** wrapped his car around a tree and ended up at Providence for a few days. Delbert and Don are both home again now. Maybe Bridal Veil could profit by buying a ward down at Providence as it seems that we are keeping one up anyway. **Harry Densmore** was also back in the hospital for a few days in February. Harry, you were just too anxious to get back to work.

Several others were sick but not in the hospital, including: **Roy Eveland** who spent several days in bed because of a back ailment. He was fishing when he felt the pain which was so intense that he began to think he couldn't get back to his car. Roy is back at work, but we notice he is still very careful to protect his back. **Martha Jones** was also on the sick list. **Ralph Mc-**

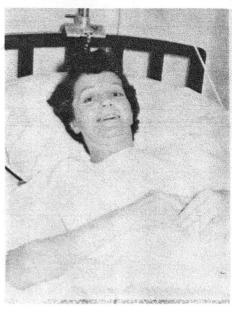

Hurry back, Mary Woodard

Credie had to take some time out due to illness. We are glad that they were not out very long.

(Continued on Page 6)

Be nice to the nurses, Delbert Duncan

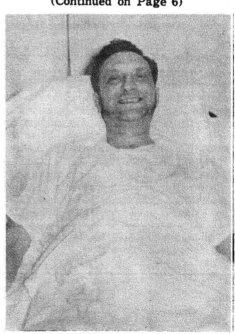

Be careful, Don Westlake

Bridal Veil
NEWS LETTER

Vol. IV, No. 10   BRIDAL VEIL, OREGON   APRIL 1959

NEWS LETTER

Published on the 10th of each month by
Bridal Veil Lumber & Box Co.
Bridal Veil, Oregon

Editor . . . . Sara Mahn

OIEA Annual Awards Dinner

The Annual Awards Dinner of the Oregon Industrial Editor's Association was held on March 16 at Henry Thiele Restaurant in Portland. As editor of the BRIDAL VEIL NEWS LETTER and a member of the Association, it was my privilege to be present for the Annual Awards Dinner.

I entered our company publication in the contest to receive some helpful criticism, not with the idea of winning an award. Our publication was in competition with publications of the U.S. National Bank, the First National Bank of Oregon, Pacific Telephone and Telegraph Company, Shell Oil Company, The Oregon Churchman, Boy Scouts of America, The Oregon Restaurant and Beverage Association, and a number of other large companies.

Therefore, it was a pleasant surprise when our BRIDAL VEIL NEWS LETTER received the award for Best Personalities Column.

— Editor

——— 36 ———

April Birthdays

Many Happy Returns of the Day!

Leo C. Hageman	Robert Reischel
Theodore Hanson	Joseph Van Orsow
Dorothy Hartshorn	John Willms
Fred Long	

Health and Welfare Coverage

All employees who worked the required number of hours in January and February will become eligible for health and welfare coverage and will be covered on the first day of April, 1959. They must have worked the required hours in both months. Additions: Joseph Cote, Ed Kinonen.

Employees who did not work the required number of hours will become ineligible the same day. Deletions: Ole K. Barto, Robert Bird, Donald Bowen, Francis Cook, Kenneth Crooke, Robert Crooke, James Dawes, Gerald Dull, Peter Graymer, Arthur V. Howell, Ronald Jackson, Floyd Jacobs, Charles Jacobson, Walton G. Jones, DeWayne Kilness, Steven Kuzmesky, Melvin Mier, Floyd F. Oden, Robert Russell, Elvin D. Smith, John W. Smith, LeRoy Sprague, Leonard Volkman.

——— 36 ———

Our Red Rivals

(Continued from Page 12)

You ask the familiar question: "Do you think Russian industry will produce as much as America in five or ten years?"

"More than America," he replies.

You think of the great contrast between Russian living and American. It is inconceivable that they could build up their total economy that fast. "That will be good for the Russian people if they can do it," you say.

But you know, too, that it will also pose a problem for America—in the world market.

(To be concluded next month)

1959 SAFETY CHART

Month	Tot. Hourly Pd. Man Hrs.	Lost Time Accidents	Accident Freq.	Days Lost	Accident Severity
January	18,468	1	54.1	1	541
February	17,904	0	0	24	1340
Total	36,372	1	27.5	25	687
1958 — 2 months	27,623	2	72.4	43	1557

A Job Is a Way of Life

At the annual meeting of the Directors of our company, I raised the question of how best to let the members of our organization know of our deteriorating competitive position. One of our directors, Mr. C. W. Kraft, agreed to tell the story. The following are his words:

The management of this Company has traditionally sought not to worry its employees with its financial problems. Perhaps this was a mistake. In any event, since we are all in this together, the time has come for a heart-to-heart talk on the seriousness of our present situation. A person who has put in 5, 10, 20 or more years in the service of a company, has an investment in it just as the people who have put money in it to provide the tools and equipment. Those investments are now in grave jeopardy here at Bridal Veil. Of the two, the loss of a job is the more disrupting and the hardest to replace. One dollar is like another to all practical purposes. Two jobs are not alike even if they paid the same per hour for the same number of hours. A job is performed at a certain place with people around you who you have come to know and with many of whom you have made friends. To a large extent, a job determines where you live. Lose that job and it will probably mean "pulling up stakes" and moving elsewhere with all that means in adjusting to new surroundings, new people, finding another place to live, maybe sacrificing on your present home. The hunt for a new job brings up all sorts of concerns. Will it pay as good? How about the hours? The working conditions? How far from home? Who with? Who for? What will it be? What will I do? Can I handle it? Then of course it means starting over again at the bottom of some one else's seniority totem pole.

Just this much of a review is sufficient to show that your job is something to value as the very foundation of one's life. And that is why we are concerned. Last year we lost $95,918.00 We think we have the answers to improving our competitive position. Basically we need to purchase a better grade of lumber, turn out a higher percentage of our production in higher grade items and improve our productivety. By so doing, we expect to improve our profit margin by widening the difference between our costs and our selling prices. To do this will require the best efforts of all of us in which it can be truly said that we all have a common aim regardless of our position in the organization — to please the customer. The customer is the real boss of this enterprise. When we please him he showers us with cash and when we don't he withholds it.

How do we please him? By making a product that he wants at a price that he is willing to pay. It's no skin off his nose if it costs us more to produce than he is willing to pay. He merely goes elsewhere, or does without. Just like you and I do when we're customers! The customer is the source of all our wages, salaries, benefits and dividends. Nobody — but nobody, will long take care of us when the customer won't. Your job is provided by a Company in the good graces of its customers, not by the Union and not by government.

In its hour of need even the government has taken pity on Bridal Veil and will refund $14,904.00 in taxes collected in prior years. This cuts the loss for 1958 to $81,014.00, which is still a lot of money that must be made back if we are to keep our doors open.

Bridal Veil pays the highest wages of any stock millwork plant in the U.S. (which means the whole world). We expect to continue to do so but the differential right now is more than we can pay and long provide any kind of a job. At the present rate of annual increases it would take our competition back East six years to catch up with us. Now nobody is going to suggest that we sit still and let them catch up but I do say we should all content ourselves with the present high rates of pay for another year and meantime improve our competitive position so we do not lose the fine jobs we already have.

We have frankly laid our predicament before you — and we would be remiss if we did not — because it is yours too. With a great cooperative effort — "and a little bit of luck" — we can get back on firm ground and that's easier than starting over again.

Chuck Kraft

Rips and Trims

The lion and the lamb have been rather well represented during this past month of March.

News has been rather scarce due to the continued lay-off because of the lumber shortage. However, the employees who have worked haven't been idle off the job.

ED KINONEN had success on his fishing trip and brought back a couple of salmon weighing 22 and 23 pounds. JERALD ROBERTS wasn't as lucky on his fishing trip out at Sauvies Island.

Working on a tractor isn't what I would call an exciting week-end, but ARCHIE DAVIES spent a recent week-end that way getting ready to put in his garden. Don't be too hasty, Archie, CLARENCE LOFSTEDT says there was still snow up on Beacon Rock when he hiked up it a couple of weeks ago.

A trip to Seattle was enjoyed by DELBERT DUNCAN to see his cousin. DURWARD and Ruth LITTON spent a couple of days in La Grande visiting Ruth's sister, Mrs. Courtney.

In spite of the rain on Easter, STANLEY and MABEL HILLS spent an enjoyable day with their daughter, Mrs. Claude Shannon, in Tigard, while ANNA and WILLIS BOWEN had their children, James and Willis, Jr., and their families at home with them.

Someone borrowed the spare tire and wheel from ROLAND MORGAN'S car out at Viking Park, but they forgot to return it.

PEARL CLOE says he has spent many happy hours playing his new Magnus Electric Organ.

Spring holidays brought a number of the college students home. Tom Cowling kept busy part of the time. He washed some of the office employees cars, and we could actually tell the colors of the red Ford, yellow Studebaker and peach Plymouth. You did a fine job, Tom. Other students home were: Jim Yerion, Bob Cowling and Gerry Kraft.

FRED HARP is looking forward to the first week-end of April when he plans to go to Puyallup, Washington, to help his mother celebrate her 93rd birthday. They plan to take pictures of five generations.

A number of employees are still on the sick list and recuperating at home.

Among them are MARY WOODARD, ELDEN GROSS, MARTHA JONES, and DON WESTLAKE.

We extend our sympathy to the wife and children of HARRY DENSMORE.

The new face at the railway station recently was Mr. G. E. Phillips, a relief man from Pendleton, who substituted for Mr. A. M. (Doc) Nelson. Doc and his wife went to Reno for a week's vacation.

DOROTHY and MERRILL HARTSHORN took a couple of day's vacation to go to the State B Tournament Basketball Game in Bend. Corbett wasn't up to their usual game.

———— 36 ————

Cute Baton Twirlers

Pat Cowling and Diana Taylor are the daughters of MR. and MRS. JAMES COWLING and MR. and MRS. RALPH TAYLOR. They have been rather popular at the recent ball games in their white suits and red leotards. Pat (right) is leader of the advanced Baton Unit at Corbett School.

1958

FIFTH ANNUAL
INDUSTRIAL EDITORS
AWARDS

OREGON INDUSTRIAL EDITORS ASSOCIATION

Best Personalities Column

BRIDAL VEIL LUMBER & BOX COMPANY NEWS LETTER

Sara Mahn, Editor

Presented March 16, 1959

Chairman, Judges Committee

"EVERY DAY OVER THE NORM," says this poster which depicts a "quota" chart like those posted in factory shops. Column at left shows "plan for the shift", second column the actual production, and third the percentage of quota achieved. Workers who beat the quota are rewarded by receiving extra pay.

Harold Mansfield, author of *Vision* and *The Challenge* (United Kingdom), is director of public relations of Boeing Airplane Company. He recently visited the Soviet Union as a member of a delegation sponsored by the International Council of Industrial Editors. Before making the trip he learned the Russian language in order to be able better to make a first-hand evaluation of Russia's efforts to surpass America industrially.

OUR RED RIVALS

© 1958, Harold Mansfield

By HAROLD MANSFIELD

Part One

of Two Parts

YOU enter Moscow with misgivings. The thousand questions stored in your mind . . . Will they be answered? The night about you . . . Will it be friendly? The silent, big-shouldered driver of the black Zim limousine that is bringing you from the airport up the dark Moscow River into the city. How does he think?

Impressive facades of brightly-lighted buildings loom along the boulevard. You try out your Russian: "New apartments?"

"Da," says the driver.

"Much progress here."

"Da, da, da." You can feel the quick pride that is tongued in that triple yes. You imagine you have already touched the keyword that is moving the Russian people: "Progress."

Two and a half years ago, you pondered the speech made by N. V.

THE MOSCOW SKYLINE, as seen from across the Moscow River through the camera of Harold Mansfield, is dominated by an elite new apartment building (center). In the foreground is one of the city's many factories.

Khrushchev at the Soviets' first Communist Party Congress since Stalin's death. Said Khrushchev then: "The principal feature of our effort is the emergence of socialism from the confines of one country and its transformance into a world system. The internal forces of the capitalist economy are working toward its downfall, while the Communist economy is steadily rising toward *its goal of proving itself to the world and transforming itself into a world system through peaceful competition.*"

" . . . Through peaceful competition." A sober challenge and a threat, aimed directly at the industrial heart-stream of America and the West. Not just defense industry, charged with the task of exceeding Soviet ingenuity in arms, but all industry and business.

Now Khrushchev has been running the show long enough to reveal how he intends carrying out his program. Could he possibly win this race for industrial supremacy, and with it his sweeping political aims? You are here to investigate.

In the days that follow in Moscow, Leningrad, Kiev, Kharkov, between supervised tours and plant visits, you prowl the streets on your own, anxious to meet and talk with workers and citizens. You find them surprisingly friendly. Using your fractured Russian in impromptu conversations, you try to sense the mood and the spirit of the people. You form some impressions.

Russia has a serious look on its face. It is a drab, purposeful, working civilization, in open-collared shirt. Its people are proud and sensitive, self-conscious about their long isolation from the West, hurt by its scorn. They are hungry for the world's esteem, and intend to win it.

"Russians are not barbarians," says a young school teacher, neat in simple skirt and wool sweater. With a slight, quick toss of blond hair and a flick of manicured fingers she adds: " . . . as you can see."

You ask a female guide if a luxurious train between Moscow and Leningrad was not German-built before the war, which it was. She is affronted. "Do you think it's too good to be Russian?"

Somehow you feel that this psychology helps explain the daring push to launch the sputniks, the jutting of astonishing white multistoried towers, nineteenth-century "monumental" in architecture, out of the otherwise flat, grey Moscow skyline. It helps explain, too, the ornate subway stations under the streets. Marble-columned, sculptured and chandeliered, they appear at once an effort to outdo the splendor of the czars, and an installment on a future-day communist millennium.

Communism exists on the basis of a great hope, a hope kept alive by show of progress, and contrasted sharply with a depressed people's past. The people go along with the objective, little complaining if it is still out of reach. They have set out on an enterprise and intend to prove they can make it go. They have lived with the system long enough now that most take it for granted, much as Americans take theirs for granted.

But the communist "millennium" is a dream. The country is poor. The government knows this and has had to take things in their order, first heavy industry, next trucks and tractors, then busses and subways for public transportation, now apart-

ments. Everywhere you see new apartments being built like mad, thrown up by brigades of mainly unskilled men and women; uninspired, square-walled masonry buildings, each a replica of the last.

By the thousands, the people are moving into these apartments from dingy places on back streets. They still offer only minimum living. You suddenly realize why they looked so dazzlingly bright that first night. No curtains. Frugally furnished, they house often two or three people to the 10- by 16-foot room. But "they're much better than what we had," the occupants tell you.

It's the progress that keeps the people going. Press and radio recite it daily. Colored charts in public buildings display it. Progress toward a goal. And always a promise. Tomorrow, refrigerators and automobiles.

You ask a worker, unshaved and in crumpled clothes: "Do you think a man with a five-room house, a car, a television set, electric refrigerator and washing machine is rich?"

"Da," he nods.

"Do you think the average American worker has these things?"

"I don't know."

"He does. Do you think the Russian worker will have them?"

"I don't know. We hope."

You ask another, better dressed, the same question.

"Da," he answers. "We will catch up with America."

In school, in the factory, at the art exhibit, *work* is touted as the basic virtue in Russia. The brass ornament on your hotel room desk consists of three men bent low and pulling a load. The sculptor has made them appear to enjoy it.

Waiting on the street, you talk with a man about jet transports and things. "Are you pleased with Russia's progress in industry and science?" you ask.

"Naturally."

"Why?"

"Because it makes more work."

By the swan pool in Gorky park you ask a keen-looking lad what field he wants to enter when he grows up.

"Science."

"Why? Because of the high pay? Fame?"

He wrinkles his forehead. "Because it is useful," he says.

On the deck of a Sunday afternoon boat up the Moscow River you slide onto the bench beside a man in work clothes, taking a bundle of berry bushes home to plant. He is a skilled mechanic in a nearby factory. You talk with him about his work. "Do you get paid more every year?" you ask.

"Not necessarily. We get paid more when we do more and better work."

"Do you think this is a good system?"

"Da. Good."

A big, brightly-colored factory poster shows a vigorous youth pointing to a minute on the clock. "Watch the working minute!" he cautions. "Time is the people's wealth." A chart shows how much steel, coal, sugar, housing is produced "in our country" per working minute.

"In our country, everyone works," the people tell you with pride.

Then they ask about your country. "Is it true there are four million unemployed?"

You explain: "At present the prices on some things have gone rather high and people are not buying as they did. Wages and prices are high. But the state pays those who are out of work."

"How much does a skilled worker make in America?" asks his Russian counterpart, who earns 1,200 rubles a month — or 60 cents an hour, figured at ten rubles to the dollar. (Tourists are given ten rubles to the dollar. Official exchange is four to the dollar, but based on prices, ten to one seems nearer correct.)

"In America he gets $2.50 to $3 per hour; maybe more," you say.

He is thoughtful, possibly incredulous.

You are thoughtful. You begin to see the problem in an unwelcome light.

Khrushchev spoke of the communist economy "proving itself" and "transforming itself into a world economy through peaceful competition." This competition, obviously, is to be in the world market. On one side is America, with its highly priced man-hour. Up to now it has made good that high cost, by machinery and tooling and mass production. But here you find Russia setting up with deliberate care the same mass - production technique, with low-cost man-hours. You quickly decide America will not relinquish its high pay, because it makes purchasing power. You see a challenge of immense proportions looming before United States industry: How to match a coming giant rival whose ideal is output, not pay.

Before your eyes, you can see the seeds of the great contest being planted. Hotel lobbies and dining rooms are teeming with foreign guests—Asians, Africans, a South American talking business with a Russian host across champagne and caviar. Seeds of peaceful competition.

A strange thought crosses your mind: a future Russia emerging from the iron curtain and America withdrawing behind the dollar curtain, priced out of the market, left

(Continued on Page 10)

trading with itself. "Could it be?" you ask yourself.

You meet a young man from West Africa, jet black, intelligent of speech, a student. He has just visited China, watched the great anti-American rally in Peking. He is touring Russia and western Europe. "I'd like to see America," he says, "but it costs too much."

"A round trip flight from London to New York is down to $450 now, economy fare," you tell him.

"But it's the hotel, the meals, the living costs," he says. "I can't afford it."

America's problem.

You consider an out. Soviet state-owned industry may fail to prove itself; may never be able to produce an equal product for less money. American ingenuity is too much for them. Or is it?

It's time to go into some Soviet plants, talk to the directors, the engineers, the trade unions. See for yourself how they're doing. You set out.

The spirit of the Russian industrial worker does not have the airy exhilaration of freedom, but it has the determination of grim reality: "There's a job to be done and it's up to us to do it."

It is a spirit that has had a frightful past: First the czarist's "Work, you devils, work." Then the revolutionist dictator's "Work with us, or Siberia!" Now the march-words, "Together workers, work." It is the song of a new Volga boatman, with the boatmen owning the boat.

At a machinery plant in Moscow, you enter a dark hallway, emerge to a sawtooth lighted factory area, dirt floored in part but orderly. Unlike the old Volga days, you see no line of men pulling together on a rope, but you quickly learn that collective discipline is the system,

though each man tends his own machine in modern plant fashion.

You spot a chart on the wall. On it are listed the names of men and women in the shop. After each is a number—the man's "social obligation" in units of work. Squares are filled to show his work performance, with a percentage over his quota.

"How do you reward them for going over the quota?" you ask the manager.

"Extra pay."

"And if they fall behind?" You find there is more to the system. Another chart with the same layout shows the weekly quota, called the "plan," for the shop itself. Chalked in adjoining columns are the shop's actual performance and percentage over plan. The shop's record is compared with other shops. Elsewhere, the record of whole departments is charted, and that of the plant itself, compared with a national plan. It is one huge, systematic, production competition, man against man, shop against shop, department against department, plant against plant. Bonus money is provided for the individuals, shops and departments that make the best record. At the end of the year the plant itself gets a bonus to distribute if it exceeds its plan.

Back to the worker who is not fulfilling his "social obligation," you find that his shop-mates, his department, and his whole plant take an interest in bringing him into line. He is holding up their own chances for a bonus, their own record for exceeding the plan. The star worker, on the other hand, is as popular as the star on a football team. The team doesn't want to lose him.

You marvel that communism has taken free enterprise's strongest drives — competition and incentive —and put them to work on an individual and group basis to an ex-

(Continued on Page 11)

tent never dared by free enterprise.

You speak to a guide about this. "I see you are making great use of competition," you say.

"Nyet," she replies. "We have no competition."

You are baffled. Then you discover there are two different Russian words for competition. The one you have been using—*konkuryentsiya*—means "rivalry," with a capitalist connotation—a bad word in Russia. The one they use—*soryevnovaniye*—means also "emulation." This they approve.

The incentives in this socialist competition are negative as well as positive, you find. You talk with the editor of the plant paper, a heavy woman and every ounce a communist. The paper is employee-run but generally sponsored by the trade union. Enthusiastically, the mother-editor explains the paper's purpose: "To criticize the work of workers and engineers, so they may be ashamed of their work and improve; to criticize the chiefs if they are not fair; to publish production plans and new ideas; to tell about the best workers in the factory so others can emulate them."

Criticism by name in the plant paper, you learn, is only part of the grim process of collective discipline. First step is reprimanding the individual before his friends. A later step, if necessary, is bringing him before a public opinion court. Removal to a lesser job, or "in rare cases," dismissal, may follow.

The head of the union, who is present, explains that the union is as anxious as the management, or "administration" as they call it, to bring forward production. You can see why. The union is closely knit with the Party, which set the objectives in the first place.

"Is union membership voluntary?" you ask.

"Yes. Voluntary. But ninety-nine and nine-tenths percent belong."

"Does the union ever strike for higher wages?"

"Strikes are prohibited by law."

The director's office in the Moscow plant you are visiting is a plain upstairs room with a desk at one end and a long table. The high window at the end has heavy, dark-blue drapes, edged with tassels. Huge on the side wall is a portrait of V. I. Lenin, looking down half sternly, half benignly, as though saying, "Remember what I taught you, boys, and you'll do fine." A man hurries into the room with an armload of red baize cloth to cover the long table and you know you're in Russia.

The deputy director is in charge in the director's absence. He is thirty-eight, with loose-combed hair, a casual but affirmative manner. He is distinguished from the rest by his necktie.

The plant director, he explains, works under an administration under the district economic council. He takes his plans there for approval, but he has the responsibility for buying his own materials, hiring his people, and negotiating the sale of his products. He is expected to meet the production plan that is established for the year, and to make a profit.

"And what if you don't?"

"We'll probably get moved to another job."

He explains that most of the workers are paid by the piece, rather than by the hour. Their pay ranges from 600 to 1,820 rubles per month. On the average they make 930 rubles per month. This would be $93 at 10 rubles to the dollar.

The deputy director says his own pay is 3,000 rubles, plus bonuses earned for "exceeding the plan."

(Continued on page 12)

"How did you get the job?" asks a member of your party. "Marry the boss's daughter?"

He laughs. The government interpreter, loyal communist, takes the opportunity to quip: "Only in your country does that . happen." The deputy director says he was graduated from an institute, went into the technologists' department, worked up to chief engineer and this.

Employee wages are established in an annual agreement with the trade union. Someone asks the executive, half jokingly, "Do you ever wish you didn't have a union to deal with?"

He doesn't smile. "The unions are helpful," he says.

"But what if the union and management disagree?"

The government interpreter looks around indulgently and explains: "They don't disagree."

Another asks: "What is the basis of wage increases?"

"Productivity. Advancement is on personal ability. General wages go up as productivity goes up."

You find the same system prevails in other plants you visit. "It's the production that pays the wages," they tell you.

You reflect, confusedly, that you have heard management in America make the same case that labor is making in a country where labor wears the hat.

When you wonder, at times, why the workers are not squawking to high heaven about wages, you remember the phrase "social obligation." In their view they are working not just for themselves. They are working together for a goal—to build Russia. "We work half for the present and half for the future," they say. Half to build their own standard of living, half to make the red star the great light of the world. To do this they know they must work to surpass America in all things, but most of all, in industry.

"Do you really think Russia can match America in production?" you ask in Moscow, Kiev, Kharkov, Leningrad.

Says a laboratory assistant: "Da. We are behind you now, but our tempo is greater. That means we will overtake you."

A university professor: "Da. Already we are nearly up to you in output of some things: milk, woolen cloth. We'll reach your standard of living in 10 to 15 years. There is a possibility of doing it faster."

A skilled worker: "It is possible. In ten years we should catch you."

A store manager: "Da, but it will take a long time."

An architecture student: "Ten to fifteen years."

A young factory worker, studying nights to finish his tenth grade: "Da, we'll catch up if you don't interfere." He means if America doesn't interfere by war. Everywhere the people tell you they want peace. But they fear America.

A student of history, candidly: "I don't like Communism. I don't like capitalism. I like freedom. But Russian industry is coming up fast. Five years, Russia will produce as much as America."

On a flight between Minsk and Kiev, you sit beside a young jet pilot of the Soviet Air Force, relaxed in a gray leisure jacket made of kapron, the Russian nylon.

"Do you think your scientists will get a rocket to the moon before the United States?" you ask him.

"Sooner," he says, with a polite but confident smile.

"Think Russia will put a man on the moon in ten years?"

"Earlier. Between five and ten years, we will do it." You sense the quiet cockiness of young Russia.

(Continued on Page 2)

Bridal Veil
NEWS LETTER

Vol. IV, No. 11   BRIDAL VEIL, OREGON   MAY, 1959

NEWS LETTER

Published on the 10th of each month by
Bridal Veil Lumber & Box Co.
Bridal Veil, Oregon

Editor . . . . Sara Mahn

Automation—Why?

Union rules that add unnecessarily to the cost of getting a job done are spurring industry into automation just as they pushed private citizens into "do-it-yourself."

If you have a leak in a water pipe at home, your inclination is to call a plumber. If he observes strict craft lines, he may call in a carpenter, plasterer, tile-setter and painter.

Industry is footing bills like this every day. Even when men qualified to do a job are available in the plant, union rules often require management to bring in other craftsmen at premium pay rates for overtime or part-day work schedules.

———— 66 ————

Automation—Why Not?

Teddy Roosevelt never heard of "automation," yet he had an answer for critics who say it will reduce the number of jobs.

Once as he watched steam shovels scooping up earth for a dam, someone said, "Think of the jobs we could create if we put men out there with shovels."

"Yes," Mr. Roosevelt replied scathingly, "and we could multiply that number a hundredfold if we equipped them with teaspoons."

———— 66 ————

15 Years of Service

Durward L. Litton observed his 15th year with Bridal Veil Lumber and Box Company on May 9.

He spent his first ten years here as a millwright and is now operating the Cleat Saw and the Variety Saw.

Durward was born in Glenwood Springs, Colorado, on June 7, 1910. His family moved to Oregon in 1922. After graduating from La Grande High School, Durward worked for Union Pacific Railroad as a machinist prior to coming to Bridal Veil.

In 1937 he married Ruth McCoch, whose home town is La Grande.

Durward lists as his hobbies fishing and raising roses. He enjoys baseball but would not speculate on who will be playing the Yankees this fall.

———— 66 ————

1959 SAFETY CHART

Month	Tot. Hourly Pd. Man Hrs.	Lost Time Accidents	Accident Freq.	Days Lost	Accident Severity
January	18,468	1	54.1	1	541
February	17,904	0	0	24	1340
March	12,994	0	0	22	1693
1st Qtr.1959	49,366	1	20.3	47	952
1st Qtr.1958	46,963	2	42.6	64	1363
1st Qtr.1957	46,788	3	63.9	5	107

A Landmark Passes

The closing of the store closes a chapter in the history of this business that has long held a sentimental attachment with the past. Bridal Veil, like most mills before the advent of modern transportation was isolated and employees depended upon the company for housing and shopping facilities as well as a job by which to pay for them. It used to be said that the only two things that were certain were "death and taxes" but in our dynamic society of today a new dimension has been added — "change".

The years have brought changes. Communities grew and along with them came services of many kinds including organizations specializing in merchandising. At the same time competition grew more intense in all lines, including our own. It finally became obvious in our own case that we would be well-advised to concentrate on doing the very best we could in the stock millwork business and leave to others more qualified the job of running stores. All angles were considered and it was decided that no great hardship would be inflicted on anyone if the store were closed. With our small volume and small purchasing power it was obvious that we could not compete for your favor with the chain stores and supermarkets.

Here in capsule form is a wonderful demonstration of the problem confronting all business. It must offer its goods or services at a price and quality that is at least as attractive as its competitors or its customers will leave it high and dry. With our small volume and purchasing power it was necessary for us to charge more than the supermarkets on many items which reduced our store to the status of a convenience for more or less "drop-in" business.

Contrary to a perfectly natural notion that because we charged more the store was a "mint" the store never made enough money to justify the money tied up in it and which could be used to better advantage in the stock millwork business which is our only justification for being here in the first place.

Last year the store "made" only $123.03. No charge was made for lights, heat, repairs or rent, costs which were buried in manufacturing operations. Even if the store had little better than broke even carrying all the expenses caused by its operation it would still have turned in too little a return on the $13,914 tied up in stock on the shelves at year's end because it was operating on funds borrowed at 6% which would have been an additional charge of something like $835.

Clearly the store was a drain on the Company, compounded by the prospect of a re-roofing job over the store building this year. That proved the last straw.

In a larger sense the Company itself faces the same problems that the store was subject to. It is not earning enough to justify the money that is tied up in it. In such a situation, the stockholders would be justified in coming to the same conclusion about it that the Company came to regarding the store.

I for one do not propose to let that happen because I like this place and my place in it. I hope you are with me on that.

Len Kraft

——————— 66 ———————

Salty Subject

Centuries ago salt was a luxury for which adventurers risked their lives and kings sold their jewels. Today in America more salt is sprinkled on slippery highways than on food.

——————— 66 ———————

MAY BIRTHDAYS

Many Happy Returns of the Day!

Frederick Bailey
Anna Bowen
Franklin Bowen
Lloyd DeMain
Leo F. Hageman
Richard Hatfield
Stanley Hills

Clif Latourell
Lawrence Peterson
Leslie Polzel
David Rees
Marvin Stolin
Ralph Taylor
Homer Walker

Farewell

Mr. and Mrs. Walter Keller are leaving the Bridal Veil Lumber and Box Company after 15 years of managing the Company Store. We will miss their smiling faces and the convenience of having a store so near.

The Kellers came to Bridal Veil in May, 1944. Prior to that time he was a truck driver for Swift and Company in Portland. He was making a delivery here when he was asked if he knew someone who might be interested in coming to Bridal Veil to manage the store. He applied for the job.

They are originally from Canada, but have been in Oregon for the past 28 years.

Ann and Walt plan to take a couple of months vacation before going into another job. They are still undecided as to what the new job will be.

———————— 66 ————————

Health and Welfare Coverage

All employees who worked the required number of hours in February and March will become eligible for health and welfare Coverage and will be covered on the first day of May, 1959. They must have worked the required hours in both months. Additions: Theophile Van Hee, Sr., Charles D. Jacobson, Walton G. Jones, Floyd Oden, Richard R. Hatfield.

Employees who did not work the required number of hours will become ineligible the same day. Deletions: Leo C. Hageman, Mary Woodard.

———————— 66 ————————

How the world shrinks. The new Boeing 707 jet plane is actually longer than the distance of Wright's first flight.

———————— 66 ————————

Rips and Trims

(Continued from Page 12)

RALPH LAMKE's son wrecked a car this past month, but came out with only bruises. TED VAN HEE's car was also wrecked.

April first was the birthdate of the new baby girl, Donna Victoria, born to Mr. and Mrs. EDSEL KINONEN. FRANK BOWEN has a new granddaughter, Donna Jean, born on April 9. She is the daughter of Donald Bowen, a former employee. And just in time to meet the deadline for publication, Mr. and Mrs. BOB LAYTON announce the birth of a boy, Daniel Allen (he thinks is the name his wife picked) weighing 7 pounds 2 ounces. He was born this afternoon, April 29.

CLAIMS

Claims allowed during the first five months of our current fiscal year are almost three times the total claims allowed during the entire year 1958.

The bulk of these claims are due to defects which may not have been evident at the time the stock was shipped. Cupping, warping and twisting in frame stock sometimes develop after the stock has been shipped. Much depends upon the handling and storage conditions in the customer's warehouse.

Some claims are debateable, such as tally differences. Even though all our production and loading tallies show the stock to have been produced and shipped, when the customer says an item was not in the car and refuses to pay, there is no way to collect short of a lawsuit. It would not pay to sue a customer in an eastern court for $111.46.

However, all claims cannot be laid at the customer's door. Millwork is a touchy and complicated product requiring close attention to detail in all stages of production.

The importance of claims is twofold. First is the amount of money involved. Claims this year almost exactly equal the wages of ten people for one month.

In the long run, the damage to our reputation is perhaps more important than the immediate cost in money. Our reputation for quality merchandise is our most precious asset. Some of these claims represent lost customers. At best, suspicion, doubt and ill-will are created in the minds of both buyer and seller that may take years to overcome.

Summary of Claims Allowed
To April 28, 1959

Louisville Sash & Door Co.
    100 door jambs twisted, cupped, bowed, warped —
    which customer converted to headers .... $ 185.00

Frank Paxton Lumber Co.
    Pairing and rebanding outside door frames incorrectly
    bundled 51.04

Louisville Sash & Door Co.
    Defective frames in CNW 962 and replacement of cupped,
    warped and twisted frames in PRR 26648 and CNW 962 .... 2475.00

McGill Metal Products
    Allowances to date for defective mouse trap bases in
    excess of normal 5% 813.14

Firpine - Campbellsville
    Rework picture sash run 3/16'' over width; charge to
    pin window divided lites not pinned, bars loose; non-
    usable check rails — top and bottom rails punched
    wrong, bottom rails run upside down; rework window
    and door frame heads cut 3/16'' too long 224.25

Firpine - Louisville
    Tally difference between what invoiced to customer
    and what customer claimed he received 111.46

Tennessee Building Supply Co.
    Sorting and reworking sills which affected brick mould length, etc 100.00

Total Claims . . . $3959.89

Opinions differ as to timing, but not one Russian you have talked with believes his country will remain behind America industrially. Most, like the young jet pilot, believe they are already leading in science. In fact, you can recall a good many Americans at home who would grant this, though you believe it to be true only in limited fields. How has the Soviet Union achieved this point of progress? How did it successfully get off a sputnik while others slept? Except for the sputnik, what you have seen in Russia so far has been short on originality. You wonder if scientists educated under communist dogma can have the imagination to produce new scientific discoveries. You want to learn more about what motivates these men.

Loitering in the main hall of Kiev University, you meet a research psychologist, a man you think should be qualified to discuss this point. "What inspires the Russian scientist?—what makes him try to discover new ideas and put them to use?" you ask him in his cluttered laboratory office next day. "Is it the money he can make, the hope of a Lenin prize and fame, love of his country, or what?"

The man across the desk has intent eyes, a lean face, and needs a shave. You are alone with him, embarking on deep waters with your frail Russian, plus his fragments of English. He leans toward you, interested: "It's all of these," he says, "but these are not all. These are not the main factors." He lays out a finger. "First, our scientists are free."

"Free? How do you mean free?"

"Free to work on things they want. If you have a new idea, you tell your superiors. If they think it is a good idea, they will say, 'Go ahead and work on it.' You are given the equipment and the facilities."

"And if they aren't interested?"

OUR RED RIVALS

© 1958, Harold Mansfield

By HAROLD MANSFIELD

Part Two

of Two Parts

"You have to try again." He continued: "I am free to experiment on what I want. My colleagues are free to work on what they want."

He put two fingers on the table: "Second: the Russian people love the scientist."

"Why?"

"They are servants of the people. They have a high and respected position. Third: Their security is provided. They are secure on account of money."

"You mean they have good material comforts."

"Very good. But this is general: You must understand. Our people are a free people."

"The Russian people—free?" It is more than you can swallow, but you are polite and let him continue. He leans closer.

"My mother and father were farmers in the Ukraine," he says.

MASSIVE MOSCOW UNIVERSITY is imposing testimony to the Soviet's intention of leading in education. Harold Mansfield describes his visit to Kiev University, where he discussed science and education.

"They can't read or write. I am a scientist. This is what I mean by a free people."

"Free to achieve, to go to a higher position?"

"Da. Also free from exploitation. A Russian is free in his capacity and ability. This freedom is the general factor—the chief factor that inspires our men of science." He adds: "I should have said first of all, we have general education. All are equal in possibilities."

You begin to see how the very things America credits for its great progress, Russia is adapting to its ends. Education and opportunity. You pursue your original question: "But you agreed the desire for money, fame, and love of country were each factors. Which of these three is more important?"

"We are talking openly, freely," he answers. "Love of our country is first. For myself, I do not think about money. For my friends in science, money is not the main thing in their thinking."

You say: "In America, I don't think the scientist is working mainly for money either. He works because he wants to discover new things, get more knowledge, learn new things. Only those who earn the least, work primarily for money."

He nods vigorously. "It is the same in our country. Only those who earn the least."

"What about wages in general. Do the unions ask an increase each year?"

"The government decides," he replies. "If I ask for myself, I may ask too much. It would make prices too high. We do not want inflation." He adds: "One day the ruble will be worth as much as the dollar."

"You think so? When? Ten years? Fifty years?"

"That's hard to say. But it will come."

Up to now, America has been the shining model before the world's eyes. Russia wants to be that model, so people and nations will be attracted to communism. It is easy to see why Russia has set as her main goal to beat America in the economic competition.

The strange contradiction is that it is the nation whose very traditions and manners Russia seeks to warn her people against, which has become the model she seeks to emulate. You think about that. Suddenly it doesn't seem so strange. You remember your puzzling encounter with the two different meanings of "competition" in Russian. The accepted word for it means emulation. It's true, you reflect, in most any competition the contender begins to emulate the successful techniques of the champion. How else can he match him? You know it has been happening for years in design and invention. There is a joke in Russia, that the country's most successful inventor is Comrade Reguspatoff (Reg. U. S. Pat. Off.).

There is other evidence of emulation. The children, better dressed than their parents, the hope of the land, choose English language study four to one over other foreign languages. You ask some of them why.

"Because it will be the most useful to me," one boy tells you. Says another: "Because America is best in technology."

In one of the schools you visit a beginner class in English, composed of fourteen-year-old girls and boys. You mention you have a daughter about their age. Two girls in pigtails step up shyly and brightly curtsy. Carefully one of them articulates: "We wish to correspondence."

The Russian people like Americans, despite all the propaganda against them. Many tell you they would like to visit your country, but few believe they will ever get the chance.

Managers of enterprises say they want to buy American products. "You have more than you can use. We have shortages of everything," they say. "We should trade with each other."

Russians like American music. University students want to buy American suits and shirts from tourists, "because they have style."

There is even something more subtle that the Russian finds attractive to him in Americans. One guide explains it simply: "They smile."

With more tourists, more trade, is there not hope Russia will also accept new ideas and ideals, you wonder? You ask a devoted communist: "Do you people think Marx's doctrines must apply to all time? Conditions change. Do you re-examine these doctrines in light of new conditions?"

"Yes. We re-examine them."

You are surprised, a little shocked, at the answer. You hadn't expected it. Yet you have seen how these people have adopted practices foreign to the original concept of communism — "from each according to his ability, to each according to his need." Competitive incentives, profit, greater freedom of individual opportunity, private ownership are examples. You meet a family which is buying its own home under a new Moscow plan — borrowing money from the government bank and paying it back over a period of fifteen years. You learn that forty million Soviet citizens have private deposits in savings banks. You become fascinated with a speculation:

Suppose Russia were to achieve her goal of full production: Would she not have to adopt more western business methods just to keep the bustling commerce straight? Would she not have to go still further from Marxist communism, still nearer to Western methods, even though she retained government ownership, as friendly countries do to varying degrees? Instead of the present queues at government shops waiting for a few shirts and shoes, would there not be need for advertising to attract buyers? To stimulate sales, would there not be need for credit buying? Wouldn't bank accounts and checks be necessary to simply handle the money traffic? You want to talk with some bank officials about these things.

When you step into a Russian savings bank, an institution rapidly growing in popularity, you think you might be in a small U. S. post office. There is the writing counter against the wall, and across from it two or three attendants' windows. Behind the partition, some women are sorting deposit slips in a shallow wood box. You watch them do their addition on Chinese abacus counting frames, adroitly clicking the beads of the ancient devices that you have also seen used in all the stores.

The manager of the bank, a man in his mid-thirties, unharried, accommodating, invites you to the back office. You feel that you have been here before, and then remember it is an old farmhouse kitchen you are thinking of, with its square-legged board table in the center. The manager apologizes for a shortage of chairs, and himself sits on the corner of the table. A government interpreter explains the intricacies of soviet banking, the six types of institutions: agricultural, state, communal, industrial, foreign trade, and savings.

You learn there is a crude approach to the use of checks, when one industrial plant writes a note to the bank which keeps its funds, asking that a certain amount of money be transferred to a bank in another city and put in the account of a plant there from which it has purchased some material. You get the manager aside.

"In the future," you say, "Russia hopes to be producing plenty of things for everyone. When that time comes, won't you need things like personal accounts at banks and credit accounts at the stores, and checks to pay for goods and services?" It is a little involved for your Russian. You repeat the question. The official interpreter hears you and comes over. You would rather have talked privately with the banker, but you put the question to the interpreter. She gives it a little laugh of inconsequentiality and turns to another man's question. Later you try it again. Finally as the visit is breaking up you insist you'd like to know the manager's opinion. She asks him. He looks at her, then at you.

"We don't have need for these things now," he says. "When we have communism," — they always speak of communism as something in the future rather than at present —"we will need neither checks nor money."

That ends the discussion. When the wall of dogma appears, communist thought will not attempt to penetrate it. But you can see clearly the contradiction. The trend in Russia is going precisely opposite to the trend planned toward pure communism. You see it further when you visit a large state bank, a more imposing institution with a long row of cashiers clicking the beads of their abacuses, but with modern bookkeeping machines behind, and a mahogany-furnished executive office, suitably adorned with portraits. The manager asks eager questions about banking prac-

(Continued on Page 10)

tices in America.

Business methods—even government business—have only started to make the improvements that Russian science and production have been making in recent years. The distance between the Chinese counting frame at the bank and the electronic computer in the Soviet science laboratory is typical of the glaring inconsistency between the country's forward drive and the cumbersome methods of communism that are dragging it back. Clumsy office methods and procedures, the bureaucratic ladder that must be climbed for policy decisions, delay, dogma and dictation, are heavy fetters on a people's push toward progress.

But Russia is getting wise to these faults. Trade with the outside world will open her eyes, sharpen her practices. To now, America has been reaping a competitive advantage from the backward cumbersomeness of communism itself, the high "overhead" cost of its supergovernment, the ponderosity of governmental control. Because of this, Americans have often wrongly assumed that Russia could never do what it says. But the streamlining is bound to come. As an example, Russian plant directors say the recent decentralization of industrial ministries has greatly speeded the process of decision.

Meanwhile America has its own trend to "big government." Even now, you reflect, there isn't too much difference between the length of the list of ministries and policy-forming institutes in Moscow and the list of agencies and committees in Washington. Different names. America is not immune to the problems of big government.

There is ample evidence that Russia is pushing resolutely Khrushchev's program to "prove communism to the world" through peaceful competition.

What of his other contention, borrowed from earlier communist theorists, that meanwhile "the internal forces of capitalism are working toward its downfall?" Can you merely pooh-pooh this brash claim? Viewed from the distance of Soviet Russia, you can see the dangers inherent in America's success. The spoil of success is indulgence. You can't for the life of you see how America can long keep its world leadership in the "peaceful competition" if it indulges the luxury of waste, the luxury of half-hearted effort, the old-style luxury of paying tribute to any group which can exact it through power, the bitterly illusory luxury of inflation. Not when Russia is living and breathing cost control.

Between acts of the opera in Kiev you follow the crowd downstairs to the drawing room where refreshments are being served. You stand in line for a thirty-cent dish of ice cream. You watch with utter fascination the apron-clad girl who is dishing it out. Each dish goes on a little balance like the one at the pharmacist's. She dips up a scoop of ice cream and puts it on the balance. If the balance is high, she adds a trifle, lightning-like because of the waiting crowd. If it is low, with one deft twist of the wrist she flicks off the half teaspoon that will bring it into balance, and returns this to the container for the next serving.

You look about at the happily chattering people. Other than you, no one in the room considers the precise weighing process in the least odd.

This balance, you can't help thinking, is emblematic of Russian effort to make cost and output meet. You have seen it in the whole Russian economy, the fight to build without inflation. You might say it is emblematic, too, of the counter scale of a new, sharp dealer down the street of nations. He is in poor quarters now, but working and saving for the day when he can buy out the rich store on the main intersection. The big store owner with his Cadillac has "had it so good" that he has not much worried about the new competition. But lately he has begun to wonder; ever since the other storekeeper shot a sputnik into the sky and began to attract customers.

The little ice cream balance, you think further, betokens a balance of power in the world: The forces of communism against the forces of freedom. Two societies basically antagonistic, though simulating each other in surprising, unacknowledged ways. Between them, there is a balancing of military power and of advancement in military weaponry: atomic stalemate. The more frightful the weapon becomes, the deeper the stalemate, because of mutual fear not so much of the other country as of the weapon itself.

You have seen, growing out of the stalemate, Mr. Khrushchev's new plan to sell communism to the world. The pharmacist's balance looms larger, filling the frame of your thought. You see everything that the communist world does and everything that the free world does as adding to one side or the other of the balance. You see everything that either fails to do as subtracting from its side of the balance.

You realize, as never before, that your country is being weighed in the balance. It has no self-perpetuating heritage of superiority. It must prove itself, year to year. It stands challenged.

Is the system of freedom and equity answering the challenge? To do so, must it not cite for its people a goal of its own—to paraphrase Khrushchev: "the emergence of freedom and equity as a world system?" Must it not sacrifice selfishness and work for its goal, as Russia has taught her people to work for theirs?

You come back to America, land of the free, to find Americans taking riotous advantage of that freedom. You realize as never before that freedom requires self-discipline. Nothing less can match the discipline of a communist regime.

And how is this related to peace? Because the road to peace is not paved with the unturned stones of idleness, selfishness or complacency.

Because atomic stalemate still leaves the Soviet Union free to gain the balance of world power by the route Mr. Khrushchev has announced.

Because, if communism gains the balance of power by any means, the peace is lost. Then freedom's great struggle will still be ahead.

On the other hand, for America to stay in the peaceful competition will mean that it will have to improve, and that the Soviet system and ideology will have to improve, through competitive emulation. If this happens, the great cause for conflict — the conflict of beliefs — may be removed and replaced by a better understanding, stone by stone.

Industry, labor, all America, have their part to play. Your sense of the unsolved problem shouts within you that Americans must work for their own future.

But not just that.

They must get interested in something besides themselves. In other countries. In the world. In people. Even Russian people. In the two little girls who "wish to correspondence."

The girls are fourteen now. In ten years they will be women. The ten years in which Soviet Russia says it will "catch America." And after that . . .?

Rips and Trims

With the fishing season open and the Corbett Centennial Parade, April was a very busy month for many of the employees of Bridal Veil.

A beautiful catch, Harold.

The trout pictured are part of the catch of Mr. and Mrs. HAROLD BURKHOLDER on their recent fishing trip over to Warm Springs. They both caught their limit. FRED HARP also reported getting the limit of trout at the P.G.E. Dam on the Clackamas. Fishing for Chinook were EDSEL KINONEN and ELDEN GROSS. They both had good success. Elden has just returned to work after his recent surgery.

Others have been on the sick list and in the hospotal during the past month. ANNA BOWEN has been spending her evenings at Portland San with WILLIS. He is doing fine and has been back helping with a little of the book work in his department. TED HANSON recently brought his wife home after a brief stay in Portland San. DONALD WESTLAKE is back on the job again after being out for a couple of months recuperating from an automobile accident.

The Centennial Parade in Corbett was a big affair. FAY and BERTHA DAVIS rode in a covered wagon. She said she had quite a time getting her centennial dress finished. MIRA NIELSON rode with ELDON in his 1930 Model A.

Now that Spring has arrived many are finding it necessary to work in their gardens again. FRED DAMERELL is doing some farming at Coopey Falls.

PAUL DETRICK has in his oats and clover. LEONARD VOLKMAN has planted barley — he says he worked until about eleven o'clock at it one evening. (Are you planning to ride that new Harley Davidson Motorcycle through the barley?) JOE COTE and FAY DAVIS have both been spending some time in the garden.

Among the handymen are ORIEN PITTS who has been painting his house and GEORGE MURRAY who put on a new roof.

Wedding bells rang on April 4 for Marilla Jean Murray (daughter of GEORGE MURRAY) and Patrick Kenneth Wagner and also Darlene Bird (daughter of VERL BIRD) and Royce Donovan Robertson.

ELEANOR and RALPH TAYLOR took a week's vacation and went down to Oroville, California, for a visit with Don and Barbara West (former sales manager here). They also went over to Reno to try their luck, but decided they would do better back here at work.

DEAN BURKHOLDER went with MARVIN JACKSON to Detroit to pick up his new blue and white Ford Custom 300. After picking up the car and seeing the sights around Detroit and a side trip into Canada, they headed south, down through Alabama, Mississippi, Texas and on over into Mexico. They traveled in twenty states, Canada and Mexico and covered 7500 miles before returning to Oregon. They also saw the Queen of Spain in Detroit, the Queen of Mexico and in Mississippi the Queen of the U.S. — Miss America. They will be real happy to tell you all about their trip; just ask them.

(Continued on Page 4)

Very neat, Eldon.

Bridal Veil
NEWS LETTER

Vol. IV, No. 12   BRIDAL VEIL, OREGON   JUNE, 1959

NEWS LETTER

Published on the 10th of each month by
Bridal Veil Lumber & Box Co.
Bridal Veil, Oregon

Editor . . . . Sara Mahn

Quite an Impact

What happens in a community when a new manufacturing business is started, or an existing one expands its operations and takes on additional employees?

The Canadian National Railways has made a study of changes that took place in nine different Canadian communities, which revealed that 100 additional manufacturing workers meant to their community:

- 427 more people
- 131 more households
- 66 more school children
- 117 more workers employed other than in manufacturing
- 187 more motor vehicle registrations
- 393 more telephones
- 3 more retail establishments
- $939,000 more retail sales per year

Studies in the U.S. tell a similar story.

———96———

IMPOSSIBLE

Just before the turn of the century Joseph Coppersmith was arrested for selling stock in a telephone company.

The charge said, "Well-informed people know that it is impossible to transmit the human voice over wires and that, were it possible to do so, the thing would be of no practical value."

No Union Contract

With the Consumer

For the last 20 years we have suffered from a creeping inflation. Many of us felt helpless to do anything about it. Some few actually may have liked it — although there is no greater threat to future personal economic security than inflation's withering effect on savings, pensions and insurance.

Some of the inflation, especially in the last three years, has been caused by wage rises too great for productivity gains to keep up with. Inflationary wage rises were forced by large unions holding monopoly powers.

But on whom were these rises forced? Not just on the companies involved. Because the wage rises could not be absorbed without price rises, the demands in effect were forced upon the people.

However — as the recession of 1957-58 proved — the unions cannot always dictate terms to the American consumer. If prices are forced too high by rising costs, people can simply refuse to buy. In the end, the welfare and security of employees depend not on the union but on the ability of the company they work for to sell its products.

———96———

Today's Motto

One can no more develop capacity by resting on his job than he can learn to spell by sitting on a dictionary.

— Arthur Dean

1959 SAFETY CHART

Month	Tot. Hourly Pd. Man Hrs.	Lost Time Accidents	Accident Freq.	Days Lost	Accident Severity
January	18,468	1	54.1	1	541
February	17,904	0	0	24	1340
March	12,994	0	0	22	1693
1st Qtr. 1959	49,366	1	20.3	47	952
April	16,596	0	0	21	1265
Total	65,962	1	15.2	68	1031

How Are We Doing?

Nearing the half-way mark for our Company year which ends November 30, 1959, we pause a bit to check our course, evaluate our strengths and weaknesses and address ourselves to the task of improving our performance in the balance of the year. We find some slight improvement over last year — a loss of $35,416 in 5 months of operation. This is at an annual rate of $84,000 compared to a loss last year of $95,918. Obviously that can't be. We cannot stand two years in a row like that and survive. What then are the chances and how do we propose to better the situation?

A Houdini-like performance in getting out of financial "binds" has enabled us to keep paying our bills — including payrolls. One of the more spectacular examples was closing out the store which freed up $15,226.52 of badly needed cash to keep the plant going. Liquidating on a "crash" basis had its cost however, in the form of a $3,635.35 loss. But helpful as these measures have been, they do not hold the fundamental answer to our problem.

Nothing but a proper relationship between sales price and cost of production will do that. This can be improved in three ways: 1) increase prices 2) hold down costs and 3) produce more per hour.

On the price front, we have been in constant touch with our customers over the past several months. As a result, we have been able to negotiate price increases averaging 5% on all products.

The easiest way to increase the general sales average is to channel the greatest possible portion of our material into millwork. On a footage basis, it costs more to produce a mouse trap or a cheese box than it does to produce a window frame. Yet the sales value of the millwork items may be as much as twice the price of the cheaper items. Progress is being made in this direction. Millwork sales through April were 64% of total sales compared to 59% during 1958. Here we need further improvement to reach the 70% figure of five years ago. We have done it before, we can do it again.

The biggest single item of cost in the stock millwork business is lumber. During the first five months of this year our lumber cost has increased 13.8%. There is every indication that the rapid rise in lumber prices has about run its course. Prices should level off for the balance of the year.

At today's lumber price, each one percent of cut-away costs from $800.00 to $900.00 per month. One of our goals for the balance of the year is to reduce lumber losses by three percent. A saving of this kind would reduce our loss by $15,000.00 to $18,000.00 during the balance of the year.

Next to the cost of lumber, people are our greatest expense. Your management believes that this is no time to "rock the boat" and as you have no doubt learned from the Union, we have requested a moratorium on wage increases until we can get back on the track. As my brother pointed out in his editorial of last April, this need not be looked upon apprehensively since what we are doing is to take steps to safeguard the best jobs in the stock mill-work business in the whole country. We're still the highest paid.

Thirdly, we can help — in fact it will be necessary, to wipe out the balance of the loss — by producing more per hour. This pre-supposes that we have the sales so we have need for the extra production. Happily, this is the case. Our order file is up 13.44%. Now we've got to find ways and means of turning this volume out at a rate that will get our costs down below our selling prices. This is most important and without this any other sacrifice we make will be nullified.

— Len Kraft

———————96———————

The federal government now spends more on the purchase of paper towels than it did on the whole federal budget in George Washington's day.

Our

ni al

ɔ marks the beginning of the Oregon
nnial Exposition and International
: Fair.

·ing the past several months many
ɔ Bridal Veil employees have been
ng beards and mustaches to cele-
the Centennial. Others have ridden
ɔntennial Parades in both Corbett
;resham. Eldon Nielson won third
 in the Gresham Parade with his
Λodel **A** and received the yellow
ι.

Recent Visitor

Mr. Spencer Wernham, president of McGill Metal Products in Marengo, Illinois, was a recent visitor at our mill.

McGill Metal Products purchases four or five carloads of mouse and rat traps from us each year.

———96———

Scientists have finally discovered how much sleep the average person needs — about ten minutes more.

———96———

Health and Welfare Coverage

All employees who did not work the required number of hours during the month of March will become ineligible for Health and Welfare Coverage on the first day of June, 1959. Deletions: Alfred L. Barnes, Roger A. Blaine, Delbert P. Cloe, Kenneth O. Craig, Marvin N. Dhone, Robert D. Godat, Theodore N. Hanson, Charles D. Jacobson, Martha A. Jones, Walton G. Jones, John Mershon, Charles H. Murphy, Floyd F. Oden, Robert W. Reischel, Donald Westlake, Jack V. Westlake.

Accident Insurance Up

Starting July 1 of this year, payments by Bridal Veil Lumber & Box Company to the State Industrial Accident Commission for Workmen's Compensation Insurance will double.

Action of the State Legislature at its last session increased the basic rate for our type of woodworking factory from $2.21 per hundred dollars of payroll to $2.61, an increase of 19%.

At the same time, our accident experience over the past several years has been such that our account with the State Industrial Accident Commission is in bad shape. To bring our account into better balance, the Commission is cutting our discount from 50% to 15%.

As a result of these two adjustments, our contribution will rise 102-1/2%, costing the Company an additional $500.00 per month or $6,000.00 per year.

Dick Hatfield

———96———

June Birthdays

Many Happy Returns of the Day!

Earl Hutchison
Harold Jacobson
James Kendrick
Durward Litton
Roland Morgan
Jerald Roberts
Raymond Schneringer
Elvin Smith

———96———

Rips and Trims

(Continued from Page 8)

Chuck Kraft left Guam on June 1 to return to the States. He didn't know whether he would be flying and be home the next day or if he would be coming by boat and be on the water for three weeks. He has just completed his tour of duty with Uncle Sam in the Navy. He plans to continue his education in the fall.

The Strong Man —
With a Weakness

FIFTY or more years ago, the industrial worker was more than likely to be a "strong man." He worked hard...too hard. And he worked long...too long. Whatever work had to be done, he did with sheer muscle power—for the most part. Only a fraction of all work was done with the help of machinery or power.

The industrial worker of the old days was a strong man—but the lack of mechanical power was his weakness. With the use of only his muscles and hand tools, he had to work about 70 hours a week. It took him that long to produce far less than the production a worker turns out in these days in 40 hours.

TODAY, we can save our muscles for fun, sports and leisure time activities of whatever sort we like. At work, we use our brains rather than our muscles, to guide the powered machinery at the disposal of industrial workers, and which today does about 96 per cent of the work.

Machinery costs money, however — it does not just come into being at the will of management. It is estimated that at the beginning of 1958, the amount of investment standing behind the average industrial worker—to make his job possible—was $17,800. Thus it is plain we must have an immense flow of investment to provide the nation's jobs and goods.

Rips and Trims

The big event for the first week of June each year is graduation. This year is no exception. So we will start by saying "Congratulations". Lyn Crouser is now a Physicist after his recent graduation from college in McMinnville. Graduating from Corbett High School are Fred Bailey, Richard Bowen, Linda Burkholder, Linda DeMain, Daniel Hills, Marvin Howell, Robert Long, Barbara Mickelson, and Patricia Westlake. Charlene Gaymon graduated from Gresham High School. Those graduating from the Eighth Grade at Corbett are Pat Kendrick, Dana Pitts, Dick Hanson, Ron Nielson and Pat Cowling. Len Ann Kraft graduated from Riverdale School and Kathleen Gaymon from Orient School.

Fishing captured the spotlight for many of the employees of Bridal Veil over the Memorial Day weekend. MARVIN VAN ORSOW and his son were at Crane Prairie and brought back blue back salmon. Most of the trout fishermen got their limits. HARRY ADOLPH at Timothy Lake, MARVIN STOLIN and ED KINONEN at State Cove Park, ELDEN GROSS at Pelton Dam, HOWARD HUNT at Tolgate Park, EUGENE McMANUS at Gordon Creek, BOB BIRD at Eagle Creek, WALTON JONES at Kingsley Resevoir, and EINAR MICKELSON at Bridal Veil Creek. JIM COWLING, ROBERT FITZGERALD, and PAUL DETRICK were also fishing. Paul said he didn't get any fish but perhaps he can do better when he gets that new boat finished and in the water.

Several were rather pink from sunburn when they returned to work on Tuesday. Among them were E. H. POTTER, MARVIN DHONE, RONALD CATLIN, BOB PATRICK and BERTHA DAVIS. Picnicking over the week-end were JOEL CROUCH at Viking Park, and ANNA and WILLIS BOWEN. Anna and Willis also enjoyed the boat riding and have selected the cruiser they hope to buy in the near future.

CLYDE HAMBRICK went to Everett, Washington, to visit his mother who recently suffered a heart attack. He says she is now doing very well.

"Happy Birthday, Dick!"

STANLEY and MABEL HILLS had two of their daughters, Beverly Steffen and Mary Jane Shannon, home over the week-end. FRED HARP had to give up his fishing trip to have time to enlarge his back steps. LEONARD VOLKMAN cycled out to Estacada Dam. He also gave his girl friend a diamond. LAWRENCE PETERSON stayed home and got his garden cultivated. ROY EVELAND spent the week-end in Seattle.

ALFRED BARNES has recently joined the Dale Carnegie Class in Portland. Have you noticed how different DELBERT DUNKEN looks since he shaved off his beard?

JERRY ROBERTS is out of the hospital and recuperating at home. MARY WOODARD and MARTHA JONES are still on the sick list.

The office workers helped DICK HATFIELD celebrate his birthday on May 21. We hope you have many more happy birthdays and chocolate cakes.

Our sincere sympathies to JOHN WILLMS and his family on the death of his son.

(Continued on Page 6)

Bridal Veil
NEWS LETTER

VOL. V, No. 1   BRIDAL VEIL, OREGON   JULY, 1959

NEWS LETTER

Published on the 10th of each month by
Bridal Veil Lumber & Box Co.
Bridal Veil, Oregon

Editor . . . . Sara Mahn

Machines Raise Number of Jobs

In the last 100 years, the U.S. population has multiplied 7 times; production has multiplied itself 25 times. There are more jobs per 1000 population available today, with machines doing 94% of the work, than there were in 1850, when machines did but 6% of the work.

In 1910 you paid more than $1 for every 100 miles of use you got out of an automobile tire. Today you can get 100 miles of use out of 10 cents worth of tire.

———— 30 ————

July Birthdays

Many Happy Returns of the Day!

Lester Anderson
Robert Bird
Willis Bowen
James Cowling
Paul Detrick
Gerald Dull
Arthur Howell
Lillie Landreth
Bob Layton
Orien Pitts
Theophile Van Hee, Sr.
Harold A. Vogel
Leonard Volkman

Health & Welfare Coverage

All employees who worked the required number of hours in April and May will become eligible for Health and Welfare Coverage and will be covered on the first day of July, 1959. They must have worked the required hours in both months. Additions: Alfred Barnes, Robert Bird, Roger Blaine, Delbert Cloe, Francis Cook, Kenneth Craig, Marvin Dhone, Gerald Dull, Peter Graymer, Theodore Hanson, Ronald Jackson, Charles Jacobson, Walton Jones, Dewayne Kilness, Floyd Oden, Elvin Smith, Leonard Volkman, Donald Westlake, Jack Westlake.

Employees who did not work the required number of hours will become ineligible the same day. Deletions: Marion E. Jones, Willis Bowen.

———— 30 ————

Rips and Trims

(Continued from Page 8)

HAGEMAN a cut hand.

Have you noticed the difference a shave made in the looks of DELBERT DUNKEN, BOB LAYTON, FRED DAMERELL, ELVIN SMITH, WESLEY ADAMS AND DAVID REES? I almost didn't recognize them.

I understand that Mrs. WALT STOLIN isn't in very good practice for baseball. At least I was told that she missed the target when she yanked the phone off the wall and threw it.

That seems to be about it for this month. So Long.

1959 SAFETY CHART

Month	Tot. Hourly Pd. Man Hrs.	Lost Time Accidents	Accident Freq.	Days Lost	Accident Severity
January	18,468	1	54.1	1	541
February	17,904	0	0	24	1340
March	12,994	0	0	22	1693
1st Qtr. 1959	49,366	1	20.3	47	952
April	16,596	0	0	21	1265
May	17,557	1	57.0	42	2392
Total	83,519	2	23.9	110	1317

These Are the Best Jobs

"These are the best jobs in the Stock Millwork industry in the United States."

I have made this statement in these pages several times before. And I have also made this statement orally to anyone who would listen. I am saying it again now because it is important.

It is important to every man and woman working at Bridal Veil. It cannot be over-emphasized.

And they are not better by just a nickel or a dime an hour. They are better by an average of forty cents an hour.

Here is one of our competitors with an entry wage of $1.37 per hour. Another at $1.25. Another at $1.41. Another at $1.44. And another at $1.46.

One of these same mills has a top rate of $1.98 per hour. Another $2.03.

However, we do not have to reach very far afield to find lower rates than Bridal Veil. Our competitors generally lie at some distance from us. I have the scale from a factory in Portland organized under a different union. The starting rate is $1.75-1/2. Cutters are on a sliding scale and are paid from $1.90-1/2 to $2.03. Fork lift operators are $1.90-1/2. Push rip sawyers $1.90-1/2.

It is my understanding that Local #1120 even has a contract in this area in which millwrights are listed at $2.20.

The point to all this is that our affiliation with Bridal Veil Lumber & Box Co. is one of which we can all be justly proud. And one which we can well do all we can to protect.

Len Kraft

Company Ownership

I have been asked who owns Bridal Veil Lumber & Box. Co. Here is the scoop:

Estate of C. H. Kraft . . . . 5096 shares
Estate of J. L. Kraft . . . . 5096 shares
Leonard Kraft . . . . 2800 shares
C. W. Kraft . . . . 1 share
H. W. Winfree . . . . 1 share

12994 shares
— Len Kraft

Where $$$ Grow

When you get your hands on that "long green" today, you can thank the chemical industry and the borough of Brooklyn, N. Y., for helping to keep our money green. The color comes from the Reichhold Chemical plant in Brooklyn, which will make 350,000 pounds of dry pigment this year so the U. S. Treasury Department can print more money than ever before.

Growing Older?

A recent analysis of achievements of 400 famous men throughout history is highly encouraging to all who think they are growing old.

The study revealed that more than one-third achieved their greatest accomplishments after they passed the age of 60. A surprising 23% scored their greatest success in life after the age of 70.

Ne

Each year during May and Jur
our group. Many of these are stu
and college in the Fall. Some of
summer.

Pictured left to right are: (Fir
Richard Bowen, Leroy Brenneke,
Cowling, Ramon Damerell, (Seco
Edward Fox, Donald Hageman, (
Larry Lamke, Robert Long, (Four
son, Roy Papin, Robert Patrick,
James Yerion.

eS

ɔf new employees are added to
ill be returning to high school
ll probably remember from last

ɹ Bailey, Jr., Donald Bowen,
ver, Robert Cowling, Thomas
ford Dawson, Laverne Fagan,
Marvin Howell, Dennis Irish,
ɟene McManus, Fred Mickel-
, Paul Watts, Dean Wilson and

Welcome and Farewell

Barbara Jean Mickelson has joined our office crew to replace Harry Densmore as Office Clerk.

Barb was born in Cathlamet, Washington on January 29, 1941. When she was four months old her parents moved to Bridal Veil where whe has spent her young life up to the present. She is the daughter of Mr. & Mrs. Einar E. Mickelson. Einar is Foreman in the Crosswork Department and Bunny is Assistant Postmistress.

The entire twelve years of Barb's schooling have been at the two Corbett schools. She graduated last month.

She has a sister, Nancy (Mrs. Dewayne Kilness) living at Coopey Falls and a brother, Fred, who is working in the mill on the cutter line for the summer.

Barb enjoys collecting the latest records and stuffed animals. When asked about her hobby, she told us about the first fish she caught just a couple of weeks ago. She plans to make fishing her hobby.

She has also been learning about the ideal way to save money and become a wealthy young lady. If you are interested in saving money, just ask Barb, she can tell you all about it.

Again we say "Farewell" to Eleanor Taylor for at least a little while.

We appreciate so much the way that she has so willingly stepped in and helped with the work in the office during the past several months.

Eleanor resigned her job in the office in 1956 so that she could spend more time at home with her daughter. However, she hasn't been able to spend much time at home because there have been very few months since that time that she hasn't been on the payroll. She has always come back when she was needed and asked to do so.

We hope she can at least have a longer vacation this time from the office. We will surely miss her ready smile and the help she has given.

Thanks again, Eleanor.

———— 30 ————

What To Do

American men, they say, never know what to do with themselves when they retire. As one put it: "I get up early and read the obituary column and if my name isn't there, I go back to bed."

1959 VACATIONS

JANUARY
1 Fred Crouser 10
8 Merrill Hartshorn 10
23 Mira Nielson 10
26 Clem Hancock 7

FEBRUARY
7 Roland Morgan 8

MARCH
1 Ralph Taylor 10
1 Leslie Polzel 8
15 Robert Fitzgerald, Jr. . . . 6
15 Stanley Hills 10
22 Edward Wendler 7
22 Fay Davis 10
23 Clifford Latourell 10
25 Harold Vogel 10
28 Marvin Stolin 10

APRIL
1 Archie Davies 10
8 Marvin Jackson 10
17 Theophile Van Hee 10
18 Theodore Hanson 10
21 Eldon Nielson 10
22 Joseph Van Orsow 10

MAY
1 Louis Bissell 10
8 Floyd F. Oden 5
6 Bertha Davis 10
6 Harold Burkholder 10
6 Edsel Kinonen 10
8 Walton Jones 5
8 Charles D. Jacobson . . . 5
9 Durward Litton 10
11 Walter Stolin 10
13 James Kendrick 10
13 Hiram Layton 10
18 Ward Dull 10
19 Lester Anderson 10
21 Fred Harp 10
27 Theophile Van Hee, Sr. . 10
27 Charles N. Gaymon 8

JUNE
3 Robert Reischel 5
3 Mary Woodard 10
8 Jarvis Kilness 10
13 Orien Pitts 8
23 Lester B. Howell 10
28 Bob Layton 10
30 Anna Bowen 10

JULY
1 Einar Mickelson 10
2 Fred Damerall 6
2 Ronald Catlin 6
8 Wesley Adams 8
10 Paul Dooley 8

JULY
14 Leo F. Hageman 10
18 J. Delbert Dunken 10
19 Lillie Landreth 10
22 Delbert Cloe 6
22 Alfred Barnes 6
22 Kenneth Catlin 6
26 Gerald Dull 5
28 Norman Van Buskirk . . . 10

AUGUST
7 Peter Graymer 5
9 Theodore V. Van Hee . . . 10
12 Marvin Dhone 6
17 Leonard Volkman 5
19 Franklin Bowen 10
21 George Murray 10
27 Ralph McCredie 10

SEPTEMBER
2 Loren Hancock 10
4 Elmer Ayles 10
8 Jerald Roberts 10
9 Fred M. Long 10
10 Joseph Cote 10
11 Roley Zumwalt 10
16 Kenneth Meyer 10
16 Robert Bird 5
20 Verl W. Bird 10
22 Harry Adolph 10
24 Lawrence Peterson 10
27 Elden Gross 10
27 Elvin Smith 5
29 John Willms 10
29 Roger Blaine 6

OCTOBER
1 Howard Hunt 10
1 Kenneth Craig 6
2 Lawrence Smazal 10
9 Ralph Ellis 10
9 Homer Walker 10
10 Louis Wilson 10
13 David Rees 10
14 Mabel Hills 10
28 E. H. Potter 10

NOVEMBER
8 Raymond Schneringer . . . 10
12 Pearl P. Cloe 10
15 Roy Eveland 10
16 Harold Jacobson 10
23 Earl Hutchison 10
24 Clarence Lofstedt 10

DECEMBER
7 Beulah Choate 10
12 Thelma Rowe 10
14 Dorothy Hartshorn 10
20 Thomas Britton 10

Rips and Trims

The sun shines bright and the rain has almost become a thing of the past. We can feel that summer is actually here. Time just doesn't stand still. Half of the year 1959 is over and the next six months will pass just as rapidly as the first half of the year passed. Have you done half of the things you planned to do in 1959?

That new Chevie Impala — a rich golden brown on the bottom and tan on the top—belongs to ANNA and WILLIS BOWEN. They just couldn't pull that new green and white 16 foot Dilbough Boat with the 40 hp Mercury outboard with their old car.

The golden brown Olds that is often parked in front of the office is the pride of MEL MALLINSON. EINAR MICKELSON recently traded his Merc for a four-door Bel-Air Chevie. Its highland green and white. He said it really used a lot of gas the first night, but it should be better now that they fixed the leak in the tank. WALTER STOLIN'S new pickup is also a Chevrolet. It is a very pretty turquoise.

June is a real nice month for vacations. MERRILL AND DOROTHY HARTSHORN, with their daughters Sharon and Becky, enjoyed their drive down to Klamath Falls and Lakeview, Oregon, and then on to Redding, California. They returned over on the coast highway. Merrill later had two days of pretty good fishing on the Deschutes River. Ruth and DURWARD LITTON spent three days of their vacation visiting with Don and Barbara West (former Sales Manager) at their home in Oroville, California. FLOYD ODEN says you can spend a lot of money on a three day vacation at Seaside, but he did say he had a good time.

BERTHA AND FAY DAVIS spent a recent Sunday over at Damascus. The entire town is decorated in Centennial Style. Bertha was very interested in the display of Antiques. ROY EVELAND and family attended the Annual Rodeo at St. Paul and enjoyed it.

CLARENCE LOFTSTEDT took six boys to the Beaver Baseball game a couple weeks ago. TED HANSON and his family were also on hand to see the Beavers get beat.

DONALD BOWEN AND RONALD CATLIN have just completed their two weeks at National Guards Camp. Don said he much preferred to work in the mill.

Among recent visitors at the Centennial Exposition were MARVIN VAN ORSOW and JIM COWLING with their families.

LEO C. HAGEMAN and his parents recently entertained two young men from the Indonesian Department of Commerce. Leo met them while he was attending the American Institute for Foreign Trade in Phoenix, Arizona. They are touring the country in the interest of the Exchange Student Program.

The EINAR MICKELSON'S spent a weekend camping out at Cove State Park. FRED HARP was also there, but didn't get his limit of fish. JIM COWLING never did explain to me how he caught nine and one-half fish in the Bridal Veil Creek.

The engagement of Eva Lipscomb to LAVERNE FAGAN has been announced. They plan an August wedding. LEONARD VOLKMAN will be married in July.

Mr. & Mrs. BOB BIRD enjoyed the visit from her parents when they came from Colorado. Mr. & Mrs. John Cosbey of Long Beach, California, were recent visitors in the home of ELMER AYLES.

PETER GRAYMER spent a recent Sunday in Pendleton visiting his son. WESLEY ADAMS and some friends went fishing in Burnt Lake on the west slope of Mt. Hood. LEONARD VOLKMAN went swimming at Blue Lake.

EUGENE McMANUS is hightly elated at receiving top market price for 160 mink pelts sold in June. ARCHIE DAVIES says he doesn't mind being awaken by the hotrodders using the road in front of his house at Springdale at 2 o'clock in the morning, but he just can't go back to sleep. ED WENDLER is painting his house light and dark green. CHARLES GAYMON is recuperating at home after his recent sugery. PAUL DOOLEY is remodeling his house and MARVIN DHONE has moved to Coopey. RALPH LAMKE is nursing a cut thumb and LEO F.

(Continued on Page 2)

Bridal Veil
NEWS LETTER

VOL. V, No. 2   BRIDAL VEIL, OREGON   AUGUST, 1959

NEWS LETTER

Published on the 10th of each month by
Bridal Veil Lumber & Box Co.
Bridal Veil, Oregon

Editor . . . . Sara Mahn

GOVERNMENT HEADS — John Quincy Adams and Dwight Eisenhower are the only baldheaded presidents the United States has ever had.

——— 60 ———

Rips and Trims

(Continued from Page 8)

HARRY ADOLPH warns against bees. One flew in his eye while he was driving and disturbed him enough so that he had to go over the embankment to keep from hitting another car. He and his car received some damage. He hopes to have his car back as good as new in about three weeks. He seems to be recuperating fairly well and was back to work after just two days.

DOROTHY HARTSHORN was off work for a week to be with daughter, Sharron, when she had her tonsils taken out.

LEONARD VOLKMAN was married on July 10 and is now living in a house trailer.

That new white Volvo in the parking lot belongs to FRANCIS COOK and he seems to like it real well.

Have you heard about BERTHA DAVIS' hobby? FAY says she is raising Bantum chickens. She now has a rooster, two hens and ten chicks. ROLEY ZUMWALT has been rather busy keeping his raspberries picked. They were really nice berries.

BARBARA and FRED MICKELSON, with their Dad's help, traded their Ford for a yellow and green '54 Chevie. They think it runs much better than the Ford did.

Mr. and Mrs. LOUIS WILSON went out to Seaside to visit their son-in-law, Jack Case, who broke his leg in a logging accident.

Congratulations to all the parents of new arrivals. ROBERT FITZGERALD has a new daughter, Sheryl Lou, born on July 28, weighing 7 pounds and 2 ounces. For MARVIN DHONE a boy, Cleave Arron, born July 27 at 3:30 a.m., weighing 7 pounds and 4 ounces. ADE JONES has a new grandson, Danny Ray Leopard, born July 8.

If you thought the mill was hot during the hot days, you should have visited HIRAM LAYTON or LAWRENCE PETERSON working on the glue clamp. They had to have the steam on while gluing up luggage shook. It sure seemed at least twenty degrees hotter over there. At least it felt fairly comfortable in the rest of the mill after leaving there.

1959 SAFETY CHART

Month	Tot. Hourly Pd. Man Hrs.	Lost Time Accidents	Accident Freq.	Days Lost	Accident Severity
January	18,468	1	54.1	1	541
February	17,904	0	0	24	1340
March	12,994	0	0	22	1693
1st Qtr. 1959	49,366	1	20.3	47	952
April	16,596	0	0	21	1265
May	17,557	1	57.0	42	2392
June	18,735	0	0	44	2273
2nd Quarter	52,888	1	18.9	107	2023
TOTAL	102,254	2	19.6	154	1506

HOUSING

The annual rate of privately financed non-farm residential construction put in place has already peaked out, so the economists tell us, and has started a gradual decline over the past several months.

There appears to be a very definite "lead and lag" relationship between residential construction and the general level of business activity. In all cases during the past ten years, residential construction has changed direction, either up or down, from six to twelve months ahead of general business.

This is not necessarily a cause and effect relationship. It would be more accurate to say that this is a historical fact that may be of some value in predicting the future.

One of the major factors affecting residential building is the availability of mortgage money. And herein probably lies the main reason why the peaks and bottoms in the home building industry do not coincide with those of the general level of business activity.

In order for someone to borrow money, someone else must save money to loan. This is true regardless of who does the borrowing. Whether it be the Federal Government, the State, a city, a business or an individual, the money borrowed represents someone's savings.

When business expands, the demand for the use of people's savings becomes enormous. Businesses need more to finance larger inventories and bigger payrolls. Expansion and modernization plans are revived and dusted off.

Governments — federal, state and local — borrow to meet demands of the people for more government services.

Consumers also pile up a demand for credit for automobiles, refrigerators, "pay later" vacations and all the other items determined advertising can sell. In 1958 people actually reduced their installment debt, but the guessers now tell us that consumer debt will go up about five billion this year.

This is the kind of competition for funds the housing industry runs into when business is good. When short term loans at a good rate of interest are available, long term mortgage loans lose their romance for the saver and investor.

When general business is sluggish and the demand for credit falls, mortgage money becomes an attractive investment. With more money available for home construction, home building then picks up before general business. And this continues until other forms of investment become more attractive and the cycle is completed.

This is not to forecast an immediate or radical change in the housing business. Though the annual rate of construction is tapering off, it is tapering off from a high level.

Probably the most significant result of all this is that saving is more attractive now than it has been for sometime. And since the demand for credit is still building up, your savings will pay better in the future.

Len Kraft

––––––– 60 –––––––

Health and Welfare Coverage

All employees who worked the required number of hours in April and May will become eligible for Health and Welfare Coverage and will be covered on the first day of August, 1959. They must have worked the required hours in both months.

Additions: Gerald G. Carver, Leon C. Dunlap, Laverne R. Fagan, Robert L. Patrick, Robert Reischel, Willis Bowen.

Employees who did not work the required number of hours will become ineligible the same day. Deletions: Roger Blaine, Loren Hancock, Ronald Jackson, Theophile Van Hee, Sr., Ann Keller, Walter Keller.

Sons Join Fathe

Cowling Family

Did you know that there are fourteen fathers working for Bridal Veil Lumber and Box Company who have sons also working for the Company? There are also four mothers here who have sons working here and one mother who has a daughter working.

Pictured are two families who are on the Company payroll. The Cowling family — Jim is head filer, Lou is postmistress and telephone operator, Bob (on the left) works on the cut off line, and Tom (on the right) is tail off on the band saws. Bob and Tom are both college students working in the mill during summer vacation.

The Mickelson family — Einar is foreman of the crosswork department, Bunny is assistant postmistress and telephone operator, Barbara is working in the office, Fred is working on the cut off line, and son-in-law Dewayne Kilness (left in back) is working in the factory. Fred also is a student working here for the summer.

Other related employees are as follows:

Fathers & Mothers	Sons & Daughters
Leo F. Hageman	Leo C. Hageman Donald Hageman
Franklin Bowen	Donald Bowen Richard Bowen
Theophile Van Hee, Sr.	Theodore Van Hee Theophile Van Hee
Fredrick Bailey	Fredrick Bailey, Jr.

in Work at Mill

Fathers & Mothers	Sons & Daughters
Kenneth Catlin	Ronald Catlin
Verl Bird	Robert Bird
Pearl Cloe	Delbert Cloe
Fredrick Damerell	Ramon Damerell
Ward Dull	Gerald Dull
Lester Howell	Marvin Howell
Jarvis Kilness	Dewayne Kilness
Ralph Lamke	Larry Lamke
Fred Long	Robert Long
Lillie Landreth	James Yerion
Mira Nielson	Eldon Nielson
Gertrude Noble	Thelma Rowe
Walter Stolin	Gary Stolin

Brothers or brothers and sisters are: Dean and Harold Burkholder and Dorothy Hartshorn, Loren and Clem Hancock, Bob and Hiram Layton, Walter and Marvin Stolin and Ralph Taylor and Beulah Choate.

Husbands and wives are: Anna and Willis Bowen, Bertha and Fay Davis, Dorothy and Merrill Hartshorn, and Mabel and Stanley Hills.

Mickelson Family

Wedding Bells

Charles Edwin Kraft, son of Mr. and Mrs. Leonard Kraft, and Jacqueline Helen Howard, daughter of Mr. and Mrs. Fred W. Howard, were married on July 25 in St. Peter's Episcopal Church. The Rev. Kent L. Haley officiated.

The couple are making their home in Eugene where he plans to continue his college courses.

August Birthdays

Many Happy Returns of the Day!

Kenneth Burkholder
Archie Davies
Marvin Dhone
Ralph Ellis
Robert Fitzgerald, Jr.
Lester Howell
Jarvis Kilness
Ralph Lamke
Theodore Van Hee
Theophile Van Hee

——— 60 ———

Growth of Taxes

The Petroleum Institute reports that taxes on gasoline alone brought more money into state and federal coffers in 1957 than the total revenue collected by the federal government from all tax sources in the first 88 years of this nation's history.

State gasoline taxes ran to $2.9 billion and federal taxes added more than $1.6 billion more. This contrasts with only $1.6 billion in total federal tax receipts for the period extending up to the Civil War.

New Employees

Leslie Nixon

Virgil McNatt

Donald King

Seniority List

1. Dull, Ward E. 5-18-36
2. McCredie, Ralph H. . 8-27-36
3. Davis, D. Fay 3-22-37
4. Jackson, Marvin T. . .4-8-37
5. Stolin, Walter F. . . . 5-11-37
6. Bowen, Franklin M. 8-19-37
7. Crouser, Fred 8-30-37
8. Bird, Verl W. 9-20-37
9. Taylor, Ralph L. . . .11-22-37
10. Hanson, Theodore N. 4-18-38
11. Van Orsow, Joseph M. 4-22-38
12. Dunken, J. Delbert . .7-18-38
13. Meyer, Kenneth L. . . 9-16-40
14. Hartshorn, Merrill . . 1-8-41
15. Harp, Fred 5-21-41
16. Mickelson Einar E. . 7-1-41
17. Roberts, Jerald G. . . . 9-8-41
18. Ellis, Ralph 10-9-41
19. Latourell, Clifford . . .3-23-42
20. Vogel, Harold A. . . . 3-25-42
21. Nielson, Eldon F. . . 4-21-42
22. Davis, Bertha M. . . 5-6-42
23. Bowen, Anna 9-30-42
24. Hartshorn, Dorothy . .7-14-42
25. Hageman, Leo F. . . 7-14-43
26. Yerion, Lillie P. . . . 7-19-43
27. Cloe, Pearl P.. 11-12-43
28. Britton, Thomas C. . .12-30-43
29. Nielson, Mira J. . . . 1-23-44
30. Litton, Durward 5-9-44
31. Peterson, Lawrence . .9-24-45
32. Hunt, Howard G. . . . 10-1-45
33. Smazal, Lawrence A. .10-2-45
34. Stolin, Marvin J. . . . 3-28-46
35. Van Hee, Theophile V. 4-17-46
36. Kendrick, James B. . .5-13-46
37. Woodard, Mary R. . . 6-3-46
38. Jacobson, Harold R. . .9-16-46
39. Choate, Beulah 10-7-46
40. Layton, Hiram 11-13-46
41. Lofstedt, Clarence. . .1-16-47
42. Murray, George . . . 4-21-47
43. Jones, Martha A. . . . 5-14-47
44. Van Hee, Theodore V. 9-9-47
45. Rowe, Thelma Y. . . .11-12-47
46. Hills, Mabel M. 1-14-48
47. Hills Stanley B. 1-15-51
48. Van Hee, Theophile, Sr. 2-27-51
49. Schneringer, Raymond 10-8-51
50. Walker, Homer F.. . . 10-9-51
51. Eveland, Roy D. 10-15-51
52. Anderson, Lester W. .5-19-52
53. Howell, Lester, B. . . .6-23-52
54. Hutchinson, Earl . . .6-23-52
55. Van Buskirk, Norman 7-28-52
56. Hancock, Loren 9-2-52
57. Long, Fred M.. 9-9-52
58. Cote, Joseph 9-10-52
59. Adolph, Harry 9-22-52
60. Willms, John G. 9-29-52
61. Potter, Eugene H. . . .10-28-52
62. Davies, Archie L. . . . 4-1-53
63. Bissell, Louis W. . . . 5-1-53

64. Layton, Bob 5-28-53
65. Ayles, Elmer L. 8-4-53
66. Gross, Elden 8-27-53
67. Burkholder, Harold . . 5-4-54
68. Kinonen, Edsel 5-4-54
69. Kilness, Jarvis 6-2-54
70. Zumwalt, Roley 9-7-54
71. Wilson, Louis A. 9-20-54
72. Rees, David 9-23-54
73. Morgan, Roland B. . .12-14-54
74. Polzel, Leslie D. . . . 1-5-55
75. Gaymon, Charles N. . 3-29-55
76. Pitts, Orien 4-13-55
77. Adams, Wesley A. . . . 5-9-55
78. Dooley, Paul D. 6-1-55
79. Hageman, Leo C. . . . 6-1-55
80. Hancock, Clem A. . . .8-15-55
81. Wendler, Ed L. 9-6-55
82. Jacobson, Rodney . . 3-11-57
83. Fitzgerald, Robert, Jr.3-15-57
84. Damerell, Fred 7-2-57
85. Catlin, Ronald E. 7-2-57
86. Cloe, Delbert P. 7-22-57
87. Barnes, Alfred 7-22-57
88. Catlin, Kenneth V. . . .7-22-57
89. Dhone, Marvin N. . . . 8-12-57
90. Craig, Kenneth O. . . .9-10-57
91. Reischel, Robert W. . . 5-1-58
92. Oden, Floyd F. 5-5-58
93. Jacobson, Charles D.. .5-6-58
94. Jones, Walton G. 5-6-58
95. Dull, Gerald V. 5-8-58
96. Volkman, Leonard F. . .5-19-58
97. Graymer, Peter J. . . . 5-19-58
98. Cook, Francis 6-26-58
99. Bird, Robert K. 7-24-58
100. Smith, Elvin E. 7-28-58
101. Dunlap, Leon C. 4-14-59
102. Carver, Gerald G. . . . 5-12-59
103. Patrick, Robert L. . . .5-12-59
104. Fagan, Laverne R. 5-12-59
105. Fox, Edward R. 5-19-59
106. Bowen, Donald M. . . . 5-20-59
107. McManus, Eugene F. . .5-25-59
108. Mickelson, Einar F. . .6-8-59
109. Bowen, Richard L. . . .6-10-59
110. Howell, Marvin 6-10-59
111. Long, Robert A. 6-10-59
112. Lamke, Larry 6-11-59
113. Bailey, Fredrick, Jr. . 6-15-59
114. Darnerell, Ramon A.. .6-15-59
115. Hageman, Donald . . . 6-15-59
116. Cowling, Robert 6-16-59
117. Yerion, James 6-16-59
118. Cowling, Thomas . . . 6-17-59
119. Watts, Paul A. 6-18-59
120. Irish, Dennis 6-18-59
121. Brenneke, Leroy 6-22-59
122. Papin, Roy L. 6-22-59
123. Stolin, Gary 6-24-59
124. Dawson, Clifford D. . .6-25-59
125. Russell, Robert 6-25-59
126. Wilson, Dean R. 6-25-59

Rips and Trims

The many sun burns and beautiful tans are proof that we have been having some real nice summer weather. However, it hasn't all been just the right temperature. There have been some cool days as well as some extra hot days. But on the whole, it has been very comfortable. It should make us feel very fortunate when we read in the papers of temperatures well over the hundred mark.

At this time of year fishing is always a big topic of conversation. LARRY and RALPH LAMKE say that the steelhead are biting pretty well in the Columbia. They recently brought home seven. MARVIN STOLIN caught an 18 pound salmon out on the coast. MARVIN VAN ORSOW caught his limit of trout out at Craine Prairie. Many others have also been fishing, but some didn't have such good luck.

Vacationing were: CLIFF LATOURELL at home, MIRA NIELSON at home, PETER GRAYMER visiting friends and relatives in Oklahoma, and EINAR MICHELSON fishing somewhere.

Centennial Activities are still popular. ELDON NIELSON drove his Ford in the recent Milwaukie Parade and ALFRED BARNES rode in the Master's Parade wearing his new cowboy boots. He didn't say whether he had a ten gallon hat to go with them. He is still finding time to attend the Dale Carnegie course he started a couple months ago and is advising everyone to take it. He says it is very interesting and educational.

LEON DUNLAP moved his house trailer out to Gladstone and lived on the camp grounds while attending the Oregon Seventh-Day Adventist Camp Meeting. He said the meetings were unusually good this year.

The newness still hasn't worn off that new boat of WILLIS and ANNA BOWENS'. They take it up the river for a ride every Sunday. It will probably be lonesome about the eleventh of August (tomorrow) when they leave on vacation to visit a son and daughter in Los Angeles and San Diego. Willis says he isn't really looking forward to driving down there. He has been to L.A. before.

James Hambrick, son of Mr. and Mrs. CLYDE HAMBRICK, is now in the Army and is in boot camp at Fort Ord. He will be home on leave the latter part of August. In the meantime, Clyde is keeping busy getting some screens made for his house in Gresham and also some screens for the Brothers House at St. Luke. He doesn't seem to like all the different sizes. He thinks it would be easier if at least two of them were the same size.

GEORGE MURRAY has been entertaining guests at his home; among them were his Uncle and Aunt from Columbia, B.C. HOWARD HUNT recently spent some time down at Newport. ED WENDLER's son with his four D's (Dean, Diane, Debbie and David) came home from Colorado for a visit. After a brief stay they took Ed's wife back with them. She planned to meet her brother and go with him to Oklahoma for a visit. So Ed is batching. TED HANSON was also chief cook and bottle washer for the eight days his wife was in the hospital for surgery. She is home again now and seems to be doing fine.

A Bee Did It

(Continued on Page 2)

Bridal Veil

NEWS LETTER

VOL. V, No. 3   BRIDAL VEIL, OREGON   SEPTEMBER, 1959

NEWS LETTER

Published on the 10th of each month by
Bridal Veil Lumber & Box Co.
Bridal Veil, Oregon

Editor . . . . Sara Mahn

September Birthdays

Many Happy Returns of the Day!

Joseph Cote
Lula Cowling
Merrill Hartshorn
Howard Hunt
Adrian Jones
Edsel Kinonen
Leonard Kraft
Floyd Oden
Lawrence Smazal
Roley Zumwalt

——— 91 ———

From Bad to Worst

Those economic terms really aren't so hard to understand. A "readjustment" is when your neighbor loses his job. A "recession" is when you lose your job. A "depression" is when your wife loses her job.

Health and Welfare Coverage

All employees who worked the required number of hours in April and May will become eligible for Health and Welfare Coverage and will be covered on the first day of September, 1959. They must have worked the required hours in both months.

Additions: Frederick C. Bailey, Jr., Donald M. Bowen, Richard Bowen, Robert L. Cowling, Thomas J. Cowling, Joel W. Crouch, Ramon Damerell, Edward R. Fox, Donald Hageman, Loren H. Hancock, Leo C. Hageman, Marvin Howell, Larry L. Lamke, Robert Long, Eugene F. McManus, Einar Fred Mickelson, James M. Yerion, Barbara J. Mickelson.

Employees who did not work the required number of hours will become ineligible the same day. Deletions: Edsel E. Kinonen.

——— 91 ———

Worse Than War

In nearly four years of battle during World War II, the U.S. Marines lost 19,733 men killed, 67,207 wounded. Last year motor accidents in the U.S. killed 37,000 crippled 1,300,000.

1959 SAFETY CHART

Month	Tot. Hourly Pd. Man Hrs.	Lost Time Accidents	Accident Freq.	Days Lost	Accident Severity
January	18,468	1	54.1	1	541
February	17,904	0	0	24	1340
March	12.994	0	0	22	1693
1st Qtr. 1959	49,366	1	20.3	47	952
April	16,596	0	0	21	1265
May	17,557	1	57.0	42	2392
June	18,735	0	0	44	2273
2nd Quarter	52,888	1	18.9	107	2023
July	22.353	0	0	23	1029
Total	124,607	2	16.1	177	1420

Safety Movies Scheduled

Our Safety Committee has made arrangements with Mr. W. G. Thorsell, Safety Representative of the Accident Prevention Division of the State Industrial Accident Commission to put on a series of six safety movies.

Plans have been completed to show a short ten to fifteen minute movie on the third Monday of each month. Projection equipment will be set in the store building and benches will be provided so that lunch can be eaten during the show.

The first movie "Falls Are No Fun" will be shown at 11:40 a.m. Monday, September 21. This is listed as "a brand new, laugh provoking cartoon type" of safety film that should prove entertaining as well as instructive.

While attendance at these shows is not required, the State Industrial Accident Commission and the Safety Committee hopes for a good attendance.

Schedule

September 21, 1959	Falls Are No Fun	10 min. black & white
October 19, 1959	An Accident Happens to Sam	13 min. black & white
November 16, 1959	Stop the Fire Thief	13 min. black & white
December 21, 1959	Foresight Not Hindsight	13 min. black & white
January 18, 1960	How to Avoid Muscle Strain	13 min. black & white
February 15, 1960	You Can Take it With You	15 min. black & white

——— 91 ———

Committee Report

Since the Safety Committee reinstituted regular monthly meetings starting April 30, 1959, a total of thirty-nine safety suggestions have been turned in by members of the Committee. Of thirty-one suggestions turned in prior to the last meeting on August 20, a total of twenty-two unsafe conditions have been corrected for a batting average of 71 per cent.

——— 91 ———

Safety Committee

Marvin Jackson, Chairman
Mel Mallinson, Secretary

Leo Hagemen   Eldon Nielson
Jim Kendrick

It Puzzles Me!

Two men have an eight-quart jug of wine. They wish to divide it equally. Besides the eight-quart jug with wine, they have two empty jugs. One jug has a five-quart capacity, and the other jug has a three-quart capacity. By pouring the wine from one jug to another, each man ended with exactly four quarts of wine. How were the men able to accomplish this?

(Answer next month)

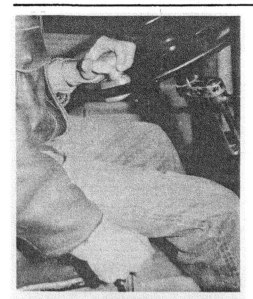

Busy A

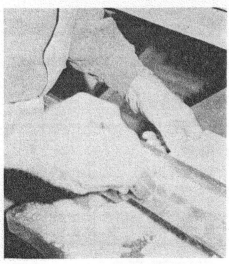

t Work

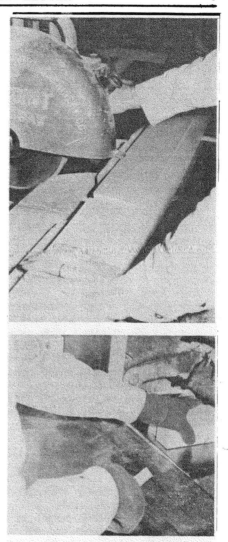

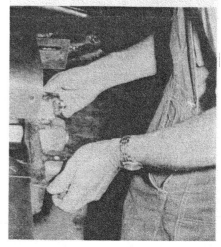

Not Santa Claus

but a Sneak Thief

Inflation is not caused by a mysterious virus which we cannot find, nor by nature's violence, like a hurricane, which we cannot control. We COULD stop inflation — or, to put it another way, inflation could be stopped if we really wanted to. Then why not?

Though they complain bitterly about rising prices, many millions of Americans don't really want inflation stopped. That fact is the greatest single handicap in the fight to halt this growing menace to our nation's security.

In an interesting analysis of the inflation problem, the family economics bureau of the Northwestern National Life Insurance Company says a plain case of mistaken identity is at the bottom of this surprising reluctance to deal with inflation. A great many people confuse inflation with genuine prosperity. But the mistake can be disastrous, for inflation actually distorts and eventually destroys genuine prosperity.

The average standard of living has risen about 50 per cent since 1939. This is not due to our having four times as many dollars in circulation, but because we are producing some 50 per cent more goods and services.

Since 1939, our total output of all kinds of consumer goods and services has approximately doubled. Meanwhile, our population has increased by only one-third. The net result is that we are now producing half again as much goods and services for each individual American.

But money has increased much faster than goods. There are now twice as many dollars for each unit of goods as there were in 1939. So — and there's no way of getting around this — each dollar can now buy only half as much goods.

Most working people's money income has gone up. But retired persons, pensioned workers, widows and orphans, anyone dependent on fixed or nearly fixed incomes not only have missed sharing in the benefits of greater production —

Wedding Bells

Tom Dull, son of Mr. and Mrs. Ward Dull, and Sandra Blackstone were married on August 8 in San Francisco.

Mr. and Mrs. Dull and his mother, Mrs. Irving, were present for the wedding.

Tom is stationed at Hamilton Air Force Base.

———— 91 ————

Ulcers are the result of mountain climbing over mole-hills.

but many have been impoverished as inflation robbed them of buying power.

The real gains have come from more efficient production of the goods and services that actually make up our American standard of living.

Inflation, says the insurance analysis, is merely an undesireable hanger-on, "promoting inefficiency, waste, extravagance, the cost-price spiral, speculation, and excessive debt."

But inflation is difficult to stop when millions of voters regard it as they would a genial, generous Santa Claus — instead of recognizing it as the sneak thief it actually is.

For Better Health

The district nurse of the Multnomah County Division of Public Health has advised us that our employees can obtain Polio, Diphtheria, Tetanus and Whooping Cough immunizations, Smallpox Vaccinations and Chest X-Rays through the clinics as scheduled below.

Schedule of Clinics

POLIO Immunization:
Children and adults - Every Thursday 1:30 to 4:30 (no appointment needed).

DIPHTHERIA, TETANUS & WHOOPING COUGH Immunization and SMALLPOX VACCINATION:
Children from age 3 months to school age - 1st and 4th Wednesday of each month - 9:00 to 11:00 a.m. (no appointment needed)

Above Clinics at
Health and Education Building
12240 N. E. Glisan Street

TUBERCULOSIS:
Tuberculin Tests - Wednesday - 1 to 4 p.m. Chest X-Ray - 21 years of age and over (no appointment needed).
Tuesday . . . . . . 9:00 to 1:00
Wednesday . . . . . 2:00 to 4:00
Thursday . . . . 12 noon to 1:00
Friday . . . . 9:00 to 12 noon

at City County Survey Center
830 S. W. 10th

——— 91 ———

Our Apologies

Through error, the name of Harold Jacobson, father, and sons Charles and Rodney were omitted from the list in the article "Sons Join Fathers in Work at Mill" last month. We are very sorry for this mistake.

Rips and Trims

(Con't from page 8)

Others who were on vacation were: LOUIS BISSELL, HARRY ADOLPH, FRANKLIN BOWEN, RALPH LAMKE, KENNETH CATLIN and LESTER HOWELL.

Several have asked me where I spent my vacation. For those interested, we went up to Canada, and drove up the Fraser Canyon, then went up to Banff and Lake Louise. We enjoyed our trip in spite of all the rain.

CLARENCE LOFSTEDT's twin brother came up from California for a visit and they attended a family reunion near Tacoma.

ROY EVELAND spent a recent weekend at Seattle visiting relatives.

PEARL and DELBERT CLOE made a rush trip to Corvallis for the funeral of Pearl's wife's brother.

ED WENDLER entertained his sister and brother-in-law, Mr. and Mrs. C. E. Wagner, from St. Louis, by taking them out to the coast and up to Mt. Hood.

Mrs. ELMER AYLES brother, Sgt. Ronald E. Moore and family from McChord Air Force Base were visitors at the Ayles' home.

MARTHA JONES is back on the job again after her illness. She and her family attended a Family Day celebration at Troutcreek Dam near Springdale the last Sunday of August.

RODNEY JACOBSON has returned to his post of duty in the Army.

LEO C. HAGEMAN has begun another five months of schooling. He is looking forward to an overseas assignment when he completes this course.

WALTON JONES said he helped the squirrels pick up fir cones while he was laid off recently. He was able to make about $15 a day at it.

Have you heard THEODORE VAN HEE, DAVID REES and BOB REISCHEL talking about their trip to Reno? Ask them about it.

Thanks to ELDON NIELSEN, who was ready with a camera when the giraffes were in our parking lot enroute to the Portland Zoo.

Rips and Trims

It's time again to let you know what the other employees have been doing recently.

First, congratulations to Mr. and Mrs. THEOPHILE V. VAN HEE. It's a son, Toby B., weighing 10 pounds 3-1/2 ounces and 24" long. They say he has a lot of hair.

ANNA and WILLIS BOWEN spent their vacation in California, visiting son, Kenneth and his family in San Diego and daughter, Mrs. Art Christman and family in Los Angeles. They enjoyed their trip and the cool pleasant weather they had there. Willis did say that you can easily get lost down there as there have been many changes in the roads recently.

GEORGE MURRAY stayed home during his vacation, due to the illness of his wife.

JERRY ROBERTS went to Oklahoma and also visited his brother in Cheyenne, Wyoming. He came back through Yellowstone National Park before the earthquake arrived.

WESLEY ADAMS enjoys working so much that he spent his vacation working on his house, the preacher's house and his mother's house (which is at Goldendale, Washington). He also found time to do some work in his garden.

Giraffes for the Zoo

FRED HARP went down by the Rogue River and back up the coast for a nice vacation. He is now excited about a visit with his sister from Iowa. This is their first visit in eighteen years.

LAWRENCE SMAZAL went to Yakima on his vacation. Have you seen the horse that his daughter Bobbi won in the drawing at the St. Paul Rodeo?

CLYDE HAMBRICK was real pleased to have his son Jim home during his vacation. Jim has just completed his boot camp at Fort Ord and now is back taking a course in Business Administration. Clyde did go up to Puget Sound and San Juan Island.

LLOYD DeMAIN went to the coast to do some fishing, but it rained. He returned home early to recuperate from the first part of his vacation.

FRED DAMERELL went up to British Columbia in Canada and took in the Expedition in Vancouver and also a Fashion Show.

MARVIN STOLIN took a very leisurely vacation in California and at Crater Lake. He said it was the first time he has had time to average traveling only about 120 miles a day.

DELBERT DUNKEN entertained his children from Nebraska and California while vacationing.

EINAR MICHELSON said fishing was good during his vacation, but not so good now.

(Con't on page 7)

Bobbi & Tony

Bridal Veil
NEWSLETTER

VOL. V, No. 4   BRIDAL VEIL, OREGON   OCTOBER, 1959

NEWS LETTER

Published on the 10th of each month by
Bridal Veil Lumber & Box Co.
Bridal Veil, Oregon

Editor . . . . Sara Mahn

Laugh You May — But Please Obey

Unless there have been some recent changes, the U. S. still has some odd laws on the books. For example: A law in Detroit regulates the size of wheat cakes. A law in Massachusetts forbids anyone to lounge on the shelves of a bakery.

A Nebraska statute forbids barbers to eat onions between 7 a.m. and 7 p.m. In Winchester, Mass., a local regulation says that a young girl cannot dance on a tightrope except in church. And a law in Ohio declares that any animal on the street after dark shall prominently display a red tail-light.

—— 122 ——

There's a line on the ocean which by crossing you can lose a day. There's one on the highway where you can do even better.

Our Cover

Do you recognize it? It is Mt. Hood as seen from Larch Mountain late in the afternoon.

The secret of a good life is not in doing what one likes to do, but in liking what one has to do.

—— 122 ——

Suggest Safety

There have been a number of suggestions made by the Safety Committee, most of which have been carried out to make our mill a safer place to work.

Those who saw the safety film last month may have noticed unsafe conditions in our mill which they also saw in the film. If so, please make your suggestions on correcting these conditions to a member of the Committee or put it in the suggestion box.

The film for this month "An Accident Happens to Sam" will be shown on October 19. Watch this picture and see how many of the same conditions shown exist in our mill and then make your suggestions for correcting them.

1959 SAFETY CHART

Month	Tot. Hourly Pd. Man Hrs.	Lost Time Accidents	Accident Freq.	Days Lost	Accident Severity
January	18,468	1	54.1	1	541
February	17,904	0	0	24	1340
March	12,994	0	0	22	1693
1st Qtr. 1959	49,366	1	20.3	47	952
April	16,596	0	0	21	1265
May	17,557	1	57.0	42	2392
June	18,735	0	0	44	2273
2nd Quarter	52,888	1	18.9	107	2023
July	22,353	0	0	23	1029
August	17,804	0	0	21	1180
Total	142,311	2	14.1	198	1391

The Road Ahead

The story has been circulating for some time that our company was planning to leave the millwork business and operate a cut-up factory.

The story is true.

Since the story is true, why the delay in making the thing official?

Many times plans are made, but in the many discussions before adoption, these plans may be abandoned. In our case, changing the product of the plant constitutes a major change of direction. And such a major change is a matter properly coming before the Board of Directors.

At the semi-annual meeting of the Board, held October 2 at Bridal Veil, the Board reviewed the decisions made to date. Under the circumstances prevailing, the Board agreed that this action appears to be the proper course. The matter was put to vote and unanimously adopted.

In view of the pace of residential building in the past couple of years, it may seem inconsistent to abandon the millwork business at this time.

As a matter of fact, our own physical business in 1958 exceeded 1957, and 1959 is running well ahead of 1958. At the same time, profit margins have disappeared.

Sales prices during 1959, on millwork items, have finally crawled back up to where they were in the early fifties. In those days we were able to earn a small profit, even with our hand-made millwork.

As of today, lumber is selling for $5.00 to $10.00 a thousand more than in the early '50's. And of course, there have been several rounds of wage increases since then.

So, in spite of the some $100,000.00 spent on new equipment and improvements since then, we have not been able to keep pace competitively.

It is interesting to note in this connection that Diamond-Gardner, located at Chico, California, who entered the frame business shortly after we did, have also and independently decided to abandon the frame business. This is an integrated operation, with their own sawmill to back them up and a somewhat lower wage scale.

It appears that by converting to cut stock, we can, among other things, level off our production to eliminate, within the limits of available lumber, the violent fluctuation in the volume of business handled from month to month. The swing from 75 employees in the winter months to 140 employees during the summer rush is not only an expensive one for the company, but also works a hardship on those who are depending upon us for a livelihood. We should end up using fewer people, but with steadier employment for those we do use.

One fact we cannot escape: the people who will be buying our cut stock for conversion to millwork will be doing the conversion at wage scales far below ours. Middle-western wage scales run from 50¢ to 60¢ per hour less than ours for entry jobs to as much as a $1.00 less than ours for skilled workers.

This is rather rough competition.

To us it seems to be a logical move to do the cutting in the West and the machining in the East.

We can set up an efficient cutting department and eliminate the freight on the 30% cutting loss. Our customers, on the other hand, can finish the machining and do the marketing far more efficiently than we can.

One efficiency we hope to gain should arise from selecting cuttings from a number of customers that will work out best from our lumber. This should help us to keep from cutting our lumber for specific items we do not wish to make but which our millwork file forces us to make.

This isn't going to be easy. Business is by its very nature competitive. There are plenty of competitors eager to knock us off. We have to be good.

For example, Weyerhauser at Klamath Falls operates the type of shop we are contemplating. Their wage scales average 5% less than ours, and on individual rates run as much as 40¢ per hour below us.

Weyerhauser's cut shop has a guaranteed source of supply. Certainly they

(Con't on page 6)

Are You

Perhaps you were on the absent list and not on the job at some time during the last few months. Was there a way that you could have prevented the absence?

Many absences could be prevented by a little extra effort on our part. Of course, when we are sick it is best to stay home and recover as quickly as possible. However, we should remember to do everything possible to keep from getting sick. Maybe you were among the missing who had the flu. Had you remembered to take time to get your flu shot? Or perhaps you thought the shot was too expensive. Have you stopped to consider the amount you lost in wages the several days you were absent?

Picture?

The average wage rate paid in our mill is $18.08 a day. If you were absent only 5 per cent or 13 days of your working time, you lost approximately $226.00 during the past twelve months. How many shots would that buy?

Do you realize what your absence means to the Company? When you are not on the job, someone else has to do your work. That means that some job is left undone, and perhaps our customer has to wait a few days longer to receive his car. Those extra days may cause his customers to buy from his competitor, and so he loses a customer because you were not on the job.

Are you doing everything within your power to stay in the picture?

Retired

Earl Hutchison exchanged his job at Bridal Veil Lumber and Box Company on September 30 for a life of relaxation, fishing and hunting. He left October 1 for a hunting trip in the John Day area.

Earl came to Bridal Veil on June 23, 1952 and has spent much of his time working on the cut-off line. He was previously employed by Wood Specialties Company in Portland.

We hope he will have many years to enjoy his retirement.

——— 122 ———

The Road Ahead

(Con't from page 3)

have vast resources of both money and technical assistance. They will not be a pushover by any means.

On the other hand, we have some advantages over Weyerhaeuser. For one thing, we are smaller, and it is easier for us to co-ordinate sales and production. When Weyerhaeuser makes a mistake, it is a whopper.

Our problems, then, are real. But not insurmountable. We have faced dark days before, as when the box business collapsed almost overnight. It will require the hearty and sincere cooperation of all.

Len Kraft

Health and Welfare Coverage

All employees who worked the required number of hours in June and July will become eligible for Health and Welfare Coverage and will be covered on the first day of October, 1959. They must have worked the required hours in both months.

Additions: Leroy H. Brenneke, Dennis Irish, Donald B. King, Virgil McNatt, Leslie M. Nixon, Gary Stolin, Paul A. Watts, and Dean R. Wilson.

Employees who did not work the required number of hours will become ineligible the same day. Deletions: Joel W. Crouch, Edward R. Fox, Charles N. Gaymon, Donald Westlake, and Jack V. Westlake.

——— 122 ———

Be a Good Neighbor

The United Good Neighbors Campaign, formerly known as the United Fund, started its drive on September 22.

As you know, the United Good Neighbors is an organization established to combine fund-raising appeals. There are 72 agencies, including the United Cerebral Palsy added this year, that receive their funds from this Campaign.

Remember to be a good neighbor and give your share to the United Good Neighbors Campaign.

——— 122 ———

It wouldn't be so bad if your take home pay stayed there.

——— 122 ———

October Birthdays

Many Happy Returns of the Day!

Wesley Adams
Kenneth Craig
Ward Dull
Peter Graymer
Sara Mahn
Jacob Van Orsow

It Puzzles Me!

A man has an old fashioned balance scale, but only four weights with which he can weigh all weights from one pound up to and including 40 pounds. One of the four weights is a one pound weight. What are the weights of the other three?

Solution for Last Month:

Step 1 – Fill 5 qt. jug from 8 qt.

Step 2 – Fill 3 qt. jug from 5 qt.

Step 3 – Empty 3 qt. jug into 8 qt. jug.

Step 4 – Pour the 2 qts. of wine left in 5 qt. jug into 3 qt. jug.

Step 5 – Fill the 5 qt. jug again from the 8 qt. jug.

Step 6 – Fill the 3 qt. jug from 5 qt. jug. Now one man has a 5 qt. jug with his 4 qts. of wine, and the other man has a 3 qt. jug with 3 qts. and an 8 qt. jug with 1 qt.

Rips and Trims

It is easy to tell by the recent weather that Fall is here, which means that Winter is not far off.

October opens deer season again and many of Bridal Veil employees were hunting on the first week-end. Among them were JIM COWLING, BERTHA and FAY DAVIS, RALPH and LARRY LAMKE, MARVIN VAN ORSOW, and EINAR and FRED MICKELSON.

ANNA and WILLIS BOWEN spent a recent week-end over at Pendleton for the Round-Up. TED VAN HEE went up on Larch Mountain pigeon hunting. He brought back 16, which he said were just one meal. MIRA NIELSON took her husband to the Veteran's Hospital in Vancouver. He seems to be getting along fine now. FRED HARP went up to Puyallup, Washington, to visit his mother and sister. MARVIN VAN ORSOW went fishing in the rain up at Crane Prairie and caught his limit. RALPH LAMKE went fishing down on the coast but then had to come home to catch fish. MARVIN STOLIN caught two salmon out at the coast. DURWARD LITTON spent a part of his vacation on the coast and in Eastern Oregon. He caught a lot of fish and said that the weather was real nice.

JIM KENDRICK spent a couple of days of his vacation on the coast in the rain. He seems to think that the mountains will be nicer next time. GERTRUDE NOBLE, with her daughter and three grandchildren spent their vacation in Bend and at Crater Lake camping out.

TED HANSON'S brother-in-law, Carl Johnson, was injured at Georgia Pacific Mills in Springfield, Oregon, when a flashfire occurred while he was eating lunch.

MARTHA JONES' daughter, Marylin, has returned to the Roecker Private Day School in Portland.

BERTHA DAVIS recently attended a meeting of Eastern Multnomah Pioneers in the Grange Hall in Corbett. This organization has been meeting for the past 43 years.

ARCHIE DAVIES is a proud grandpa. It was a girl, Cindi Lee, born September 8 at 8:20 p.m. to Mr. and Mrs. Bruce

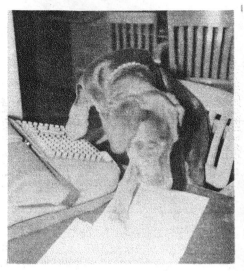

"Office Mascot"

A. Young. She weighed 6 pounds 10-1/2 ounces.

HARRY ADOLPH has his car back again after his recent accident. It looks much different from the way it looked in the picture last month.

Ramon Damerell, son of FRED DAMERELL, is back at Portland State to continue his education.

HAROLD VOGEL and LARRY SMAZAL'S niece and her husband from Wisconsin were recent visitors at Bridal Veil, while on their honeymoon. Mr. and Mrs. Clarence Beatty, brother of Mrs. PEARL CLOE, were also visiting from Washougal, Washington. MARTHA JONES and family recently entertained at their home Mr. and Mrs. Earl Christianson and son Tommy from Portland.

Bob Bird, son of VERL BIRD, and former employee of Bridal Veil Lumber and Box Company is now employed by the Kinzua Lumber Company in Kinzua, Oregon.

Have you heard FRED MICKELSON singing or whistling "Anchors Aweigh?" He reported for induction in the Navy on October 7.

The office mascot is Tippy and belongs to Doc Nelson, local agent for Union Pacific Railroad Company. Tippy likes to visit the office, especially during lunch time.

Bridal Veil NEWSLETTER

VOL. V, No. 5   BRIDAL VEIL, OREGON   NOVEMBER, 1959

NEWS LETTER

Published on the 10th of each month by
Bridal Veil Lumber & Box Co.
Bridal Veil, Oregon

Editor . . . . Sara Mahn

Our Cover

This picture was taken on the Oregon Coast on a private beach near Otis Junction.

Health and Welfare

Coverage

All employees who worked the required number of hours in July and August will become eligible for Health and Welfare Coverage and will be covered on the first day of November, 1959. They must have worked the required hours in both months.

Additions: Charles N. Gaymon, Rodney Jacobson.

Employees who did not work the required number of hours will become ineligible the same day. Deleteions: Dennis Irish, Donald King, Robert Long, Eugene McManus, Robert L. Patrick, Elvin Smith, Norman Van Buskirk, Dean R. Wilson.

November Birthdays

Many Happy

Returns of the Day!

Harry Adolph
Alfred Barnes
Verl Bird
Louis Bissell
Harold Burkholder
Ronald Catlin
Fay Davis
Clem Hancock
Fred Harp
Kenneth Meyer

————43————

"My wife has been nursing a grouch all week."
"Do you feel better now?"

1959 SAFETY CHART

Month	Tot. Hourly Pd. Man Hrs.	Lost Time Accidents	Accident Freq.	Days Lost	Accident Severity
January	18,468	1	54.1	1	541
February	17,904	0	0	24	1340
March	12,994	0	0	22	1693
1st Qtr. 1959	49,366	1	20.3	47	952
April	16,596	0	0	21	1265
May	17,557	1	57.0	42	2392
June	18,735	0	0	44	2273
2nd Quarter	52,888	1	18.9	107	2023
July	22,353	0	0	23	1029
August	17,804	0	0	21	1180
September	17,706	1	56.5	29	1638
3rd Quarter	57,863	1	17.3	73	1262
TOTAL	160,117	3	18.7	227	1418

Competition

In some quarters the idea prevails that an industry prospers and makes a profit simply because it is in business.

Nothing could be farther from the truth.

It is no more true of a manufacturing industry than it is of a filling station. As I understand it, it is easy to lose money operating a filling station.

Bridal Veil has just left the millwork business because of our apparent inability to remain competitive. Now we are engaged in another approach to the lumber conversion business. Whether we are successful will depend upon our ability to compete with others with the same idea. Whether we are successful will determine our ability to buy materials and supplies, provide employment and sell our product.

For whatever consolation there is in it, we are not alone in our troubles. The profitable era of scarcity, artificial and otherwise, has given way to new and more demanding times. In most markets, normalcy, so to speak, has returned. Competition, both at home and abroad, has grown fierce.

Domestic steel finds itself beset not only by plastics and aluminum, but also by the mounting flow of imported metal.

Alpha Portland Cement, one of the leading concerns in the industry, laments that it is losing customers on the east coast to a cheaper foreign product which is every bit as good as its own.

A recent survey by a leading business daily discloses the remarkable gains made by imports in department and specialty stores and mail order houses.

Competition has been called the life-blood of trade. In this country it has also turned to be a powerful antidote for inflated prices and costs.

Inflated prices and costs sparked the decision made by National Homes, one of our country's larger home prefabricators, to use all aluminum sash and frame starting the first of the year.

The lessons to be learned are clear. It has been estimated that housing starts in 1960 will run well behind 1959 — as much as ten percent. Somebody is going to get hurt in the scramble. The efficient will prosper and grow. The inefficient will fall by the wayside.

Your management pledges its best efforts in the struggle for survival. We are betting that you are behind us all the way.

— Len Kraft

Many Heart Beats

Make a Week Day

Have you any idea how many times your heart beats during an average 8-hour day? A study shows it's about 63,894 times. During an ordinary 8-hour period of sleep, it "idles" along with an average of about 50,357 beats — a load reduction of 13,537 beats.

Awake or asleep, your heart expends a tremendous amount of energy. That is why it is essential to get enough sleep each day to avoid building up fatigue and putting extra strain on this hard working muscle machine.

Americans Spend

Billions for Fun

Never before have so many people spent so much money having so much fun, the American Investor reports.

Americans today have an average of 1040 more hours yearly in which to dispose of the $32 billion they spend for recreation alone. Of this, $2.8 billion goes to hunting and fishing. Photography, the nation's number one hobby, keeps about 60 million cameras clicking; golfers will soon support 900 new golf courses (for a total of 6,568) while bowling, now drawing 22 million people annually, will lure 13 million more by 1966.

We Salute

The Becker B
of Wilmingto

During the past seven years, appro
mately twenty cars of window and d
frame parts have left Bridal Veil going
south eastern North Carolina.

The Becker Builders Supply Comp.
has a complete shop specializing in st.
dard and custom made "Becker Be
Built Window Units." They have b
buying their stock — approximately th
to four cars a year — from Bridal
since they first started fabricating th
own units in 1952. Prior to that time t.
were also using Bridal Veil stock, bu
was purchased on a sub-contract ba:

Beckers carry a complete line of bu
ing materials, serving eastern North
South Carolina and the southern edge
Virginia. They have five full time sa
men and a total of approximately thir
five employees.

The Becker Builders Supply Comp

Dispina Tripodes, former Stock Record
Clerk, in front of the office. The two warehouses are directly behind the office.

Window units are being assembled in the shop.

mer . . . .

ers Supply Co.
orth Carolina

founded in 1917 by Mr. Charles J.
er. It first operated under the name
ecker Coal Company and was later
ged to Becker Coal & Builders Supply
pany when building materials were
d to the line. After the death of Mr.
er in 1937, the business was oper-
by his heirs until 1943 when it was
ired by a group headed by Mr. E. R.
on, at which time the name was
ged to The Becker Builders Supply
pany.

. Wilson served as manager until
retirement in 1954. Mr. Ralph M.
h was named manager at that time
is still serving in that capacity.

. Smith says of his relations with
al Veil, "The association has been
e than satisfactory in every way.
ice and shipments are on schedule
the quality of material is tops. We
e our association very much."

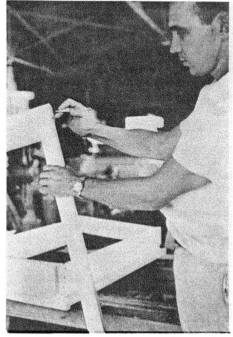

Danny Powell marks a frame as it is being
assembled in the shop.

A twin unit is being loaded on the truck for delivery to the job.

You Are Involved in Political Affairs

You are involved in political affairs, whether you want to be or not. The only question is whether you intend to have a voice in determining the kind of public policies you are going to have to live with.

Most political issues these days are also economic issues. For example, the level of taxes you pay certainly has a direct influence on your standard of living. And the amount of federal government spending inevitably affects the value of the dollars you have left after taxes — and these dollars have been losing value continually in the last two decades.

Voting once a year is fine. So is taking part in local civic activities, such as fund-raising or other voluntary work.

But these things are not enough to help shape the course of political events which will affect the living standards, and perhaps the individual liberties, of you and your family. When you take an active interest in politic al affairs all the year 'round — let your representatives in federal, state and local governments know your views . . . then you can look at the improving 'state of the nation' and say to yourself: "I have been a part of this.'

———————43———————

Midweek Holiday Or Long Weekend?

Several states are considering proposals to rearrange holidays so that they fall on Monday every year instead of "floating" through the week. Industry likes the idea because it would avoid the costly process of shutting down for one day in the middle of the week. Most employees like it because it would give them long weekends instead of one-day holidays.

Massachusetts, for instance, is considering permanent Monday observance of five holidays — Washington's Birthday in February, Patriot's Day in April, Memorial Day in May, Columbus Day in October, and Veterans' Day in November.

———————43———————

Heredity: Something you believe in when your child's report card is all A's.

———————43———————

When the Indians ran this country, there were no taxes and the women did all the work — and the white man thinks he has improved on that system!

———————43———————

It Puzzles Me!

A man owns an island that has a canal around it exactly 14 feet wide on each of the four sides of the island. He goes to this island often. However, he only has two planks, each exactly 12 feet long, on which to cross over the water. How does he use these two planks to get to the island?

SOLUTION FOR LAST MONTH

The four weights were: 1 pound, 3 pounds, 9 pounds and 27 pounds.

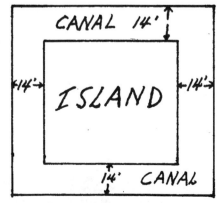

Fishing off the Grand Banks: one risky form of enterprise

Risks Grow Bigger but Rewards Shrink

YEARS ago, a man could set himself up in a business, such as a small machine shop, for an investment of a few hundred dollars. Virtually all the work was done with hand tools and inexpensive equipment. If he failed, the owner could sell those tools and try something else, without having suffered any serious loss. If he succeeded, all his earnings were his own.

Back in the mid-1800's investment per worker was almost negligible, by comparison with the cost of equipping a worker with today's complex and highly efficient machines. Nowadays it takes an investment of $17,800 to make the average industrial worker's job possible.

IN the last few decades, the effect of federal tax policy and big union leadership has been to multiply the risks of business, and to reduce the incentives. Wage boosts running ahead of productivity have increased costs and squeezed profits. And more than half of corporation earnings are taken away in taxes.

Americans are still willing to take business risks. Thousands of new businesses are started every year; others are expanded. But as the risks grow bigger, and the rewards shrink, we face the danger that investment and enterprise will dwindle, along with the growth and job-making ability of our economic system.

Rips and Trims

Here it is November already and the month of Thanksgiving, with Christmas just around the corner. Where has time gone?

The big news of last month seemed to be hunting season and deer. Two of the lucky hunters are pictured here with their deer. Among those who were hunting were: JERRY ROBERTS who got his deer at Burns, MARVIN STOLIN got his up by Mt. Hood, HARRY ADOLPH in Eastern Oregon, ROLEY ZUMWALT near Mt. Vernon, EINAR MICKELSON and DEWAYNE KILNESS both at Tillamook Burn, JIM COWLING also in Eastern Oregon, and LESLIE POLZEL near Kinzua. There were six hunting in the group with Leslie and they got five deer including the one his twelve year old nephew got.

BERTHA and FAY DAVIS were also hunting while on vacation, but didn't get their deer. MABEL and STANLEY HILLS failed to get their deer when hunting up at Bend. They spent the first part of their vacation in Reno and ended it out at the Coast.

ANNA and WILLIS BOWEN entertained her brother and his wife, Mr. and Mrs. Everett Clymer from Seattle. He is a copilot for Northern Air Lines flying from Seattle to Anchorage, Alaska.

MARTHA JONES and family were re-

NICE DEER, EINAR

cent guests of Mr. and Mrs. Ed Loe and daughter Carol at Molalla. Martha also seemed well pleased that Corbett won the home-coming football game, which she attended.

WARD DULL helped put the new roof on the V.F.W. Building at Corbett on a recent Saturday night. They finished the job about 12:20 A.M. and then enjoyed a Chili Dinner.

FRED HARP and his wife each caught their limit of trout during several of the past week-ends.

ARCHIE DAVIES is happy to have his daughter, Mrs. Marvin Link, back from Oklahoma. She plans to stay here while her husband is in Korea.

JIM HAMBRICK, CLYDE's son, has recently transferred to Fort Lee, Virginia where he will attend Quartermaster School. He plans to be home for Christmas.

Our sympathies to TED HANSON. His brother-in-law passed away after what had seemed to be a fine recovery from the explosion he was in a couple of months ago.

Our sympathies also to the family of PETER GRAYMER.

Have you noticed the diamond that BARBARA MICKELSON is wearing? Did she say a spook (Leslie Nixon) gave it to her on Halloween?

DEWAYNE'S FIRST

Bridal Veil
NEWS LETTER

VOL. V, No. 6   BRIDAL VEIL, OREGON   DECEMBER, 1959

NEWS LETTER

Published on the 10th of each month by
Bridal Veil Lumber & Box Co.
Bridal Veil, Oregon

Editor . . . . Sara Mahn

CORRECTION

The statement in the October issue of
the NEWS LETTER that Diamond-Gardner
had discontinued the production of frames
was in error.

————— 10 —————

December Birthdays

Many Happy Returns of the Day!

Clyde Hambrick
Hiram Layton
Eugene Potter

————— 10 —————

The simplest way to better your lot is
to do a lot better.

Health and Welfare Coverage

All employees who worked the required
number of hours in August and September
will become eligible for Health and Welfare Coverage and will be covered on the
first day of December, 1959. They must
have worked the required hours in both
months.

Additions: Martha A. Jones.

Employees who did not work the re-
quired number of hours will become in-
eligible the same day. Deletions: Fred-
erick Bailey, Jr., Donald Bowen, Leroy
H. Brenneke, Francis P. Cook, Robert L.
Cowling, Thomas J. Cowling, Ramon A.
Damerell, Leon C. Dunlap, Charles N.
Gaymon, Donald Hagemen, Leo C. Hage-
man, Merrill B. Hartshorn, Rodney Jac-
obson, Walton Jones, Larry L. Lamke,
Virgil McNatt, Einar Fred Mickelson,
Gary Stolin, Eleanor Taylor, Paul Watts,
James M. Yerion.

1959 SAFETY CHART

Month	Tot. Hourly Pd. Man Hrs.	Lost Time Accidents	Accident Freq.	Days Lost	Accident Severity
January	18,468	1	54.1	1	541
February	17,904	0	0	24	1340
March	12,994	0	0	22	1693
1st Qtr. 1959	49,366	1	20.3	47	952
April	16,596	0	0	21	1265
May	17,557	1	57.0	42	2392
June	18,735	0	0	44	2273
2nd Quarter	52,888	1	18.9	107	2023
July	22,353	0	0	23	1029
August	17,804	0	0	21	1180
September	17,706	1	56.5	29	1638
3rd Quarter	57,863	1	17.3	73	1262
October	16,246	0	0	52	3201
Total	176,363	3	17.1	279	1582

Can We Win the Economic War?

From Babson's WASHINGTON FORECAST

The Ike-Khrushchev conversations have given birth to a great hope in America . . . a hope that East and West, Communism and Capitalism, can agree on a policy of co-existence.

This, they reason, will eliminate the fear of war . . . which they feel is the only threat to our freedom and our way of life.

Is this a sound conclusion? Can we beat Communism in an economic battle "with one hand tied behind our back?"

Are we just as much in danger of losing our freedom in economic battle as in atomic warfare?

For the past several decades, the United States has led the world by a wide margin in gross national product. We have had vast natural resources, great wealth for investment, and an enterprising citizenry.

This combination has permitted us to "run rings around" the other free nations of the world. And — until a few years ago — impoverished Red Russia was so far behind that she was "not in the same league."

Our world leadership has made us justifiably proud . . . but it has also made us unrealistically overconfident that no other nation, no other system, can beat us at the economic game.

CONFUSED PRIDE: We love our way of life . . . and with good reason.

It has provided a great measure of individual freedom . . . and a constantly advancing standard of living.

Our big error is that we tend to tie the two inalterably together. We have reached the conclusion that it is our freedom— and our freedom alone — which is responsible for our status as the economic giant of the world.

We are sure that some of our clients rise in indignation at our suggestion that this is not so. We merely ask that you "hear us out."

VALUE OF INCENTIVE: It is unquestionably true that any man will expend greater efforts — and produce greater results — if he is given an incentive to do so.

Pure Communism and theoretical Socialism have "fallen on their faces" everywhere they have been tried . . . because of this lack of personal incentive.

There are few workers in the United States — or in the world — who would not be willing to work harder and longer if such effort could reasonably be expected to produce a great economic reward.

THE U. S. TREND: Despite the above truism, the American political-economic pattern has been undergoing modifications which are leading to a substitution of security for incentive . . . rather than a combination of the two.

Our tax system has become an instrument of wealth equalization. Profit — the prime economic incentive — has become a "dirty word." Incentive has been dulled by a constant increase in direct and indirect taxation on anything above subsistence income.

Our American working men have been taught to scorn attempts by business management to increase individual productivity thru the offer of rewards to those who can do a better or bigger job.

Any such proposal is viewed as a "sweat shop" technique . . . and it is expressly forbidden in most union contracts.

These two forces have brought about a great lessening of the rate of increase in individual productivity and in our gross national product.

THE PRICE FACTOR: The relative economic strength of any nation is affected by its ability to sell its goods to other nations.

Because of the wide gap in labor costs between the U. S. and all other nations, we are finding it increasingly difficult to attract overseas customers for our products.

And . . . American producers in ever-larger numbers each year are being undersold in our own domestic markets by importers of foreign merchandise.

Our policy of gradual reduction of tariffs has not been the primary cause of the "invasion" of foreign goods.

We have failed to understand that our continuous wage-price spiral can put us at such a competitive disadvantage in world makets as to threaten the future of American industry.

COMMUNIST CAMOUFLAGE: None of the nations in the Red bloc is truly Communist . . . not even Soviet Russia.

(continued on page 6)

A Nice Smooth Finis

The dump truck backs up to the asphalt spreading machine . . .

which spreads it in s

On Monday m
began to arrive
asphalt for the p
lumber shed and
lumber shed. 1
for the job had
before. So a mu
begun.

Many truckloa
in and dumped ir
the asphalt. The
ing asphalt, as
and packed it do

Warren North
job of paving th
work in the lum
hip boots and get
them now.

and empties the load of asphalt into the hopper of the machine . . .

A Job Long Needed

as the steam rises from the hot asphalt.

ur feet wide . . .

ıber 16, trucks
filled with hot
ırd between the
ıe inside of the
ipment needed
: in on Friday
ırovement was

lt were brought
e that put down
all day spread—
ıe behind them

ıd a very fine
w the men who
ake back their
hey won't need

This roller packs and smooths it into a real nice surface.

Can We Win the Economic War?

(continued from page 3)

Top Reds freely admit that they are not ready for the institution of a real Communist society . . . and probably won't be until all the world is under their domination.

Actually, the Soviet-bloc nations are operating under the strictest form of dictatorship . . . one which owns all property and completely controls the activity of the people.

Text-book Communism calls for self-rule by the proletariat . . . not domination by a self-perpetuating ruling individual or clique.

It also prescribes the distribution of goods "to each, according to his needs."

Red leaders have stolen a page from the book of Capitalism . . . and have been moving away from, rather than toward, the latter goal.

In all so-called Communist nations, those who produce more than their fellow-workers become state heroes and are given great material rewards.

Slackers are considered enemies of the state . . . and are treated as such.

Classism in Communist countries has been developing with great strides . . . particularly in the growth of a large upper-middle class made up of military specialists, scientists, successful industrial managers, and outstanding workers.

The economic incentive for Soviet citizens is relatively far greater, therefore, than that available to most Americans.

Note that we use the word "relatively." It is true that those in the upper-middle class in Russia do not enjoy most of the comforts, conveniences, and material goods which are available to our medium-low-income families.

However, the status of these privileged Reds is so far above that of the ordinary Soviet citizen that the incentive to produce is very real and very great.

The possibility of "jumping" into this life of comparative luxury is enough to create tremendous zeal on the part of the average Russian worker — whose standard of living is still far below that of the lowest income group in the United States.

INCENTIVE TO LIVE: In judging the economic capacity of Communist countries, we also fail to realize the power of the incentive to live.

Human life is considered of importance by Red leaders only when that life is devoted exclusively to the purposes of the state.

Unwillingness or failure to produce creates a burden which the state cannot afford to tolerate. Therefore, it deliberately transfers that burden to the "offending" individual himself.

The result is work in a slave-labor camp under abject conditions of misery.. or starvation.

The fear of such a fate probably serves as an even greater incentive to produce than does the lure of the "hero's" reward.

LUXURY OF FREEDOM: It is important that all Americans realize that the freedom we enjoy is a luxury . . . one that we pay for dearly.

In a period of war or other strife, our government sometimes finds it necessary to restrict that freedom by a system of controls . . . of the type which are a part of the daily life of the Soviet people.

We know — as the Kremlin rulers do — that such controls increase our national efficiency and, therefore, our output.

We abhor the idea of a government which has the power to tell us where we must work, what type of work we must do, how much we must produce, what we will be paid, and how we will spend the money we earn.

Yet, let's not kid ourselves into thinking that such a system is inefficient . . . particularly when the welfare — and even the life — of the worker depends entirely on his strict conformance to such orders.

Our freedoms — to plan our personal future, to change jobs, to bargain for working conditions, to go on strike, to spend our money as we choose — all these are privileges which are paid for in terms of productive waste and inefficiency.

We are not arguing that these freedoms should be abolished. They should be defended with all the vigor at our command.

They are costly . . . but they are worth the cost.

The important point is that we should not delude ourselves by thinking that these freedoms are responsible for our national economic success . . . that they are the very economic tool with which we will

Can We Win
The Economic War?

(continued from page 6)

"bury" the Communists.

Actually, our liberty is the "hand that's tied behind our back" insofar as our productive achievement is concerned.

If we win the economic war, it will be despite our freedoms — not because of them.

SOVIET PROGRESS: There is irrefutable tangible proof that the Communist empire is increasing its productivity and output at a rate far exceeding that of the Free World.

In countless activities, the Reds are still pitifully far behind us. But — in every one — they are catching up.

And — under present conditions and methods — they will continue to catch up in the years ahead . . . eventually moving ahead of us.

If both East and West continue to play the economic game under the rules they are each presently employing, a victory for the Free World is far from assured.

THE WAY OUT: Because economic domination of the world by the Communist empire would necessarily lead to political domination, it is vital that we face the challenge.

It would be ridiculous for us to switch over permanently to a controlled economy and a controlled people in order to battle the Communists on even terms. That would be tantamount to surrendering the way of life which we were striving to defend.

We must, instead, provide our people with sufficient spiritual and material incentive to outmatch the efforts and results of those in Red-dominated countries at every turn.

The spiritual incentive can be supplied by a candid scotching of the myth of American invulnerability . . . and a reawakening of our people to the fact that the great prize of freedom is at stake — whether the war be fought with missiles or machines.

The material incentive must come as the result of soul-searching reappraisal of our goals and methods . . . a new sense of fairness and honesty to each other . . . and a realization that the fruits of our labor must necessarily be in proportion to the effort we expend.

This would result in an eagerness on the part of our workers to do a good day's work for a good day's pay . . . with security assured by the great advance that would be seen almost immediately in our national standard of living and with sizable individual material rewards to those who expended the greatest efforts and achieved greatest productive results.

It would be necessary for government, too, to join in this team effort of management and labor . . . protecting each against specific instances of unfairness by the other . . . and providing new additional incentive for achievement by a revised tax structure designed not to confiscate but to build.

Is this a dream? Yes, we guess it is. But . . . it's far more reasonable and acceptable than the nightmare which could prove to be its only alternative.

———————— 10 ————————

Retired

Joseph H. Cote took his doctor's advice and retired from active work the first of November.

Joe came to work at Bridal Veil in September, 1952 as a band saw hike-away. Recently he has been doing a fine job of cleaning around the machines in the factory.

Joe thinks he will be able to find plenty to keep him busy around home and we hope he will have many years to enjoy taking life easy.

Rips and Trims

Here we are with another Christmas almost upon us, and I just hope that you are better prepared for it than I am.

Thanksgiving is over, but many will remember that good Thanksgiving Dinner they enjoyed. Mr. and Mrs. JERALD ROBERTS had as dinner guests his father and brother Keith and the ELDON NIELSON family. ANNA and WILLIS BOWEN ate dinner with her sister and family, Mr. and Mrs. Neil Wolff in Portland. The FRED HARPS had dinner with their children.

There is still some hunting being done. WILLIS BOWEN, Doc Nelson, Jimmy Bowen and Max Bissell were hunting up at Mosier but had no luck. HOWARD HUNT was in the Desolation Area, but didn't get his elk either. MARVIN STOLIN was luckier; he got his elk. RALPH LAMKE got his deer near Sweet Home and ORIEN PITTS' daughter got her deer even though Orien wasn't that lucky. TED HANSON said he was driving near Bridal Veil when a deer ran into the side of his car. It evidently didn't do as much damage as the car that ran into the back of his car. His wife and son both received some injuries.

CLARENCE LOFSTEDT went down to Salem on Veterans Day just for the drive. MARTHA JONES says she had a very enjoyable day in town shopping on the Monday that the paving was being done at the mill. BERTHA DAVIS took her grandsons, Gordon Timothy and Richard Scott Davis, to the Fairy Tale Parade and to see Santa Claus. FAY DAVIS reports that the recent ice was too heavy for his fruit trees and broke some of them.

Congratulations to the new Grandfathers who both gained their new titles on the twenty-fifth of November. HOMER WALKER'S grandson was born on Homer's 35th wedding anniversary, weighing 8 pounds and 11 ounces, but he forgot his name. RALPH TAYLOR'S grandson is Jeffrey Raymond. Eleanor is down in California seeing that Jeff is taken care of properly and plans to return about the thirteenth.

DELBERT DUNKEN spent his recent vacation near home so that he could spend as much time as possible at the hospital with his wife. She is now home and seems to be doing fine. DOROTHY HARTSHORN is still on the sick list but seems to be improving. CLYDE HAMBRICK is back on the job after his recent bout with the flu and a skin infection. MARVIN VAN ORSOW is a patient at Gresham General Hospital.

A number of you asked me about my accident. I was driving to work on the morning of November 18 on the ice when I started to skid a half-mile past Rooster Rock. I immediately took my foot off the accelerator as I skidded out of the right lane over into the left lane. Just as I started to put my foot back on the accelerator, the semi (tractor and two trailers) which had been following me in the right lane, plowed into the back of my car pushing the front of my car into the posts in the center of the highway. I then bounced over and the side of the car hit a post, then the other side of the car hit another post and I came to a stop on the other side of the posts, still headed East. My Studebaker is completely totaled and I spent five days at the Portland San. I am still taking treatments for the back injury I received, but feel very fortunate that I am still alive.

"You should see the front and both sides."

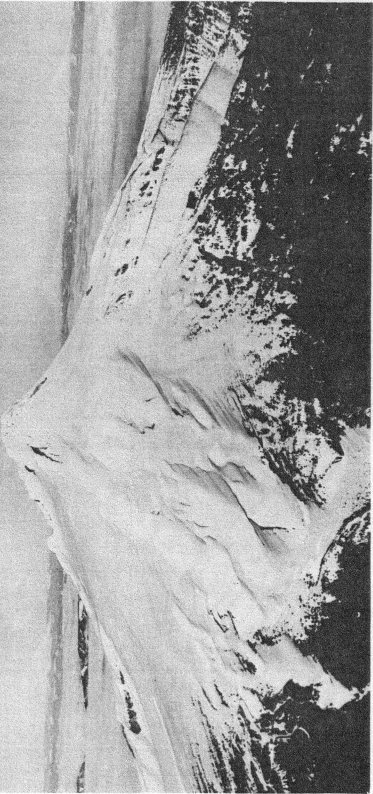

Bridal Veil NEWS LETTER

Vol. V, No. 7

BRIDAL VEIL, OREGON

January, 1960

NEWS LETTER

Published on the 10th of each month by
Bridal Veil Lumber & Box Co.
Bridal Veil, Oregon

Editor . . . . Sara Mahn

January Birthdays

Many Happy Returns of the Day!

Thomas Britton
Gerald Carver
Pearl Cloe
Bertha Davis
Roy Eveland
Loren Hancock
Marvin Jackson
Charles Jacobson
Dewayne Kilness
Clarence Lofstedt
Melvin Mallinson
Ralph McCredie
Barbara Mickelson
Eldon Nielson
Mira Nielson
Thelma Rowe

Our Cover

This month our cover is an aerial view of Mt. St. Helens, Mt. Rainier and Mt. Adams in the background. Photo courtesy of George Diel.

———— 13 ————

Patriots Would Rue Changes

It was Patrick Henry, born on May 29, 1736, who stood up in Saint John's church in Richmond, Va., 184 years ago and proclaimed "Give me liberty or give me death."

Henry was objecting to the taxes and restrictions imposed on the American colonies by the British government. His stirring words helped touch off the war for Independence.

Wonder what this champion of freedom would think today of the taxes and restrictions which free Americans have allowed their own government to impose on them in the 160 years since his death?

1959 SAFETY CHART

Month	Tot. Hourly Pd. Man Hrs.	Lost Time Accidents	Accident Freq.	Days Lost	Accident Severity
January	18,468	1	54.1	1	541
February	17,904	0	0	24	1340
March	12,994	0	0	22	1693
1st Qtr. 1959	49,366	1	20.3	47	952
April	16,596	0	0	21	1265
May	17,557	1	57.0	42	2392
June	18,735	0	0	44	2273
2nd Quarter	52,888	1	18.9	107	2023
July	22,353	0	0	23	1029
August	17,804	0	0	21	1180
September	17,706	1	56.5	29	1638
3rd Quarter	57,863	1	17.3	73	1262
October	16,246	0	0	52	3201
November	12,955	1	77.2	24	1853
Total	179,318	4	22.3	303	1690

1960

Elsewhere in this NEWS LETTER we have included a group of pie charts. These pie charts show the nature of our sales over the past several years.

Also included is a pie chart showing our best guess as to how 1960 should shape up. This isn't necessarily the way we want 1960 to look, nor is it likely to be the way 1960 actually will look.

It is just the best estimate we can make at the present time.

Of course, our prime object in making a radical change of this nature is to create a profit.

However, we anticipate other advantages which are also of concern to all our employees.

The millwork business has always been an extremely seasonal thing. No one wants to buy millwork in the winter when the snow is knee-deep. On the other hand, everyone wants millwork during the summer months.

This situation has always resulted in violent expansion and contraction in the size of the crew needed to get out the work. Some summer months have seen as high as 192 employees. And some winter months have been as low as the 50 to 60 range.

———— 13 ————

Under the present program we hope to level off so that total employment, summer and winter, will be much the same.

This is possible because our major cut stock customer recognizes that we cannot produce his requirements in the summer months. In order to guarantee a steady production, then, this customer levels off his buying to regular quantities the year around. All our other items will also be geared to the cut stock requirements of our major customer.

A program of this nature should help us to level off our lumber needs. It may well develop that we will be able to contract for regular year around deliveries of lumber, and thus help to prevent lay-offs due to lumber shortages.

Expense wise, leveling off the inbound lumber shipments should do big things in the way of reducing our demurrage bill.

However, the important point here is that while we should be using fewer people, the ones we do use should get much closer to a full year's employment.

This is a highly desireable goal for all of us. We pledge our best efforts to the realization of this goal.

Len Kraft

———— 13 ————

Health and Welfare

All employees who worked the required number of hours in September and October will become eligible for Health and Welfare Coverage and will be covered on the first day of January, 1960. They must have worked the required hours in both months.

Additions: Merrill B. Hartshorn, Larry Lamke, Ray Leopard, Virgil McNatt.

Employees who did not work the required number of hours will become ineligible the same day. Deletions: Robert K. Bird, Louis W. Bissell, Marvin N. Dhone, Gerald V. Dull, Earl Hutchison, Fred M. Long.

This Is How You Spend Your Time

The term "spending time" has a real meaning — and the more money our governments spend, the more time we must spend paying taxes.

The Tax Foundation extimates the average worker now toils 2 hours and 29 minutes in each 8 hour day to earn enough to pay his taxes. This compares with 1 hour and 39 minutes spent earning his food, 1 hour 25 minutes for rent or house payments, 37 minutes for clothes, 42 minutes for transportation, 24 minutes for medical care, 20 minutes for recreation and 24 minutes to pay for other purchases.

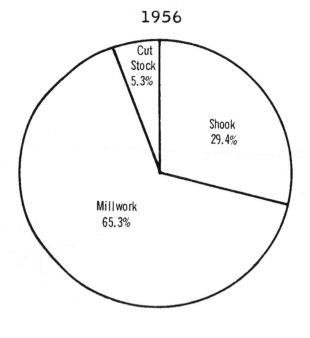

1956

Cut Stock 5.3%

Shook 29.4%

Millwork 65.3%

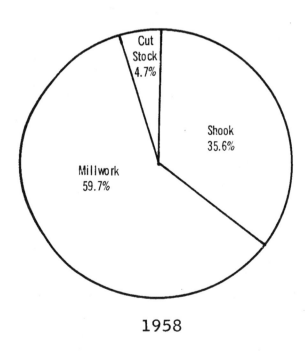

Cut Stock 4.7%

Shook 35.6%

Millwork 59.7%

1958

Cut Stock 48.5%

A Glanc

As Compar

Perhaps you h.
ference the recent ch
sales policies have
shipments. Here we
with an estimate for

You will note :
a high of 65.3 per (
23.5 per cent in 1
stock increased fr(
1957 to an estimate

(E

▶he Future

'ith The Past

▶ wondering what dif-
▶ our production and
▶ the nature of our
▶ the past four years

▶ millwork sales from
956 to an estimated
t the same time cut
of 1.7 per cent in
per cent in 1960.

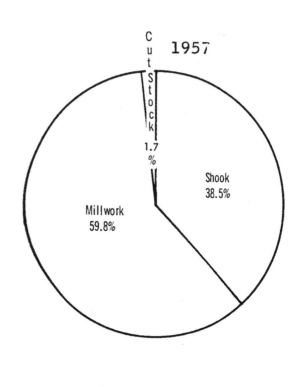

Cut Stock
1.7%

Shook
38.5%

Millwork
59.8%

Shook
28.0%

Millwork
23.5%

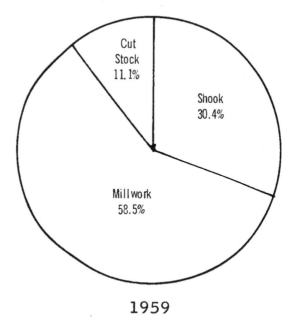

Cut
Stock
11.1%

Shook
30.4%

Millwork
58.5%

1959

Rips and Trims

(Continued from Page 8)

JIM KENDRICK spent the day with their wives' folks in Tacoma; ORIEN PITTS was at the Bob Rice home in Springdale; the RALPH TAYLORS were at Eleanor's parents' home in Cathlamet; JOHN WILLMS was at his wife's mother's home in Oregon City; WESLEY ADAMS at his mother's at Goldendale; TOM BRITTON at his daughter's, Mr. and Mrs. JOSEPH VAN ORSOW (Tom spent his recent vacation moving to Corbett, at the Chet May place); ADE JONES, together with his family and daughter's family, Mr. and Mrs. RAY LEOPARD, were with his mother at Oregon City; ROBERT FITZGERALD with his Aunt and Uncle, Rev. and Mrs. Sutton at Deming, Washington (his Christmas present from them was about $50 worth of groceries); HOWARD HUNT was with his daughter and five grandchildren at Springfield (and he talked long distance with his son at the Naval Air Base in San Diego); LESTER HOWELL was at the Max Bissell's; LESTER ANDERSON was in Tigard; RALPH McCREDIE was with his brother and family in Hood River; ROY EVELAND visited with relatives in Seattle; LEO HAGEMAN was with his mother in Seattle; MARVIN JACKSON visited relatives in Vancouver; DELBERT DUNKEN was with his brother in Corbett (his sister and her husband were also here from California); LAVERNE FAGAN spent Christmas with his girl friend's family; and Nancy and DEWAYNE KILNESS were with her family, the EINAR MICKELSONS.

TED HANSON'S son was home from Laurelwood Academy. Fred Mickelson was home from San Diego. He has now gone to Norfolk, Virginia, where he will start his course in radar. CLYDE HAMBRICK'S son, Jimmy, also planned to be home for Christmas, but Uncle Sam had other plans. He is now in Korea, after a stopover in Hawaii and Japan. (Did Clyde tell you about the birthday card he got from Hawaii?)

LEONARD VOLKMAN stayed home, however, to liven things up he got a

Recent Visitor

Mr. Burton R. Pease Millwork Company in Hamilton, Ohio, recently visited our mill.

He was touring the mills of the Northwest in an effort to replace his source of supply on window frames, since we have discontinued the manufacture of this item. However, we will continue supplying their door frames.

---

nail in his hand while tearing down an old barn. BOB REISCHEL also stayed home, but he wouldn't tell me where he got that shiner.

At the WARD DULL home, it is traditional for her relatives to come and celebrate Christmas together. Those who were there were daughter Val Rae, son Gerald with his wife and baby daughter Valerie, and Mr. and Mrs. Fred Sanders all of Portland; Thelma's mother, Mrs. Alma Harrison of Gresham; and Mr. and Mrs. Linn Harrison and children Terrence, Tee, Tamara and Tait of Sandy. Ward's sister, Mr. and Mrs. Thomas Stewart and son Terry of Portland, also joined the family for dinner.

Did ROLAND MORGAN tell you about the turkey he won at the raffle at the High School?

FAY DAVIS reports that there was 14 inches of snow on Larch Mountain during Christmas. He made it all the way up by having four-wheel drive.

WALT STOLIN and son Garry both got their elk during December. (Or was it late November?)

And that about winds up the employee news for the year 1959.

1960 VACATIONS

JANUARY
- 1 Fred Crouser 10
- 5 Martha Jones 10
- 8 Merrill Hartshorn 10
- 23 Mira Nielson 10
- 26 Clem Hancock 8

FEBRUARY
- 7 Roland Morgan 10

MARCH
- 1 Ralph Taylor 10
- 1 Leslie Polzel 10
- 15 Robert Fitzgerald, Jr. 7
- 15 Stanley Hills 10
- 22 Edward Wendler 8
- 22 Fay Davis 10
- 23 Clifford Latourell 10
- 25 Harold Vogel 10
- 28 Marvin Stolin 10

APRIL
- 1 Archie Davies 10
- 8 Marvin Jackson 10
- 17 Theophile Van Hee 10
- 18 Theodore Hanson 10
- 21 Eldon Nielson 10
- 22 Joseph Van Orsow 10

MAY
- 6 Floyd F. Oden 6
- 6 Bertha Davis 10
- 6 Harold Burkholder 10
- 8 Charles D. Jacobson 6
- 9 Durward Litton 10
- 11 Walter Stolin 10
- 12 Gerald Carver 5
- 12 Laverne Fagan 5
- 13 James Kendrick 10
- 13 Hiram Layton 10
- 18 Ward Dull 10
- 19 Lester Anderson 10
- 21 Fred Harp 10

JUNE
- 3 Robert Reischel 6
- 13 Orien Pitts 10
- 23 Lester B. Howell 10
- 28 Bob Layton 10
- 30 Anna Bowen 10

JULY
- 1 Einar Mickelson 10
- 2 Ronald Catlin 7
- 8 Wesley Adams 10
- 10 Paul Dooley 10
- 14 Leo F. Hageman 10
- 18 J. Delbert Dunken 10

- 19 Lillie Landreth 10
- 22 Delbert Cloe 7
- 22 Alfred Barnes 7
- 22 Kenneth Catlin 7

AUGUST
- 9 Theodore V. Van Hee 10
- 17 Leonard Volkman 6
- 19 Franklin Bowen 10
- 21 George Murray 10
- 27 Ralph McCredie 10
- 27 Lloyd De Main 10

SEPTEMBER
- 2 Loren Hancock 10
- 4 Elmer Ayles 10
- 8 Jerald Roberts 10
- 11 Roley Zumwalt 10
- 14 Dewayne Kilness 5
- 16 Kenneth Meyer 10
- 20 Verl W. Bird 10
- 22 Harry Adolph 10
- 24 Lawrence Peterson 10
- 27 Elden Gross 10
- 29 John Willms 10

OCTOBER
- 1 Howard Hunt 10
- 1 Kenneth Craig 7
- 2 Lawrence Smazal 10
- 5 Ray Leopard 5
- 9 Ralph Ellis 10
- 9 Homer Walker 10
- 10 Louis Wilson 10
- 13 David Rees 10
- 14 Mabel Hills 10
- 28 E. H. Potter 10

NOVEMBER
- 8 Raymond Schneringer 10
- 12 Pearl P. Cloe 10
- 15 Roy Eveland 10
- 16 Harold Jacobson 10
- 24 Clarence Lofstedt 10

DECEMBER
- 7 Beulah Choate 10
- 12 Thelma Rowe 10
- 20 Thomas Britton 10

Date Undetermined
- Louis Bissell 10
- Edsel Kinonen 10
- Theophile Van Hee, Sr. 10
- Mary Woodard 10
- Fred M. Long 10
- Dorothy Hartshorn 10
- Jarvis Kilness 10

Rips and Trims

Christmas, with its true meaning "Good will toward all men," has come and gone. Again we face a new year full of hope and promise.

Many of the employees just spent the holiday at home enjoying their turkey with their family, while others had guests and relatives in, and some visited elsewhere.

Among those just staying home were: LAWRENCE PETERSON, LARRY HANCOCK, CLIFF LATOURELL, BOB LAYTON, PAUL DOOLEY, HARRY ADOLPH, MIRA NIELSON, BEULAH CHOATE, MERRILL and DOROTHY HARTSHORN, THEODORE VAN HEE, CONNIE MEYER, DURWARD LITTON, CLEM HANCOCK, RALPH LAMKE, DAVID REES, LESLIE POLZEL, ROLEY ZUMWALT, HOMER WALKER, ED WENDLER, EUGENE POTTER, ELDEN GROSS, KENNETH CATLIN, ALFRED BARNES, DELBERT CLOE, RONALD CATLIN, HAROLD BURKHOLDER, DEAN BURKHOLDER, FRANK BOWEN, FLOYD ODEN, KENNETH CRAIG, ARCHIE DAVIES and CHARLES JACOBSON.

Those entertaining over the holiday were: WILLIS and ANNA BOWEN had their sons Willis, Jr., and Jim and their families home, with a total of seven grandchildren. HAROLD VOGEL had relatives in, including an aunt, Laura DeLong from Wisconsin. MARVIN STOLIN'S wife's brother, Ernest Rowland of Beaverton, was with them. The COWLING FAMILY had a house full, including Jim's brother-in-law, Jack Kennedy of Medford, Mr. and Mrs. Fred Larsen and daughter Vicky, Jan Hinton, and, of course, Tom and Bob were home for the holidays. BERTHA and FAY DAVIS had their sons home. (By the way, in a couple of months if you go by the Davis residence and hear lovely organ music, you will know that Fay has learned to play the Thomas Organ his brothers and sisters gave him for Christmas.) MARTHA JONES entertained her sister, Mr. and Mrs. Arden Wedwick and family from Brookings, and also Mr. and Mrs. Ed Loe and Carol Jean of Molalla. LILLIE LANDRETH had son Jimmy home from college. MABLE and STANLEY HILLS

had their daughters and families, Mr. and Mrs. William Steffen from Tacoma and Mr. and Mrs. Shannon from Tigard, and also son Danny, who is living in Portland and attending Portland State. GEORGE MURRAY'S daughter and her husband were home. Mr. and Mrs. JERRY ROBERTS and brother Keith were with the ELDON NIELSONS for Christmas dinner. The FRED HARPS had their children home for dinner. (Fred recently purchased a portable TV for his house trailer, getting prepared for those fishing trips this coming spring and summer. Maybe that's where that cuckoo clock he received for Christmas will go. Does it still wake you up in the middle of the night, Fred?)

FRED CROUSER'S son and his girl friend were home. RAY SCHNERINGER'S children were all home. GERALD CARVER'S sister spent Christmas with them. LARRY SMAZAL'S niece and her husband were up from Newberg. MARVIN VAN ORSOW'S whole family was with them. LLOYD DeMAIN'S father was here from Portland.

And then there were those who spent Christmas away from home. They include PAUL DETRICK, who was at his nephew's; CLARENCE LOFSTEDT and

(Continued on Page 6)

JIM HAMBRICK

Bridal Veil NEWS LETTER

VOL. V, No. 8   BRIDAL VEIL, OREGON   FEBRUARY, 1960

NEWS LETTER

Published on the 10th of each month by
Bridal Veil Lumber & Box Co.
Bridal Veil, Oregon

Editor . . . . Sara Mahn

February Birthdays

Many Happy Returns of the Day!

Elmer Ayles
Kenneth Catlin
Beulah Choate
Debert Cloe
Fred Crouser
James Dunken
Laverne Fagan
Mabel Hills
Edward Wendler
Louis Wilson

Our Cover

This month we look at the ice at Cape Horn across from Bridal Veil. Our thanks to Ralph Taylor.

———— 44 ————

Correction

The mountain on our cover last month was Mt. Hood, showing Mt. St. Helens, Mt. Rainier and Mt. Adams in the background.

———— 44 ————

The number of words in the English language has quintupled since Shakespeare's time, increasing from about 140,000 to somewhere between 700,000 and 800,000.

1959 SAEETY CHART

Month	Tot. Hourly Pd. Man Hrs.	Lost Time Accidents	Accident Freq.	Days Lost	Accident Severity
January	18,468	1	54.1	1	541
February	17,904	0	0	24	1340
March	12,994	0	0	22	1693
1st Qtr. 1959 . . .	49,366	1	20.3	47	952
April	16,596	0	0	21	1265
May	17,557	1	57.0	42	2392
June	18,735	0	0	44	2273
2nd Quarter	52,888	1	18.9	107	2023
July	22,353	0	0	23	1029
August	17,804	0	0	21	1180
September	17,706	1	56.5	29	1638
3rd Quarter	57,863	1	17.3	73	1262
October	16,246	0	0	52	3201
November	12,955	1	77.2	24	1853
December	14,846	1	67.4	5	337
4th Quarter	44,047	2	44.6	81	1839
1959 Total	204,164	5	24.5	308	1509
1958 Total	229,349	10	43.6	209	911
1957 Total	211,225	9	42.6	124	587
1956 Total	226,656	4	17.6	19	84

At Random

Last month we pointed out here that one result of our change in product mix, we hoped, would be to level off our production. Stated another way, we hope to ship more in the winter and less in the summer.

In terms of footage shipped, this appears to be true so far as December, 1959, and January, 1960, are concerned.

December shipments of 678,417 FBM was the best footage volume for any December since December of 1954. Likewise, our January footage volume of 622,274 FBM was the best since January of 1956.

The combined footage for December, 1959, and January, 1960, of 1,300,691 FBM was the best shipments for this two month period since the winter of 1954-55.

Lest we get the wrong impression, we hasten to point out that basically we are still tied in with the general market for residential building. Although we are no longer involved in the direct production of window frames, something like one half our production will be used by companies that are.

All we have accomplished is to sell our product to converters whose volume is large enough to permit them to buy steadily the year around.

* * * * * * * *

By way of miscellaneous information, we used a total of 2,104,800 KWH of electrical power during 1959. Power used in 1959 was equal to 10.31 KWH per man hour. The same figure for 1955 was 5.54 KWH and for 1956 was 5.48 KWH.

This is another way of saying that on the average, every employee had the help of almost twice as many horse power in 1959 as in 1955 and 1956.

* * * * * * * *

Safety-wise the year 1959 was a mixture of the good and the bad. In terms of the number of accidents per million man hours, we were better off in 1959 than for several years. Our accident frequency of 24.5 per million man hours was the best since the all-time low of 17.6 achieved in 1956.

In terms of severity, however, 1959 was the worst year we have ever had. Although we had fewer accidents, the ones we did have resulted in more lost time than ever before.

Insofar as our accident severity rating is a measure of human suffering, we can take no pride in our 1959 safety record. Here is an area that will require the best efforts of all of us during the coming year.

Also, we need to take advantage of all the services made available to us by the State Industrial Accident Commission. Of particular value are the monthly safety movies put on by the Commission during lunch period.

It would be a shame for anyone to incur a crippling injury that might have been prevented by attendance at the safety movies.

Len Kraft

——— 44 ———

Health and Welfare Coverage

All employees who worked the required number of hours in October and November will become eligible for Health and Welfare Coverage and will be covered on the first day of February, 1960. They must have worked the required hours in both months.

No additions.

Employees who did not work the required number of hours will become ineligible the same day. Deletions: Richard Bowen, Joseph Cote, Fred Damerell, Peter J. Graymer, Dorothy Hartshorn, Marvin Howell, Larry L. Lamke, Virgil McNatt, Leslie Nixon.

Multnomah Falls

Wea

January was
the Bridal Ve
and the roads
as you looke
beauty that s

Many of y
January of 1
were taken sl
snow and ice
Taylor for the

Tug pulling barge

Wise

vinter month in
ome snow fell
ous. However,
d you see the
;?

ably remember
these pictures
y of beautiful
anks to Ralph
e pictures.

Wahkeena Falls

ar Cascade Locks

Visitors

Recently Mr. W. D. McNee and Mr. Fred McBride, both sales representatives of Oregon Moulding and Lumber Company in Portland, visited our mill. Mr. McNee, formerly from Klamath Falls, recently joined Oregon Moulding and Lumber Company and was here in the interest of cut stock buying. Mr. McBride is presently buying jambs from us.

———— 44 ————

What's Behind
A Dividend Dollar

To pay one stockholder a divident of one dollar, the average company must make a net profit of $2.00. (Half the net is plowed back to replace equipment or for expansion.)

To make a net profit of $2.00, that company must earn $4.16 before taxes. (Corporate taxes are generally 52 per cent.)

To create one new job in industry, the company, it has been estimated, must find $16,000 in net new investment — either from profits or from borrowing that ultimately must be repaid from profits. (This is the average cost of tools, training, plant overhead, etc., behind each American worker.)

To have available $16,000 out of profits to create a new job, the company must do $528,000 worth of business.

So take another look at that $1.00 dividend check. It represents America at work.

It Won't Work

Is inflation the price of "good times"?

Contrasting the depressed 1930's to the 1940's and '50's, with generally rising prices, many people would say "I'll take inflation." But that isn't the choice. Inflation will not work in the future as a means of maintaining business and high employment.

After World War II we were the only industrial nation producing. All our products could be sold, even if our economic policies were sloppy. Today the nations of Europe and Japan have adopted sound economic policies and are able to compete both as to quality and price. We can't afford to be careless in our economic practices; even those who may have benefited briefly from inflation can no longer afford it.

Another reason inflation won't work is that creditors have been punished enough; they've "caught on" to inflation and will be reluctant in the future to provide capital for business expansion.

———— 44 ————

There is no right way to do the wrong thing.   — Anon.

BOISE CASCADE CORPORATION

January 22, 1960

Bridal Veil Lumber and Box Company
Bridal Veil, Oregon

ATTENTION: Mr. Leonard Kraft

Gentlemen:

Our cut stock foreman, Frank Chapin, and our
shipping superintendent Stan Bolinger, felt
that the very fine loading of your portion of this
car of cut stock for Weyerhaeuser was worth the
mention. They wanted to pass along the information that the car arrived in perfect condition.
This was car UP 500059, shipped to the
Turner Manufacturing Company, Chicago,
Illinois.

> Yours very truly,
>
> BOISE CASCADE CORPORATION
>
> W.W. Ford
> Assistant Sales Manager

WWF: aj

cc: H.L. Grove

Rips and Trims

It seems that news for the past month is very scarce. The weather seemed to be the topic of conversation and that is covered elsewhere in this issue.

Mr. and Mrs. PAUL DOOLEY do have a new baby girl, but I don't know what they named her or how much she weighed.

MARVIN VAN ORSOW and GEORGE MURRAY were both absent several days due to illness. TED HANSON and RALPH ELLIS were slated for surgery the end of January or first of February.

HOWARD HUNT has a new station wagon. He'll be happy to tell you all about it.

Richard Bowen, son of FRANK BOWEN, is in the army and is stationed at Fort Ord.

There were two weddings recently. ROLEY ZUMWALT married Leala Thompson of Troutdale. Linda Burkholder, daughter of DEAN BURKHOLDER, married Gene Stewart in Washington.

They say there is still a cougar wandering around the hills above the mill; I just hope he stays up there.

That's about all I could find for this time.

Fred Mickelson is in Norfolk, Virginia, engrossed in his studies in radar.

BOY SCOUTS 50th Anniversary

Readers' Comments

Tom Cowling loves to hear from his readers! Simply email him at tom@bridalveiloregon.com, putting the title of the book in the subject line, and your comments in the body. Be sure to include your full name, current email and postal addresses, and a statement saying that Tom Cowling has your permission to use your comments. Read what other readers are saying about Tom's book, **STORIES OF BRIDAL VEIL.**

"I'm really looking forward to receiving the book."

~Annette Kraft

"Hi Tom: I was wondering how your book is going? It sounds exciting but exhausting. Kind of like my new job. I had no idea it would be so intense but exhausting too. I would love to have a copy when you are published. Can't wait to read it and better yet have you come by and sign it. I am doing my office in Salem in Gorge stuff, pictures, books, etc. and I would love to have one for my collection. I am getting a lot of comments from people who actually only hear on the news about the Gorge so our history is special."

~Patti Smith, State Representative

"Thanks for your creative efforts, Tom. This is priceless!"

~Pat Smith (Tom's sister)

"I've been looking at your beautiful book, **STORIES OF BRIDAL VEIL,** for the last two hours. You did a good job. It was an interesting and informative format the way you included the family stories. For some reason I never seem to tire of looking at old logging pictures of bulls, horses and steam donkeys. I congratulate you in doing the book. It will be a real treasure as time goes by. One has only to look at some old account of the pioneers writing on the trail to Oregon to realize the value to history that things become after a century."

~Dow Beckham, author

"Just a quick note to thank you for the copy of **STORIES OF BRIDAL VEIL**. You can be proud of your achievement to put this together. I love the history and pictures it contains, and I look forward to driving to see the sights and locations where this once-vibrant community produced lumber for decades."

~Jim Schlauch

"Congratulations! What an effort! I'd like copies for Dad and myself. Can't wait!"

~Arlene Williams

"Received your book, **STORIES OF BRIDAL VEIL**, very impressive! So far, I haven't had time to read much of it but did read the stories that you, Bob and Pat wrote. They bring back memories."

~Wes Post

"How I have enjoyed your book, **STORIES OF BRIDAL VEIL**. It is a phenomenal treasure of research. Your layout of the book makes it very readable. The "Timeline" helped me understand the history of the area. I referred back to it often. The interviews, documents and photos give a better understanding of the hardships these hardy pioneers endured. And the way you introduce each family, and explain their part in the community, makes one feel as they, too, were living, playing and working in this close-knit company town. I bought a copy for each of my four siblings and am looking forward to your next book."

~Lloyd Davis, Postmaster
Bridal Veil, OR 97010

THE BRIDAL VEIL HERITAGE COLLECTION

Yes, I want to order books about Bridal Veil's heritage.
__STORIES OF BRIDAL VEIL:
   A Company Mill Town (1886-1960) $23.95

__LETTERS FROM A DYING TOWN:
   Bridal Veil, Oregon (1955-1960) $20.95

Discounts: 15% for libraries, schools and non-profits, 25% for 5 books of same title.

Trade-ins: Cars aren't the only things you can trade in! Is your copy of this book dog-eared and shabby? Whether or not you ordered the book directly from us, just send us $15 (plus shipping) and the front cover. We'll send you a brand-new edition!

To order: (1) List the book titles and quantities you want to order along with your name, address, telephone and email address. Mail it and your check or credit card information (including expiration date) to:

Acorn Publishing Co.

3140 SW 97th Ave.

Portland, OR 97225

Be sure to include $4.05 for priority mail for one book and $2.00 for each additional book.

<u>OR</u> **(2)** Visit our website at www.bridalveiloregon.com to place your order online.

To receive our **FREE** <u>**Bridal Veil Newsletter**</u>, with stories of Bridal Veil's rich history, book announcements and other news of interest, email info@bridalveiloregon.com or register at our website, www.bridalveiloregon.com.